CHINESE CULTURE AND MENTAL HEALTH

CHINESE CULTURE
AND
MENTAL HEALTH

Edited by

Wen-Shing Tseng
Department of Psychiatry
School of Medicine
University of Hawaii
Honolulu, Hawaii

David Y. H. Wu
Institute of Culture and Communication
East-West Center
Honolulu, Hawaii

1985

ACADEMIC PRESS, INC.

(Harcourt Brace Jovanovich, Publishers)

Orlando   San Diego   New York   London
Toronto   Montreal   Sydney   Tokyo

ACADEMIC PRESS, INC.
Orlando, Florida 32887

United Kingdom Edition published by
ACADEMIC PRESS INC. (LONDON) LTD.
24–28 Oval Road, London NW1 7DX

LIBRARY OF CONGRESS CATALOGING-IN-PUBLICATION DATA

Main entry under title:

Chinese culture and mental health.

Derived from a conference held in Hawaii, Mar. 1–6,
1982, and sponsored by the Culture Learning Institute of
the East-West Center, the Dept. of Psychiatry, University
of Hawaii School of Medicine, and the Queen's Medical
Center in Honolulu.
  Includes index.
  1. Mental health—China—Congresses.   2. National
characteristics, Chinese—Congresses.   3. China—
Civilization—Congresses.   4. Family policy—China—
Congresses.   5. Community mental health services—China—
Congresses.   I. Tseng, Wen-Shing, Date
II. Wu, David, Y. H.   III. East-West Center. Culture
Learning Institute.   IV. John A. Burns School of
Medicine. Dept. of Psychiatry.
RA790.7.C6C49   1985   362.2'0951   85-3927
ISBN 0-12-701630-9 (alk. paper)
ISBN 0-12-701631-7 (paperback)
PRINTED IN THE UNITED STATES OF AMERICA

85 86 87 88   9 8 7 6 5 4 3 2 1

CONTENTS

Contributors   xiii
Preface   xv
Glossary   xix

PART I
CULTURE, SOCIETY, AND PERSONALITY   1

1.   Introduction: The Characteristics of Chinese Culture
David Y. H. Wu and Wen-Shing Tseng

Background   3
Different Courses of Sociocultural Change   4
Common Characteristics of Chinese Culture   6
Concluding Remarks   12
References   12

2.   The Emergence of the New Chinese Culture
Godwin C. Chu

Introduction   15
The Concept of Culture   16
Social and Economic Transformations   18
Initial Ideological Campaigns   20
Impact of the Cultural Revolution   21
Response by the Chinese People   22
Cultural Transition   26
References   27

3. **The Confucian Paradigm of Man: A Sociological View**
Ambrose Y. C. King and Michael H. Bond

Introduction	29
The Confucian Conception of Humanity	30
Family Structure and the Individual	32
The Problematic of the Confucian Paradigm	36
The Self and Relation-Construction	38
References	42

4. **A Preliminary Study of the Character Traits of the Chinese**
Song Weizhen

Introduction: Research on Personality	47
The MMPI	48
Preliminary Findings on the MMPI in China	50
Discussion and Cultural Explanation	53
References	55

5. **Social Change, Religious Movements, and
Personality Adjustment: An Anthropological View**
Yih-yuan Li

Introduction	57
Theoretical Framework	58
Ritualized Society	60
Antiritualism Cults	60
Social Hygiene Cults	62
Millennial Cults	62
Nativistic Movements	63
Discussion	64
References	66

6. **Traditional Chinese Beliefs and
Attitudes toward Mental Illness**
T'ien Ju-k'ang

Introduction	67
Ancient Records of Mental Illness	67
Review of Traditional Medical Books	69
Emotional Disorders as Described in Literary Writing	75
Conclusion	79
References	79

PART II
FAMILY AND CHILD 83

7. **The Effect of Family on the Mental Health of the Chinese People**
Li Xintian

Background	85
The Role of the Family in Child Rearing	86
The Role of the Family in Married Life	87
The Role of the Family in the Care of the Elderly	88
Family Construction among Strangers	89
Discussion	92
References	93

8. **The Chinese Family: Relations, Problems, and Therapy**
Jing Hsu

Introduction	95
The Concept of Family Health and Pathology	96
Chinese Family Structure and Relationships	98
Common Psychological Problems	102
Usual Coping Patterns	104
Clinical Significance and Application	105
Summary	109
References	110

9. **Child Training in Chinese Culture**
David Y. H. Wu

Background	113
Research Methods	114
Theoretical Considerations	115
Chinese Child Rearing and the Development of the Mother–Child Bond	117
Situations That Arouse Fear and the Susceptibility to Fear	121
Aggression	129
Conclusion	131
References	132

10. **Characteristics of Temperament in Chinese Infants and Young Children**
Chen-Chin Hsu

Introduction	135
Report of Chinese Studies	143

Discussion   148
References   150

11. The One-Child-per-Family Policy:
    A Psychological Perspective
    Tao Kuotai and Chiu Jing-Hwa

Introduction   153
A Need for Better Family Planning   153
Recent Developments in Family Planning   155
Advantages and Disadvantages of Only Children   157
Causes of Negative Behavior Patterns in Only Children   160
Special Aspects of Early Childhood Education   161
Conclusion   164
References   165

12. Child Mental Health and Elementary Schools in Shanghai
    Xu Taoyuan

Introduction   167
The Elementary School System in China   168
An Example of the School Mental Health Situation in Shanghai   171
Psychiatric Disorders among Students   175
Closing Comment   177
References   178

PART III
ADJUSTMENT IN DIFFERENT SETTINGS   179

13. Language and Identity: The Case of Chinese in Singapore
    Eddie C. Y. Kuo

Introduction   181
The Sociolingusitic Situation in Singapore   182
The Policy of Multilingualism   184
The Trend of Language Shift   187
The Chinese Dilemma   189
Language and Identity: Some Considerations   190
References   192

14. Social Stress and Coping Behavior in Hong Kong
    Rance P. L. Lee

Introduction   193
Prevalence of Psychiatric Stress   195

High-Density Living and Adjustment 196
Material Aspiration and Adjustment 199
Concluding Remarks: The Fading of Immigrant Culture 209
References 211

15. **Chinese Adaptation in Hawaii: Some Examples**
Kwong-yen Lum and Walter F. Char

Introduction 215
Background: The Chinese in Hawaii 217
Successful Examples: The Subjects of the Interviews 219
Results of the Interviews 221
Discussion 225
References 226

PART IV
MENTAL HEALTH PROBLEMS 227

16. **Mental Health in Singapore and
Its Relation to Chinese Culture**
Wing Foo Tsoi

The Singapore Chinese 229
Mental Health Services in Singapore 234
Conclusion 247
References 248

17. **Psychiatric Pathology among Chinese Immigrants in
Victoria, Australia**
Edmond Chiu and Eng-Seong Tan

Demographic Sketch 251
Historical Background 252
Current Psychiatric Survey 253
Findings 255
Summary 261
References 262

18. **Sociocultural Changes and Prevalence of
Mental Disorders in Taiwan**
Eng-Kung Yeh

General Social and Health Background 265
Prevalence of Mental Disorders 267

Discussion   279
References   284

19. An Overview of Psychopathology in Hong Kong with
     Special Reference to Somatic Presentation
     Fanny M. Cheung

     Introduction   287
     Manifestation of Mental Disorders   288
     Psychological and Cultural Explanations   292
     Treatment Resources   296
     Methodological Issues   298
     References   300

20. An Epidemiological Study of
     Child Mental Health Problems in Nanjing District
     Yu Lian

     Introduction   305
     Description of the Method   306
     Results of the Investigation   306
     Discussion   311
     Comment   313
     References   313

21. An Investigation of Minimal Brain Disorders among
     Primary School Students in the Beijing Area
     Yang Xiaoling

     Introduction   315
     Investigations in Elementary Schools of Different Areas   318
     Summary   321
     References   322

22. Some Psychological Problems Manifested by
     Neurotic Patients: Shanghai Examples
     Yan Heqin

     Introduction   325
     Common Psychological Problems   328
     Comments   333
     References   336

PART V
MANAGEMENT AND PREVENTION OF
MENTAL ILLNESS 339

23. The Mental Health Delivery System in Shanghai
   Xia Zhenyi

   Introduction 341
   A Three-Level Scheme of the Mental Health Care System 346
   Summary and Future Perspectives 353
   References 355

24. The Mental Health Home Care Program:
   Beijing's Rural Haidian District
   Shen Yucun

   Introduction 357
   General Information about the Haidian District Project Area 359
   Procedures Used in Setting up the Community Mental Health
     Care Network 359
   Findings of the Psychiatric Survey in the Haidian District 361
   Development of the Home Care Program 362
   Results of the Home Care Program 363
   Discussion 365
   References 366

PART VI
SUMMARY AND SUGGESTIONS FOR THE FUTURE 367

25. Mental Disorders and Psychiatry in Chinese Culture:
   Characteristic Features and Major Issues
   Tsung-yi Lin

   Introduction 369
   Characteristic Features of Mental Disorders among the Chinese 370
   Treatment Modalities of Mental Disorders 379
   Coping, Help-Seeking, and Delivery of Mental Health Services
     for the Mentally Ill in Chinese Culture 382
   Theories and Hypotheses about Mental Disorders 385
   Concluding Remarks 387
   References 388

26. Directions for Future Study

Wen-Shing Tseng and David Y. H. Wu

Introduction	395
Important Approaches to Studying Culture and Mental Health	396
Future Directions	399
Chinese Culture and Mental Health: Review	403
References	405

Index 407

CONTRIBUTORS

Numbers in parentheses indicate the pages on which the authors' contributions begin.

BOND, MICHAEL H.(29), Department of Psychology, The Chinese University of Hong Kong, Shatin, New Territories, Hong Kong

CHAR, WALTER F.(215), Department of Psychiatry, School of Medicine, University of Hawaii, Honolulu, Hawaii 96813

CHEUNG, FANNY M.(287), Department of Psychology, The Chinese University of Hong Kong, Shatin, New Territories, Hong Kong

CHIU, EDMOND (251), Department of Psychiatry, University of Melbourne, St. Vincent's Hospital, Fitzroy, Victoria 3065, Australia

CHIU JING-HWA (153), Nanjing Child Mental Health Research Center, Nanjing, China

CHU, GODWIN C.(15), Institute of Culture and Communication, East-West Center, Honolulu, Hawaii 96848

HSU, CHEN-CHIN (135), Department of Psychiatry, National Taiwan University Hospital, Taipei, Taiwan, China

HSU,JING (95), Department of Psychiatry, School of Medicine, University of Hawaii, Honolulu, Hawaii 96817

KING, AMBROSE Y. C.(29), New Asia College and Department of Sociology, The Chinese University of Hong Kong, Shatin, New Territories, Hong Kong

KUO, EDDIE C. Y.(181), Department of Sociology, National University of Singapore, Singapore 0511, Republic of Singapore

LEE, RANCE P. L.(193), Institute of Social Studies and Department of Sociology, The Chinese University of Hong Kong, Shatin, New Territories, Hong Kong

LI XINTIAN (85), Institute of Psychology, The Chinese Academy of Sciences, Beijing, China

LI, YIH-YUAN(57), Institute of Ethnology, Academica Sinica, Nankang, Taipei, Taiwan, China

LIN, TSUNG-YI (369), Department of Psychiatry, University of British Columbia, Vancouver, British Columbia V6T 2A1, Canada

LUM, KWONG-YEN(215), Department of Psychiatry, School of Medicine, University of Hawaii, Honolulu, Hawaii 96813

SHEN YUCUN (357), Institute of Mental Health, Beijing Medical College, Beijing, China

SONG WEIZHEN (47), Institute of Psychology, The Chinese Academy of Sciences, Beijing, China

TAN, ENG-SEONG (251), Department of Psychiatry, University of Melbourne, St. Vincent's Hospital, Fitzroy, Victoria 3065, Australia

TAO KUOTAI (153), Nanjing Child Mental Health Research Center, Nanjing, China

T'IEN JU-K'ANG (67), Department of History, Fudan University, Shanghai, China

TSENG, WEN-SHING (3, 395), Department of Psychiatry, School of Medicine, University of Hawaii, Honolulu, Hawaii 96813

TSOI, WING-FOO (229), Department of Psychological Medicine, National University of Singapore, Singapore 0511, Republic of Singapore

WU, DAVID Y. H.(3, 113, 395), Institute of Culture and Communication, East-West Center, Honolulu, Hawaii 96848

XIA ZHENYI (341), Department of Psychiatry, Shanghai First Medical College, and Shanghai Psychiatric Institute, Shanghai, China

XU TAOYUAN (167), Department of Psychiatry, Shanghai First Medical College, and Shanghai Psychiatric Institute, Shanghai, China

YAN HEQIN (325), Department of Psychiatry, Shanghai Second Medical College, and Shanghai Psychiatric Institute, Shanghai, China

YANG XIAOLING (315), Section of Child Psychiatry, Institute of Mental Health, Beijing Medical College, Beijing, China

YEH, ENG-KUNG(265), Department of Psychiatry, National Taiwan University, and Taipei City Psychiatric Center, Taipei, Taiwan, China

YU LIAN (305), Nanjing Child Mental Health Research Center, Nanjing, China

PREFACE

There are many ways to explore the subject of culture and mental health. Often the choice falls on one of two frequently used methods: the cross-comparison of culture and mental health in different samples or the intensive, in-depth exploration of certain topics in a single culture. We chose the latter approach and explored the culture and mental health of Chinese people in varying times, geographic areas, and settings.

Chinese culture is an appropriate focus for studying the relationship between mental health and customs, beliefs, and philosophies. The Chinese have a history of at least 5000 years of civilization. Today, with one-quarter of the world's people, China has one of the largest populations in the world. Chinese people are also scattered throughout the world in a variety of social settings. As a whole, they provide a unique example for the study of cultural aspects of adaptation. The Chinese also provide a model for studying how cultural factors influence psychosocial stress, contribute to the formation and manifestation of psychopathology, and determine the patterns of coping mechanisms. Knowledge of these reactions and the factors that cause them offer valuable guidance in planning culturally acceptable styles of mental health care delivery.

This book is divided into six parts. The first reviews traditional and contemporary Chinese culture, explores Chinese concepts of personality, and describes a profile of Chinese character traits. This is followed by an examination of religious movements associated with social change, and traditional concepts and attitudes about mental illness.

The second part addresses specific family–child issues, reviewing both the characteristic relations and psychological problems commonly observed in the Chinese family, and the impact of family on the mental health of people. It concludes with an examination of child rearing, child temperament, and psychological aspects of children in the family and school.

In Part III, the adjustment of Chinese in different sociogeographical circumstances is revealed, with a special focus on language and identity, stress and coping mechanisms, and successful adaptation. Part IV begins with a general review of mental health problems in various areas. Considered in the chapters following are special issues in mental health such as patterns of symptom presentation, common psychological problems, and psychiatric problems observed in students.

The sociocultural aspects of management and prevention of psychological problems are dealt with in the fifth part. Two psychiatrists report on how community- and family-oriented mental health programs are developed in Mainland China. Cultural assets are utilized so that mental health care systems fit the social and community needs. In Part VI, Chinese and Western psychiatry are contrasted regarding manifestations of psychopathology, service delivery modality, and the need for theoretical exploration. Finally, suggestions are offered for future studies of Chinese culture and mental health.

This book is derived from the Conference on Chinese Culture and Mental Health held in Hawaii, March 1–6, 1982. The conference was jointly sponsored by the Culture Learning Institute of the East-West Center, the Department of Psychiatry of the University of Hawaii School of Medicine, and the Queen's Medical Center in Honolulu. Brought together were 28 psychiatrists and other distinguished behavioral scientists of Chinese ethnic background from various areas, including Mainland China, Taiwan, Hong Kong, Singapore, Australia, Canada, and the United States (both mainland and Hawaii). The conference was a unique and historic event. Scholars of many disciplines from many locations overcame various barriers to meet and discuss their common concern: how Chinese culture affects the behavior, emotions, and mental health care of the Chinese people.

We are very proud and delighted that after long and careful preparation, the conference finally took place and that this book is a result. The success of the conference is due to many persons and organizations. We greatly appreciate the support given by President Victor Li of the East-West Center, Dean Terence A. Rogers of the University of Hawaii School of Medicine, and President Will J. Henderson of the Queen's Medical Center for their enthusiastic sponsorship. Many thanks are due Mr. Gregory Trifonovich, head of the Culture Learning Institute; Dr. John F. McDermott, Jr., Chairman of the Department of Psychiatry; and Dr. K. Y. Lum, former Chief of Psychiatry of the Queen's Medical Center for their kind support and administrative assistance.

We also express our appreciation to Mrs. Ruth M. Ono, Vice-President of the Queen's Medical Center, for her kind assistance in fund-raising from the community. We are grateful for generous contributions from the Stanley N. Barbee Memorial Fund, the Davies Charitable Trust, the Harry S. K. Zen Memorial Fund, Kuan Yin Temple of Honolulu, Mr. and Mrs. Yao-Tsai Huang, and Mrs. Lily Sui-Fang Sun Wong.

Our thanks are extended to Mrs. Lyn Anzai, program coordinator, and Mrs. Lyn Moi of the East-West Center Culture Learning Institute; Mrs. Kathy Awakuni, administrative officer, and Miss Rose Fuse, both from the Department of Psychiatry, for administrative assistance; and to Mrs. Joy Ashton, also of the department, for her help in preparing and organizing the reference literature for preparation of the conference. Special thanks are due Mrs. Wei-lang Wang-Wu for recording and organizing the conference discussion for editing purposes.

Last, but not least, we express our sincere and deep appreciation to all the distinguished conference delegates for their enthusiastic interest and cooperation in participating in this historically significant conference. They have indeed helped to develop mutual professional working relationships, facilitate the exchange of academic knowledge, and stimulate the development of further study to promote our knowledge of culture and mental health. Their contributions will be useful for the improvement of the mental health of Chinese as well as of people all over the world.

GLOSSARY

Pinyin transliteration is followed by Wade–Giles transliteration in parentheses.

A

An pin (an p'in)　安貧

B

Ba gua (pa kua)　八卦
Bao (pao)　報
Bei (pei)　悲

C

Che gong (cho kung)　車公

D

Dai (tai)　呆
Dao (tao)　道
Dian (tien)　癲
Diu lian (tiu lien)　丟臉
Du jin (tu chin)　渡金

E

En-zhu-gong (en-chu-kung)　恩主公

F

Fa pi qi (fa p'i ch'i)　發脾氣
Fan bu (fan pu)　反哺
Feng (feng)　風．瘋

Feng pai (feng pai)   風派
Feng shui (feng sui)   風水
Fu (fu)   符
Fu-ji (fu-chi)   扶箕

G

Gan (kan)   乾
Gan huo (kan huo)   肝火
Gan huo shen (kan huo shen)   肝火盛
Gan qin (kan ch'in)   乾親
Gong xi fa cai (kung shi fa tsai)   恭禧發財
Guan-xi xue (kuan shi hsue)   關係學
Guang-zong-yao-zu (kuang-tsung-yao-tsu)   光宗耀祖

H

He (ho)   和
Huang da xian (huang ta hsien)   黃大仙

J

Ji (chi)   己
Jia (chia)   家
Jie bai (chi pai)   結拜
Jie-bai-xiong-di (chieh-pai-hsiung-ti)   結拜兄弟
Jin (chin)   晉
Jing (ching)   驚

K

Kai (Cantonese word; naughty, misbehaving, and bad)   不乖
Kang-Xi (Kang Hsi)   康熙
Ke-ji (k'o-chi)   克己
Kong (kung)   恐
Kuang (k'uang)   狂
Kuang yan (k'uang yuan)   狂言

L

Le dao (le tao)   樂道
Li (li)   禮
Lun (lun)   倫

N

Ning ke xin qi you, bu kevxin qi wu (ning ko shin ch'i you, pu ko
    shin ch'i wu)   寧可信其有‧不可信其無
Nu (nu)   怒

P

Po-si-li-gong (puo-ssu-li-kung)   破私立公

Q

Qi (ch'i)   氣
Qi ding (ch'i ting)   氣頂
Qi fu zi (ch'i fu tsu)   契父子
Qi mu nu (ch'i mu nu)   契父母
Qi qing (ch'i ch'ing)   七情
Qi-gong (ch'i-kung)   氣功
Qin (ch'in)   親‧泰
Qing chi (ch'ing chih)   情痴
Qu (ch'u)   匪

R

Re nao (je nao)   熱鬧
Ren (jen)   仁‧人
Ren wei cai si, niao wei shi wang (jen wei tśai ssu, niao wei shih
    wang)   人為財死‧鳥為食亡

S

Sang keng (sang keng)   三綱
Shan-shu (shan-shu)   善書
Shen (shen)   神臀
Shen kui (shen k'uei)   賢虧
Shen yang (shen yang)   腎陽
Shi (shi)   詩
Shu (shu)   疏
Shu zhong zi you huang jin wu, shu zhong zi you yan ru yu (shu
    chung tsu you huang chin wu, shu chung tsu you yen ru yu)
    書中自有黄金屋‧書中自有顔如玉
Si (ssu)   思
Suo-yang (so-yang or shung-yang, Cantonese)   縮陽

T

Tai-ji (tai-chi)　太極

Tang-ki (tong-ji in Southern Min [Fujian] dialect)

Tian hou (tien hou)　天后

Ting hua (t'ing hua)　聽話

Tong-ji (t'ung-chi)　童乩

Tu di shen (tu ti shen)　土地神

W

Wai-ren (wai-jen)　外人

Wan ban jie xia pin, wei you du shu gao (wan pan che hsia pin, wei you tu shu kao)　萬般皆下品, 唯有讀書高

Wu chang (wu ch'ang)　五常

Wu di (wu ti)　吾弟

Wu lun (wu lun)　五倫

Wu xung (wu-hsiung)　吾兄

X

Xi (hsi)　喜

Xian (hsian)　瘋縣

Xiang-yuan (hsiang-yuen)　鄉愿

Xiao (hsiao)　孝

Xie bing (hsieh ping)　邪病

Xin (hsin)　信

Xin feng (hsin feng)　心風

Xin yu (hsin yu)　心臟

Xing shan yi hua yuan (hsing shan yi hua yuan)　行善以化緣

Xing-ji (hsin-chi)　行己

Xiu-ji (hsiu-chi)　修己

Xuan-yuan-jiao (hsuan-yuan-chiao)　軒轅教

Xue er you ze shi (hsueh erh you tse shih)　學而優則仕

Xung di ban　兄弟班

Y

Yi (i)　義, 儀

Yi ming, er yun, san feng shui, si ji yin de, wu du shu (i ming, erh yun, san fung shui, suchi yin to, wu to shu)　一命二運, 三風水、四積陰德, 五讀書

Yi-guan-dao (i-kuan-tao)　一貫道

Yin (yin)　陰

You lian (yu lien) 有臉

You qian yi tiao long, we qian yi tiao chong (you chíen i tíao lung, we chíen i tíao chúng) 有錢一條龍, 無錢一條蟲

You yuan qian li neng xiang hui, wu yuan dui men pu xiang feng (you yuan chian li nengvshang hui, wu yuan tui men pu hsang fung) 有緣千里能相會, 無緣對門不相逢

Youyi (you i) 有誼

Yu (yu) 鬱

Yuan fen (yuan fen) 緣份

Z

Zao jun (tsao chun) 灶君

Zhan yan (chan yuan) 讒話

Zheng ming (cheng ming) 鄭聲

Zheng shen (cheng sheng) 正名

Zhi (chih) 制, 知

Zi min (tzu ming) 子民

Zi-ji-ren (tzu-chi-jen) 自己人

CULTURE, SOCIETY, AND PERSONALITY

In order to understand fully the cultural aspect of mental health, it is essential to have adequate knowledge about the society, culture, and people we are concerned with. It is the aim of this introduction to address the Chinese background.

In the first chapter, Wu and Tseng begin by pointing out that there are different courses of sociocultural change undertaken in different Chinese communities. Then they describe common characteristics of Chinese culture shared by all ethnic Chinese, whether in the homeland or other settings.

Chu (Chapter 2) analyzes the emergence of a new culture in mainland China, which was brought about by the process of social reform and indoctrination and was influenced by cultural revolution. As a result of the emergence of this new culture, varying elements of Chinese culture are discerned in different generations: Both tradition and change shape the future of culture in China.

In Chapter 3, the concept of Chinese personality is elaborated by King and Bond, both sociologists. Most scholars view Confucianism as a social theory that tends to mold the Chinese into group-oriented, socially interdependent beings. However, King and Bond point out that the Confucian paradigm of man has the theoretical thrust, as well as a built-in structural imperative, to develop humans into relation-oriented individuals who are

1

CHINESE CULTURE
AND MENTAL HEALTH

not only socially responsive and interdependent, but also capable of assuming self-directed roles in constructing their social world.

In Chapter 4, Song describes her psychometric study of the character traits of the Chinese people. Using the Chinese version of the Minnesota Multiphasic Personality Inventory (MMPI), she found that the Chinese character profile contrasts with its American counterpart in several aspects. The Chinese are emotionally more reserved, introverted, fond of tranquility, overly considerate, socially overly cautious, and habituated to self-restraint. These traits are not only manifested in the test results, but also are corroborated in the daily lives of the Chinese people.

Following this discussion of personality, is Y. Y. Li's (Chapter 5) review of social change and religious movements and their relation to personality adjustment. From the anthropological point of view, he describes and categorizes the religious cults prevailing in the rapidly changing society of Taiwan. Li then correlates the various types of cults with the personal adjustments to social change of their members and with shifting patterns of the society itself.

Part I concludes with T'ien's study of traditional views on mental illness in Chapter 6. From ancient records and medical books, he draws the basis for formulating the ancient Chinese concept of mental disorder. He also uses descriptions of emotional disturbance in the popular literature of premodern times to present insights into the psychic unity of the Chinese people.

CHAPTER 1

Introduction: The Characteristics of Chinese Culture

David Y. H. Wu
Wen-Shing Tseng

BACKGROUND

Whether it is published in Chinese or English, the literature relevant to Chinese culture and mental health is scarce. Thus, the essays in this volume, which focus upon contemporary situations in Chinese culture and which relate to social structure, sociocultural change, and the relationship of these factors to the current state of mental health of the Chinese people, afford valuable scholarly insights unlikely to be otherwise encountered. This volume records a unique meeting of Chinese minds, a congress of scholars who dealt with the issues of mind, body, and behavior.

Mental health issues most often deal with the normal and abnormal states of the mind (see Kleinman and Lin, 1981), with culture being seen as the arbiter of rules of conduct in the minds of individuals in a particular culture (Geertz, 1973; Keesing, 1974). In this overview of Chinese culture

3

and mental health, we present case after case showing that the cultural framework is of central concern to this group of Chinese participants, whether they be social scientists, humanists, or clinical psychiatrists. Chinese culture as a way of thinking appears to affect the state of body and health, parent–child interaction, social relationships, individual and group aspirations, models of health care services, and above all, as emphasized in several parts of this volume, the patterns of disorders as well as methods of coping under the impact of migration, industrialization, and urbanization. It is striking to see here the convergence of scholarly views from experts in Chinese communities that are physically distant from each other as well as disparate in social systems. It also appears that the sociobehavioral scientists and psychiatrists represented in this volume more often than not agree on the importance of the impact of cultural tradition upon perception, behavioral orientation, pathology, coping, and help-seeking. Throughout this volume, common concerns addressed by our authors can be summarized in the following questions:

1. What are the characteristics of the Chinese culture? What are some of the recent changes in different Chinese communities? How are these changes related to mental health issues?
2. Are these mental health or psychological problems peculiar to the Chinese? What are common factors of mental illness that are evident in Chinese society?
3. What kinds of coping methods in response to environmental and cultural change are distinctively culturally related?
4. What are some of the popular ways of delivering mental health services in the Chinese society?

DIFFERENT COURSES OF SOCIOCULTURAL CHANGE

Before we attempt to answer these questions, it is appropriate for us to know whether the various Chinese societies represented in the present volume are comparable units for comparison. In other words, do they all reflect the same Chinese culture on the basis of which an investigation of the behavioral and mental health issues can be conducted? We cannot deny the fact that all the societies under discussion share certain common features in their cultural backgrounds, but we cannot ignore the separation in time and space of these societies, in addition to the effects of recent socioeconomic changes. If indeed we could document a variety of patterns of changes occurring in these societies and if we could note the persistence of common cultural characteristics, we could then discuss those mental health issues pertinent to a contemporary Chinese culture.

A quick review of the recent history of the Chinese societies represented here leads us to see three kinds of sociocultural change: One can be observed in mainland China; one is characteristic of Hong Kong and Taiwan; and another is found in immigrant Chinese communities overseas, such as those in Australia, Singapore, and the United States. These three categories of change have given rise to dissimilar social as well as individual problems that warrant the attention of mental health professionals and researchers.

In mainland China, dramatic change has taken place in both the sociopolitical system as well as in social ideology. However, it is uncertain to what degree these changes have affected the cultural behavior, or rules of conduct, of the population. Until recently, little research information in this area has been available. Given the fact that 75% of the population remains involved in agricultural production, with little change noticeable in the agrarian way of life, we might not anticipate the kind of change occurring elsewhere due to forces of industrialization, Westernization, and urbanization. This is why the term *Chinese model of development* has been used in the literature. The mental health concerns that are relevant to the population of mainland China, as indicated in several chapters by resident specialists contributing to this volume, are related to the recent dramatic socialist revolution and particularly to the 10-year period of the Cultural Revolution. While the legacy of the Cultural Revolution has not been specifically dealt with by the mental health professionals from China, certain legacies of such a drastic sociopolitical movement—explicit societal concern for the general moral order and education for the young—have been quite revealing in our discussions. In short, a concern for constructing (or reconstructing) society for the future generation of Chinese has become the central issue with regard to maintaining good mental health.

In the decades after World War II, Hong Kong and Taiwan shared a similar course of socioeconomic development. Both underwent rapid growth in light industry and expanded export-oriented international trade. The two societies also share the demographical feature of a large, dislocated migrant population. While mental health problems are often associated with migration in Western literature, they did not surface as serious issues for the Chinese society in Hong Kong or in Taiwan. The more salient issue is the impact of economic development and population growth on the urban centers, where the change of life-styles due to economic affluence may have caused many of the mental disorders and social ills that are new to the society. One important issue that requires further research is the macropolitical situation in the society. How does individual concern with continuing political instability and uncertainty affect the mental health of the entire society? Investigation relevant to this question may well yield clues to the more profound problems of group and individual well-being. (If the concepts *health, adjusted,* and *well* can be linked to the improving economic situation and rising standard of living, the people in Hong Kong and Taiwan could be said to be coping quite well.)

Among the immigrant Chinese in Australia, Singapore, and the United States, cultural adjustment and cultural identity have deep meaning even after the passing of several generations. The successful, socioculturally adjusted, elite Chinese in Hawaii (see Lum and Char, Chapter 15, this volume), take pride in a Chinese culture they claim to possess but find difficult to pinpoint. As generations pass, the roots of Chinese culture begin to disappear, yet individuals continue to express their interest in maintaining a Chinese identity.

In contrast to these nostalgic sentiments concerning cultural identity expressed by Chinese Americans, the cultural adjustment process among the Chinese in Singapore takes the form of official state-level planning and intervention. In Chapter 13, Kuo deals with language policy and shows that the selection of an official language can be considered one index of cultural or behavioral norms. Therefore, speakers of Mandarin in Singapore could be seen as subscribing to a traditional Chinese cultural norm. Yet it is clear that the effects on individual identity and on behavioral norms in the society are far more complicated than was anticipated by those leaders who saw a simplistic relationship between language and culture.

Tsoi, in Chapter 16, offers an intriguing revelation about the superficial Westernization of a society in which traditional religious behavior is closely related to mental illness as well as to processes of healing. The Singaporean Chinese case thus provides us with one of the most interesting cases for examining further the study of culture identity and mental health.

COMMON CHARACTERISTICS OF CHINESE CULTURE

From the point of view of population adjustment and adaptation to culture and sociopolitical changes, we recognize the three previously mentioned types of process. We must ask what characteristics of Chinese cultural behavior, as manifested in individual behavior, group organization, social relationships, and emotional and psychological concerns, have persisted in the face of such changes and what is prototypically Chinese. We find it interesting that, indeed, we are able to extract some common characteristics of Chinese culture as we go through each chapter in this volume. We abstract some of these common features.

Family and Collective Responsibility

Perhaps most central to Chinese culture is the value of the family as the fundamental unit of the society. This concern permeates all sociopolitical activities. J. Hsu (Chapter 8) recognizes the Chinese family system, not the individual, as the focal point of psychotherapy. King and Bond (Chapter 3) discuss Confucian ethics and emphasize the collective quality in the nature of the individual's life and behavior. The meaning of *face*, for example, should be viewed in relation to the gain or loss of the status of the family, not just of the individual. Though King and Bond argue for the existence of individuality and initiative under the Confucian paradigm, the existing literature often associates individual achievement and proper conduct with that of the family.

Family relationships are, to this day, perceived as essential in mainland China, despite the extreme changes that have taken place in the sociopolitical structures beyond family. X. T. Li (Chapter 7) reports recent occurrences of individuals coming together to construct a family by uniting members who have no actual kin relationship. The significance of these remarkable examples lies in the fact that caring for family structure and relationship is dear to the hearts of the Chinese people. Therefore, we are not surprised to learn from the overseas ethnic Chinese, as shown in the Hawaiian case in Chapter 15, that a strong sense of obligation and responsibility to one's family is still cherished as Chinese virtue, whereas values in other areas may have given way to Western influence.

However, psychological problems may be generated in a seemingly closely knit family. On the one hand, J. Hsu (Chapter 8) lists the following as common problems in the family: inadequate parent–child communication, the generation gap, split loyalties, and sibling rivalries. Hsu holds that these problems may be considered inherent in Chinese family relations, especially as they concern relationships between parents and children. Wu (Chapter 9), on the other hand, emphasizes the parent–child bond in early childhood. The paradox in the Chinese family of bonds and interdependence versus lack of communication and the generation gap perhaps will be better understood if future studies concentrate on the Chinese style of nonverbal emotional expression. The fact that Chinese patients are inclinded to exhibit somatic compliance rather than to express problems in emotional or psychological terms, as indicated in earlier literature and in Cheung's Chapter 19, serves to suggest the existence of interpersonal communication patterns that are peculiarly Chinese.

Emphasis on the Parent–Child Bond

The process of child socialization may provide clues to the reasons for the persistence of a closely knit family as the center of Chinese culture. Wu (Chapter 9) describes in detail the ways in which children are encouraged to be both physically and emotionally close to their parents through sharing common as well as social activities. During the conference discussion, C. C. Hsu confirmed that child-rearing patterns in Taiwan are quite similar to Wu's ethnographical report on an overseas community.

Since we presently have no research information about the child's socialization process in mainland China, we hope that very soon research will be undertaken and that the kind of rudimentary data presented by Wu will be made available. Such research would help to establish some analysis as to whether the prevailing cultural values in China have indeed shaped the current child-rearing and training practices. It also would be hlepful if C. C. Hsu's (Chapter 10) research methods in assessing infant temperament could be used among various mainland Chinese communities in a way that would test some of the mental health hypotheses associating early childhood emotion and temperament.

As the size of the Chinese family changes, because the official policy limits a married couple to one child, the mainland Chinese are now preoccupied with the task of properly rearing a healthy and disciplined only child. This fact increases the significance of Tao and Chiu's (Chapter 11) discussion of the one-child family. Consistency and variation in child rearing, differences in training practices between rural and urban areas, and variations in rearing between the one-child families and multiple-child families remain to be studied. Certainly, there are other interesting potential consequences if the one-child family should become the norm in mainland China. The role of kinship and the relationships of the parent to the child and the grandparent to the grandchild need to be researched. Some of the resulting societal changes may well be unprecedented in human social and cultural history.

Another question worth pondering with regard to the Chinese family and culture involves the antecedents of culture change. Chu (Chapter 2) sees the change taking place in mainland China as having its source in the younger generation. He attributes the changing perceptions and cultural values of rebellious youth in contemporary China to the lack of socialization provided by traditional culture. This suggestion leads us to a more profound theorizing in testing the relative influences of early child socialization as compared to the effect of a powerful sociopolitical movement.

The Art of Social Interaction and the Importance of the Personal Network

Another aspect of Chinese culture that surfaces in our discussions in various chapters is the Chinese art of handling social interaction and personal relationships. King and Bond (Chapter 3) illustrate an important aspect of Chinese culture as revealed in the seemingly oppressive Confucian cultural ideal. Because this ideal is not to be found in actual cultural behavior among Chinese individuals, Confucian conformity to cultural norms is nothing more than superficial conformity.

If one accepts this superficial conformity to sociocultural norms of conduct as a prevailing force in shaping Chinese perception and behavior in social interaction, it is not surprising that many social and political movements aimed at making fundamental changes in mainland Chinese society have not worked. Indeed, many traditional patterns of social interaction that are diametrically opposed to the new sociocultural ideals—such as using the "back door" (i.e., unorthodox approaches) or personal ties for one's gains—have once again surfaced in the aftermath of drastic political reform.

Pragmatism is perhaps a better term to characterize this discrepancy between cultural ideal and actual behavior. One finds a similar attitude expressed in the Chinese concept of a greater personal network outside of the family structure. In Chapter 14, Lee makes a convincing presentation on this point in analyzing Hong Kong's Chinese society. The distinguishing of insider from outsider (non–family member) was a traditional, ideal practice, which seems now to have given way to a more personalized network that serves pragmatic purposes. However, the situation may not be due to sociocultural change but may simply reflect the perception of the researchers.

In Y. Y. Li's Chapter 5, we again find evidence of the use of a nonkinship group as a means of adjusting to urban life among the increasing number of religious cult groups. These groups consist predominantly of migrants from rural areas and form the lower socioeconomic stratum of the industrialized society. Some of these new religious cults are more successful than others in attracting followers, and this fact further illustrates that the continuity of certain personality types are associated with traditional values and conform to collective group norms.

Control of Emotion and Cultivation of Morality

From childhood, Chinese are trained to control emotions that are considered adverse and disruptive to harmonious social interaction. Punishment of aggressive behavior among children is a characteristic Chinese child-training technique that may account for the learning of self-control and emotional restraint at an early age (see Wu, Chapter 9). Emotional control among the Chinese may also be seen in the report that in Hong Kong, despite the extreme population density of the dislocated migrants from the mainland, the rate of occurrence of emotional problems is lower than that for Thais, Malays, and Indians in their homelands (Lee, Chapter 14).

Song's findings in this regard (Chapter 4) were based upon data provided by the Minnesota Multiphasic Personality Inventory (MMPI) tests, the first MMPI tests ever done on the mainland of China. In contrast to the personality profile reported for Westerners, the mainland Chinese are still found to be "emotionally more reserved, introverted, fond of tranquility, overly considerate, socially overcautious, habituated to self-restraint." This finding adds additional evidence to our confident assertion that there is continuity of certain culture values and cultural behavior on the Chinese mainland despite some four decades of dramatic political and social reform.

Song attributes this continuity in personality traits to Confucian thought, which for two thousand years has dominated the Chinese code of conduct and which never ceased in its influence on Chinese society.

The data from the MMPI tests conducted in mainland China reveal one kind of change that must have been the result of conscious official social intervention. This is shown in the higher masculinity score of Chinese women as compared to women in Hong Kong, Japan, and Europe and America. Women who are liberated from the passive domestive role are now actively participating in sociopolitical life and in productivity. It would be interesting for our cross-cultural study of mental health to evaluate the next generation of Chinese women and compare our findings with those of studies of other societies.

Song's chapter parallels several other chapters in which the authors from China pay marked attention to the question of the moral standards of the current younger generation (see Tao, Chapter 11; Xu, Chapter 12). Viewing this concern with social order and moral standards in social conduct in the context of a long Confucian moral tradition in China, current societal concern for the moral development of citizens can be understood from the point of view of the continuation of a Chinese cultural value, rather than the novelty of the development of a socialist state. Related to the overall development of social order and moral standards is another Chinese value—that of educating the young generation. This value of learning and achievement prevails in every Chinese society covered by the discussions in this volume.

Value of Education and Achievement

Many authors in this book touch on the issue of educating the young, particularly Tao (Chapter 11), Xu (Chapter 12), Yu (Chapter 20), Kuo (Chapter 13), and, in part, Lum and Char (Chapter 15). Such attention was not the result of prior selection of arrangement for the conference meeting; it was a coincidence. But the fact that so many authors chose to discuss the education issue is not accidental, for it ties in to the traditional cultural value of enhancing the welfare of the next generation by focusing on its education.

In the family, Chinese parents pay special attention to training children to adhere to socially desirable and culturally approved behavior. One way to measure the success of parental intervention is the ability of children to perform well in school. Children who fail to live up to adults' standards of performance in school are often viewed as expressing abnormal, deviant, or antisocial behavior. Once we understand this point, it is not difficult to understand why both social scientists and psychiatrists in Chinese society, as represented by our authors in this volume, treat the education and learning issues as if they are mental illness issues. Some of the chapters give us the impression that when children fail to achieve a certain standard in school in both grades and proper conduct by, for example, showing dis-obedience and stubbornness, and being over-demanding, these failures may sometimes be considered abnormal in almost mental pathological terms. The chapters concerning the issue of school behavior in mainland China demonstrate, though implictly, certain efforts of socially engineering the state in expectation of producing desireable child behavior and values. This issue is also noticeable in Singapore, as is already common knowl-edge.

Even without state intervention in a direct way as seen in mainland China, Lum and Char (Chapter 15) provide some indication of the Chinese perception in the United States of the special value of education. The authors see a correlation between the Chinese value of education for the young and their achievement in adulthood in the areas of business success and upward social mobility. This view reflects a common belief shared by many Chinese overseas.

CONCLUDING REMARKS

Although many scholars have attempted to study and describe the characteristics of Chinese culture, most of them focus on and elaborate on these characteristics from different angles. Some approach the subject of conceptualizing culture as civilization (Qian, 1969), while others focus on the dimensions of thought and philosophy and have reviewed such matter mainly from historical aspects (de Riencourt, 1965; Greel, 1953; Wei, 1979). In contrast to this, by comparing the different lifestyles of Chinese and Americans, Hsu (1981) make an attempt to describe the Chinese culture as reflected in behavior and ways of life. Furthermore, in concentrating on the personality, a group of behavioral and social scientists has tried to describe the characteristics of the Chinese personality (Li and Yang 1972), and the subject of normal and abnormal behavior in Chinese culture has been dealt with by Kleinman and Lin (1981).

From a mental health point of view, it is more useful and pertinent to understand how a culture affects the mind, behavior, and mental health of an individual, a group of people, and a society as a whole. More specifically, personal development, personality formation, family, and social behavior are some of the subjects needing investigation. It is also necessary to elaborate on how cultural factors influence the nature of stress in society, how the manifestation of psychopathology is created, and how cultural factors determine patterns of coping mechanisms and styles of adjustment. Particularly pertinent to the contemporary time is our understanding of how the processes of cultural change and modernization affect our emotional life and mental health and what ways of coping are available in such processes of change. Throughout this volume, authors explore all these themes from the point of view of their own disciplines, based on their work in different settings of Chinese communities, both on the mainland and overseas. It is hoped that this volume will help us to understand the common characteristics of Chinese culture and its impact on mental health.

REFERENCES

de Riencourt, A.
    1965   The soul of China: An interpretation of Chinese history (Rev. Ed.). New York: Harper and Row.
Geertz, C.
    1973   *Thick description: Toward an interpretive theory of culture.* In C. Geertz (Ed.), *The interpretation of cultures.* New York: Basic Books.
Greel, H. G.
    1953   *Chinese thought: From Confucius to Mao Tse-Tung.* New York: The New American Library.

Hsu, F. L. K.
    1981   *Americans and Chinese: Passage to differences* (3rd Ed.). Honolulu: University Press of Hawaii.
Keesing, R. M.
    1974   Theories of culture. *Annual Review of Anthropology, 3,* 73–97.
Kleinman, A. and Lin, T. Y.
    1981   *Normal and abnormal behavior in Chinese culture.* Dordrecht, Holland: Reidel.
Li, Y. Y., and Yang, K. S. (Eds.)
    1972   *The character of the Chinese: An interdisciplinary approach:* Taipei: Institute of Ethnology, Academia Sinica.
Qian, M.
    1969   *Zhongo wun hua contang* [The collection of essays on Chinese culture]. Taipei: Sanmin Shu Ju.
Wei, Z. T.
    1979   *Zhongo su siang shi* [The history of Chinese thought]. Taipei: Daling.

CHAPTER 2

The Emergence of the New Chinese Culture*

Godwin C. Chu

INTRODUCTION

Since 1949, important changes have taken place in the social, political, and economic structures in China. This chapter represents an attempt to analyze the impact of these major structural changes on Chinese culture.

I begin by presenting a paradigm that views the concept of culture in a structural perspective. Next, I analyze the more salient structural changes in mainland China since the 1950s, including the social and economic transformation in the early 1950s, the political and ideological campaigns of the late 1950s, and finally, the 10 eventful years that began with the Cultural Revolution in the summer of 1966. Finally, I discuss the implications of these structural changes on Chinese culture. Cultural change in China is described in broad terms; and because of the scarcity of available data, my observations should be more appropriately regarded as hypotheses that await further verification, rather than as empirical statements.

* This manuscript was prepared in December 1981.

15

CHINESE CULTURE
AND MENTAL HEALTH

THE CONCEPT OF CULTURE

Culture is a way of life. It embodies consistent patterns of behavior that are distinctive of a particular group of individuals, in this case the people of mainland China. We recognize diversities in the behavioral patterns of any group. We assume, however, that despite the range of individual diversities, we can identify elements of consistency and uniformity that are common to many members of a cultural group. It is this uniformity within a range of diversities that must be discovered to provide for a basis for understanding contemporary Chinese culture.

The behavioral patterns of a group are built around social relationships between the individual self, as a hypothetical prototype, and the individual's significant others. These relationships take place in the context of two major components: (1) materials and objects in the physical environment that the self relies on for survival and that, through the extent of technology, mediate social relations; (2) ideas including ideology, values, and religious beliefs—both cognitive and evaluative—that influence the way the self perceives the social and physical environments and that set priorities for social relations and the pursuit of materials and objects in the physical environment.

The relationships between the self, on one hand, and the significant others, materials and objects, and ideas, on the other, are represented in Figure 2.1. The solid lines represent the direct relations, that is, how the self interacts with the significant others, how the self utilizes the materials and objects in the physical environment and is in turn influenced by them, and how the self embraces certain ideas as relevant for social and material relations. The broken lines represent perceived relations, or linkages, that exist in the perceptual field of the self. They are important even though they may not fully correspond to reality, because it is often the perception rather than reality that influences our behavior. Are the significant others seen as endorsing the same ideas the self embraces? Are the significant others seen as cooperating or competing with the self in the pursuit of material relations? Is the self's pursuit of materials and objects seen as consistent with the prevailing ideology?

Culture, expressed as a way of life, encompasses the totality of these complex relations, both substantive and perceptual, which regulate the behavioral patterns of a group. These relations are so intricately intertwined that they tend to be fused at the observational level. Conceptually, they are distinguishable and can serve as a useful framework in which we sort out and organize our empirical observations. These relations form a holistic structural entity. The social relations, which are the human ties

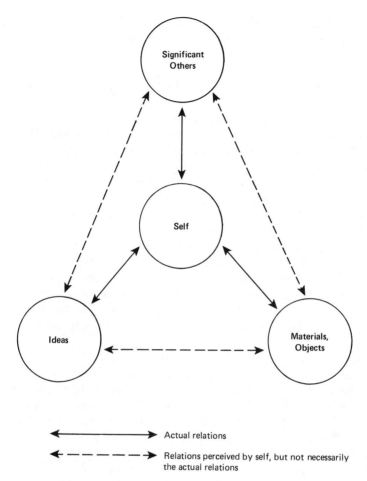

Figure 2.1 Concept of self in relationship to significant others, materials and objects, and ideas.

that by and large hold a cultural group together, are built upon the two other components as cornerstones: The material component provides for physical survival and nurture, and the ideological component gives life a measure of meaning. It is in the context of the social relations that material life is sustained and ideologies are maintained. When changes occur in either the material relations or the ideological domain, the social relations will adapt and adjust, often haltingly and laggardly. By cultural change, we mean change in the basic patterns of social relations due to changes in either material relations or ideological perception.

SOCIAL AND ECONOMIC TRANSFORMATIONS

In traditional China, material relations were subjugated to ideologies. This does not mean that material relations were not important. Without an adequate material basis, the Chinese culture could not have survived. But the Chinese seem to have been content with a margin of material subsistence that would strike people in other cultures to be rather meager. Chinese were taught to find peace in poverty (*an pin*) and to derive pleasure in mental cultivation (*le dao*). Mental cultivation (*dao*), seemed to be earthbound and rooted in ancestor worship. To the Chinese, the extended family not only provided for material subsistence but, perhaps more importantly, also acted as the primary environment in which a strong bond held together the generations of the past, present, and future. Instead of turning to God, the Chinese sought and found security in the ancestors' shadow (Hsu, 1967). Credit for achievements went to the ancestors, as exemplified by the popular saying, *guang zong yao zu* ('to glorify clan and honor ancestor').

Failure was considered a disgrace to the ancestors. That disgrace, however, was not the burden of any single individual, but rather was collectively shared by the members of the extended family. The traditional Chinese culture provided little impetus for change, and collectively, the Chinese society was able to maintain a status quo for centuries. Individually, the Chinese lived with relatively low personal aspirations and, at the same time, experienced relatively low personal anxiety. Even though China was a society of scarcity, the Chinese were able to endure their sufferings because their hearts were set on nonmaterial ideas.

With the founding of the People's Republic of China in 1949, sweeping changes were introduced to the material life of the Chinese. In the rural countryside, material relations were freed from landlord domination by the land reform of 1951–1952 and progressed from individual small farming to mutual aid teams, and finally, to the agricultural cooperatives by 1956. During the same period, industrialists and businessmen in towns and cities were expropriated and their properties taken over by the state. These measures eliminated two of China's perennial sources of inequity and put the peasants and urban workers closer to the means of production and the fruits of their labor.

On one hand, these radical changes in the material relations literally wiped out the social and economic influences of the landed gentry in the countryside and greatly reduced, if not totally obliterated, the positions of the urban business elite. To the extent that China's traditional kinship networks were partially built on such economic foundations, these measures weakened the influence of the kinship groups. Although kinship ties still exist today on an attenuated basis, extended families have disappeared as a coherent formal group and the kinship groups are no longer able to apply economic sanctions to enforce their norms and demands as they did in the past.

On the other hand, these early measures of social and economic reforms tied the mass of people closely to the national efforts of socialist reconstruction, with the state acting as a main provider of means of subsistence. Nearly all urban workers have become wage earners employed by the state. In the villages, the peasants derive their income largely from state-owned land in the communes, supplemented by earnings from private plots and sideline productions.

In these changes, one sees a thread of continuity with the past. Just like the traditional ones they displaced, the new material relations are subjugated to ideologies, except the new ideologies have been anchored on state-inspired collectivism instead of on kinship loyalty.

Motivated partly by patriotism and partly by a sense of purpose after a whole generation of war and internal strife, the people of mainland China initially met the challenge of national reconstruction with a high spirit and sustained efforts. The experience of a college girl during the Great Leap Forward illustrates this point:

> Well, we were supposed to work eight hours a day but there were so many challenges and counter-challenges between the various units that we were frequently told to work extra hours. There were three eight-hour shifts but those with high political consciousness refused to stop work when their time was up—and their display of enthusiasm spurred on the less active students, because no one wanted to be criticized as ideologically backward. How I remember those cold wet early spring days when we slipped and fell under our heavy loads, covering our faces and clothes with mud. But we all worked like mad because we wanted to prove our political soundness. . . .
>
> When we discussed the work amongst ourselves we were always careful to say something like, "It's rough, but nothing is insurmountable in the socialist society, and nothing is difficult for one with noble ambitions." (Harper, 1964)

The importance of group pressure in maintaining high spirits is clearly demonstrated in that example. Later on, beginning with the three years of natural calamities from 1959 to 1961 and aggravated by the Cultural Revolution, such high spirits were to become gradually dissipated to the point where the party had to launch one production campaign after another in order to maintain productivity at an acceptable level.

The Communist revolution and the measures of economic and social reform indeed changed the face of China. They raised the aspirations of the Chinese people, instilling in them high hopes and lofty ideals. For the first time in history, the Chinese were no longer content to find peace in poverty (*an pin*) or derive pleasure in mental cultivation (*le dao*). They wanted to rebuild their country. A legacy of the extreme leftist policies, beginning with the hasty moves to establish the Peoples' Communes in the fall of 1958 and culminating in the 10 years of Cultural Revolution, was to dampen the high hopes and frustrate the new aspirations.

INITIAL IDEOLOGICAL CAMPAIGNS

Shortly after the founding of the People's Republic, the Party began a series of ideological campaigns, directed mostly at intellectuals and cadres. To understand these campaigns, we need to go back in history to the midnineteenth century, the period of the Self-Strengthening Movement, during the reign of emperor Tung Chih. China had suffered two humiliating defeats in wars with Britain and France. There was a general feeling among Chinese intellectuals and officials that China must recover and restore its past glory. The Self-Strengthening Movement, which was short-lived and unsuccessful, was the beginning of an agonizing process of awakening and protest that lasted nearly a century. Kang Yu-wei and Liang Chi-chao attempted to capitalize on these popular sentiments in their Hundred Day Reform but failed because the Dowager Empress intervened. Sun Yat-sen rode on the crest of the same nationalist emotions and succeeded in toppling the Manchu dynasty. Essentially the same mixture of patriotism and nationalism enabled China to sustain the 8 years of war that ended with Japan's defeat in 1945. So when the Communist party introduced the bold economic and social reforms soon after 1949, the Chinese intellectuals responded with enthusiasm and support. In that sense, the ideological campaigns initiated by the party could have a receptive audience.

But the campaigns went a step further. The party leadership wanted more than enthusiatic support of and active participation in these reform movements. Relying on the methods of criticism and self-criticism, borrowed largely from Soviet Russia, these campaigns aimed at the perpetuation of self-sacrifice and the establishment of collective will (*po si li gong*).

It was obvious from the beginning that these campaigns were going to have rough sailing through the traditional minds of the Chinese because a tendency of simulation, which was apparently widely known, seems to have persisted over the years. The latest manifestation was a trend, revealed after the purge of the Gang of Four, known as *feng pai* (wind group), rolling in the direction of the gusty wind: If the wind happens to be blowing eastward, lean eastward; if the wind happens to be blowing westward, lean westward. The best way of survival was to follow the mainstream.

One particular campaign in the early years deserves special mention because of its impact on China's intellectuals: the Hundred Flowers Movement in the spring of 1957. Sensing an atmosphere of unrest in the large cities in China following the Hungarian Revolution, the party urged the intellectuals to speak their minds. When the criticisms became an outpouring and reached a level far beyond anybody's expectations, party authorities reacted by launching the Anti-Rightist Movement, and many who had spoken up were purged. This campaign is now recognized as having caused damage to the relations between the party and the intellectuals. The trend was further aggravated in the Cultural Revolution, when Chinese intellectuals were condemned as "stinky Number 9," a derogatory term that treated the intellectuals as the lowest of all undesirables.

It is difficult to assess the effectiveness of these ideological campaigns without empirical evidence. The general impression from events since the 1950s as well as revelations in the mainland Chinese press now and then is that these campaigns fell short of their professed goals of transforming the Chinese self. Two factors may be relevant. First, what the campaigns advocated were not always consistent with what was seen in the physical environment. Second, due to the simulation tendency, the perceptual linkage between the significant others and the new ideology was not firmly established. It is important to note that the current Party leadership has vowed not to wage such criticism campaigns anymore.

IMPACT OF THE CULTURAL REVOLUTION

I briefly discuss the impact of the Cultural Revolution on Chinese culture. When millions of young Chinese responded in 1966 to the call of Mao Tse-tung to join the Cultural Revolution, they were inspired by the same brand of patriotism and idealism that had fueled the revolutionary fire several generations ago. But events soon got out of control, and the initial spirit of revolution turned into massive violence and chaos. What was originally proclaimed to be a movement to restore the spirit of revolution and to purge the ills of bureaucratism was turned into a struggle for power by Chiang Ching, Lin Piao, and other leftist leaders. Many of the old party leaders who had defended the cause of the party were purged and persecuted. Some committed suicide. Others died in prison. Opportunist like Wang Hung-wen, who took advantage of the confusion to join the leftist group, were able to rise so fast that the Chinese coined the phrase "going up by helicopter" to describe their ascendance.

While the power struggle was going on in party branches and government offices, millions of Red Guards roamed the country in a wanton rampage to destroy the old customs and old culture. Books were burned; objects of art smashed; temples and historical relics wrecked. Intellectuals who were considered to be links with the past were humiliated and paraded in the streets. After the Red Guards had served their purpose as an instrument of disruption and destruction to facilitiate the seizure of power by the leftists, they themselves were dispersed and sent to the countryside. Their prominence as a new force of political actors was short-lived.

This is a very sketchy summary of the violent and complex events during the initial years of the Cultural Revolution. To the people of China, these events contributed to a few major perceptions. On one hand, there was no longer any doubt that the old way of life, to which the Chinese had been accustomed for many generations, had finally been cast in disgrace. On the other hand, there was confusion about the meaning of the new ideology. Veteran party members who had joined the Communist movement in the 1920s and 1930s suddenly became renegades. Yet new party leaders like Wang Hung-wen did not inspire confidence and respect: They preached revolution but lived a life of corruption. The perceptual uncertainty was further aggravated when the Chinese learned of the death of Lin Piao after his abortive attempt to assassinate Mao had failed. This was the man who called himself Mao's closest comrade.

It is now known that for 10 years the Chinese people lived in chaos. Mao was isolated from reality by the leftist clique that supplied him with misinformation about the conditions in the country. Meanwhile, injustice and corruption prevailed. Those who knew how to please the leftist clique were able to retain their positions and even to gain promotions. Those who dared to speak the truth became the targets of persecution. Those 10 years, now recognized as a period of calamities rather than revolution, were a low point in the saga of Chinese culture.

RESPONSE BY THE CHINESE PEOPLE

Any general observations about the way the Chinese people responded to these changes would be inadequate in view of the diversities of personal experiences and situations. The changes the vast rural population went through were quite different from the agonies of the urban residents. Even within urban areas, to which our discussion mainly applies, party cadres, intellectuals, and workers had different experiences. With these qualifications in mind, I suggest three kinds of behavioral and attitudinal responses that can be roughly identified with three age groups: the older generation, most of whom grew up before 1949; the middle generation, whose coming of age was caught up in the Cultural Revolution; and the younger generation, to whom the Cultural Revolution is only a nightmare retold by the elders. The dividing points between groups are not clear-cut.

For the older generation, the response was largely one of endurance and resilience. They were saddened when the high hopes they had developed in the 1950s were destroyed by the extreme leftist policies. But they had lived with suffering before and were able to endure and persevere. They had learned to be patient, to wait for a change for the better. Since the downfall of the Gang of Four, most of those in the older generation have returned to their original posts. Their primary aspiration is to cultivate a generation of successors who can absorb their work experience and take over the responsibility of building a socialist state. If there is one group that has retained some latent elements of the traditional Chinese culture, it is probably the older generation Chinese.

The middle generation is quite different. Most of them were young and impressionable when the Cultural Revolution began, and they had their brief moments of power and glory. When Mao reviewed them at Tien An Men Square, they went wild in their frantic pledge of loyalty and support. They were taught to challenge the authorities, to tear up anything that stood in their way. They were willing to sacrifice for the cause of revolution. They disdained material comfort. Even when they were sent to the countryside, many still maintained their high spirits. They wanted to prove what they could do for their country. To them, nothing seemed impossible if there was a will. But as time went on, when they had to deal with inhospitable environments and uncooperative local bureaucracy, they became frustrated, and their frustration eventually turned into bitterness. After the downfall of the Gang, some writers of the middle generation have poured out their afflictions and frustrations in a brand of literature known to be marked with scars. Recently, many in this generation have returned to cities like Shanghai, where they are impatient with the authorities, rather than submissive, and they do not hesitate to speak up. During the nationwide pay raises in 1979, many in that generation argued forcefully with their supervisors, making demands for more pay, which they considered to be their right. It was essentially people in this generation that joined the mass rally in April 1976 in Tien An Men Square that eventually erupted into riots. If there is any general way to characterize the middle generation, it seems that they are more outspoken, less submissive, and take ideology more seriously than the older generation. They are not as patient and are more ready to commit themselves to actions in order to achieve their objectives of building a socialist China. They embody some budding new elements of Chinese culture, but as of now, they are a partially lost generation.

When the Cultural Revolution started in the summer of 1966, the younger generation of today had barely begun school. Most of them were still in junior high school when the leaders of the Gang of Four were arrested. Thus, they have been sheltered from the harsh realities of the leftist policies that ended with the downfall of the Gang. The policy of sending high school students up to the mountains and down to the villages, for example, was discontinued before most of them became eligible. Thus, they have not experienced the hardships that their older brothers and sisters had to go through. At the same time, they have not acquired in their socialization process a firm imprint of the traditional culture, which their parents had. They did not have an opportunity to read the many popular traditional novels that dwelt on the old values and beliefs. Nor were they old enough to see any of the traditional Chinese operas that espoused such long-established morals as loyalty to the emperor, filial peity, ancestor worship, chastity, and personal integrity. Yet whatever radical ideology they learned in school under the leftist influence has now been repudiated. In a sense, it is almost as if they were brought up in an atmosphere of moral ambiguity.

Their experience with the material environment is also quite different from that of the older and middle generations. They never knew the suffering of the past, except through school sessions on "remembering the bitterness [of the past] and thinking about the sweetness [of the present]." At best these sessions provided secondhand understanding, and they lack the ingrained feeling of nationalism that the older generation developed through personal experience during the Sino–Japanese War or from humiliation inflicted by Western imperialists. They grew up in a China that was already a world power. However, the benefits of opportunism that the followers of the Gang enjoyed until 1976 were probably not lost on their young minds. Their aspirations seem to be largely materialistic, often expressed for immediate gratification.

In the spring of 1981, the *People's Daily* published the results of a survey on the characteristics of the young people of China (Huang, 1981). The survey was conducted in 1980 by three researchers (Huang Chi-chien, Cheng Li-Hua, and Fan Hsin-ming) among 987 young respondents interviewed in factories, communes, schools, and residential districts in two provinces, Fukien and Anhui. The findings, presented here in translation, are summarized in five parts.

1. Young Chinese overwhelmingly reject leftist radicalism and broadly support the party's new directions and policies. However, among some of

them there exist in varying degrees inadequate understanding of the superiority of the socialist system and insufficient confidence in China's Four Modernizations.

2. Young Chinese are concerned with the future of China. Their thinking is critical and lively. They demonstrate a greater ability for independent thinking and less inclination for conservatism and traditionalism than the past generation. They are in the forefront of ideological liberation. However, some of them lack a clear-cut direction in their ideology. They lack stability in applying standards of right and wrong. Some even demonstrate certain erroneous tendencies.

3. Young Chinese are pragmatic. They are concerned about the economic development of their country. They are concerned about their own realistic benefits. They are enthusiastic about learning science and technology, about acquiring useful skills. The empty political rhetoric of the ultraleftists has no following among them. Among some of the young people, however, there is a feeling of boredom about politics. They lack lofty ideals. The stimulation of political activities and the appeals of charismatic leadership are losing ground among these young people.

4. Young Chinese are expressing greater and greater demands in the material and cultural areas of life, they show an increasingly stronger desire for what is aesthetic and beautiful and they abhor the life of poverty, the material abstinence, and the cultural dictatorship advocated by Lin Piao and the Gang of Four. However, some form of excessive desire divorced from the reality of China's economic development is gaining ground among some of the young Chinese. They lack a persevering, enterprising spirit. Capitalism and other forms of nonproletarian ideology are still seriously eroding some of the young.

5. Moral standards are gradually improving. Many young people have played an exemplary role in establishing a new moral code in society. But the 10 years of turmoil (the Cultural Revolution from 1966 to 1976) have created a dilution of legal concepts. The lack of moral cultivation remains to be further remedied. The abnormal psychology among some young people requires further healing.

In full recognition of this need for healing, the party launched an educational campaign in the spring of 1981 to help the young people. The movement promotes five moral standards and four "beauties." The five standards are civility, courtesy, sanitation, orderly conduct, and morality. The four beauties were the following:

1. *Beauty in heart and spirit.* This requires cultivation of an upright personality and ideology in support of the leadership of the party and socialism. This beauty is to be demonstrated in patriotism, integrity,

and honesty. Any behavior that is a blemish on national honor and personal dignity or that is self-centered and couched in falsehood must be avoided.

2. *Beauty in language.* This requires the use of polite language that is harmonious, graceful, and modest, rather than rude and profane. One should not twist words and argue without reason.

3. *Beauty in behavior.* This requires diligence, friendliness, discipline, and behavior that will not harm the collective interest but will promote the welfare of the people and society. One must not damage public property nor violate law and order.

4. *Beauty in environment.* This requires sanitation and cleanliness in one's own home, place of work, and any public gatherings.

It was recognized that this new movement must begin with children in the formative years, from the time they learn to talk. This movement has been carried to the families, schools, factories, stores, and any other places where people gather. All the available media of communication, including art, literature, music, drama, dance, and television, have been pressed into service to carry out this movement of civility and courtesy.

CULTURAL TRANSITION

My hypothesis is that mainland China is in the throes of cultural transition. The old traditional culture is declining, partly as a result of social and economic transformations and partly due to the adverse impact of the Cultural Revolution. The traditional patterns of social relations that espoused filial piety and respect for elders and that deterred innovation no longer dominate life in contemporary China. If the erosion of traditional Chinese culture began even before the Communist revolution, the weakening of the social and economic ties in the kinship networks since then has quickened the pace of its decline. For most urban residents, the chaotic turmoil during the Cultural Revolution caused the residual traditional culture to totter further.

Parodoxically, the older generation Chinese, who still embody some traditional culture in varying degrees, were the ones who built up high hopes in the 1950s. They helplessly stood by when these hopes were dashed by the leftist radicals. The middle generation Chinese had a brief moment of ideological fervor at the height of the Cultural Revolution. Many now live in frustration and disappointment. The new Chinese culture thus rests in the younger generation.

On the bright side, the younger generation Chinese are not burdened by the conservatism and traditionalism that stood in the way of innovation and progress. If the old kinship obligations weighed heavily on the past generations, then the younger people have been freed of that bondage. One question is whether the denial of kinship constraints may go so far as to reject the traditional Chinese virtue of caring for one's elderly parents. There is some indication that this is becoming a problem among some young urbanities. The party leadership has recently begun to publicize caring for elderly parents as a virtue, without suggesting total obedience toward parents in one's adulthood.

The younger generation Chinese are recognized to be pragmatic, a clear evidence of their rejection of conservatism and traditionalism. Pragmatism without a foundation of moral principles, however, can border on utilitarian manipulation. Unless guided by appropriate moral standards, a pragmatic life could turn into a ruthless pursuit of limited material goods and services. The consequence could be an enormous burden on the existing mechanisms of social control. But the basic issue here goes beyond the mere maintenance of social order. Even if a society could maintain perfect order and harmony, pragmatism without meaningful public goals and ideals can be like a boat drifting without direction: It would end up in nothing more than consumerism. This prospect would be contrary to China's ambition of accomplishing the Four Modernizations.

Three decades after China's revolution, we see the budding emergence of a new Chinese culture, standing, as it were, at a crossroad. The new emerging culture has traveled a tortuous journey. It is finally leaving behind some of the restraining forces of the traditional past that was anchored on kinship obligations. But in so doing, it seems to edge toward ignoring the care of elders as a family responsibility. It has parted with traditional Chinese conservatism and embarked on a new course of pragmatism. But it has yet to rebuild a foundation of socialist moral principles and a bastion of public goals so that the energy freed from kinship constraints and the leftist yoke can be put to creative uses.

REFERENCES

Hsu, F. L. K.
    1967   *Under the ancestors' shadow—Kinship, personality, and social mobility in village China.* Garden City, NY: Doubleday.
Harper, F. (Ed.)
    1964   *Out of China—A collection of interviews with refugees from China.* Hong Kong: Dragon Books.
Huang, C. C.
    1981   How should we understand our younger generation? *People's Daily,* February 24.

CHAPTER 3

The Confucian Paradigm of Man: A Sociological View*

Ambrose Y. C. King
Michael H. Bond

INTRODUCTION

While we fully appreciate that Chinese culture is a far from homogeneous system (Wright, 1957:71–104), it seems to us that Confucian values have nevertheless played a predominant role in molding Chinese character and behavior. Therefore, it is legitimate to anatomize the structural pattern of Chinese attitudes and behavior by analyzing the Confucian paradigm of man, although this method is neither exclusive nor exhaustive.

Admittedly, Confucianism, which is enormously rich and complex, defies any simple characterization, and there are different articulations of

---

* In this chapter, the term *man* is used to refer to the individual in accordance with Confucian terminology. However, it should be understood that in most cases, it refers both to man and to woman.

29

Confucian theory of society and the individual. Most of the literature, sociological or not, depicts Confucianism as a social theory and a social force that tends to mold the Chinese into group-oriented or, more specifically, family-oriented and socially dependent beings (Solomon, 1971). Unquestionably, this view has a good deal of sociological truth and has been more or less borne out to date by empirical studies (Bond and Wang, 1983).

Nevertheless, the typical presentation grasps only a part of the total complexity. In this chapter, we attempt to show that the Confucian paradigm of man has the theoretical thrust as well as a built-in structural imperative to develop a person into a relation-oriented individual who is not only socially responsive and dependent but also capable of asserting a self-directed role in constructing a social world. This feature of Confucianism has been relatively neglected in theoretical analyses and unexplored in empirical research.

THE CONFUCIAN CONCEPTION OF HUMANITY

The fundamental fact of Confucianism is that it is primarily a secular social theory, the foremost purpose of which is to achieve a harmonious society. Indeed, harmony is the most treasured social value (Bodde, 1953:19–80). But how is a harmonious society possible? To this question, Confucians invariably answer that if every individual were to act towards others in a proper way, then an orderly world would be achieved. The proper way is prescribed by the dictates *li* (propriety), a set of rules for action (Fingarette, 1972:53). In sociological terms, Confucianism perceives the ideal society as a massive and complicated role system. The conception of role system is in fact embedded in the doctrine of *zheng ming* (rectification of names; Mote, 1972:49).

"Let the ruler be a ruler, the father a father, the son a son," and so forth. (Lau, 1979:Chapter 12, paragraph 11). The guidelines for instantiating these various roles are defined by *li*, which can be conceptualized as the grammar of relationships.

In a thought-provoking article, Francis Hsu (1971:23–44) argues that personality is a Western concept rooted in individualism, and he proposes that the central ingredient in the human mode of existence is man's relationship with his fellow men. Accordingly, Hsu proposes the *ren* (humanheartness) approach of Confucianism in contrast to the Western approach, which focuses on anomic individuals and their intrapsychic dynamics. Indeed, it seems to us that the Confucian conception of man cannot be neatly characterized by Western concepts of individualism or holism and should be considered in its own terms (King, 1981).

In Confucian social theory, the individual is never conceived of as an isolated, separate entity; man is, by Confucian definition, a social, or interactive, being (Moore, 1967:5). Using the words of Hu Shih (1919), the late contemporary Chinese philosopher, "In the Confucian human-centered philosophy, man cannot exist alone; all actions must be in a form of interaction between man and man" (p. 283). Not unlike Emile Durkheim, Confucians (at least, Confucians of Hsun-Tzu's persuasion) see society as a humanizing agent: to them, being human is conditional on a man's being obedient to social norms in daily interactions (Bauman, 1976:26–57). It is no accident that the Chinese character *ren* means two men. As Lin Yusheng (1974–1975) put the matter, "*Ren* can only be cultivated and developed in inter-human relationships in a social context" (p. 193).

Indeed, Confucius, the founder of Confucian School, is concerned with the nature of *humanity* rather than the polar concepts *individual* and *society* (Fingarette, 1972: 72–73). Liang Shu-ming (1974:94) presents a perceptive thesis that the traditional Chinese society is neither individual-based nor society based, but relation-based. Liang writes that in a relation-based social system, "the emphasis is placed on the relation between particular individuals" (p. 94). The focus is not fixed on any particular individual but on the particular nature of the relation between individuals who interact with each other (see also Solomon, 1971). Put differently, in the Confucian paradigm of man, man is socially situated, defined, and shaped in a relational context. In brief, man is a relational being (King, 1981:19–24). A relational being is sensitive to his relations with others, above, below, or on equal footing with him. He sees himself situated symbolically in the web of a relational network through which he defines himself.

It must also be acknowledged, however, as de Bary (1970) correctly notes, that "the relations alone . . . do not define a man totally. His interior self exists at the center of this web and there enjoys its own freedom" (p. 149). Confucians recognize and attach great importance to the *ji* (self). While stressing, on the one hand, the importance of relations between and among individuals, Confucians emphasize, on the other, that the individual is not simply a being shaped and determined by his role-relational structure. Ultimately, the individual is more than a role-player mechanically performing the role-related behavior prescribed by the social structure. To use Median terminology, the individual consists of a self (*ji* in Confucian terms) that is an active and reflexive entity. Confucians assign the individual self the capacity to do right or wrong, and, ultimately, the individual alone is responsible for what he is. This voluntaristic view of the individual is crystalized in the unique Confucian concept of *xiu-ji* (self-cultivation). Self-cultivation is a process that involves a subtle interplay between role and identity. And in the process, the ideal of sincerity is essential. The attainment of sincerity is the way of men. The Doctrine of the Mean says, "He who attains to sincerity is he who chooses what is good and firmly holds it fast" (Legge, 1960:324). For Confucians, sincerity is indispensable to the achievement of true self. In the eyes of Confucius, nothing is more unbearable than a *xiang-yuan* who was condemned as "the thief of virtue" simply for his lack of moral autonomy and courage in being unable to hold a consistent stand towards right and wrong (Legge, 1960:324).

The Confucian paradigm of man, in short, is sociological but not sociologistic. It basically sees man as a relational being, who achieves his humanism through interaction with other particular individuals. His self-image and character are shaped by his role in this relational structure. But the individual is not merely a player of roles prescribed by *li*; he has an active self that is capable of shaping the role-relationship he enters. To this often neglected aspect of Confucianism we return in the final section of this chapter.

FAMILY STRUCTURE AND THE INDIVIDUAL

The preceding analysis shows that in the Confucian paradigm the individual is conceptualized as a relational being. According to Confucians, certain relationships are of paramount importance, they are the so-called Five Cardinal Relations (*wu lun*), namely, those between sovereign and subject, father and son, elder and younger brother, husband and wife, and friend and friend. Of these five basic dyads, three belong to the family and the other two are based upon the family model.[1] In Confucian social theory, the family occupies a central position; it is not only the primary social group, but it is the prototype of all social organizations (Mei, 1967:331). In the words of Fung Yu-lan (1948), "The family system was the social system of China" (p. 21). In earth-bound China, family was the primary reality of the Chinese people. Apart from the kinship system, there was rarely a secondary organization or association outside the family to serve the individual's social needs (C. K. Yang, 1959:5). Indeed, there was no major aspect of traditional social life that was not touched by the ties

---

[1] The relationship between sovereign and subject is in terms of father (i.e., *chun-fu*) and son (i.e., *zi-min*), and the relationship between friend and friend is in terms of elder brother (i.e., *wu-xung*) and younger brother (i.e., *wu-di*).

and influence of the family. It is then entirely understandable why the Five Relations were predominantly familistic in conceptualization and role relationships were couched in kinship terms.

It should be emphasized the in the original Confucian paradigm of the Five Relations, role relationships were symmetrical and interdependent. Each party in the relation was expected to perform his role according to the norms prescribed by *li*. In these role dualities, each actor was required to honor his role requirement. Otherwise, his counterpart was not obliged to honor his responsibility. This implicit contract lay at the heart of the doctrine of Rectification of Names.[2]

After the East Han dynasty, however, the concept of *san-keng* (three bonds) gradually emerged as the dominant ideology for the political system as well as the family. According to *san-keng*, the ruler and father were given absolute authority over the subject and the son, respectively. Additionally, the father's position was buttressed by the Confucian virtue of *xiao* (*hsiao* or filial piety). It is convincingly argued by Hu Shih that this principle of filial piety was only later elaborated in the hands of Confucius' disciples, especially Tseng Tzu. What *ren* was to Confucius is what *xiao* was to Tseng Tzu and later Confucians. Confucuis certainly did not fail to recognize that the father–son relation was one of the basic human relations. Yet, it was the later Confucians who attached singular importance to the father–son relationship. They came to conceive of filial piety as the foundation of *ren*, elevating *xiao* as a preeminent virtue (Hu, 1919:128). According to Hu Shih, Confucius' social philosophy of *ren* was transformed into a social philosophy of *xiao*, and *xiao* became the most powerful social dictate (Hu, 1919:126). Indeed, filial piety had become so powerful and pervasive that Fung Yu-lan (1949:18) called it "the ideological basis of traditional [Chinese] society."

It was only logical that the father–son relationship became what students of Chinese society called the model structural unit (Solomon, 1971:78). Lifton (1967) is certainly right in saying, "Whatever its strains, filialism was the source of the predominant identity of traditional China, a basic ideal against which any other form of self-image had to be judged" (p. 419).

Nevertheless, it should be remembered that status and authority in the Chinese family was not solely based upon filial piety; it was also based upon age and the principle of kinship proximity. The veneration of age can be seen as a value concomitant to filialism. According to Confucian teach-

---

[2] In such a symmetrical relationship, if the father or elder brother failed to perform his required role, then the rebellion of the son or younger brother would be accorded a certain degree of legitimacy (see Solomon, 1971:56).

ing, family members should be arranged into proper hierarchic order by their age, with age referring both to generational and chronological age. These two factors formed the foundation for the hierarchy of status and authority in the family. Outside the family the principle of kinship proximity operated, requiring that children be trained to distinguish the degree of *jin* (closeness) and *shu* (distance) in their contacts with his kinsmen in order to show the proper amount of deference and obedience. As C. K. Yang (1959:89) writes: "The interlocking operation of these three factors, generation, age, and proximity of kinship resulted in a system of status and authority that assigned to every person in the kinship group a fixed position identified by a complex nomenclature system." Thus we can see that under the sway of Chinese familism, each individual was locked into an elaborate role structure. Throughout his life the individual constantly struggled with problems concerning his relations with others in this complex kinship circle.

At this juncture, it should be pointed out that the general value of *he* (*ho* or harmony) was emphatically stressed at the family level (Abbott, 1970). That the family thrives and prospers where there is harmony is a deep-seated tenet of conventional Chinese wisdom. Indeed, family harmony itself became a goal. Given and primacy of family models throughout society, harmony became the touchstone for all interpersonal behavior; and the way to achieve this harmony was through the practicing of *li*.

To speak of *li* is to speak of conformism, that is, conforming with the rules. These rules structure family relations into hierarchical dualities: son–father, younger brother–older brother, wife–husband, nephew–uncle, and so forth. Children are taught respect for this ordering throughout the socialization process but particularly after about age five (Ho, 1980). Interpersonal communication is nonreciprocal in the sense that children are discipled not to take initiative in respect to adults and they are not supposed to talk back to parents or other elders. This pattern of passivity is expressed in the Chinese phrase for obedience, *ting-hua* (listen to talk; Solomon, 1971:49–52). In child-rearing practices, a fundamental concern is to inhibit open emotional expression of hostility or aggression towards authority or even peers (Bond and Wang, 1983). There is in fact no prescribed and sanctioned way for the expression of such feeling and behaviors (Abbott, 1970; Wilson, 1970). This lack is certainly consistent with the logic of filial piety. Restraint (*zhi*) is a highly desirable trait in Chinese culture. Controlling emotions is a condition necessary for proper behavior; it is believed that if a man is under the undue influence of passion, he will be incorrect in his conduct and incapable of objective assessment (Tseng, 1973).

Lifton (1967:453) labels the Chinese cultural pattern—moderation, balance, and harmony—a cult of restraint. Self-expression or the strivings for autonomous behavior on the part of the children are discouraged or suppressed as nothing more than selfishness (Solomon; 1971:69). This is certainly fundamental to the concept of *Keji* (*k'o-chi*, conquering or overcoming one's individuality; Wilhelm, 1965:293).

At this point, it should be mentioned that the social forces pressing for hierarchical order are not without their counterpoint. Confucian teaching does recognize the legitimacy of nonconformism. As Rubin (1976) rightly points out, the ideal Confucian is one who aims at harmony; not uniformity; and in the *Analects*, "the message concerning obedience is balanced by one concerning disobedience" (pp. 20–27). This potential for disobedience functioned socially to help individuals mobilize resources for overpowering tyrannical leaders who had exceeded the bounds of legitimacy. In fact, the right of rebellion against tyrannical leaders was fully endorsed in Confucian social–political thought (Hsiao, 1954, Vol. 1:90). Therefore, Confucianism can hardly be accused of being an intellectual system lacking concepts of individualism (Metzger, 1977:42).

The self-oriented precepts became especially vital for the individual when he was caught in a dilemma resulting from divided loyalties. Traditional Confucian scholar–bureaucrats were often under cross pressures coming from the family group, for which the ethical principles were particularistic, and from bureaucratic organizations, for which the ethical principles were universalistic. There was no easy solution for the individual scholar–bureaucrat in passively conforming to ready social guidance; the resolution of such conflicting demands required active struggle and individual choice (C. K. Yang, 1959:158). We believe that the extensive explorations into Chinese conformity have failed to tap the potential for disobedience in the Chinese by constructing demonstrations where no serious moral choices were involved. Hopefully, this incomplete picture of the Chinese as dependent and conforming will be fleshed out by studies more sensitive to the full range of the Confucian influence.

One further word about Chinese conformity is that it is often nothing more than surface conformity, that is, compliance without internalization (Kelman, 1961). Chinese persons are not subject to the same pressures for consistency between inner beliefs and outer behavior as are Westerners (Hiniker, 1969). One generally responds to the dictates of the situation, rather than to the dictates of one's self (Hsu, 1953). Such behavior is not construed as hypocritical or insincere as it would be by Westerners; rather it is a culturally sanctioned mechanism enabling the individual to maintain a harmonious relationship with the external world. In a way, formalistic conformity has a ceremonial function in maintaining social harmony (see also Doi, 1974).

This observation is not to deny that Chinese have a sense of self with associated attitudes, beliefs, and opinions. We have not yet, however, begun to investigate when these internal characteristics come to be relevant in guiding behavior. Until we do so, comparisons of conformity in Chinese and Westerners will be incomplete.

THE PROBLEMATIC OF THE CONFUCIAN PARADIGM

One of the enduring observations of Western analysts is that Chinese people have a strong sense of belonging to a group. Wilson (1970) writes, "What differentiates the Chinese is the singular focus of Chinese group loyalties and the intensity with which ideals of loyal behavior (such as sacrifice for the collective good) are held" (p. 20). Compared with the individualistic culture of the West, this can hardly be debated (Bond, 1983; Bond, Leung, and Wan, 1982; Hofstede, 1980). However, in comparison with the Japanese, the Chinese seem to us less group centered. Nakane (1973) perceptively points out:

> In the Japanese system all members of the household are in one group under the head, with no specific rights according to the status of individuals within the family. The Japanese family system differs from that of the Chinese system, where family ethics are always based on relationships between particular individuals such as father and son, brothers and sisters, parents and child, husband and wife, while in Japan they are always based on the collective group, i.e., members of a household, not on the relationship between individuals. (p. 14)

Perhaps the source of the difference between Chinese and Japanese culture is the consideration given within Confucianism to the individual.

The Confucian version of individualism has, however, a relational emphasis. As Bodde (1957) summarizes it, "Confucian 'individualism' means the fullest development by the individual of his creative potentialities— not, however, merely for the sake of self-expression but because he can thus best fulfill that particular role which is his within his social nexus" (p. 66). This particular role is often incongenial to the development of individual autonomy and initiative. The family produces structural effects that tend not only to make child develop a dependency social orientation towards authority but also to make the members develop a group orientation towards the family. In traditional China, it was the family, not the individual, that was the important unit in social transactions.[3] Whenever there

[3] Johnson wrote, "Nothing is more important for an understanding of the wonderfully stable and long-lived social system of China than this fact: that the social and the political unit are one and the same, and that this unit is not the individual but the family." (1910:135)

was conflict between individual members and the family, "it sought the solution from the self-sacrifice of the individual for the preservation of the group" (C. K. Yang, 1959:172). Family socialization practices were marked by a particular stress on the cultivation of collective consciousness and responsibilities of the members. This same strategy is being used in contemporary China to sharpen the individual's sense of responsibility towards that larger group of the commune, district, and the country (Ho, 1979).

The much-discussed concept of *face* is a case in point (Bond and Lee, 1981). Face concerns are certainly no monopoly of Chinese people (Ho, 1976). Part of what differentiates the Chinese concept of face from that of the Westerner, however, lies in the fact that face is more a concern to the family than to the individual. Face-losing or face-gaining concerns not only the person directly involved but also the family (King and Myers, 1977). Such sayings as, "The children's misbehavior is the fault of the father," or, "The ugly things [of the family] should not go out of the family gate," underscore the sense of joint responsibility and shared fate involved in family membership. One's face is a collective property. For this reason children must be taught that, "A man needs face like a tree needs bark." Believing this, children are likely to be cautious and avoid any rash behavior that may adversely reflect both on them and on their family.

We have briefly outlined the hierarchical and collective pressure inherent in Confucian social philosophy. The family, as the primary social reality for Chinese, was chiefly responsible for socializing its members to function within these restraints to achieve harmony. Often this harmony was purchased at the price of individual interests, despite the considerable emphasis given by Confucian teachings to the need for individual development and cultivation.

It is understandable, then, why scholars advocate the discovery of the individual as the main theme of Confucius (Hughes, 1937), yet hold the view that the individual can never be discovered in Confucian culture (Liang, 1974:260). Indeed, this is the problematic of the Confucian paradigm (Schwartz, 1959). We venture to argue that the Confucian paradigm for man is not totally compatible with Confucian familistic structure and concerns. And it is here the so-called three contradictions of the Confucian tradition argued by Solomon become crystalized.[4] These contradictions and their practical resolution have never received adequate attention from scholars. We hope that this chapter helps stimulate that interest.

---

[4] According to Solomon (1971:78–80), the three contradictions inherent in the Confucian tradition are (1) dependency on hierarchical authority versus self-assertion, (2) social harmony and peace versus hostility and aggression, and (3) self versus group.

THE SELF AND RELATION-CONSTRUCTION

In the preceding analysis, we argue that the Chinese individual was locked into a hierarchical and cohesive family structure. There is no denying that family harmony was supported by asymmetical norms of *xiao* (obedience); we should not, however, overlook the fact that family harmony was also maintained by care and intimacy among the family members. Warmth and mutual love are outstanding characteristics of the Chinese. Consistent with this caring is the probability that the Chinese family has greater tolerence than most for deviant behavior (Lin, 1953:333). So family life was not an oppressive burden by any means for its individual members.

However, the structural restraints of the Chinese family have produced a tendency to subordinate the individual to the wishes of superiors as well as to those of the group (family), and it is no accident that the self's emancipation was widely believed to be possible only through normative and structural changes in the family system (C. K. Yang, 1959:11, 168) With the increasing influence of Western individualistic values since the early twentieth century and the inexorably evolving forces resulting from industrialization and urbanization, the Chinese family system has slowly, but definitely, been eroded (Wong, 1972, 1975).

Moreover, it is not only that the internal family structure has been weakened; the individual's life space has been extended more and more from this primary group into secondary groups. As a result, the Chinese individual is no longer tightly locked in a family structure but finds himself in quite a new social situation where the individual is given a much broader scope for self-expression. To put it differently, the individual is now relatively more free from the restraints of familism, thus shifting the Confucian agendas to a new and different structural base. And it is here that we turn our attention.

To be sure, social relations were never confined exclusively to the sphere of the family in traditional China (Fried, 1953:218–232). Of the Five Cardinal Relations, the Confucian paradigm explicitly recognizes relations among friends. The Chinese proverb, "Relying on parents at home, and on friends outside of home," testifies clearly to the recognition of the need for transcending the family boundary in coping with life situations. Of course, friendship is a universally recognized human phenomenon. What is probably a distinctive characteristic of Chinese friendship is that its nature is always couched in kinship terms. That is, relations among friends are constructed along the pattern of elder brothers and younger brothers: Friends treat each other as brothers. So, three friends became the three blood-brothers immortalized in *The Romance of the Three Kingdoms.* Expressions such as, "Friends are as close as brothers," and, "Within the four seas, all men are brothers," emphasize this familistic conception of friendship. So the less well articulated form of relationship is modeled along the lines of a more familiar *lun*, that of elder brother and younger brother.

Nowhere does Confucius discuss relations among strangers. Not surprisingly, Chinese people are uneasy in such social transactions. Abbott (1970:304) writes, "Heavy reliance on the family and primary group seems to make functioning in outside groups in Chinese society an uncomfortable process even for people with healthy ego-structure and who enjoy associating with others." In the case of the Chinese, the individual's discomfort with strangers lies partly in the fact that he is unable to relate to strangers through any *lun* prescribed by Confucian ethics. Because Confucian ethics are particularistic, but not universalistic, in nature (L. S. Yang, 1957), the stranger as a role category is too ambiguous to be placed in any role structure. This is one reason why Chinese have used the intermediary widely as a cultural mechanism in social relation-construction. Solomon (1971), who is aware of this phenomenon, writes, "Given the importance which Chinese attach to status deference in social contact, in instances of dealings with unknown individuals they tend to seek out a mutually known third party who understands the "face" expectations of all involved to mediate the relationship" (p. 128). We might also add that the third party acts as a bridge to integrate one's relationship to the other indirectly into some prescribed *lun*.

Given the hierarchical nature of the established *lun*, the individual would be relatively uneasy relating with a friend or peers of equal or near-equal social status (Solomon, 1971:126). In this respect, Fairbank observes, "An equal relationship has little precedent in Chinese experience. Their relation (to politics) began with the observation that the order of nature is not egalitarian but hierarchic" (1966:12). This aspect of Chinese relation-construction has important implications for interactions between Chinese and persons from more egalitarian cultures. Mutual accommodation is probably required. The strategy of adopting a Western given name in dealing with Westerns is one such adaptation and is in part a device for managing this unusual relationship between equals.

Another important feature of relationship building is that once outside the rigid role requirements of the immediate family structure, the individual self has considerable freedom in constructing the relational network. What cannot be overemphasized is that the boundary of the Chinese relation network is highly elastic in the sense that it can be expanded or contracted according to the decisions of the self (Fei, 1967:22–37). It is significant to note that even the Chinese basic and primary social group, *jia* (family), is in fact an elastic entity. It can mean only the members of a nuclear family, or it may also mean all members of a lineage or a clan. This ambiguity or elasticity of the family gives the individual ample room for maneuver in kin-relation network construction. What constitutes the boundary of family is very much dependent upon the purposes of the ego. Chinese kinship relations, C. K. Yang writes, "take on the form of a series of concentric circles with Ego as the Center" (1959:89). At the center of the elastic relation network, as Fei (1967:27) rightly argues, there is always the self.

The self-centered voluntarism of the Chinese, which is underdeveloped in the family system, manifests itself in various ways when the individual is free from the bonds of the family. Eberhard (1971) is not incorrect, though exaggerating somewhat, when he says,

> As the Chinese must suppress all aggression within the family, the outer world is the field in which aggression finds its outlets. . . . Only with complete strangers, such as in encounters in a modern big city, or in a foreign country where one is sure that the contact is casual and not lasting, is the individual free and can discharge his aggression directly as the individual in Western society may feel free to do. What counts in such contacts is aggressive intelligence, making the most of every chance as often as one can without risking too much. The biographies of Chinese immigrants, especially Chinese businessmen in other societies, testify to this. (pp. 8, 11)

It is a widely recognized social phenomenon that Chinese individuals unabashedly show a kind of egocentric behavior outside the family, particularly in a nonkin social context (Fei, 1967:27–30). Instead of Western individualism, one finds what is called individual firstism, meaning "placing personal honors, status and interest above other things" (Lifton, 1967:435). We are here indeed suggesting that when the Chinese individual is not structurally situated in a relation-based social web, Confucian values and norms cease to be morally binding or, more accurately, cease to be morally relevant. The popular saying, "If one does not think of his own interest, neither Heaven nor Earth will save him," can hardly be slighted as of no social consequence. Indeed, this egoistic aspect in the development of the Chinese individual, though utterly non-Confucian, is rooted in the very body of the Confucian social theory, which gives a central place to the individual self.[5] Ironically, this type of Chinese characteristic, though often seen as pathological, seems to be socially acceptable in competitive societies.

What interests us here, however, is the relation-construction project, which seems to be of vital importance for the individual engaged in social engineering in a modern world. As mentioned above, the Chinese individ-

---

[5] Fei (1967:27) goes so far as to suggest that *tzu wo chu i* (egotism) lies at the very heart of Chinese social thought, including Confucianism.

ual has a strong relational orientation, which conceives the other person in concrete, differentiated terms. According to the Confucian paradigm, every individual is related with others in the context of *lun*; some *luns*, such as the father–son relation, are preordained givens, while others, such as the friend–friend relation, are voluntarily undertaken. In the former type, the individual has little or no option; he is expected to perform his prescribed roles in these structured relations. However, in the latter type, the individual is very much on his own; he is the initiator of social communication; he is the architect in relation-construction.

It is in this vortex of voluntary network building that the Chinese have demonstrated impressive and sophisticated skills. As one Western anthropologist notes, "Chinese culture has developed inter-personal relationships to the level of an exquisite and superb art" (La Barre, 1946:215). In Western societies, one noted Chinese sociologist writes, "People struggle for rights, while in China, people are concerned with relation construction, affectionate ties" (Fei, 1967:26). This Chinese concern makes very good sense, of course. In a society where civil law was relatively undeveloped (Bodde and Morris, 1967; Hulsewe, 1955) and bureaucratic corruption was rampant (Lau and Lee, 1981), a reliable friendship network was of considerable advantage in protecting one's personal and family interests.

It is therefore no surprise that in effecting a social transaction, personal relational networks, which are based upon particularistic ties, have taken precendence over universalistic legalistic relationships (Bloom, 1977). It is surprising perhaps, this cultural phenomenon has not only survived in socialist China but has become increasingly rampant. "Walking through the back door" and other practices are almost the norm rather than the exception in mainland China.[6] The phenomenon is so widespread that a new term, *guan-xi-xue* (relationology), has been coined for it (*Peking Daily News*, 1981). However, it should be noted that this phenomenon is no monopoly of the mainland Chinese; it is a phenomenon of all Chinese communities. In the achievement-oriented and highly competitive, capitalist society of Hong Kong, this relation-oriented behavioral pattern continues to be a viable cultural phenomenon coexisting with the universalistic, rational pattern of behavior. It is important to bear in mind that traditional familism has been eroded in Hong Kong due primarily to vast institutional processes of industrialization and urbanization. The ascriptive aspect of Chinese familism is fading (King and Leung, 1975). A new kind of familism in which utilitarian considerations are the hallmark of relation-

---

[6] This salient social phenomenon was officially recognized and criticized. See the speech given by Priemier Zhao to the annual session of The Fifth National People's Congress (*People's Daily News*, 1978).

construction has emerged in Hong Kong (Lau, 1981). Due to war and geographical mobility, traditional kinship ties have ceased to have an impact on individual family members. This structural loosening allows for greater flexibility to kinsmen's selectivity in their relation-construction (L. Y. K. Fung, 1981). In Hong Kong, the Chinese individual has not infrequently constructed relation networks through the mobilization of kinship ties, ethnicity ties, friendship ties, and work ties.

So regardless of the political setting, the Chinese cultural dynamic continues to operate. This kind of highly personal relation construction constitutes an important cultural strategy for securing social resources towards self-advancement. To be sure, it is not merely a rational, calculative process; such "engineering" is conditioned by Confucian norms of *bao* or reciprocity (King, 1980; L. S. Yang, 1957). What we argue is that the Chinese individual living under Confucian guidelines is entirely capable of asserting a self-directed role in constructing vast relational networks outside his family. The individualism forming a part of Confucian social philosophy can be realized in this important social arena. Undoubtedly, there are many other such arenas. We hope that this chapter with its relative emphasis on Chinese individualism may stimulate others to examine these other social avenues for self-expression among the Chinese. Previous analyses of Chinese culture have been guilty, we believe, of focusing exclusively on the dependent aspects of Chinese behavior. Such unbalanced presentations are not in keeping with the Chinese imperative of "keeping to the middle way."

REFERENCES

Abbott, K. A.
    1970   *Harmony and individualism.* Taipei: The Orient Culture Service.
Bauman, Z.
    1976   *Toward a critical sociology.* London: Routledge Kegan Paul.
Bloom, A. H.
    1977   A cognitive dimension of social control: The Hong Kong Chinese in cross-cultural comparison. In A. A. Wilson, S. L. Greenblatt, and R. W. Wilson (Eds.), *Deviance and social control in Chinese society.* New York: Praeger.
Bodde, D.
    1953   Harmony and conflict in Chinese philosophy. In A. F. Wright (Ed.), *Studies in Chinese thought.* Chicago: University of Chicago Press.
    1957   *China's cultural tradition.* New York: Holt, Rinehart and Winston.
Bodde, D., and Morris, C.
    1967   *Law in imperial China.* Cambridge: Harvard University Press.
Bond, M. H.
    1983   How does cultural collectivism operate? The impact of task and maintenance contributions on reward distribution. *Journal of Cross-Cultural Psychology, 14,* 41–63.

Bond, M. H., and Lee, P. W. H.
   1981   Face saving in Chinese culture: A discussion and experimental study of Hong
           Kong students. In A. Y. C. King and R. P. L. Lee (Eds.), *Social life and develop-
           ment in Hong Kong.* Hong Kong: Chinese University Press.
Bond, M. H., Leung, K., and Wan, K. C.
   1982   The social impact of self-effacing attributions: The Chinese case. *Journal of
           Social Psychology, 118,* 157–166.
Bond, M. H., and Wang, S. H.
   1983   Aggressive behavior in Chinese society: The problem of maintaining order and
           harmony. In A. P. Goldstein and M. Segall (Eds.), *Global Perspectives on Aggres-
           sion.* New York: Pergamon.
de Bary, W. T.
   1970   Individualism and humanitarianism in late Ming thought. In W. T. de Bary
           (Ed.), *Self and society in Ming thought.* New York: Columbia University Press.
Doi, T.
   1974   Some psychological themes in Japanese human relationships. In J. C. Condon
           and M. Saito (Eds.), *Intercultural encounters with Japan.* Tokyo: Simul Press.
Eberhard, W.
   1971   *Moral and social values of the Chinese: Collected essays.* Taipei: Cheng-wen.
Fairbank, J. K.
   1966   How to deal with the Chinese Revolution. *The New York Review of Books, 6*(2),
           12.
Fei, H. T.
   1967   *Hsiang-tu Chung-kuo*[Peasant China]. Taipei: Lu-Chou Ch'u-Pan She.
Fingarette, H.
   1972   *Confucius—The secular as sacred.* New York: Harper Torchbooks.
Fried, M.
   1953   *Fabric of Chinese society: A study of the social life of a Chinese seat.* New York:
           Octagon Books.
Fung, L. Y. K.
   1981   Strategies for occupational mobility in Hong Kong: A biographical approach.
           Unpublished master's thesis, Sociology Department, The Chinese University of
           Hong Kong.
Fung, Y. L.
   1948   *A short history of Chinese philosophy* (D. Bodde, Trans.). New York: MacMillan.
   1949   The philosophy at the basis of traditional Chinese society. In F. S. C. Northrop
           (Ed.), *Ideological differences and world order.* New Haven: Yale University Press.
Hiniker, P. J.
   1969   Chinese reactions to forced compliance: Dissonance reduction or national char-
           acter. *Journal of Social Psychology, 77,* 157–176.
Ho, D. Y. F.
   1976   On the concept of face. *American Journal of Sociology, 81,* 867–884.
   1979   Psychological implications of collectivism: With special reference to the Chi-
           nese and Maoist dialectics. In L. H. EcKensberger, W. J. Lonner, and Y. Poor-
           tinga (Eds.), *Cross-cultural contributions to psychology.* Lisse: Swets and Zeitlinger.
   1980   *Chinese patterns of socialization.* Unpublished manuscript, Psychology Depart-
           ment, University of Hong Kong.
Hofstede, G.
   1980   *Culture's consequences: International differences in work-related values.* London:
           Sage.

Hsiao, K. C.
    1954   *Chung-kuo cheng-chih ssu-hsiang shih* [A history of Chinese political thought]
            (Vols. 1–6). Taipei: Chung-Hua Wen-Hua Chu-Pan She.
Hsu, F. L. K.
    1953   *Americans and Chinese: Two ways of life.* New York: Abelard-Schuman.
    1971   Psychosocial homeostasis and jen: Conceptual tools for advancing psychologi-
            cal anthropology. *American Anthropologist 73,* 23–33.
Hu, S.
    1919   *Chung-kuo che-hsueh shih ta-keng* [An outline of the history of chinese philoso-
            phy]. Shanghai: The Commercial Press.
Hughes, E. R.
    1937   *The individual in East and West.* London: Oxford University Press.
Hulsewe, A. F. P.
    1955   *Remnants of Han law.* Leiden: Mouton.
Johnson, R. F.
    1910   *Lion and dragon in northern China.* New York: Dutton.
Kelman, H.
    1961   Processes of opinion change. *Public Opinion Quarterly, 25,* 57–78.
King, A. Y. C.
    1980   *Jen chi kuan-hsi chung jen-ching chi fen-hsi* [An analysis of *jen-ching* in interper-
            sonal relationships]. Paper presented at the International Conference of Sino-
            logy, Taipei.
    1981   *The individual and group in Confucianism: A relational perspective.* Paper presented
            at the Conference on Individualism and Wholism, York, Maine, June 24–29.
King, A. Y. C., and Leung, D.
    1975   *The Chinese touch in small industrial organizations* (Occasional Paper). Social
            Research Center, The Chinese University of Hong Kong.
King, A. Y. C., and Myers, J. T.
    1977   *Shame as an incomplete conception of Chinese culture: A study of face* (Occasional
            Paper). Social Research Center, The Chinese University of Hong Kong.
La Barre, W.
    1946   Some observations on character structure in the Orient: II. *Psychiatry, 9,* 215–
            317.
Lau, D. S.
    1979   *The analects.* New York: Penguin.
Lau, C. C., and Lee, R. P. L.
    1981   Bureaucratic corruption and political instability in nineteenth-century China.
            In R. P. L. Lee (Ed.), *Corruption and its control in Hong Kong.* Hong Kong: The
            Chinese University Press.
Lau, S. K.
    1981   Utilitarianistic familism: The basis of political stability. In A. Y. C. King and R.
            P. L. Lee (Eds.), *Social life and development in Hong Kong.* Hong Kong: The
            Chinese University Press.
Legge, James
    1960   *Chinese classic: Vol. 1. Confucian analects.* Hong Kong: Hong Kong University
            Press.
Liang, S. M.
    1974   *Chung-kuo wen hua yao-i* [The Essential Features of Chinese Culture]. Hong
            Kong: Chi-Cheng T'u-Shu Kung Hsu.
Lifton, R. J.
    1967   *Thought reform and psychology of totalism.* Harmondsworth, England: Penguin.

Lin, T. Y.
   1953   A study of the incidence of mental disorder in Chinese and other cultures. *Psychiatry, 16,* 313–336.
Lin, Y. S.
   1974–   The evolution of the pre-Confucian meaning of jen and Confucian concept of
   1975   moral autonomy. *Monumenta Sinica,* 31, 172–204.
Mei, Y. P.
   1967   The status of the individual in Chinese social thought and practice. In C. A. Moore (Ed.), *The Chinese mind.* Honolulu: University of Hawaii Press.
Metzger, T. A.
   1977   *Escape from predicament.* New York: Columbia University Press.
Moore, C. A.
   1967   Introduction: The humanistic Chinese mind. In C. A. More (Ed.), *The Chinese mind.* Honolulu: University of Hawaii Press.
Mote, F. W.
   1972   *Intellectual foundations of China.* New York: Knopf.
Nakane, C.
   1973   *Japanese society.* Harmondsworth, England: Penguin.
Rubin, V. A.
   1976   *Individual and state in ancient China* (S. I. Levine, Trans.). New York: Columbia University Press.
Schwartz, B.
   1959   Some polarities in Confucian thought. In D. S. Nivison and A. F. Wright (Eds.), *Confucianism in action.* Stanford: Stanford University Press.
Solomon, R. H.
   1971   *Mao's revolution and the Chinese political culture.* Berkeley: University of California Press.
Tseng, W. S.
   1973   The concept of personality in Confucian thought. *Psychiatry, 36,* 191–202.
Wilhelm, H.
   1965   Chinese Confucianism on the eve of the Great Encounter. In M. B. Jansen (Ed.), *Changing Japanese attitudes towards modernization.* Princeton, NJ: Princeton University Press.
Wilson, R. W.
   1970   *Learning to be Chinese.* Cambridge, MA: M.I.T. Press.
Wong, F. M.
   1972   Modern ideology, industrialization, and conjugalism: The Hong Kong Case. *International Journal of Sociology of the Family,* 2, 139–152.
   1975   Industrialization and family structure in Hong Kong. *Journal of Marriage and the Family,* 37, 985–1000.
Wright. A. F.
   1957   The formation of sui ideology. In J. K. Fairbank (Ed.), *Chinese thought and institutions.* Chicago: University of Chicago Press.
Yang, C. K.
   1959   *Chinese Communist society: The family and the village.* Cambridge, MA: M.I.T. Press.
Yang, L. S.
   1957   The concept of pao as a basis for social relations in China. In J. K. Fairbank (Ed.), *Chinese thought and institutions.* Chicago: University of Chicago Press.

CHAPTER 4

A Preliminary Study of the Character Traits of the Chinese

Song Weizhen

INTRODUCTION: RESEARCH ON PERSONALITY

Since the 1970s, in response to practical demand, psychologists, sociologists, and clinical medical workers of China have gradually realized that the scientific study of the personality characteristics of the people is of profound significance.

Personality is a complicated subject of inquiry. It is a subject of both psychological and sociological research. Personality is studied from the psychological point of view by taking a person to be the embodiment of the sum of his or her psychological traits or characteristics. The depth and extension of these traits and characteristics varies among individuals. Psychology is the study of these traits and characteristics as manifested in the person and in the course of their formation. In other words, psychology is the study of individual differences among people, while sociology studies personality traits from the nonindividual and extrapersonal perspective and considers personality as a particular social representation. The funda-

47

CHINESE CULTURE
AND MENTAL HEALTH

mental trait of this representation is the product of a defined status within the social structure that is conditioned by economic development, historic and cultural considerations, and customs and conventions. There are certain common spirits and temperaments specific to a particular ethnic group. Ethnic groups are formed in the historical course of national development, develop common conditions, and tend to possess great stability. Sociologists study such common traits of social communities. Since the formation of personality traits is inseparable from social practice, the study of personality and its structure and activities is consciously or unconsciously conditioned by philosophical viewpoints, whether through the approach of psychology or sociology. The difference lies in the fact that some researchers are conscious of such connections and the manner in which they conduct their studies within the perspective of a definite world view, while others are unconscious of such connections and formulate theories by reliance on facts and test materials. But, the analysis and treatment of the facts and test materials are, nevertheless, inevitably conditioned by certain philosophical viewpoints.

Since 1979, members of the Pathological Psychology Section of the Institute of Psychology of the Chinese Academy of Sciences, have taken the initiative in developing a personality inventory that would be suitable for testing the personality traits of the Chinese people. It is hoped that the inventory and test will lay the foundation for further studies on some of the theoretical issues in personality from the point of view of psychology. As a first step, psychology testing was employed in sample populations. Experiences gained from these tests have helped in developing a set of personality inventories that is suitable for applied research on the Chinese people. Furthermore, the testing has helped to lay a foundation for further studies on the theoretical issues of personality psychology. During the 2-year testing period, the test results among the Chinese people indicated significant differences when compared to people in Western countries. Among Chinese (chiefly people of the Han ethic group), certain common personality traits were found in the northerners and southerners and in the young and the old. This finding may provide some referential data for sociologists in their exploration of the social traits.

THE MMPI

Since we are in the process of establishing a model scale and since a standardization is to be achieved, the present findings can be regarded as a general pattern of reference. I now briefly explain work being done.

There are two basic types of personality testing methods: One is a projective test; the other involves use of the questionnaire. Recently, questionnaire methods, especially the Minnesota Multiphasic Personality Inventory (MMPI), have been popular internationally. We have applied this inventory in our testing.

The MMPI, which allows respondents to make a self-report, was first published in 1943 as a result of the need felt in mental health clinics (Hathaway and McKinley, 1967). Since then, due to its popularity this inventory has attracted the attention of scholars from many disciplines in many countries (Butcher 1979, Butcher and Pancheri, 1976; Dahlstrom, Welsh, and Dahlstrom, 1972). In some countries, the inventory has been translated into the native language, and its application in research is seen in the fields of anthropology, psychology, and medical science. The MMPI is especially popular in diagnosing of mental health patients.

This inventory contains 550 statements written from the subject's point of view. The respondents can answer "yes," "no," or "uncertain" to each item. The results are scored according to 14 scales, and a profile can be established for each respondent. The first four parts of the profile are based on validating scales, and the last 10 are based on clinical scales.

The validating scales represent the following areas: Q, question; L, lie; F, validity; and K, correction. The clinical scales represent the following areas: Hs, hypochondriasis; D, depression; Hy, hysteria; Pd, psychopathic deviate; Mf, masculinity–femininity; Pa, paranoia; Pt, psychasthenia; Sc, schizophrenia; Ma, hypomania; Si, social introversion.

In addition to these 14 scales, many additional scales of measurement have been developed by scholars, such as the Es scale to measure self strength, the Dy scale to measure dependency, and the Pr scale to measure prejudice.

Testing for possible use of this inventory began at the end of 1979.[1] The Chinese version was translated by Fanny M. C. Cheung of Hong Kong. Cheung completed a validation test between her Chinese version and the English version before she finalized the inventory in Chinese (Cheung, 1979). We, therefore, made few changes in her Chinese text, except where the phrasing or ideas did not fit the common usage in China. To check the usability of this Chinese inventory in China, a pilot test was conducted in Beijing and Tienjing with a sample of 62 normal males, 70 normal females, 47 male schizophrenic mental patients, and 45 female schizophrenic mental patients. During the pilot test, we found that the respondents could give appropriate answers to most of the items. However, due to the differences in social customs and life habits, we had to revise a few items with regard

---

[1] Assistance was provided by Professors J. N. Butcher of the University of Minnesota and R. D. Fowler of the University of Alabama.

to religion and sex, as well as those questions that proved to be difficult to answer or unanswerable. After a proper test of validity, both in terms of relevance and effectiveness, we believe the final version of the Chinese MMPI can be used in mainland China (Song, 1980).

In 1980, a national coordination team was formed under the auspices of the Institute of Psychology of Chinese Academy of Sciences to explore the relevance of the MMPI in personality studies (National Coordination Group of MMPI, 1982). The coordination team consisted of 32 units distributed among six regions in China: northern China, eastern China, mid-southern China, southwestern China, northwestern China, and northeastern China. It was required that each unit complete a sample of at least 30 normal respondents. Because the instruments were in the pilot-testing stage, the samples were conditioned in terms of the respondents' age, sex, ethnicity, and educational level. A stratified sample on the basis of census was not employed and has to wait for the next stage of work.

As this inventory was originally designed for clinical application, only 10 of the most fundamental clinical scales were employed in analyzing the test results. Therefore, the common traits observed are reflective of only selected character traits of the people of the Han nationality in China. The following interpretation can only be regarded as tentative, that is, as based on the assumption that the Chinese MMPI measures what it has been demonstrated to measure in the United States and in other societies.

PRELIMINARY FINDINGS ON THE MMPI IN CHINA

Since people of the Han nationality account for 94% of the total population of China, 1791 people of Han nationality in the previously mentioned six major areas of China were initially selected as test subjects. This number included 909 men and 882 women whose ages ranged from 16 to 55, with educational levels above junior middle school (equivalent to U.S. grades 7–9). Two MMPI profiles have been formed by the test results according to the Minnesota T-Score Conversion Table (Figures 4.1 and 4.2). Comparing these profile types with test results from people of several Western countries (Butcher and Pancheri, 1976), we see striking differences. On the D and Sc (depression and schizophrenia) scales, two peaks appear, and their forms approximate those found for the people of Japan, Hong Kong, Pakistan, and other oriental countries. These data are in agreement with the results we obtained in Beijing and Tianjin districts in 1980. Statistical treatment of the collected data from the six major areas of China showed the same results. To determine if there is some age-related difference

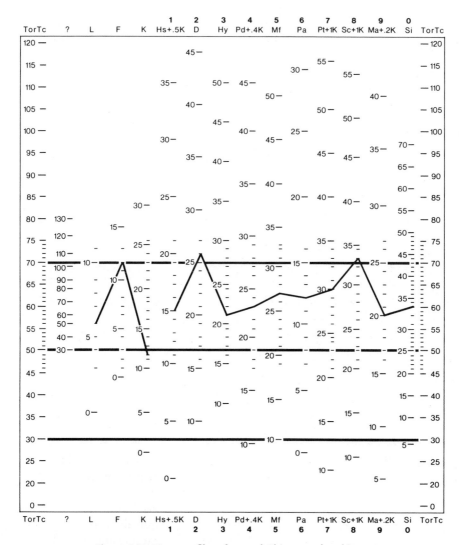

Figure 4.1   Mean profiles of normal Chinese male subjects.

among subjects, we tested 106 youths (59 males and 47 females) whose ages ranged from 18 to 30 with educational levels above senior middle school (equivalent to U.S. grades 10–12). The MMPI Profiles formed by the test results were essentially similar. Hence, we can see that the appearance of these profile types may reflect certain character traits of the Chinese with higher stability.

How can we account for the appearance of these two peaks? Is it that the

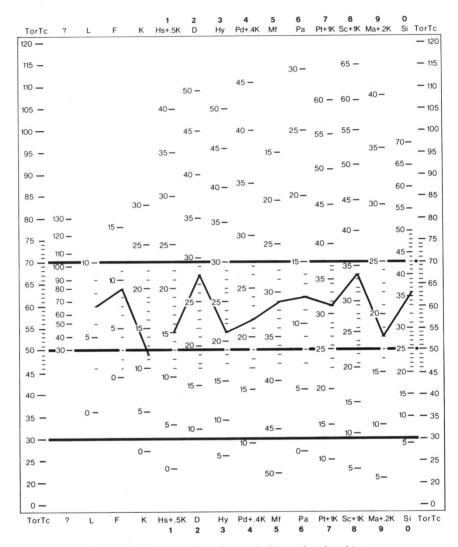

Figure 4.2   Mean profiles of normal Chinese female subjects.

Chinese are more depressive or schizophrenic? We have analyzed the answers of the Chinese subjects according to the method used by Cheung (1981). First, the percentage of "true" answers to each question given by the male and female subjects was calculated. Then, a comparison was made, item by item, with the answers given by American subjects. Taking a difference above 25% as the criterion of existence of difference, there were

72 such items (16.8% of the total) in the test results of men and 81 such items (24.3% of the total) in the test results of women. According to the method of MMPI scoring, most of the these mentioned items are within the D and Sc scales and are reflective of the character traits of normal Chinese people. For example, such items as, "I brood a great deal," "I am never happier than when alone," "I dislike having people about me," "I have difficulty in starting to do things," "I prefer to pass by school friends, or people I know but have not seen for a long time, unless they speak to me first," "My conduct is largely controlled by the customs of those about me," and similar items were largely given affirmative answers by the Chinese subjects. To such items as, "At times I feel like swearing," "Sometimes when I am not feeling well I am cross," and "While in trains, busses, etc., I often talk to strangers," and so forth, most of the Chinese subjects gave negative answers. The answers given by the Chinese subjects tend to differ greatly from or to be opposite to those given by American subjects to the same or similar questions.

Thus, it can be seen that the Chinese people have some character traits that are utterly different from those of Westerners. For example, Chinese are emotionally more reserved, introverted, fond of tranquility, overly considerate, socially overcautious, habituated to self-restraint, and so forth. These character traits are not only manifested in the test results but are also corroborated by the daily lives of Chinese people. Therefore, we believe that the two peaks on the profile types do not indicate that Chinese people are of a more depressive or more schizophrenic character than Americans: They are simply reflective of the differences between the national characters of the two peoples. Therefore, when the scales of the other countries are used, the test results must be carefully analyzed in light of the character traits of the particular nation.

DISCUSSION AND CULTURAL EXPLANATION

The causes of the differences are manifold and include the natural environment, the means of material production, the mode of life, the traditional culture, and the historical background of the nation. Among these, the profound influence of Confucian thought is a significant factor. Confucian philosophical thought and ethical concepts were esteemed highly by the feudal rulers of successive dynasties and were regarded as sacred and inviolable dogma that the people were compelled to profess. Like the dogma of a dominant religion, they have imposed ideological rule over the Chinese people for more than 2000 years and have permeated the people's spiritual life in every respect, leaving deep tracks on the mental outlook of the Chinese people. Confucianists taught people, "Neither see, nor hear, nor speak, nor act against propriety." Confucianism advocates mildness, goodness, courtesy, thrift and modesty. It demands that a woman be obedient to her father, husband, and son and to cultivate chastity, speech, artistry, and demeanor. These teachings became, in the long-standing feudal society, the code of conduct and rule of moral cultivation among the Chinese people. The influence of Confucian thought on the formation of the character of the Chinese people is complex and diverse. Thus, the Chinese people are expected to become sober-minded, reasonable, and prudent; but the development of their nature has, as a result, been restrained, which has inhibited the full display of their feeling, intellect, and initiative.

Following changes in the means of material production and in living conditions, the ideology and character traits of people also change. Since 1949 in the course of critically examining ancient cultural legacies, the Chinese people have reevaluated long-accepted Confucian thoughts and have rejected the undesirable while recognizing the rational factors and endowing them with new content. A fine example is the present social movement, Five Stresses and Four Points of Beauty. The Five Stresses are cultural emphases on decorum, manners, hygiene, discipline, and morals. The Four Points of Beauty relate to beautification of the mind, of language, of behavior, and of the environment. These precepts serve to educate the people, especially the younger generation, to values, and they promote traditional virtues while setting demands on them in accordance with modern social moral standards. Of course, socialist thought opposes the Confucian doctrine of universal love, which obliterates class contradictions. Additionally, the negative Confucian attitude toward women has already been changed radically due to the Chinese women's right to participate in work equally with men. In the test results, it was also found that the masculinity score of the female subjects in China is in general higher than that in Western countries and even higher than that in Japan or Hong Kong.

Education for several decades after 1949 cultivated certain new character traits in the mainland Chinese. Still, it can also be seen in the test results that some influence of Confucian thought still exists in the character of the Chinese people. It requires the efforts of psychologists, sociologists, and educators to analyze such influences, to promote the development of the inherent strong points in the national character of our people, to overcome the shortcomings, and to cultivate those character traits that will meet the demand of the present. Such efforts will enhance the cause of China's four modernizations.

Finally, it must be understood that the previously discussed character traits are those revealed by the test among people of the Han nationality in China. The problem of explicating the character traits of the people of the various nationalities (ethnic groups) of the country through a comprehensive and developmental approach remains. We must encourage scientific researchers to carry out more extensive studies.

REFERENCES

Butcher, J. N.
　　1979　*New developments in use of MMPI.* Minneapolis: University of Minnesota Press.
Butcher, J. N. and Pancheri, P. A.
　　1976　*A handbook of cross-national MMPI research.* Minneapolis: University of Minnesota Press.
Cheung, F. M. C.
　　1979　*MMPI profile and analysis of the normals in Hong Kong.* Paper presented at the Sixth International Conference on Personality Assessment. Kyoto, Japan, July 12–16.
　　1981　*Development of the Chinese MMPI in Hong Kong.* Paper presented at the International Conference on Personality Assessment. Honolulu, Hawaii, February 27–28.
Dahlstrom, W. G., Welsh, G. S., Dahlstrom, L. E.
　　1972　*An MMPI handbook* (Vol. 1). Minneapolis: University of Minnesota Press.
Hathaway, S. R., and McKinley, Z. C.
　　1967　*Minnesota Multiphasic Personality Inventory manual* (rev. ed.). New York: The Psychological Corporation.
National Coordination Group of MMPI
　　1982　*The revision, employment and evaluation of MMPI in China.* Beijing: Institute of Psychology, Chinese Academy of Sciences.
Song, W. Z.
　　1980　Application of the Minnesota Multiphasic Personality Inventory in some areas of our country. *Chinese Journal of Neurology and Psychiatry, 13,* 157.

CHAPTER 5

Social Change, Religious Movements, and Personality Adjustment: An Anthropological View

Yih-yuan Li

INTRODUCTION

Instead of dealing with Chinese personality adjustment directly, this Chapter does so through analysis of special religious cult movements among the Chinese on the island of Taiwan during the last thirty years. I discuss the kinds of personalities and the functional adjustments of people who join the religious activities in various cult groups. The underlying philosophy is that religious beliefs and their related ritual activities can be considered symptoms of group reaction under the stresses of social change. From an analysis of 12 religious cult movements, including indigenous folk cults and foreign sects in Taiwan, I developed a scheme for interpreting personality adjustment traits among the Chinese in Taiwan. The religious cults discussed in this paper fall into two categories.

57

1. Indigenous folk cults: group shamanism, individual shamanism, compatriot–territorial, I-Kuan-tao, En-Chu-Kung worship complex, and Hsuan-yuan Chiao.
2. Christian denominations: the Assembly Hall, the True Jesus church, the Unification church, the Children of God, Jehovah's Witnesses, and the New Testament church.

THEORETICAL FRAMEWORK

The theoretical framework used for the analysis is based on the Douglas (1966, 1973, 1978) group-grid quadrant scheme. The scheme represents a way to perceive and to classify social experience in that "the symbols based on the human body are used to express different social experiences" (Douglas, 1973:vii). According to Douglas, the more the social situation exerts pressure on people, the more the social demand for conformity tends to be expressed by a demand for physical control; in other words, the more value people set on social constraints, the more they value symbols of bodily control. Douglas suggests that in the investigation of social constraints or social pressures exerted on people, two dimensions of force should be distinguished: group and grid. *Group* refers to the dimension of social incorporation, and *grid* to the dimension of individuation. Group is here defined in terms of the claims it makes on its constituent members, the boundaries it draws around them, and the rights it confers on them to use its name and other forms of protection. Grid refers to the cross-hatch of rules individuals are subject to in the course of their interaction (Douglas, 1978:5–8). By representing the dimension of group as a horizontal line and the dimension of grid as a vertical one, we can draw a quadrant with four squares, A, B, C, and D, representing four social types (see Figure 5.1).

Square A represents a society with both strong group and strong grid, where formal behavior is highly valued and patterns for interpersonal

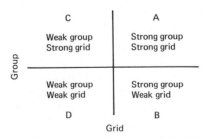

Figure 5.1 The intersection of two dimensions of social constraint, group and grid, produces four social types.

transaction and transactions between gods and people are ritualistic. Since formality and ritualism are emphasized, the following traits tend to be characteristic of this type of society:

1. In ritual and in daily life, abundant care is taken in physical appearance.
2. Many taboos and the ritual avoidance of pollution are exhibited.
3. Symbols are used to express the high value set on control of consciousness.
4. A routinized piety toward authority and its symbols and belief in a punishing, moral universe and a regulative supernature are shown.
5. The idea of wrong-doing takes no account of internal motivation; blame is placed automatically on sin.

In contrast to square A, the society represented in square D is weak both in group and in grid. This is an individualistic society where informality is encouraged; therefore, it tends to be antiritualistic. The following traits tend to be exhibited:

1. Physical appearance is not emphasized; people look unkempt.
2. There is a preference for spontaneous expression and no interest in ritual differentiation.
3. Control of consciousness is not emphasized; the favored patterns of religious worship include trance or glossolalia, trembling, shaking, or other expressions of incoherence and dissociation.
4. Direct contact between men and gods is emphasized.
5. The idea of wrong-doing is entirely concerned with state of mind. The actual consequences of the act are of less concern than the wishes and intentions of the actor.

Square B represents societies that are strong in group but weak in grid. Here we have social units whose external boundaries are clearly marked but whose internal relations are confused. Their theory of evil generally exhibits itself in fear of witchcraft. Their cosmos is dominated by ill will and jealousy. This type of society tends to have the following characteristics:

1. The people believe themselves to be in a dangerous universe, threatened by sinister powers controlled by fellow human beings.
2. Instead of prayer, fasting, and sacrifice to the deity, ritual activity is devoted to witch-hunting, witch cleansing, and healing the effects of witchcraft.
3. The idea exists of a boundary dividing good and bad; "inside" is good, "outside" is bad. (These are Douglas's terms.) This can apply to human bodies, villages, or social groups.

4. The "inside" is under attack and is in need of protection.
5. Human wickedness exists on a cosmic scale.

The last square, C, represents societies with a strong grid but a very weak sense of group. These are societies in which people never submit to the pressure of group boundaries and are free from group constraints; however, the society emphasizes a network of interpersonal transactions. This is a society with millennial characteristics as follows:

1. People deal with each other through the strong bond of interpersonal exchange.
2. Religion is pragmatic, the cosmos amoral, and ritual is highly magical. Religion is also ego-focused.
3. The society is competitive; a person can achieve leadership through interpersonal transaction.
4. When a new leader is successful in replacing a former one, the whole social network will be turned over, as will the rituals people use in dealing with their god.

RITUALIZED SOCIETY

Traditional Chinese society falls into the category of square A, that is, a society with a strong group boundary and strict rules for personal interaction. In traditional Chinese society, there was strong emphasis on formality and ritualism, and people behaved scrupulously according to the dyadic father–son rule as suggested by Hsu (1965). People were required to act toward each other according to *li* (propriety) or *yi* (ritual). Therefore there were endless rules, taboos, and the ritual avoidance of pollution in every sphere of life.

The Chinese believe in a punishing, moral universe and a regulative supernatural being; and the cultivation of a moral life through fixed ritual behavior is highly valued. However, due to the drastic sociocultural changes during the past hundred years, especially Taiwan's change from an agricultural to an industrial society since 1960, the traditional ritualistic patterns have also gone through severe changes, and these religious movements can be seen as different responses to this change among various subsections of the population. The next section explores in some detail how these religious movements fit into the four categories.

ANTIRITUALISM CULTS

The first group of cults can be called individualistic or antiritualism cults, the opposite of traditional ritualism. In this group are included one indigenous cult—group shamanism—and two independent Christian churches—the True Jesus church and the Assembly Hall.

The group shamanism cult exists in Taiwan's urban areas, particularly in Taipei City. This cult is similar to the individual shaman or *tang-ki* cult in its manner of curing the sick but is different in that not only the shaman but also his patients or followers go into a trance. Every evening in the temple, 20 to 30 patients are gathered, jumping about and speaking in tongues around the altar. The patients who come to consult the shaman are mostly new migrants from rural areas who have not yet settled down or found a permanent job in the city. In addition, these people are mostly illiterate, and about two-thirds of them are women. They are the minority, the poor, and the misfits who have lost their group identity and have no social status; therefore, they prefer direct contact with gods. They go into a trance easily, because the inarticulateness of the social organization in itself gains symbolic expression in bodily dissociation. This is one way that a religious cult can be used by some sectors of the society (Kleinman, 1980, Li, 1976).

The True Jesus church, which is a sect of Pentecostal revival, is the third largest Christian church in Taiwan and has a membership of around 35,000. As the name Pentecostal revival shows, it is a cult aiming to free itself from traditional Christian ritualism, and members try to contact God individually through trembling, shaking, and other expressions of bodily dissociation. It is interesting to note that about two-thirds of the churches and half of the members of this indigenous Christian sect are aborigines who live mostly in mountainous areas of Taiwan. The aborigines are a cultural minority and are in the last stage of the acculturation process. It is no wonder that these people, who are facing a cultural identity crisis, have become followers of what Durkheim (1912) called an effervescent cult.

The Assembly Hall cult, established in 1927 in China as a reaction to Western Christian formality and ritualism, emphasizes praying and reading the Bible. When this Christian sect moved to Taiwan in 1948, it gained popularity very quickly among the new migrants from the mainland. This Pentecostal-like church is now the second largest Christian sect on the island, and its membership is still drawn almost exclusively from mainland Chinese, most recently from among young college students. A likely explanation is that the mainland Chinese converted to this sect when they first moved to Taiwan because since they were new immigrants, they had temporarily lost their sense of group and category. However, the reason for college students converting is more difficult to discover. It seems to me that this group of young believers may fall into the category of those reactionists who protest the emptiness and inhumanity in their schools and professional lives. This group of youngsters may, in some sense, correspond to the hippies of the 1960s in Western society (Li, 1978).

SOCIAL HYGIENE CULTS

While some people belong to antiritualistic cult movements, others concentrate on witch-hunting, or the social hygiene cult. Included in this category of cult are individual shamanism (tang-ki; tong ji, t'ung-chi), and the compatriot-territorial cult.

The individual shamans (tang-ki, in the southern Fujian dialect of the Taiwanese) are spirit mediums whose practice includes two functions: group festivals and curing the sick. At the annual village festival, the tang-ki travels in a sedan chair in a long procession and patrols the village boundary. The tang-ki's main job in the procession is to implant spirit flags on the boundary line around the village to ward off malevolent ghosts and keep the boundary free from outside intruders. In the healing rites for the sick, no matter what the diagnosis or explanation for the illness is, the treatments used by the tang-ki mainly emphasize protecting the bodily boundary (symbolizing the territorial boundary) and cleans it of the sources of evil. In a sense, this is seeing the human body as analogous to society and adopting the same principle of social hygiene in dealing with sickness (Li, 1976).

The compatriot–territorial cults appear more often in urban areas. These are cults organized by members of the same dialect group who live in one borough of the city. In the annual ceremony for their tutelary deity, there is also a procession around the territorial boundary. But instead of a tang-ki in a sedan chair, there are the deity's spiritual detectives, Generals Fan and Hsieh and eight generals, whose task is to sweep out or purge the evils, which is equivalent to the tang-ki's work in the village (Feuchtwang, 1974).

Both the group practice of tang-ki and the compatriot-territorial cult procession were very popular in traditional China but are now declining. However, the tang-ki's curing practices have become even more popular both in rural and urban areas. This phenomenon seems to be related to a modern revival. The present-day social situation in Taiwan is very close to the model of society with strong group but low grid, so a kind of purging ritual or ritual of social hygiene fits the general social mood; therefore, the tang-ki's practice of sweeping out devils is not an isolated phenomenon in a modern setting; it should be considered a kind of folk practice that reflects the social rituals of society in general.

MILLENNIAL CULTS

A third group of religious cults that can be clearly identified is the millennial movement. In this category are included the Unification church, Jehovah's Witnesses, the Children of God, and the New Testament church.

The first three churches are sects derived from foreign denominations, so are known to the Christian world. The history of mission work by these three sects in Taiwan is rather short and limited. The Unification church and the Children of God were banned by the police after less than 5 years of preaching in Taiwan. They were accused of breaching Chinese ethics and persuading young students to leave their schools and families in order to work exclusively for the church. The Jehovah's Witnesses, however, established their churches mostly in the aboriginal area in Taitung. There they caused trouble with the government because their converts refused to go into military service and would not pay respect to the national flag.

The New Testament church is an indigenous sect founded in the late 1960s, and one of the prophet leaders of this church has recently announced that holy Mount Zion has been moved to southern Taiwan by God's command. The followers of this church are mostly fanatics and new converts from other denominations; and the police, who are worried about members' fanatical behavior, have tried to prohibit them from crowding on the "holy mount."

In sum, the people who are inclined to join the millennial cult movements are usually young students, cultural minorities, or religious fanatics. Although membership in these cults is rather small compared with other orthodox churches, it represents a trend that emphasizes the responsibility of interpersonal transaction on the one hand and tries to forecast the renewal of the social system on the other (Li, 1978).

NATIVISTIC MOVEMENTS

The biggest group among these religious movements is the category of cult we may refer to as the "return to roots" or nativistic movement. In this category are included the following: the I-Kuan-tao cult, the En-Chu-Kung worship complex, and the Hsuan-yuan Chiao or Yellow Emperor's cult.

These cults have established temples or congregational gathering places all over Taiwan. Some of them have secret society overtones, and others can be considered pro-state or literati cults. But all of them try to combine aspects of the major religions—Confucian, Buddhist, Taoist, Christian, and Moslem doctrines—into one. In other words, they are examples of true syncretism.

One of the common characteristics of these nativistic cults is that they claim to be working toward a return to Chinese tradition or toward restoring traditional Chinese morality through religious belief and practices. To this end, every day they read God's edicts and Confucian or Lao-tzu classics. The headquarters of these sects usually publish a monthly journal and books with sacred edicts known as Shan-Shu to be distributed free among their followers. The publishing, distributing, and reading of these edicts has developed into a moral act in itself, leaving the moral deed per se forgotten. This is an example of typical formality or a return to traditional ritualism in a real sense.

These sects all have some sort of reformist inclination. Some of them reject the burning of paper money in traditional rites, and most of them refuse to accept offerings other than fruit and vegetables. All the cult temples are kept orderly and are meticulously clean. Most important, the practitioners and service people in the temple always maintain a tidy appearance and wear special blue gowns in performing rituals. These practices show the cult members' strong belief in avoiding pollution and maintaining ritual taboos.

All these nativistic sects emphasize the importance of maintaining consciousness and denounce the behavior of going into a trance as in *tang-ki* or other shamanistic practices. In order to show evidence of communication with the gods, they prefer spirit writing (*fu-ji; fu-chi*), in a sand pan.

These cults' advocacy of a return to traditional moral standards is a demonstration of their inclination toward a social level with a strong group boundary and strict rules for interpersonal transactions. This is a trend many official campaigns support on Taiwan (Li, 1978).

DISCUSSION

In conclusion, the foregoing analysis of religious movements is summarized in Figure 5.2. Since 1960, Chinese society in Taiwan has undergone drastic changes: from an agricultural to an industrial society, from predominantly relying on primary relationships to relying to some degree on secondary relationships, and from traditional value orientation to a more Western value orientation. These changes have occurred very rapidly and on a very wide scale, particularly since 1970. The reaction of the people to these new experiences and new pressures is inevitably uneasiness; they need a mechanism for adjustment, and religious movements provide an important means of adjustment.

One of the most obvious phenomena since industrialization is the heavy migration of peasants to the urban areas. The new migrants to the cities have lost their primary relationships while their secondary relationships have yet to be established; they may not drop their traditional values, but new values put heavy pressure on them. To these misfit minorities, lonely and anxious, religious faith and participation is undoubtedly a mechanism for adjustment, since established formality and complex ritualism are abso-

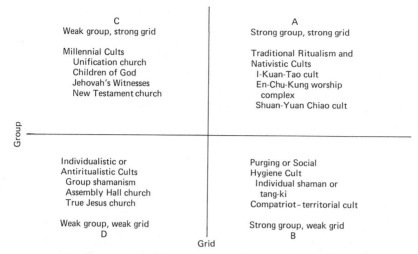

Figure 5.2   Group–grid categorization of religious movements.

lute nonsense to them. Therefore, when they need religion for adjustment, they tend to join religious sects that have overtones of antiritualism, that is, those sects in square D in Figure 5.2. Believers in these sects prefer direct contact with God and go into a trance easily. In other words, they depend upon bodily dissociation to gain symbolic expressions. While in that state, they feel more confident and comfortable, since they have used their own resources rather than relying on others in dealing with their new environment.

In square C are those millennial cults that draw their followers mostly from ethnic or cultural minorities and religious fanatics. For them, religion is attractive, not for escape, but for changing the social system. Since these people are mostly dissatisfied with their present social existence, their devotion to the millenial cult may provide satisfaction because of the forecast of social renewal by the prophet of the cult.

In square B is the cult of social hygiene, which includes individual shamanism and the compatriot-territorial cult. The latter has turned away from the modern setting, while the former's curing practices have become more popular both in urban and rural areas. As mentioned previously, the present social and political situation in Taiwan is very close to the model of society with strong group but low grid, so a kind of purging ritual like the *tang-ki*'s curing practice is not an exceptional or isolated phenomenon. Rather, the shaman's practice of sweeping out internal evils should be considered a kind of folk ritual that reflects the secular social ritual of society in general.

However, in the opposite direction, the nativistic cult groups are not seeking new means of adjustment but are trying to return to their roots. Most of the members of these cults are middle-class urban residents who still hold quite firmly to traditional values and ethics. They believe that uplifting the moral standard is the only way to save the modern world, and they may have tried other ways to achieve this goal. But the religious means is the easiest and most popular way to reach it, since the religious means lets them express their deepest feelings even if only symbolically.

REFERENCES

Douglas, Mary D.
   1966   *Purity and danger: An analysis of the concepts of pollution and taboo.* London: Routledge & Kegan Paul.
   1973   *Natural symbols.* New York: Vintage.
   1978   *Cultural bias* (Occasional Paper No. 35). London: Royal Anthropological Institute of Great Britain.
Durkheim, E.
   1912   *The elementary forms of the religious life.* New York: Collier Books.
Feuchtwang, S.
   1974   City temples in Taipei under three regimes. In M. Elvin and W. Skinner (Eds.), *The Chinese city between two worlds.* Stanford: Stanford University Press.
Hsu, F. L. K.
   1965   The effect of dominant kinship relationships on kin and non-kin behavior: A hypothesis. *American Anthropologist, 67,* 638–661.
Kleinman, A.
   1980   *Patients and healers in the context of culture.* Berkeley: University of California Press.
Li, Yih-yuan
   1976   Shamanism in Taiwan: An anthropological inquiry. In W. Lebra (Ed.), *Culture-bound syndromes, ethnopsychiatry, and alternate therapies.* Honolulu: The University Press of Hawaii.
   1978   *Xin-Yang yu wen-hua* [Belief and culture]. Taipei: Chu-liu Publisher.

CHAPTER 6

Traditional Chinese Beliefs and Attitudes toward Mental Illness

T'ien Ju-k'ang

INTRODUCTION

The history of mental health is an important subject for study, since knowledge about it can enhance our understanding of current mental health concepts and practice. In this chapter, the origins of traditional Chinese beliefs and attitudes about mental disorders are examined by reviewing the ancient records, traditional medical books, and popular literary writings. I show that these findings given in these sources were empirically based, but it also emerges that the reflection of these beliefs and attitudes in Chinese literature served psychological functions of transcultural significance.

ANCIENT RECORDS OF MENTAL ILLNESS

The earliest reliable Chinese data on illness are found in characters engraved on oracle bones of the Shang dynasty (c. 1600–1066 B.C.). Among the 1220 pieces that have been deciphered by reliable scholars to date, only 36 are said to be connected with illness, but none of them concerns mental illness.

According to Liu (1981), the word *kuang* (probably meaning insane with excitation) first appeared in 1100 B.C. in *Shangshu* (The Book of Historical Documents), which is one of the famous Five Classics of ancient China. The word *dian* (probably meaning either insane without excitation or epileptic) first appeared between 781 and 771 B.C. in *Shi* (The Book of Songs), another book of the Five Classics, but there was no description of the symptoms of either conditions.

It is in the Qin dynasty (221–207 B.C.), when the first Emperor of China caused all the characters to be standardized in what is now known as the small seal form, that the characters for mental health became popular. It must be emphasized that their appearance in the standardized characters does not necessarily mean that the phenomenon of mental illness did not begin to fall popularly within Chinese cognizance until as late as 200 years B.C. Presumably, the characters for mental illness, kuang and dian, were in use for a considerable time before the official standardization.

In the *Kang-xi* dictionary, compiled (A.D. 1716) during the reign of Emperor Kang-xi (Qing Dynasty) and containing 47,021 characters, there are altogether 445 characters in connection with illness and disease. Among these characters, some like *dian, kuang,* and *feng* were used as medical terms for specific mental illnesses by the authors of ancient medical classics and as descriptions of emotional states in a general sense by the common people.

The Original Meaning of Mental Illness in Chinese Characters

In the Chinese language, the general description of mentally disordered behavior is *kuang*. This character is composed of two parts: The left radical resembles a dog, the right is an ancient character, no longer used, called *huang*, signifying flourishing grass and herbage, which according to the *Shuo Wen* dictionary, compiled in A.D. 120, indicates that a dog bites fiercely and undiscriminatingly. This interpretation apparently tells us that the Chinese idea of madness derived from the rabies of dogs. *Rabies* comes from the Latin verb *rabere,* meaning to rage, which is in conformity with the meaning of *kuang.* We do not know how this process of conceptualization was formed. Did the ancient people attribute madness to rabies, or were they unable to make a distinction between human mental illness and the syndrome of a rabies victim?

According to the *Jayi Jing on Acupuncture* written by *Huangfu Mi* (1967;

fl. A.D. 215–282), the crucial symptom of mental illness was a spasm of the muscles of the larynx and the pharynx, which is similar to one of the most prominant symptoms of rabies in modern medical diagnosis.

We know for certain, however, that the rabies of dogs constituted a great menace to health in the old days. It was recorded in the ancient Chinese chronicles of Zuo Chuan (Zuoqu, 1931) which covered the period 770–476 B.C., that the people of the country of Lu made a great effort to drive out mad dogs, chasing them to the territory of the nobleman Hwa Chen. Hwa Chen was so terrified at the people's hot pursuit that he escaped to the country of Chen.

In the *Han Shu* (The History of the Han Dynasty; see Ban, 1962), the violent death of dogs was linked with the permutation of the five primary elements. It claims that the violent death of dogs often occurs in years of drought and that unfavorable weather accounts for these calamities.

A well-known Chinese physician of the fourth century, Ke Hung (1923), summarized the experience of the previous 300 years and discovered what he considered to be an effective way of curing this fatal disease. The therapy was to kill the mad dog and to use its brain to dress the region of the wound. This method has been regarded as the forerunner of Chinese immunotherapy.

Sun Si-miao (1955) the eminent author of medical prescriptions in the sixth century, gave this advice: "When spring ends and summer begins, dogs tend to become mad. Young children should carry sticks for protection."

In summary, the Chinese character for madness had its origins in the rabies of dogs. There is no evidence to prove that the earliest etiological explanation for mental illness was attributed to rabies, though the prevalence of rabies was no doubt one of the major concerns at that time.

REVIEW OF TRADITIONAL MEDICAL BOOKS

The Development of Mental Illness Concepts

A review of the development of psychiatric concepts in traditional Chinese medicine, reflected in materials appearing in Chinese medical books of various periods, indicates that diagnostic classification and terminology suffered from lack of precision and theoretical systematization.

Huangti Neijing Suwen (Yellow Emperor's Elementary Questions of Internal Medicine; 1967b) thought to be the first work summarizing traditional Chinese medicine in antiquity, known in China since the second century B.C. at the latest, records only the *dian–kuang* type of rare illness. The syndrome is described thus:

When the illness is grave, [the patient] always takes off his garment and walks away, or ascends heights chanting songs, or even refuses to eat for several days. [The patient] can also climb over the walls and roofs, which were beyond his usual capability. [Some patients] may make wild statements and heap abuses on others indiscriminately.

From the above symptoms, it is impossible to identify the illness in modern diagnostic terminology except that it refers to psychotic behavior.

From the *Nan Jing* (*Difficult Classic,* also called the *81 Difficult Questions of Huangti*) compiled by Bien Jao (1961), *kuang* appears to have been distinguished from *dian*—the morbid condition of the former was excess of positive force, while the latter was excess of negative force. "The patient suffering from *kuang* initially cannot sleep or feel hungry, often self-dramatizing himself as being a man of excellent virtues, self-proclaiming as a nobleman, or self-glorifying as a person of great wisdom and talents. [The patient] continuously sings and laughs strangely and acts without due consideration." For the disease of *dian*, "The initial symptom is an unhappy feeling and falling down suddenly to the ground with eyes wide open."

It is very difficult to describe *kuang* and *dian* diseases as results of mental disorder or physiological dysfunction in accordance with the description of *Huangti Neijing Suwen* and *Nan Jing* because the syndrome of *dian* given by *Huangti Neijing Suwen* are said to be similar to that of epilepsy, and its etiology is attributed to a hereditary factor: "This rare disease is styled as a disease in the womb and traces its origin to the time inside the mother's womb. When the mother was very frightened it caused the ostruction of the vital air, which in turn affected the fetus to contract this illness" (1967: Chapter 13, No. 42, p. 62).

In *Jinkui Yaolue* (Golden Box Summary), written by Zhang Zhong-jing (1971), the foremost physician of the second century A.D., we come across a kind of mental illness called hurrying-pig sickness. The name of this peculiar disease has two different meanings; one describes the patient's pulse beating like a running pig, the other indicates a mental illness percipitated by conscious fright or unconscious fear. In the sense of the second explanation, when this illness occurs, the patient may be almost terminally sick, with the heart beating like a hurrying pig, but will soon recover. Because some paragraphs concerning this illness have been left out in Zhang Zhung-jing's book and also because hurrying-pig sickness appeared only in *Jinkui Yaolue* and was never recorded in any other ancient Chinese medical books of the later periods, this sickness has presumably been considered no more than another colloquial name for *dian*. *Jinkui Yaolue* gives another case worth noting: "A woman contracting the "malady of hasty organ" feels so sad that she wants to cry, as if she is bewitched by spirits, and she yawns frequently" (Zhang, 1971). It seems that a case of mental disorder like this could be identified as hysteria, but, unfortunately, except for the etiological explanation, *Jinkui Yaolue* does not develop a classic diagnostic name for it.

Even as early as the seventh century, the first Chinese pathologist Cao Yuan-fan (1601) had reached the conclusion that *xian* is a specific sickness suffered by children. He made a distinction within this sickness according to age—for those who suffered over the age of ten, he called it *dian*, while for those under ten, he called it *xian*. Apparently, he made a demarcation between physical diseases and mental disorder.

However, since *Huangti Neijing Suwen* was regarded as the bible of Chinese medicine, in which *kuang* and *dian* were put together to designate mental disease in general, not many Chinese physicians were able to deviate from its statements. The debate on the nature of *kuang* and *dian* continued for a considerable time. Some claimed that *dian* was induced by *kuang*, while some maintained that *dian* actually belonged to *kuang*. Some even felt that a patient might contract both *kuang* and *dian* at the same time (Lou, c. 1332–1401).

From the tenth century on, Chinese physicians, after many years of observation, began to realize that the symptoms had distinctive features. Li Gao (c. 1180–1251/1967), a remarkable physician of the Jin dynasty, made distinctions among the verbal symptoms of mental disorder. According to his diagnosis, if a patient talks about something from hallucination, with his eyes wide open, it is *kuang yan* (nonsense talk). If a patient talks to himself alone, with his eyes closed, about the daily routine that he has seen or in which he has taken part, it is *zhan yan* (delirium talk). If a patient talks with a throaty, tremulous voice and with disconnected words, it is *zhen sheng* (lewd voice).

As a result of careful diagnosis, some Chinese physicians, who claimed that *dian* and *kuang* were one illness, as did Liu Wan-su, who lived c. 1120–c. 1217, began to be criticized for the following reason: "It has been known to physicians that those who go mad and talk nonsensically never become chronic *dian* [epileptics], while those who indulge in silly behavior for a considerable time, never develop to be *kuang*. . . . Therefore, *kuang* is an acute and dramatic sickness and *dian* a slow and insidious sickness." (Y. Li, 1577). "Those who suffer from *dian* but are not noticed can be regarded as *dian* of a minor type, while those who are unable to suppress sudden outbursts are *kuang* of the violent type" (Shen, 1962).

At last, Zhang Jinyue (J. B. Zhang, 1970), who lived 1561–1639, concluded the long-standing debate by the following remark:

> *Dian* and *kuang* are different sicknesses. The onset of *kuang* is through a gradual process of being ill-behaviored, but with persistent attacks, and is very difficult to

heal. The attack of *dian* starts with a sudden fall and appears to be intermittent. . . .
Kuang often remains awake and irritable, while *dian* always lies asleep, feeling very
tired. . . . Children never contract *kuang,* but often suffer from *dian.* (J. B. Zhang,
1970)

In *Lingshu Jing,* also attributed to the legendary Huangti, wind (*feng*) was
mentioned as the cause of various diseases (Haungti, 1967a), so the term
xin feng (wind–heart disease) was employed to signify a patient whose
heart had been affected by the wind in the height of summer (*Haungti
Neijing Suwen*). More than 1000 years later, Yu Tuan (1515), who lived
1438–1515, began to use the term *xin feng* in his book *Yixue Zhengzhuan*
(Orthodoxy of Medicine) to denote a special mental illness called heart
insanity. According to his description, the prominent syndromes of *xin feng*
are "trance, changeable mood and silence, and sometimes a state of nervous disorder. The patient may have some symptoms similar to *dian,* but
not so serious." Whatever it was, Yu Bo at least had noticed a specific type
of mental illness in contrast with the general *kuang* and *dian.*

Later, in the period of Emperor Kang-xi (1662–1722), a physician
named Chen Shitou (c. 1662–1722) gave an example of another type
of mental illness called *dai* (stupid insanity). The symptoms of *dai* are said
to be

sitting in silence and behaving in a sort of absent-minded manner. . . . The patient
may sleep for several days without a break and then stay awake for a subsequent
period. [In some cases,] the patient may stitch carefully the hem of his clothing for
protection or secretly hide something from others. When meeting people, the suf-
ferer may keep silent, without paying any attention; while alone, he may talk about
his own misfortunes to himself in tears. When food is offered, he may refuse to eat,
but will happily swallow something like charcoal when he feels hungry.

From Chen Shitou's point of view, this type of mental illness is due to
unrelieved feelings of melancholic anger or shameful regrets. However,
since no further detailed description was given, it is difficult to identify this
type of mental illness in terms of contemporary psychiatric concepts.

The preceding survey shows that it took a period of several centuries for
Chinese physicians to distinguish neurological dysfunction (*dian*) from
mental disorder (*Kuang*) and then gradually to differentiate other kinds of
mental disorders with different terms, such as *xin-feng* or *dai,* which did not
meet with common acceptance (Tseng, 1973).

Explanation of Illness Etiology
and Legendary Treatment

From the preceding account, we see that even as early as the second
century B.C., the Chinese knew how to distinguish medicine from divina-

tion. At that time, mental illness was regarded as being caused by environmental disturbances. *Huangti Neijing Suwen* (1967b) stated that *kuang* could be produced by oppressive air, caused by abnormality in the weather.

In the seventh century, emotional imbalance derived from human relations was emphasized as the main factor giving rise to insanity. Sun Simiao (1955) pointed out in his book *Qenjin Yaofang* (A Thousand Important Golden Remedies) that "the patients with *dian–kuang* should be treated with medication as well as acupuncture. For those who practice sorcery, they should get rid of the evil winds instead of exorcizing ghosts." Han Yu (1938), one of the eight great men of letters of the eighth century, once wrote to his superior to complain about the malicious rumors against him, stating that the coercive measures would drive one to madness. (A statement like this might be accepted by present-day Western psychiatrists.) The renowned therapist Zhu Tanxi (1601), who lived A.D. 1281–1358, went further and openly declared that "all cases concerning *dian–kuang* should be regarded as purely normal human affairs; their treatment is quite beyond the area of medicine and acupuncture." He emphasized the humanistic treatment of insanity and recorded his successful therapeutic method in his book, *Xin Fa* (Methods of Curing Mental Illness), which served as a guide for later physicians.

After the seventh century, the general opinion among Chinese physicians was that the factors that caused imbalance in the physical harmony of the body were psychogenic. Unsatisfied desires, repressed anger and pent-up feelings lay at the root of mental disturbance. Accordingly, despite numerous prescriptions cited in the classics, the most effective cure seems to have been to appeal to human feeling (D. Wu, 1982). For example, they used such techniques as medically induced sleep, change of environment, self-realization, self-revelation, and so on. The physician frequently adjusted the method of therapy to the patient's response.

Some interesting cases exemplifying the treatment of disorders of behavior in traditional China follow:

> One summer, a woman named Jin attended a banquet. When she returned home, her mother-in-law inquired about where Jin had been invited to sit and thought it a total violation of etiquette for her to have taken the seat assigned to her. Jin, extremely ashamed of her bad manners and feeling that she was to blame, began to deviate significantly from normal behavior, saying repeatedly to herself, "It was my own fault. It was my own fault." In exasperation, her family invited a doctor, Zhu Tanxi, for treatment. Zhu, after feeling her pulse, diagnosed her bizarre behavior,

not as possession by evil spirits, but as a severe sickness, pointing out that with timely medical care, she would be able to make a recovery within a few days. Her family, however, did not accept Zhu's diagnosis. Instead, they decided to ask a witch doctor for exorcization. Unfortunately, Jin died about 10 days later. (M. L. Chen, 1959)

The brother-in-law of doctor Zhu Tanxi suddenly went insane after having a full meal and plenty to drink. The patient declared that he was possessed by his deceased elder brother and behaved as if he were communicating with him, recounting his brother's life history in detail. His uncle, living nearby, did not believe that this was due to possession, but rather to debauchery. Thus, a large bowl of salty soup was prepared, which the patient was forced to drink and which made him spit several mouthfuls of phlegm and become dripping wet with sweat. After a good night's sleep, the patient was cured of his madness. (M. L. Chen 1959)

A monk, Yin Hui, of Xiang Kuo temple suffered from mental derangement for 6 months, trying various well-known medicinal preparations without effect. The monk's rich lay brother Pan invited doctor Sun Simiao for treatment. Sun answered the request in a very casual manner, saying that if the monk could sleep, he might be cured in 2 or 3 days. Pan begged Sun for a prescription and expressed his wish to pay him a high fee. However, Sun's advice was simply to give him some salty food first; but if he should feel thirsty, then Sun would come for medication. As expected, Yin Hui felt thirsty in the middle of the night. Sun came and gave him a sedative pill with warm wine. As a result, the monk slept continuously for 2 days and was normal afterwards. Pan was very thankful and wanted to know why the remedy was so effective. The answer was: "Other doctors tried to tranquilize his mind but failed to induce him to sleep." This remedy proved to be equally effective in the case of the honorable Wu, posthumously granted the title Zhen Su (a person who is righteous and serious). In his younger days, Wu also had some mental trouble. He took the same kind of pill given by Sun and fully recovered after 5 days' sound sleep. (Wei 1970)

Wang Zhong Yang (late thirteenth century) had a case concerning a woman who suspected her husband of having an affair with another woman. This suspicion caused disturbance in her mind and, consequently, she became insane. She raved wildly day and night. Her whole family was puzzled and did not know what to do. After taking 80 pills prescribed by Wang for reducing phlegm, she immediately fell asleep and then expectorated all the filth from her body. The patient began to feel terribly ashamed of herself and started to eat and live as a normal person. She was able to embroider 5 to 7 days after receiving this treatment. Nevertheless, she was still in an unhappy mood. Wang, entertaining some apprehension of recurrence, secretly sent someone to talk to others in her presence concerning the piteous story of a certain woman (the one of whom the patient was suspicious) who had suddenly died as the result of a violent summer epidemic. The patient was very pleased at the news and was anxious to have it confirmed. And it was confirmed by the informant, who said that he had seen the dead woman's husband preparing for her funeral. The patient was very happy that the fundamental cause of her illness had finally been eliminated. Wang made further inquiries of her family members about the patient's menstrual condition. Her mother-in-law replied that her daughter-in-law had been sick in bed for a month without eating, which had undoubtedly weakened her constitution, making her very feeble; and this might be the reason that her menstruation was dysfunctional. Wang advised that when the patient's menstrual fluid seemed more or less fresh, they should send someone to fetch medicine. Soon came the news that her menstruation had gradually turned to a normal color, at which point Wang ordered medicine and gave instructions that she should take it for 2 weeks. From then on, the patient was perfectly well, and her illness never recurred. (Z. Yu, 1959)

Noteworthy is a finding by Chinese physicians in the sixteenth century concerning the difference in the rates of cure or improvement in mental illness between the rich and the poor: Regarding effectiveness of treatment, the receptivity to treatment among the rich is much lower than among the poor. The reason given is that a luxurious life-style induces the rich to be more prone to disease and to have exhausted the powers for recovery; the opposite is true for the poor (Xu, 1556).

EMOTIONAL DISORDERS AS DESCRIBED IN LITERARY WRITING

Now, I shift the focus to review how mental disorders are described in Chinese literary writings, which may help us to view the subject discussed here in a new dimension.

As pointed out earlier, traditional physicians were very sympathetic toward the patients in their care; this was even more true of literary writers. In traditional Chinese fiction, almost all the eccentric figures and animals were transformed into enchanting heroes and heroines. Some of the typical examples can be found in the following cases.

In the fifth century A.D., a well-known literary text called *Shi Shuo Xin Yu* (New Anecdotes of Social Talk) tells of the exploits of some of the notorious dipsomaniacs in Chinese history. For instance, Ruan Xian and his clansmen, so deeply indulged themselves in drinking that they were no longer satisfied with ordinary cups and preferred to use a large earthenware vat filled with wine, sitting around it and drinking heavily. Once a herd of pigs came to drink and went directly to the vat, whereupon, men and pigs drank happily together. Ruan liked to drive a cart by himself, roaming alone without destination as far as he could go. When the path was blocked, he would burst into tears of disappointment and turn back. One of Ruan's friends, Ji Kang would not take the trouble to wash his face for sometimes as long as $1\frac{1}{2}$ months. He was even lazier about taking a bath, so his body was covered with lice. He was seen scratching the itchy spots constantly, whether sitting or walking.

To most Westerners, these characters are utterly disgusting. The Chinese, however, respect these eccentrics and regard them as their sages because of their literary value. Their extraordinary behavior has been interpreted as justifiable because they keep clear of intrigues and power struggles within the high ruling circles. Such an attitude resembles some present Western opinions toward hippies, but China accepted activities not conforming with the standards of ordinary society more than 1000 years ago!

Bu Song-ling (1630–1715), author of *Liao Zai Zhi Yi* (Unusual Tales for the Leisure Studio; Bu, 1958) is famous for fictions of supernatural beings. In his writing, fox fairies appear invariably charming and approachable rather than frightening. This often makes the reader think that they belong—not to the world of fantasy—but to the real world. Contrary to the general pattern of folklore on fox fairies all over the world, marriages between human and supernatural beings are allowed to run their happy course, and these couples can even bear children. At the end of the story, however, the author always introduces some strange event to remind his readers that our beloved heroes and heroines are supernatural beings after all. Likewise, these eccentric characters, ridiculous and laughable as they may be, are also sympathetic. Bu's humane touch made abnormal beings into normal ones, and thus, he received applause from readers, amid laughter and tears.

In the same way, one of the most popular novels, *Ru Lin Wai Shi* (Informal History of a Literate), by Wu Jing-zi (1972) (who lived 1701–1750), a novel well-known among the Chinese for many centuries, is an excellent satire on a fit of madness. It portrays a pedantic scholar named Fan Jin who continually failed the civil service examination until his hair turned gray. At last, when he learned that he had finally passed the prefecture examination with honors, he became demented due to overhappiness.

The story goes on in the manner of traditional Chinese medical classics. The heralds who came to report the glad tidings suggested that Fan had only been thrown off his balance by a sudden fit of joy that made him choke on his phlegm. If his family could get someone whom Fan feared to slap him on his cheek and say that it was all a joke, that Fan actually had not passed any examination, the fright would make the pedant cough up his phlegm and return to his senses. Ultimately, Fan's father-in-law, the butcher Hu, was persuaded to carry out this therapy of "counterbalancing the excess of joy with either rage or fear." Hu rolled up his dirty sleeves and slapped Fan's cheek with his greasy hand. Fan reacted miraculously to this therapy and was cured immediately.

The great achievement of this episode lies in its appealing description of the effect of a fit of madness, a common occurrence and yet a shock to human emotion, which an individual always wants to be rid of. It is this aspect that caused this short piece of social satire to become so much appreciated in China.

Hong Lou Meng (Dream of the Red Chamber; transalted by Kuhn, 1958) is considered by many to be the best novel ever produced in China. We find almost all the classic behaviors of mental disorders, such as obsession, use of gibberish, self-castigation, convulsions, talking to oneself, compulsive phobia, fugue, and homosexuality, in this book. The hero, Bao Yu, who has been the most beloved character of many Chinese, is a typical case of *qing chi* (love sickness). It is said that he "behaved like a depraved idiot from birth." He was born with a piece of jade in his mouth, symbolizing his previous existence, but lost it. Thus, the occurrence of his mental illness, which was similar to epilepsy, was always associated with the loss of the piece of jade. Throughout the novel, the adjectives employed to describe Bao Yu, such as foolish, crazy, silly, naïve, and idiotic, relate to mental disorders. He is symbolized as an insensate stone and is identified by his idiocy, with which he gains laurels as well as brings shame to himself.

From Bao Yu's point of view, females are made of water—very clean and pure—and males from clay—dirty and filthy; therefore, he always wished he had been born a female. He was very fond of licking the rouge from the lips of the young ladies of his entourage. At the same time, he showed a strong contempt for the stupidity of sitting year after year practicing the sterotypic "Four Paragraph Essay," demanded at the civil service examination. Ultimately, because of the frustration of his marriage, he escaped from the secular world and was a wandering monk until the end of his life.

In the opinion of Western critics, the story of *Hong Lou Meng* is no more than "a case history of a highly gifted but degenerate young aristocrat, a psychopath and a weakling, asocial, effeminate, plagued by inferiority complex and manic depression, who, though capable of a temporary rallying of energies, founders among the demands of reality and slinks cravenly from human society." (Kuhn, 1958). The judgment of the Chinese is quite different. At present, more than 1000 books and articles referred to as "Red [Chamber's] Learning," have been published to assert the story's significance. These concentrate on the social—economic background on which this novel is based and stress particular interest in identifying all its characters as historical figures. These writings unanimously praise Bao Yu for his inestimable courage against the iniquitous feudal system of his time. Moreover, since the 1980s, on the recommendation of Chinese higher authorities, *Hong Lou Meng* has been much more widely circulated than ever before. The questions arise: For what reason is a novel describing disorders of thought, feeling, and behavior acclaimed as the best novel ever produced in China? Will ordinary Western readers ever enjoy reading it as much as their Chinese counterparts do? If not, how can we explain the divergent opinions existing between different cultures?

Evidently, the disordered and unbalanced characters in the preceding survey are beloved by Chinese readers, because they enjoy a vicarious pleasure in mental conflicts and emotional sufferings. Every individual has had a similar experience and, according to Freudian theory, has been compelled to repress it into his or her subconcious.

Ever since the time of ancient Greece, the performance of drama and tragedy has been interpreted as a channel for satisfying and pacifying the turbulence of human passion through pity and fear. The Freudian interpretation of the tragic work of art goes even deeper, attributing to it the function of releasing tensions resulting from the repression of traumatic experiences in the subconscious mind. Not many Chinese literary writings, however, possess the powerful magnitude and intensity to meet this universal human need of releasing tensions, because most place the stress on amiable relationships among individuals and on the harmony of individual emotions, emphasizing the moral effect strongly and emotional gratification hardly at all. To fill the painful void in individual hearts, the previously cited novels and other fiction provide tragedy that regulates and dispels readers' hidden insidious impulses.

The unusual pleasure experienced by the present generation in China in reading *Hong Lou Meng* demonstrates the novel's power, notwithstanding the inconsistency between an essentially decadent literary work and the readers' objective social environment. Moralists, both Chinese and Western, may be concerned that a novel of this kind, traditionally condemned as obscene by the old Chinese gentry, would incite the younger generation to a decadent life. However, since the later part of the Cultural Revolution, when *Hong Lou Meng* was selected as the first fashionable novel to be printed on an unprecedented scale, observations have shown that people, on the whole, have not been excited into indulgence and reveries by reading it. They enjoy reading it without wishing to behave like Bao Yu. We have not heard of any offenders who have licked rouge from the lips of young women comrades!

CONCLUSION

This brief survey treats the subject of traditional Chinese beliefs and attitudes toward mental illness, together with their expressions in Chinese letters, as a topic of profound cultural interest. One may hope that, despite the cultural differences that are still apparent worldwide, a more detailed study will deepen our view of the psychic unity of mankind.

REFERENCES

Ban, Gu
    1962   *Qian han shu* [The history of the early Han Dynasty], Vol. 27, *Wu xin zhi* [Essays on *Wuxin*]. Beijing: Zhonghua Bookstore.
Bien, Jao
    1961   *Nan jing* [Classic of difficulties] *Dao can ben (Daocan* edition). Taipei: Yiwen.
Bu, Song Ling
    1958   *Liao Zai Zhi Yi* [Unusual Tales for the Leisure Studio]. Shanghai: Zhonghua.
Cao, Yuan Fang
    1601   *Zhubing yuan hou lun* [Treatise on the etiology and manifestations of disease].
Chen, Meng Lei
    1959   *Yibu quanlu* [A complete collection of medical works]. Beijing: People's Health Publishing House.
Chen, Shi Tou (c. 1662−1722)
    n.d.   *Shishi milu* [Secret records from the stone chamber].
Ge, Hong
    1923   *Zhou hou bei ji fang* [A handbook of prescriptions for emergency] *(Daocan* edition) Shanghai: Han-fen Lo.
Han, Yu
    1938   *Changli Xiensheng Ji* [The collected essays of Master Changli]. Reprinted from *Shi Cai Tang* copy of the Sung Dynasty, Vol. 17. Shanghai: Shangwu.
Huangfu, Mi
    1967   *Zhenjiu jayi jing* [Classic of acupuncture and moxibustion]. Reprinted from *Guang Shu* copy of the Qing Dynasty, Collection of *Gujin Yitung Zhengmai* [A

complete book of ancient and contemporary orthodox medical work], Vol. 2. Taipei: Yiwen.

Huangti (pseudonym; author unknown)

1967a   *Huangti neijing lingshu jing* [The Yellow Emperor's classic of internal medicine, miraculous pivot]. Reprinted from *Guang Shu* copy of Qing Dynasty, Collection of *Gujin Yitung Zhengmai*, Vol. 2. Taipei: Yiwen.

1967b   *Huangti neijing suwen* [The Yellow Emperor's classic of internal medicine, plain questions]. Reprinted from *Guang Shu* copy of the Qing Dynasty, Collection of *Gujin Yitung Zhengmai*, Vol. 2. Taipei: Yiwen.

Kuhn, Franz

1958   *Dream of the red chamber*. New York: Pantheon Books.

Li, Gao

1967   *Shi shu* [Ten books]. Reprinted from *Guang Shu* copy of the Qing Dynasty, Vol. 2. Taipei: Yiwen.

Li, Yan

1577   *Yixue rumen* [An introduction to medicine].

Liu, Xie He

1981   Psychiatry in traditional Chinese medicine. *British Journal of Psychiatry*, 138, 429–433.

Lou, Ying (c. 1332–1401)

n.d.   *Yixue gangmu* [Outline of medicine].

Shen, Jin Ao

1962   *Zabin yuanliu xizho* [Enlightenment on the origin and evolution of miscellaneous diseases]. Shanghai: Shanghai Press of Science and Technology.

Sun, Si Miao

1955   *Qenjin yaofang* [Prescriptions worth a thousand gold for emergency]. Beijing: People's Health Publishing House.

Tseng, Wen-Sheng

1973   The development of psychiatric concepts in traditional Chinese medicine, *Archives of General Psychiatry*, 29, 569–575.

Wei, Zhi Xiu

1970   *Xu mingyi leian* [Continued volume of the classified case records of famous doctors]. Vol. 3. Taipei: Shangwu.

Wu, D. Y. H.

1982   Psychotherapy and emotion in traditional Chinese medicine. In T. Marsella and J. White (Eds.), *Cultural conceptions of mental health and therapy*. Dordrecht, Holland: Reidel.

Wu, Jing Zi

1972   *Rin Lin wai shi* [Informal history of a literate]. Hong Kong: Zhonghua.

Xu, Chun Pu

1556   *Kujin yitung* [Encyclopedia of ancient and contemporary medical work].

Yu, Tuan

1515   *Yixue zhengzhuan* [Orthodoxy of Medicine], Chapter 2, Section of Xin Feng.

Yu, Zhen (fl. 1778)

1959   *Gujin yian an* [Interpretation of ancient and contemporary case records]. Shanghai: Shanghai Press of Science and Technology.

Zhang, Zhong Jing

1971   *Jingui yaolue* [Synopsis of golden cabinet]. Copy of *Si ku quan shu zhen ben*, Vol. 14. Taipei: Shangwu.

Zhang, Jie Bin
    1970   *Jingyue quanshu* [A complete book of jingyue]. Shanghai: Shanghai Press of
            Science and Technology.
Zhu, Tan Xi
    1601   *Tanxi xinfa* [Mastery of Danxi's medical experience]. Collection of *Gujin Yitung
            Zhengmai*.
Zuoqu, Min
    1931   *Zuo Chuan* [Zuo's history], *The 17th year of Xang Gung*. Shanghai: Shangwu.

PART II

FAMILY AND CHILD

Childhood is not just the beginning of the life cycle: It is the essential stage in molding future behavior patterns. The family is not only the basic social unit through which the element of culture is transmitted; it is also the central matrix in which psychopathology occurs. Therefore, family and child are the two important foundations of our examination of culture, behavior, and mental state.

One of the characteristics of traditional Chinese culture is the strong emphasis on the family system. However, this emphasis has been influenced by the process of modernization, industrialization, and urbanization. At one period in mainland China, the importance of the family was challenged by political ideology. There is strong interest in knowing how the family is perceived and how it functions in mainland China of the present. Xintian Li (Chapter 7) responds to this interest. Using cases that dramatize his conclusions, he notes that the family is presently emphasized as the base of social relations and that marriage is regarded as the foundation of human life. He stresses the point that the family still has tremendous impact on the mental health of people in mainland China.

There are many ways to analyze and investigate the family system. By utilizing the family therapist's framework, Jing Hsu (Chapter 8) examines the characteristics of interpersonal relations patterns in the Chinese family in terms of power structure, cohesiveness, individualization, and coalition. She then describes the usual psychological problems observed, such as

83

CHINESE CULTURE
AND MENTAL HEALTH

inadequate communication, gaps in value orientation, split loyalties, and sibling rivalries, and suggests ways to provide culturally suitable therapy.

Wu (Chapter 9) provides his anthropological observations of the Chinese child-rearing pattern, which still prevails among the overseas Chinese in Papua New Guinea. This is characterized by a large number of caretakers, frequent and immediate response to a child's need or demand, frequent feeding, and close attachment between mother and child day and night. Training for older children emphasizes obedience to parents, but with little discipline in minor matters. To Wu, the bonding behavior in Chinese child rearing is a key to understanding mental health and well-being.

In the field of child devlopment, attention has been given recently to the study of inherited temperament, which can be identified even in early infancy and remains fairly consistent later. Chen-chin Hsu (Chapter 10) presents the findings from the first study of temperament in Chinese infants and young children. He then raises the question of how to explore and investigate character formation from a more integrated genetic-and-cultural point of view.

This is followed by two chapters addressing a significant issue: family planning and school systems and the effect of both the mental health of the child in mainland China. To avoid the future consequences of population explosion, there is an urgent necessity to enforce a strict family plan. Each married couple is encouraged to have only one child. Tao and Chiu (Jing Hwa; Chapter 11) focus on this important matter. They report on their study of the possible psychological hazards of being an only child and discuss factors that minimize the potential ill effects.

Concluding this section is Xu's (Chapter 12) description of the school system in China. He discusses recruitment, curriculum, and the emphasis on thought education, and interprets the sociocultural implications of the system. His review of the general mental health situation among school children in mainland China is based on his experience as a school consultant.

CHAPTER 7

The Effect of Family on the Mental Health of the Chinese People

Li Xintian

BACKGROUND

From the point of view of medical psychology, this chapter focuses on how the mental health of the Chinese people is affected by the family and how the manifestations of Chinese mental health problems differ from those of Westerners.

With regard to the family in China, it is essential to take into consideration the cultural background from which China has developed. For more than 2000 years, since the Spring and Autumn Period and the Warring States (403–221 B.C.) until the mid-nineteenth century, China was a feudal society based on a small-scale peasant economy with Confucianism as the predominant doctrine of its culture. The national cultural tradition framed during this 2000 years is deeply rooted in every Chinese family and every individual in the family. After the Opium War in the mid-nineteenth century, Western culture, together with Western capitalism, invaded China, and the ancient Chinese empire fell to the status of a semifeudal and

85

semicolonial society. After the overthrow of the autocratic monarchy in the 1911 revolution, Western culture penetrated China on a large scale. Nevertheless, the Chinese traditional culture, morality, and customs remained unchanged. Although the Chinese culture was being remolded step-by-step on the basis of a socialist economy following the revolution in 1949, the essence of traditional Chinese culture has been well preserved and carried forward. This can be seen, for instance, in the persistence of the traditional cultural value of family. The family plays a significant role in child rearing, married life, and in the care of the elderly in contemporary China.

THE ROLE OF THE FAMILY IN CHILD REARING

In China, the family is still the basic unit of society in which children receive great care. Throughout life, one has countless ties with the family, and it is impossible for one to be free from family influence, which brands one's mind deeply. In most ordinary Chinese families, children are the apples of their parents' eyes. They receive the best care possible, materially and spiritually. In China today, children are considered metaphorically to be the flowers of the motherland.

To emphasize the mental and physical growth of children, 7842 youth palaces, homes for youth, youth activity centers, and youth service centers have been established throughout the nation. They provide young people under age 14 with extracurricular activities and learning centers. Beijing City, for example, has a youth palace in each of the districts (*qu*) and counties (*xian*). Statistics show that together Beijing City's 15 youth palaces occupy an area of some 130,000 square meters. The interior of each of these children's activity centers covers 47,000 square meters. In 1980, nearly 2400 reading materials for children were published, and 1,560,000,000 copies of these publications were distributed. There were 66 nation-wide journals and newspapers in circulation for the youth audience. Among them, 25 were published in the cities of Beijing, Shanghai, and Tienjing.

Children are encouraged to participate in urban conservation activities. In 1981 in the city of Chengdu, many schools established tree-protecting teams for the purpose of protecting trees and flowers from damage and to educate children in habits of appreciating nature. By 1982, the greenery conservation teams had expanded in number to more than 200. No less than 106,000 youth team members have actually stood guard by the trees and plants and thus they created a joyful scene of "flowers of the motherland treasuring flowers" (*Zhungguo Qingnian-Bao*, 1982). This kind of activity is beneficial to children's mental and physical health and has been encouraged in every city of the nation.

In the pediatric department of a general hospital, 143,049 patients were recorded for 1981. Only 0.08% of the child patients among them were diagnosed as having behavioral and neurotic disorders (Shenyang Chinese Medical University, personal communication). In a mental hospital, it was noted that among 3304 inpatients, only 36 cases (1.08%) of the mental patients were below the age of 15 (Tienjing Psychiatric Hospital, personal communication). Among them schizophrenics accounted for only 26 cases (0.78%). This figure may not accurately reflect the higher incidence of mental illness that may occur outside the hospital environment, because parents are usually reticent to take their children to a mental hospital as inpatients. However, when children show signs of even slight physical discomfort, they are readily taken to a general hospital for treatment. This practice makes the figure from the general hospital for behavioral and psychological disorders a more reliable one.

THE ROLE OF THE FAMILY IN MARRIED LIFE

Marriage is regarded as a serious and sacred event. At present, young people go through the process of getting to know each other well, then falling in love before they actually get married. They can choose their partner in accordance with their own wishes. They may choose to have more than one friend of the opposite sex; and as long as they behave properly and avoid falling in love with two persons simultaneously, they are not reproached. But once they are married, unfaithfulness of a spouse is met by personal condemnations from relatives and friends as well as from the public, such as the authorities of the work unit. Sexual life after marriage is restrained. Couples seek to keep the family in harmony and happiness. If the spouses lose affection for each other, they will not readily divorce, especially if they have children.

When a marriage is about to break up, relatives, friends, organizations, and, finally, a judge try their best to mediate. If a third party is involved in a divorce case, people tend to resort to "educating" the third party through the authorities, to prevent the break-up of the family. Should the court grant a divorce due to irreconcilable differences between partners of the marriage, child care must be a part of the negotiation. An agreement must be reached in which one party takes the responsibility of raising the child, while the other party must share child-care expenses until the child reaches the age of 18.

Generally, the divorce rate in China is lower than in Western countries.

Accordingly, there are fewer children in China than in Western countries who suffer mental trauma resulting from their parents' divorce or from being abandoned by one of the parents.

THE ROLE OF THE FAMILY IN THE CARE OF THE ELDERLY

From early childhood, children in China are taught to respect the elderly and to show filial obedience. Even when they are grown and have formed their own family and are earning their own living, children give regular material and psychological support to their parents. At the same time, they may receive material and psychological support from their parents. In the socialist society of China, the meaning of *xiao* (*hsiao*; filial piety) is three-fold: to have gratitude for the care given by one's parents, to respect and love parents, and to be considerate and attentive to parents' desires. When children grow up and leave their parents' home to form their own nuclear families, they should regularly attend to their parents' economic and psychological needs. The civil code of marriage states: "Children have as their obligation the provision of support and help to their parents." Children, in turn, may depend upon the support, both economic and emotional, of their parents.

The idea that when old, one has to depend on his or her children is still prevalent, particularly in the countryside. Despite the fact that the well-being of many elderly people is guaranteed through their pensions and other sources of income, people still prefer to live close to their children so that they can visit and interact with them frequently. In China, elderly people are permitted to make arrangements for at least one of their children to be assigned to work post near the parents' residence.

In rural villages where people can build their own houses, the possibility that aged parents will live with their adult children is much higher than in the cities. Retired city dwellers often participate in public volunteer work for the community in which they reside, serving residents or students by, for example, organizing nurseries or similar service centers. Many aged people go to the parks in the morning to join *tai-ji* (*tai-chi*) or *qi-gong* (*chi-kung*) (breath and meditation) exercises, which are organized public sports. Few elderly people are idle. Therefore, markedly fewer cases of senile psychiatric disorder resulting from loneliness and being forsaken are found in China than in Western countries. According to one study (She-nyang Psychiatric Hospital, personal communication), there were four patients over age 65 admitted to a mental ward in 1981, a figure that accounts for only 0.26% of the total inpatient group of 1517 persons. One was diagnosed as senile, two as schizophrenic, and one as schizophrenic with alcoholic tendencies. This figure is lower than might be expected. As long as elderly persons are not disorderly, children take care of them at home rather than send them to a hospital.

There is also a low incidence of suicide among the elderly. In the emergency ward of a general hospital, three persons above the age of 65 were recorded as having committed suicide. This number accounted for only 1.8% of the total death count (162) in that year (Shenyang Chinese Medical University, personal communication).

FAMILY CONSTRUCTION AMONG STRANGERS

To most Chinese, home is the source of mental consolation, support, and motivation. When unexpected disasters take away their beloved ones and breakup the family, people very often try to reconstruct a family. In the countryside of China, one seldom fails to find a family made up of members of different families and with different surnames. For instance, in the countryside in Shandong, an old woman named Chang had only one daughter. For the sake of her mother, the daughter planned to have her fiancé move to her house after marriage. Unfortunately, the girl was killed in a car accident before she was married, so her fiancé, Wang, moved into her house and took care of her mother. Liang, a girl from another village, fell in love with him. She not only married him but also became the old woman's adopted daughter. The bride later had a son and instead of naming the baby Wang after the father or Liang after the mother, she permitted the boy to carry on the family name of his adoptive grandmother, Chang, and named him Chang Youyi—*youyi* (*you i*) means friendship—to commemorate the extraordinary friendship among the members of this family (*Zhongguo Funu*, 1979).

After the earthquake in Tangshan, thousands of people, having lost their families, quickly reconstructed families. Families may be formed by people known to each other (such as neighbors or friends) or by total strangers. One may lose a spouse and join another widow or widower and her or his children or parents. Or a widowed person may form a family with in-laws. Members of even three or four families may combine into one; and grandparents, parents, sons, and daughters from different families may make up new families. In this way, they are able to console and help each other survive the catastrophe. When the tremors of the Tangshan earthquake died down and life began to return to normal, about half of the reconstructed families separated for various reasons (e.g., some were reunited with their family members; others could not get along with the new family members).

In Chinese society, interpersonal relationships cannot be removed from the influence of the family. The relationship between families in the same village, residential district, or community, as well as the relationship among family members, that is, the relationship between relatives, friends, and neighbors, is still the fundamental element of social behavior in the village, district, or community. This interpersonal relationship greatly affects the mental health of the Chinese people. To live in harmony, to respect the elderly and cherish the young, to show concern for each other, to help the unfortunate—these are still the main trends of Chinese national morality that affect the thought of the Chinese people. The following examples illustrate these trends.

Respect for the Elderly

A high school student, a girl named Bian Ting-min, lived in the country-side of Shandong. She read an article in the newspaper in August 1980 concerning how Chang Xiang-ling had done everything possible in caring for her parents-in-law with filial devotion for 40 years. Chang, a commune member in the countryside in Hebei Province, joined the Communist party in 1939 during the Sino-Japanese War at age 18. Her husband left to fight the Japanese invaders not long after their son was born. Unfortunately, her husband was killed in the battlefield; and 23 years later, his only son died from a brain tumor, and her father-in-law passed away soon after that. Chang Xiang-ling said to her mother-in-law, "Don't worry, Mother, so long as I'm here, I won't let you go hungry. And I will always be at your service." In 1969, Chang remarried, and she and her new husband continued to look after her mother-in-law. Now Chang and her husband are both over 60, and her mother-in-law is 88 years of age. Although the three have been living well in harmony, all of them are elderly and need to be looked after. On reading the article about Chang Xiang-ling, the girl was deeply moved. She thought to herself: "Auntie Chang had been taking care of her mother-in-law for so many years, but who will take care of her when she is old? And who will take care of her if she is ill?" Auntie Chang needed somebody young to be with her. An idea was beginning to form in her mind. She wrote to Chang Xiang-ling with fervor, hoping that she would accept her as a daughter, and soon she got the answer. Bian Ting-min was the youngest daughter in her own family. She said to her grandmother, father, brother, and sister: "Grandma and Father have my brother and sister to look after them; therefore, I won't worry about them. But I couldn't bear to see the three people in Auntie Chang's family, old and lonely, left without anybody to take care of them. Grandma often tells me that grandpa died at the point of a bayonet of the Japanese invaders.

Auntie Chang's husband was also killed in the battle during the Sino-Japanese War. National sufferings have linked our two families. I want to go to Heibei to look after Auntie Chang's family so as to do my part and express my filial piety." Her words brought the whole family to tears, and they all agreed with her. So in April 1981, Chang Xiang-ling came from Hebei to Shandong to take her "daughter" home. The story of Bian Ting-min, who came a great distance and volunteered to take care of the three elderly people to whom she was not related spread far and wide, and people from all around came to see the person who seemed to them to have appeared like an angel. Somebody asked Bian what had made her take this step and she answered: "When I wrote to Auntie Chang in August of last year, my school was just carrying out discussions about the philosophy of life. I agree that a person should live a life that can make others live more happily. Auntie Chang has devoted all she has to the revolution. It is my responsibility and my pleasure to look after the three old people. And I'm willing to dedicate my youth to ordinary work" (*Renmin Ribao*, 1981).

This story led to the following example. In the ancient city of Xian, there was a 75-year-old retired clerk, Wang Zeng-wu. Wang had no son or daughter, and his 70-year-old wife had recently been paralyzed due to a stroke. This elderly couple had nobody to take care of them. How were they going to deal with such a hardship? When the man read about the Shandong girl who "flew" to Hebei to serve the three elderly people in Chang Xiang-Ling's home, he was deeply moved. He took out his pen and wrote a letter: "I also wish to have a daughter fly to me." The letter was publsihed in the November 30, 1981 issue of the Xian evening paper. Within 20 days, more than 800 girls had written or had come to visit the old man, competing to be his daughter. The girls who wrote came from 14 provinces, cities, or autonomous states. Within 200 meters of the man's home, there was a school of health. The 600 girl students as a group requested to become this old couple's daughters. A month later (on December 30) in that school, a most unusual, elaborate ceremony was held for the elderly couple to welcome the 600 daughters to their home. The representative of the "collective daughters" said emotionally: "We are the youth of the 1980s. We want to be Father Wang's collective daughters. We will treat these two old folks the same way we would treat our own parents to ensure they have a happy time in their old age"

Thereafter, every day there were two or three girls who came to the couple's home to cook, to do the laundry, to serve soup and medicine; and they never missed a day, not even on holidays. In this case, these two elderly people—one over 75 and the other paralyzed—had over 1400 young girls wanting to be their daughters. This reflects a new trend in

China that demonstrates the spiritual beauty of the current younger generation (*Shanxi Ribao,* 1981; *Yangcheng Wanbao,* 1982). We can imagine how much influence it will have upon the health of elderly people in China.

Respect for the Disabled

In Dandong, there was a girl who suffered from paralysis of her lower extremeties. She finished high school with the help of her classmates. After she graduated in 1968, there was no one in the family to take care of her, for her father was old and ill and her mother had to work. She had trouble taking care of herself and she felt lonely. Often, tears coursed down her cheeks. Just at that time, a neighbor girl of 13 named Long Yan came to cheer her up, "Please don't cry, sister," she said, "now that I've grown up. I'm old enough to take care of you. From now on, I'll look after you." Because the paralyzed girl needed care day and night, Long Yan willingly moved in to stay with her. Every day and night, Long Yan helped her to turn over, to wash her face, and to comb her hair and helped her to the hospital by cart. She also subscribed to magazines and borrowed books for her to read. And whenever she learned there were books, films, or plays about disabled people, she would try to get the books or tickets for the girl so that she could draw strength and courage from them. For years Long Yan helped the girl cheerfully and with perseverance. In 1978, Long Yan started to work in the city transportation company and, in addition, was required to do chores in her own home. She asked the company to schedule her work in the early morning and late evening so that she could then look after the girl during the daytime. In 1979, television became popular in the city. By doing some extra work in her spare time for a year and a half, Long Yan saved enough money to buy a television set for the girl to watch, a generous act that moved the recipient to tears. Long Yan is now 26. Quite a few people tried to help her find a boyfriend, but whenever she noticed that the potential boyfriend was not very enthusiastic about her caring for the girl, she refused to have further contact with him. She finally found a boyfriend who fulfilled her most important requirement that he should heartily support her in taking care of the girl forever. Thus, for 13 years from her teens through young womanhood, Long Yan willingly dedicated herself to the neighbor girl, who was not related to her. And for 13 years, her tender love and care have cheered the heart of a girl who was hovering at the edge of despair (*Renmin Ribao* 1981).

DISCUSSION

From these examples, it is easy to see that interpersonal and family relationships of this kind are very common in mainland China. They are the crystalization of the general mood of the society in China. At present, China is advocating the concept of Five Stresses and Four Points of Beauty. The Five Stresses are stress on decorum, manners, hygiene, discipline, and morals. The Four Points of Beauty are beautification of the mind, beautification of language, beautification of behavior, and beautification of the environment. Thus, the spirit of deriving pleasure from helping people is encouraged. With this cultural background, distrust between people and a sense of insecurity and loneliness seldom become the mental burdens of the Chinese people. Compared to the situation in Western countries, loneliness is not a major cause of mental disorders.

Presently, China is striving for four modernizations. Will the family structure in China be affected by highly modernized industry as in Western countries? China has too large a population and is now advocating the policy of one child per couple. The questions now arise of how to educate the only child and of how that child can relate to parents and in-laws after he or she grows up and marries. And further, because of the improvement of the economic, cultural, and living standards, the proportion of elderly people in China will increase gradually; and like Western countries, China will become an aged society in the near future. In the family, there will be relationships among the spouses; the four parents, and the child. Will these potential developments affect the traditional family and interpersonal relationships in China, and will they produce an adverse effect on the mental health of the people? These are new possibilities we are aware of and subjects that require further investigation.

REFERENCES

Renmin Ribao [People's Daily Newspaper], November 11, 1981.
Shanxi Ribao [Shanxi Daily Newspaper], December 31, 1981.
Yangcheng Wanbao [Yangcheng Evening Newspaper], January 10, 1982.
Zhongguo funu [Women of China]: *Vol. 4. Xin ja* [New Home]. 1979.
Zhonggua Qingnian Bao [Chinese Youth Newspaper], May 13, 1982.

CHAPTER 8

The Chinese Family: Relations, Problems, and Therapy

Jing Hsu

INTRODUCTION

Since the 1960s, one of the major advances in the mental health field has been the proliferation of theories and clinical practice in family therapy. (Group for Advancement of Psychiatry, 1970; Guerin, 1976) Individual behavior patterns are now being evaluated within the context of the family unit and treated by intervening in the family's current patterns of interaction. This approach is very different from that of traditional individual psychotherapy. From the psychoanalytical point of view, the individual is the focus of concern, psychopathologies are seen primarily as intrapsychic processes, and therapists are discouraged from having contacts with the patient's family.

Family scholars believe that humans are not isolates. They are acting and reacting members of a social group and are influenced by the social context. The family is the basic unit of the social group: It is the group with which an individual has the earliest, longest, and closest contact. The

95

CHINESE CULTURE
AND MENTAL HEALTH

family, to a certain extent, governs its members' experience and behavior: "It can be seen as the extracerebral part of the mind" (Minuchin, 1974:7). Individual symptoms may be the manifestations of the family's dysfunction and can also be maintained by the family's pattern of interaction (Ackerman, 1958; Jackson, 1957).

The family is particularly important in the individual's life in the Chinese social system. It is the center of most social functions—political, financial, educational, and recreational—and is the foundation of all social relations. From birth, individuals are under the continuous influence of the family (Chai, 1964b). Therefore, an adequate understanding of Chinese family structure and relations is essential for better diagnosis and treatment of individual and family problems of the Chinese.

Different aspects of the family can be and have been studied, for example, the kinship system (F.L.K. Hsu, 1972), family structure and function (Fei, 1982), family development, and family subsystems (relations between family members). The health and psychopathology of the family and the effects of modernization on the family are interesting subjects to family scholars. Data about the family can be collected in various ways, for example, through direct observations of family–group interaction (Farina, Conn, and Dunham, 1963, Haley 1967, Oliveri and Reiss, 1981), through investigating an individual family member's views of their family, through analyzing social systems, such as custom, rites, and law, to see how the matter of family is dealt with by such social systems, through analyzing cultural products, such as children's stories (Tseng and J. Hsu, 1972), the plots of operas (J. Hsu and Tseng, 1974), novels (Chin, 1970), or proverbs to examine how the issue of family is reflected in such cultural products, and finally, through clinical experience of treating dysfunctional families. By utilizing such variable sources of information, I examine some special aspects and common psychological problems of the Chinese family and attempt to uncover characteristics that are significant in clinical practice.

THE CONCEPT OF FAMILY HEALTH
AND PATHOLOGY

First, I briefly present current trends of thought in the field of family health and pathology, for families, like individuals, can be healthy or pathological. It is believed by some family clinicians that the characteristics associated with family health can be reviewed in several areas, which include family power structure, degrees of individual differentiation, family cohesiveness, coalition within the family, and interaction with the outside world (Lewis, Beavers, Gossett, and Phillips, 1976).

Power Structure. This refers to the distribution of parental power that can be seen in how family is organized, how hierarchy is maintained, and in the ways major decisions are made in the family. The continuum of family power can range from unstructured, chaotic, and leaderless to highly structured to the extent of rigidity and the inflexible holding of power by the dominant. In the most flexible family, power is shared by both parents. The parents are in charge, but not in an authoritarian way. The children's opinions are listened to and considered in final decision making. Differences are resolved by respectful negotiation and mutual compromise.

Family Cohesiveness. In a healthy family, the members have a sense of belonging. Each members's psychological and physiological needs are acknowledged and cared for. Mutual concern and support are given. In the dysfunctional family, members seldom communicate with each other. Blaming and scapegoating are common (Wynne and Single, 1963).

Degree of Family Individualization. Family systems vary in the degrees that they tolerate or encourage individualization. This tolerance is closely related to the autonomy of family members. The healthy family helps its members develop personal autonomy. Each person knows what he or she feels and thinks and takes responsibility for personal actions. In the dysfunctional family, individual ideas and feelings are unclear, family members speak for each other and mind-reading and intrusions are common. In general, in such dysfunctional families, any attempt to be autonomous is seen as a threat to family harmony and must be prevented. The family is emotionally fused like an "undifferentiated family ego mass" (Bowen, 1978:107).

Family Alliance and Coalition. This is a process of choosing sides within the family. Certain family members side with each other, or form an alliance. Coalitions and alliances exist in both healthy and pathological families. In healthy families, the coalitions are flexible and functional. For example, a strong parental coalition—parents work together and support each other—can help the family to bring up the children successfully; siblings can form an alliance to support each other's special needs or to challenge an unreasonable parental decision. This peer process can be an important part of growing up and becoming independent.

Family alliance can also become rigid and dysfunctional. For example, a mother consistently siding with the son against the father or a father with the daughter against the mother interferes with the parental discipline of children.

Family Interaction with the Outside World. A healthy family views human encounters as affliliational and tends to seek and make friends outside the family and take part in community activities.

CHINESE FAMILY STRUCTURE AND RELATIONSHIPS

The dimensions of family interaction previously discussed are used as a framework for examining the Chinese family. This study highlights certain specific characteristics of the Chinese family that are different from their Western counterparts.

Equalitarian but Authoritarian Power Structure

In the traditional Chinese family system, the distribution of power is based on generation, age, and gender. In this system, the eldest man of the top generation usually has the ultimate power to make final decisions regarding important matters. According to an old Chinese saying "Women are supposed to obey not only their husbands, but also must obey their adult sons if their husbands have passed away (*Fu zai cong fu, fu si cong zi*)". This male-dominant hierarchy system is changing. For example, recent surveys in Taiwan indicate this saying no longer holds true. The majority of elementary and junior high school students surveyed felt that both parents in their home usually shared in decision-making concerning family affairs and discipline of the children (Chai, 1964a). Therefore, it can be assumed that with modernization, the power structure of the Chinese family has moved from a patriarchal to an equalitarian relationship between parents, similar to that in the West. However, there are still some differences, particularly as to the manner in which the parental leadership is administered. In the Chinese family, the power is wielded in an authoritarian way. The parents make the decisions; the children are expected to obey. If there is a "discussion" between parents and children, it generally follows that the parents lecture the children on proper patterns of thought and behavior. No questioning or challenges are encouraged as they are in Western families (Wu, 1965).

Family Solidarity and Loyalty

The Chinese family is extremely cohesive. Family members depend on each other for support, both emotional and in carrying out daily tasks. Family closeness and loyalty may have been weakened because of changes in family structure caused by modernization, urbanization, migration, or changes in political ideologies or systems, but they certainly have not disappeared. For example, Chinese who move to the United States continue to send money to their parents as a token of their filial piety. Chinese in Singapore, even though separated from their kin because of the newly built highrise housing, continue to visit their relatives every week rather than establish new friends in the neighborhood (Wong and Kuo, 1981). Young mainland Chinese still try to live near their parents whenever possible even after they are married. And the sight of loving grandparents caring for affectionate grandchildren is common in mainland Chinese garden parks and streets. The form of extended family may be eroded due to physical impossibility, but it continues to exist in substance.

It is worth mentioning that the way in which Chinese family members show affection for each other is often quite different from Western ways. Instead of expressing emotions in words, the Chinese tend to show concern for and take actual care of another's physical needs (Tseng and J. Hsu, 1970). This may have root in the prolonged breast feeding of infants, as well as having children sleep in the parents' bed so the parents can add more blankets if the child seems cold. In the traditional children's classic, *24 Examples of Filial Piety,* the most common way for children to show their affection and devotion toward their parents is through taking care of the parents' physical needs. This included warming the father's mat with one's own body, tasting the parents' medicine before giving it to them, and even cutting a piece of flesh from one's own body to make a medicinal brew for the mother (Tseng and J. Hsu, 1972).

Uniformity and Propriety

The degree of family individualization within the Chinese family has a definite characteristic pattern. Generally speaking, the Chinese demand collective uniformity in terms of ideas and behavior but allow individual privacy and differences in the terms of emotion, while the opposite seems to be true in the West. For example, within the Chinese family, siblings are expected to show proper respect and good behavior toward each other; in the Western family, parents are apt to say, "Now, you must *love* your brother or sister."

Both traditional Chinese and modern Western concepts of family agree on the important role the family plays in individual behavior. However, the Chinese carry this further. The Chinese concept holds the family to be inseparable from individual behavior. This concept sees the individual's behavior as representing the collective qualities of the family, including the faults or virtues of the ancestors. If one family member accomplishes some extraordinary achievement or demonstrates virtuous behavior, then the whole family gains face (*you lian*). If one member fails or shows unacceptable, deviant behavior, the whole family loses face (*diu lian*). A serious way of criticizing people is to say, "There is a lack of virtue in your past eight generations of ancestors" (*Zu zong ba dai que de*). Thus, in the Chinese social system, the consequences of individual family members' behavior are shared by the whole family. The family members are judged as one by the larger society, and this collective presentation of the family to the outsider—face—is a shared quality. Adapting the Bowen (1978:107) concept, the Chinese family shares, instead of an "undifferentiated ego mass," an undifferentiated family face.

This face-sharing is far from disappearing at the present time and has generated many conflicts within the family. For example, some of the most common psychological problems among children and adolescents in Taiwan are those created by the pressure parents put on their children to achieve high grades so that the social status of the family, including that of the parents, will not be damaged. One mother complained to a child psychiatrist that "he [the son] gets *me* such low grades," literally considering the son's grades as her own (C. C. Hsu, 1980:169; italics added). Similar themes are found in parent–child relationships in stories published in newspapers and magazines in China. A father talking to his daughter about her difficulty in gaining admission to a dance academy says, "Do not lose face for your elders" (Chin, 1970:106).

Family sharing, however, does not apply to emotion. In the Chinese family, open expression or discussion of emotion is generally not encouraged, except in certain ritualistic situations, such as funerals when the women are supposed to cry loudly to demonstrate their grief (Tseng and J. Hsu, 1970). The Chinese believe that excess emotion endangers health. For example, losing one's temper is described in Chinese as the discharge of spleen element (*fa pi qi*). The common belief is that it is a result of too much fire element in the liver (*gan huo shen*). An overt expression of emotion, such as anger, may cause inner organ damage and, therefore, ought to be discouraged.

Thus, the lack of differentiations in the Chinese family tend to be more in the area of ideas and behavior, while the lack of differentiation in the Western family tends to be more in the emotional aspect of life.

"Central Tower" Interaction

It is hard to apply the Western concept of coalition in the Chinese family situation. In the Western family, coalition is based on dyadic relationships with great emphasis on the husband–wife dyad. In the Chinese family, the spousal relationship is deemed secondary to the parent–child relationship; and within the parent–child relationship, the mother–child relationship is the closest (J. Hsu and Tseng, 1974). However, this parent–child coalition, when present, does not necessarily compete or interfere with parental coalition or impair family function.

Sibling coalition is not prominent in the Chinese family. Chinese children are assigned different roles according to their gender and age. This hierarchy among siblings may serve to prevent the siblings from forming a strong peer group. In fact, each child tends to report directly to the parents and quite commonly betrays confidences of other siblings.

We might visualize the Chinese family's interactions as following a "central tower" pattern, with the mother as the center of the tower, the father on the side, keeping some distance from the children, while all the children are at the bottom of the tower.

"Own-People" and "Outsiders"

In general, the Chinese view of human encounters follows the family network. Within the network, the encounters are seen as affiliational. As the Chinese feel that relatives are most trustworthy and dependable, they often extend kin relationships to nonkin and form pseudokin ties. Instant kinship can be established by making people sworn brothers (*jie bai xiong di*) or "dry relatives" (*gan qin; dry* means no blood tie). Friends are introduced also as relatives, using kinship terms. This wider use of kinship terms has survived even after drastic sociopolitical changes in mainland China. On a recent trip there in 1981, I, as the only Chinese in a group of Caucasian-American physicians, was pleased and surprised when we visited a nursery and the children there called me "Aunty," while the others were all addressed as "American guests." The people one knows who have been made pseudokin are classified as *zi ji ren* (own people), and all strangers *wai ren* (outsiders). If one is *zi ji ren*, all can be accommodated; if one is *wai ren*, then it is a different matter. Westerners at Chinese bus stops in Taiwan were often amazed to see a crowd of people, pushing their way through to get on the bus, stop and politely ask someone they know to get on first. The explanation of such a drastic behavior change is simple: The acquaintance is *zi ji ren*; all the others are *wai ren*.

As a result of strong family orientation and ties, the Chinese are less enthusiastic about participating in nonkinship organizations that work toward a common cause. Chinese also believe that the family should take care of its own members and one should not intrude into other people's affairs. A Chinese maxim says: "Sweep the snow in front of your own dwelling, but don't bother about the frost on the roof of others" (*Ge ren zi sao men qian xue, bu guan ta ren wa shang shuang,* F.L.K. Hsu, 1981).

COMMON PSYCHOLOGICAL PROBLEMS

Each family system, based on its different style, may inherit certain functional assets but at the same time, may be associated with certain dysfunctional problems. The characteristics of the Chinese family structure may affect the nature of the common psychological problems arising within the family, the culturally defined clinical manifestations, and their coping responses.

Some of the psychological problems common to contemporary Chinese families are inadequate communication, generation gaps in value orientation and expectations, split loyalties, and sibling rivalries.

Inadequate Communication

As the Chinese family organizes itself in an hierachial way, with the parents, usually the father, playing an authoritarian role, communication usually means parents questioning and lecturing children. Seldom do children talk spontaneously or communicate their opinions or feelings to their parents. This can result in a lack of understanding and parental empathy for children and it can prevent the children from feeling emotionally close to the parents. Therefore, there are strong needs to search for emotional closeness and guidance elsewhere. This is demonstrated by the success and popularity of a telephone counseling service, "Dial Teacher Chang" (*zhang lao shi dian hua*) available to young people in Taiwan.

Also, as parents usually respond to misbehavior in similar ways—with criticism rather than understanding and empathy—children generally avoid telling their parents about their emotional problems. One parent may withhold information about a child when she or he is afraid that the child will be harshly punished by the other parent. One is often surprised by the many secrets family members keep over relatively minor issues.

Gaps in Value Orientation and Expectation

As the older generation still holds a more traditional view of the family, the younger generation has become more Westernized and thus views family relations and obligations differently. These differences often cause problems in the family. Take marriage as an example. While the younger generation sees mate selection as primarily an individual choice, the older generation may still feel it is a family issue that needs to be considered and decided upon based upon family interests. Interference by parents usually generates much resentment from the adult children. Chinese parents often expect their children to "feed them in return" (*fang bu*)—support and take care of them—after the children grow up. Yet the younger generations may be more independent or individual-oriented and tend to plan their life accordingly. The parents are usually disappointed and angry when they find out they are not included as an essential part in their adult children's future planning. One mother quit her job after her son went to the United States, assuming that he would bring her over and support her. When this turned out not to be the case, she became depressed and angry and accused him as being unfilial and ungrateful.

Split Loyalties

Chinese families, like other families, have interpersonal conflicts; however, since the Chinese family structure commonly involves more than just the nuclear family and also since the family member shares activities and responsibilities more often, there tend to be more conflicts, especially with in-laws and between siblings.

Because the Chinese stress obligation and loyalty to family members and also because the vertical ties in the family (parents–children) are seen as more important than the horizontal ties (husband–wife, brother–sister), it is more difficult for a newly married couple to establish identity as a new family. Members of the original family do not hesitate to remind the newlyweds of their obligation and loyalty to the family that brought them up. There is a Chinese maxim, "Siblings are hands and feet, while wives are only clothes" (*Xiong di ru shou zu, qi zi ru yi fu*), implying that one can always dispose of used clothes but cannot sever limbs. It is considered a moral disgrace if a son "forgets his mother after he gets a wife" (*qu la xi fu, diu la niang*). Thus, conflicts are generated by the in-laws on both sides who are jealous over and competing for the loyalty of the couple. Conflicts also arise within the couple because of stronger loyalty to the original family than to the spouse.

For example, one woman told me that her brother had recently separated from his wife and that she was tired of making excuses for him in front of her husband when he showed up alone at family gatherings. I asked her why she did not simply tell her husband that her brother was considering divorce. She gave me a stern look and replied, "Then my husband might look down on my family." To her, kinship bonds are stronger than marital bonds.

Another couple joined a group tour organized by the husband's company and were "ordered" by the husband's older brother to bring their widowed mother along because the mother had never visited the United States. Upon hearing this, the wife's older sister recommended that the wife also bring her parents along. The couple left for the trip with three elderly parents, two of them in wheelchairs.

Sibling Rivalries

Even though traditional Chinese teaching emphasizes filial piety to parents and harmony between siblings, sibling relations as portrayed in literature and as observed in true life reveal the contrary. There exist significant conflict and bitterness among adult siblings (J. Hsu and Tseng, 1974; Wolf, 1970). Competition for parental favoritism is a commonly cited reason, and incompatibility between sisters-in-law is another. The first is not difficult to understand in view of the Chinese family structure, in which the parents enjoy tremendous power and make most decisions and in which communication is commonly through parents and vertical ties are considered more important than horizontal ones.

USUAL COPING PATTERNS

When problems arise in the Chinese family, members involved generally do not confront each other or deal with them directly. Help from extended family and friends is usually enlisted first without the knowledge of the other members involved. At the same time, the relationship becomes cold and distant. For example, a wife discovered that her husband was romantically involved with a younger woman. Instead of confronting her husband, she discussed the situation with her adult children, her relatives, and her friends, as well as the family and the superiors of the young woman involved. Another wife who had long wanted a divorce planned a trip to California so she could "just stay there" without revealing her intention to her husband.

Occasionally, there is an attempt at direct confrontation, which usually results in explosive outbursts of anger, denial, or withdrawal of the party who is confronted.

In the Chinese family, negotiations are most fruitful if they are mediated by a mutually respected third party, such as an uncle. When direct confrontation, mediation, and other indirect maneuvers fail to solve the problem, the "final common pathway" is usually somatization. It is common for the physician to be consulted for somatic symptoms, such as headaches and general malaise, and only after a negative physical evaluation does one begin to suspect psychological causes.

It is a common observation that somatic complaints are more prominent among Chinese patients with psychological problems (Kleinman, 1979, Tseng, 1975). Explanations of this phenomenon include (1) somatization, when the patient experiences only the physical symptoms and psychological problems are repressed; (2) somatic presentation, when the patient is aware of the psychological symptoms but chooses instead to present somatic components of the psychological symptoms in the help-seeking processes (Cheung, Lau, and Waldmann, 1980); and (3) somatic symbolism, when somatic symbols are used as a symbolic network to describe and/or to understand psychological problems. From our understanding of Chinese child-rearing practices and family interaction, it may be said somatization is in part caused and/or maintained by the characteristic family structure and interaction in the Chinese family. As discussed previously, Chinese parents, especially mothers, demonstrate love and care through expressing concerns over and taking care of their children's bodily functions and needs. In the meantime, overt expression of affection and discussion of psychological issues are discouraged. Investigations have shown that a relationship exists between deficits in expression of affect and psychosomatic symptoms (Anderson, 1981). Somatized presentation and behavior is created by blocking expression of emotion while simultaneously sanctioning and nurturing somatic preoccupation. A child who complains of abdominal cramps will be given warm soup to eat and tenderly cared for, while a child who expresses fear will probably be scolded. Verbal expression of emotions in the Chinese language is still predominantly somatic oriented. Even though there are written characters designating states of depression, there are no equivalent expressions in the spoken language. The closest to such an expression is *xin ging bu hao* (the condition of my heart is not good), a somatic description. Studies that claim that there are many emotional expressions in the Chinese language fail to make this distinction (Kwong and Wong, 1981).

Minuchin, Rosman, and Baker (1978) observed four characteristics in the family process that may encourage somatization. They are enmeshment, overprotectiveness, rigidity, and lack of conflict resolution. Each can be found to a certain degree in the interaction of the Chinese family.

CLINICAL SIGNIFICANCE AND APPLICATION

Now that we have examined Chinese family structure, relations, and common psychological problems and have found that they differ in many ways from their Western counterparts, it is useful to discuss some of the clinical significances and applications.

Assessment and Interpretation

It is necessary, when assessing deviant behavior, to consider the cultural norm. Sometimes a seemingly deviant behavior or relationship in one culture is quite normal in another. This is particularly true regarding the matter of children's separation from parents. For example, a mature, 25-year-old man still living at home with his parents, attending to his parents' needs, and with little outside social contact would be thought of as dependent and lacking in autonomy in a contemporary Western culture. However, within the Chinese family system, which encourages mutual dependency and obligations, a son taking care of his parents in this way would be exhibiting normal behavior.

Similarly, an interaction pattern may have quite a different significance in different cultural groups and needs to be interpreted differently. As discussed previously, the Chinese family system is a child-centered system in which the parent–child relationship takes precedence over the spousal relationship. When observing Chinese family interaction, it is not uncommon to observe that the major portion of interaction is between parents and children and that there is relatively little spousal interaction, particularly in a public setting. In the Western family, on the other hand, similar behavior patterns may indicate a weak parental coalition or a poor husband–wife relationship. This interpretation is not necessarily true for the Chinese family. The spousal relationship can be good and the husband–wife bond can be strong in spite of the parents' investing so much in the children. Clearly, culturally appropriate assessment of the family is necessary.

Therapeutic Relationships and Modality of Treatment

One of the essential factors in helping an individual or a family is establishing good therapeutic relationships. The therapist must establish himself or herself as being trustworthy, caring, and willing and able to help. In the Chinese cultural setting with reference to the Chinese family system, it is preferable that the therapist be close kin or a part of the social network and that he or she be relatively authoritative. This is directly contrary to what is generally considered appropriate in the West, where the cultural emphasis is on individuality, the therapist is encouraged to remain purely professional and—with some exceptions—to be strictly nonauthoritarian.

My own cultural ignorance in my early days of practice illustrates the distinction. When I returned to Taiwan immediately after the completion of my training in Boston, I was eager to practice psychotherapy the ''right'' way. I was newly *du jin* (gold-polished), the old Chinese description of a

Western-trained person. Thus, I was bombarded with requests to see patients. However, the requests were not, as I expected, directed to the university clinic where I was working but came through calls from the deans of the medical school, high offices of the government, my parents, and my uncles and aunts. I suddenly found myself seeing patients, who called me "big sister," in my family's living room. Being brainwashed with traditional analytical propriety, I deemed all this "manipulation" or "resistance." I insisted that my visitors return to the clinic and register formally as my patients. None returned. Years later, I was told that people felt I "had become an American" and no longer cared about them. If I had known better, I would probably have made full use of the pseudokin relationship and adapted my therapeutic approach to the cultural expectations of the patients and their families.

Different modalities of therapy may also suit certain culture groups better than the others. The democratic peer approach, much valued in individual, analytically oriented psychotherapy, does not suit the Chinese orientation well. Parents and physicians are expected to make decisions and give instructions. Failing to do this, they are viewed as weak and incompetent. If—in the Western technique—the Chinese patient is asked, "What do you think is wrong or can be done?" the response is likely to be a puzzled look. The Chinese patient does not come to tell the doctor what he thinks is wrong or can be done but to listen to the doctor's advice. In the Western therapist's view, such a patient would very likely be thought dependent, passive, and lacking in motivation. But to the Chinese patient, to challenge the therapist, impose his or her own opinions, or take an active part in the therapy is inconceivable. The more recent forms of goal-focused, change-oriented, task-giving psychotherapy (Haley, 1976) are certainly more applicable to the Chinese patient. Group therapy, a form of therapy that requires the participant to share private emotions with strangers and to learn from peers, does not quite suit the Chinese either. The group leader often becomes the center of attention; participants, instead of talking to one another, address the group leader directly, seeking directions and advice. Family therapy, which limits itself to family members and which follows the family patterns of communications, may be more appropriate, at least at the beginning.

Therapeutic Strategies

One of the goals of psychotherapy is to facilitate culturally sanctioned behavior. Therefore, adequate understanding of the sociocultural norm is essential for successful treatment. Western psychotherapy stresses individualization and autonomy, seeing them as major developmental tasks to be completed during adolescence. Thus, it is common practice to encourage an adolescent to challenge parental authority and to establish a separate identity. However, in the Chinese family, where harmony, mutual obligation, and family solidarity are valued, such behavior can only create more conflict and more bad feelings among family members and within the individual. A young Chinese woman's letter to the editor of a youth magazine describes how she handled conflict with her parents. This incident sheds considerable light on Western–Chinese difference in human relations. The young woman wanted to share her successful experience with other young men and women whose parents opposed their choice of mates. She wrote:

> I fell in love with a young man; my parents were strongly against our courtship as he did not have the proper background. Instead of arguing with my parents, like most other young people, and making things worse, I deliberately demonstrated even more "filial piety" toward them than before. I did chores for them, bought delicacies for them, and eagerly attended to their needs. Eventually, my parents gave up their objection, because I had proved myself to be such a good daughter.

The Chinese family system stresses mutual obligation, believing that "a kind father has a filial son and vice versa" (*fu ci zi xiao*). Thus, when the daughter fulfilled her role as a filial daughter, the parents naturally had to be reasonable and kind.

As the result of modernization and urbanization, the traditional extended family has very often been replaced by the nuclear family, consisting of parents and their children only. However, the relationship to the extended family continues to be very close. There still exists a loyalty based on kinship ties.

The intrafamily kinship ties also prescribe proper behavior and interaction. Many Chinese wives complain that their husbands' sisters manage the family properties, while they, themselves, know very little and have little to say in their disposition. In the Chinese view, to encourage the wife to confront the husband or the sister-in-law on her own behalf would make her appear very greedy and virtueless. However, if she brings up this issue to her husband on behalf of her children, it is accepted as a part of her maternal duty to protect the welfare of the children.

The Chinese define intimacy in terms of primary groups rather than of individuals. Thus, one may be more open and direct with one's closest kin than to others. To suggest otherwise would be inappropriate. For example, in a family session, the wife was very upset with her husband about her sister-in-law. The sister-in-law had stored a considerable amount of furniture in their house. The wife wanted the husband to call his sister and tell her to remove the furniture and became angry at him when he failed to do so. My cotherapist, a Caucasian, asked the woman, "Why don't you call her [the sister-in-law] yourself?" Such a recommendation was quite appropriate for the Caucasian, but not quite so for the Chinese. I invited the husband to respond. He appeared puzzled and said, "I don't understand why is it that she wants me to call my sister. When they are together they appear to have such a good relationship." The wife responded, "Because she is your sister. If you tell her to remove the furniture, she will not be mad at you; but if I tell her, she will not talk to me for days. As she is my sister-in-law, I have to treat her politely, but you two are *zi ji ren* [own people] you can speak the truth to her."

In this Chinese situation, the appropriate action was for the husband to call his sister. The wife's direct confrontation of the sister-in-law would be socially inappropriate. It not only could increase the interpersonal conflict but would also make the wife feel bad about herself. In the Caucasian family, the wife might be encouraged to call the sister-in-law herself.

The Family's Utilization of Mental Health Services

The utilization of mental health services may also differ because of different cultural beliefs. As mental illness is often manifested in socially disturbing, deviant behavior, it often brings extreme shame and guilt to the family. The presence of a mentally ill person in the family is interpreted as the consequence of family ancestors having done something wrong in the past. As a result, the family's feeling of shame and its desire to keep the disturbed members' behaviors from public attention may inhibit utilization of professional mental health resources. A good illustration of this was given in an interview with an elderly Chinese couple who resided in Canada. They had taken care of their psychotic grandson and had hidden him from the social agencies and health professionals. When questioned about this, they explained: "We don't want other people to know about him; they may think there is something wrong in our family. . . . Someday his sense might come back, as our ancestors and we have done nothing wrong" (Lin and Lin, 1981).

Because the Chinese family relies first and primarily upon family members for support and help, early case findings and treatment seeking may be facilitated if the existing social network in the Chinese community is utilized for such tasks.

SUMMARY

The Chinese family system stresses family solidarity and loyalty. There is a clear boundary between the family and the outside world. However, the outside world is often integrated into the family network through pseudo-kin relations. Within the family, there is a clear power hierarchy based on generation, age, and gender. While there is parental coalition in terms of child rearing, the spousal relationship takes a second role to the parent–child relationship.

Though the Chinese family demands uniformity in terms of ideas and behavior, it allows ample space for private emotion. The family supports and nurtures its members, not through emotional expression but via practical help and concern over their physical needs. The kinship bonds remain strong in spite of urbanization and industrialization. These characteristics seem to be common to Chinese families in all parts of the world.

Because the Chinese family continues to play an important role in the individual's life, it is essential that mental health professionals who have the responsibility of working with Chinese patients have adequate understanding of the Chinese family system and its relationships in order that culturally appropriate mental health services can be provided for the Chinese population.

REFERENCES

Ackerman, N. W.
    1958   *The psychodynamics of family life.* New York: Basic Books.
Anderson, C. D.
    1981   Expression of affect and physiological response in psychosomatic patients. *Journal of Psychosomatic Research, 25,* 145–149.
Bowen, M.
    1978   Intrafamily dynamics in emotional illness. In M. Bowen (Ed.), *Family therapy in clinical practice.* New York: Jason, Aronson.
Chai, W. H.
    1964a   The attitude of high school students toward marriage and family. *Thought and Word, 2*(3), 333–336.
    1964b   Change of Chinese family system. *Thought and Word, 2*(1), 207–215.
Cheung, F., Lau, B., and Waldmann, E.
    1980   Somatization among Chinese depressives in general practice. *International Journal of Psychiatry in Medicine, 10,* 361–374.
Chin, A. L. S.
    1970   Family relations in modern Chinese fiction. In M. Freedman (Ed.), *Family and kinship in Chinese society.* Stanford: Stanford University Press.
Farina, A., Conn, S., and Dunham, R.M.
    1963   Measurement of family relationships and their effects. *Archives of General Psychiatry, 9,* 64–73.
Fei, X.
    1982   Changes in the Chinese family structure. *International House of Japan Bulletin, 2*(2).
Group for Advancement of Psychiatry
    1970   *The field of family therapy* (Rep. No. 78, Vol. 7). New York.

Guerin, P. J., Jr.
    1976   Family therapy: The first twenty-five years. In P. J. Guerin, Jr. (Ed.), *Family therapy: Theory and practice.* New York: Gardner.
Haley, J.
    1967   Speech sequences of normal and abnormal families with two children present. *Family Process, 6,* 81–97.
    1976   *Problem-solving therapy.* San Francisco: Jossey-Bass.
Hsu, C. C.
    1980   *He chu shi er jia* [Where is home?]. Taipei: Health World Press.
Hsu, F. L. K.
    1972   Kinship and ways of life: An exploration. In F. L. K. Hsu (ed.), *Psychological Anthropology.* Cambridge, MA: Schenman.
    1981   Chinese weakness. In F. L. K. Hsu (ed.), *Americans and Chinese.* Honolulu: The University Press of Hawaii.
Hsu, J. and Tseng, W. S.
    1974   Family relations in classic Chinese opera. *The International Journal of Social Psychiatry, 20,* 159–172.
Jackson, D. D.
    1957   The question of family homeostasis. *The Psychiatric Quarterly Supplement, 31,*(1), 79–90.
Kleinman, A.
    1979   *Patients and healers in the context of culture.* Berkeley: University of California Press.
Kwong, B., and Wong, S. W.
    1981   Physical presentations of psychological problems among Hong Kong Chinese: Cultural implications. *Journal of the Hong Kong Psychiatric Association, 1,* 33–39.
Lewis, J., Beavers, W. R., Gossett, J. T., and Phillips, V.A.
    1976   *No single thread: Psychological health in family systems.* New York: Bruner/Mazel.
Lin, T. Y. and Lin, M. C.
    1981   Love, denial and rejection: Responses of Chinese families to mental illness. In A. Kleinman and T. Y. Lin, (Eds.), *Normal and abnormal behavior in Chinese culture.* Dordrecht, Holland: D. Reider.
Minuchin, S.
    1974   *Families and family therapy.* Cambridge, MA: Harvard University Press.
Minuchin, S., Rosman, B., and Baker, L.
    1978   The psychosomatic families. In S. Minuchin, B. Rosman, and L. Baker, *Psychosomatic family.* Cambridge, MA: Harvard University Press.
Oliveri, M. E., and Reiss, D.
    1981   A theory-based empirical classification of family problem-solving behavior. *Family Process, 20,* 409–418.
Tseng, W. S.
    1975   The nature of somatic complaints among psychiatric patients: The Chinese case. *Comprehensive Psychiatry, 16,* 237–245.
Tseng, W. S., and Hsu, J.
    1970   Chinese culture, personality formation and mental illness. *The International Journal of Social Psychiatry, 16,* 5–14.
    1972   The Chinese attitude toward parental authority as expressed in Chinese children's stories. *Archives of General Psychiatry, 26,* 28–34.
Wolf, M.
    1970   Child training and the Chinese family. In M. Freedman (Ed.), *Family and kinship in Chinese society.* Stanford: Stanford University Press.

Wong, A. K., and Kuo, E. C. Y.
    1981   The urban kinship network in Singapore. In E. Kuo and A. Wong (Eds.), *The contemporary family in Singapore*. Singapore: Singapore University Press.
Wu, D.
    1965   Chinese child rearing—An anthropological point of view. *Thought and Word, 3*(6), 741–745.
Wynne, L. C., and Single, M. T.
    1963   Thought disorder and family relations of schizophrenics. *Archives of General Psychiatry, 9,* 191-206.

CHAPTER 9

Child Training in Chinese Culture

David Y. H. Wu

BACKGROUND

In the past, the relationship between culture and child socialization has fascinated psychologists, psychiatrists, and anthropologists alike. Through the study of child rearing and child training, anthropologists have attempted to explain cultural behavior, psychologists have attempted to understand personality, and psychiatrists have attempted to account for mental illness. Unfortunately, research has declined drastically in the field of culture and personality, which enables interdisciplinary collaboration of these disciplines.

From the anthropological point of view, discontent with culture and personality studies derives from earlier work that was methodologically oversimplified and conceptually inadequate. While Francis Hsu was criticized along with other researchers identified with national character studies, he, in fact, advocated changing the term culture and personality to psychological anthropology. He is also critical of the basic concept of *personality*, saying it is an intellectual product of Western individualism (F. Hsu, 1971; I return to this point later). Psychologists abandoned the field

113

on the grounds, as summarized by Draguns (1979), that traditionally, personality was rigidly regarded as a stable construct that is slow to change; and psychologists doubt the usefulness of personality as a concept without taking situational factors into account. However, psychologists admit that the study of antecedent conditions in personality research is still important and socialization variables hold the crucial keys to understanding the conditions. Thus, Draguns (1979:134) sees the need to extend the kind of research that relies on concrete investigations of specific parent–child interactions. Anthropologists also realize the need to examine the influence of rapid sociocultural change on the socialization process and on cultural behavior (Barnouw, 1973). Anthropologists continue to emphasize research based on observation in natural settings (LeVine, 1982).

Aside from these methodological concerns, there is still a basic question to be raised with particular regard to this book. Given the fact that the Chinese under our current investigations inhabit vast geographical areas and live in discrete physical, cultural, and sociopolitical environments, what are the so-called Chinese cultural characteristics? If there are commonalities in values and behavior, how are these common characteristics transmitted to individual Chinese in different places? If there are changes, how do they occur?

Certainly, the present chapter cannot provide answers to all these broad questions, but I present a case study of child training in one overseas Chinese population in order to illustrate the maintenance of tradition in consonance with ongoing change. Other investigators may draw implications from my presentation in future research elsewhere on child rearing in a Chinese cultural ambience. We are, in particular, awaiting scientific information with this focus from China.

RESEARCH METHODS

From 1971 to 1973, I carried out anthropological fieldwork in Papua New Guinea, studying the overseas Chinese community that has resided there more than 80 years (Wu, 1982). Throughout my stay among these overseas Chinese, I was fascinated with their expressions of values, behavior, and personality that so much resembled those of the mainland Chinese with which I am familiar, although in some respects they showed clear differences. A familiar behavioral mode is their group-oriented conduct. They have been successful in commercial enterprises that have been undertaken with partners, especially kin. In political activities, actions and interactions within any community-wide social–political organization almost always center on a number of factions headed by a few leaders.

Table 9.1   Age and Sex Distribution of Sampled Children

Age	Local mother		Hong Kong mother		Total
	Male	Female	Male	Female	
4 and under	3	6	2	4	15
5 and over	5	2	2	2	11
Total	8	8	4	6	26

Another familiar behavioral characteristic of this overseas community is the existence of long-lasting ties between parents and children and the constant social involvement throughout an individual's lifetime with family members and other kin. However, their aggressiveness, outspokenness, and quickness to display negative emotion struck me as not being typically Chinese.

Although my initial observation was comparative—between China and Papua New Guinea—I decided to examine the setting specific to this Chinese population. My interest was to examine how and in what forms changes have occurred in the context of their socialization. In this chapter, I use as data for analysis information obtained both from my field observations in natural settings and from interviews with mothers. In two urban towns, Rabaul and Kavieng, I interviewed 26 Chinese mothers, of whom 16 were locally born (referred to as *local mothers*) and 10 were born in China or Hong Kong referred to as *Hong Kong mothers*). I was interested in finding out whether child-rearing and training methods are similar or different in certain aspects between these two groups of mothers. Interview schedules were constructed on the basis of those developed by Sears, Maccoby, and Levin (1957), Wu (1968), and Lloyd (1970). Interviews were conducted predominantly in Cantonese, some in English, and some in both languages. The results are tabulated according to the mothers' coded responses, and statistical calculation was not attempted due to the small size of the sample (see Table 9.1). Observation of mother–child interaction was also conducted for each mother that was interviewed, but the result was fragmented and used here only to supplement the interview data.

THEORETICAL CONSIDERATIONS

My data are presented in conjunction with analysis conducted with reference to the theoretical framework postulated by child psychiatrist John Bowlby (1971, 1973), who in his research deals with two different yet interrelated phenomena of human behavior—attachment and fear. Bowlby's theory was chosen because, first, he explains human behavior in terms of a powerful evolutionary theory that has been neglected in the study of culture and personality;[1] and second, his theory differs from Freudian theory and will raise interesting, and perhaps controversial, discussion among psychiatrically oriented researchers.[2]

Bowlby is especially concerned with early infancy. Attachment behavior, in which crying, smiling, babbling, sucking, clinging, and following are part of the behavioral system, is most prominent in early infancy. The manner in which a mother figure responds to an infant's attachment behavior plays a decisive role in shaping the personality. It is important to note that a mother figure is distinguished from, but includes, the biological mother. Through attachment behavior, an infant establishes a profound bond with its mother figure, but the experience of separation from (short-term) or loss (long-term) of the bonded mother figure causes anger, distress, and anxiety. Separation from the mother figure is not only a key variable in determining a child's emotional state and behavior, but it is also decisive in personality development and the behavior manifested in adult life. Bowlby's conclusion is that a child who has been soundly bonded to a mother figure is less susceptible to fear of being separated from the mother; and a child less susceptible to fear will become a happier and more confident adult, who is more likely to develop relationships of mutual reliance with other people within society and so become more able to deal with the world at large—or, in mental health terms, a healthier person.

I now examine Bowlby's theory step-by-step in the context of child-rearing methods—mother–child interactional behavior among the Papua New Guinea Chinese. Child training as regards aggressive behavior towards parents and other children are also discussed. The limited scope of this chapter does not permit me to describe the full range of child-training behavior; therefore, I address points especially relevant to the main issues raised previously and summarize other related aspects. In several examples, I demonstrate how changes in cultural values as well as environmental factors may alter traditional mothers' behavior in contrast to that of their elders.

[1] While anthropologists debate the meaning of sociobiology (E. O. Wilson, 1975, 1978), pervasive evidence indicates a genetic basis for differences in temperament between newborn Chinese and Caucasian infants in the United States (see D. G. Freedman 1971; 1974). To what degree these genetic determinants challenge culturally determined behavior is still open to verification, but, nevertheless, biological factors in personality formation need to be investigated.

[2] For instance, I note with interest that C. C. Hsu's (1963) article on school phobia emphasizes sociocultural causes instead of the popular psychiatric explanation of separation anxiety, a major point of my discussion.

Table 9.2   Amount of Infant Caretaking by Mother

	Local mother	Hong Kong mother	Total
Practically none	—	—	—
About half, with considerable help during the day	7	5	12
More than half, but still with considerable help	5	2	7
Most, but some help	4	3	7
Nearly all; help rare	—	—	—
Total	16	10	26

CHINESE CHILD REARING AND THE DEVELOPMENT OF THE MOTHER–CHILD BOND

Few traditional Chinese taboos related to pregnancy and childbirth are observed in Papua New Guinea; instead, the modern Western idea of regular medical checks is valued by almost every mother, and babies are mostly delivered in hospitals. Most babies are breast-fed for periods of 2 weeks to 3 months, their mothers believing human milk to be more nutritious than cow's milk. The overall consensus derives partly from tradition and partly from the teaching of the physicians or nurses in the hospital. However, the majority of mothers gave the same reason for an early termination of breast feeding: They had to work—many of them worked in their stores—and a scheduled bottle-feeding would not interfere with their work as would breast-feeding. In this matter, as in others, environmental factors have changed the mothers' values and pratices on child rearing.

All the mothers indicated that they were the major caretakers when the child was an infant. But answers to further questions on the amount of caretaking actually performed by the mother—holding, feeding, bathing, changing diapers—indicate variations in the degree of mothering, as shown in Table 9.2.

It was observed that the majority of the mothers took most of the responsibility for caring for the baby when it was less than 6 months old. When the baby grew older, a larger number of persons gave a hand. These included the father, a native nurse, and other adult family members. The number of caretakers of a child under the age of 1 ranges from one to seven. The significance of this great number of caretakers for some of the children is dealt with later.

It is noteworthy that nine of the local mothers reported that there were

Table 9.3   Early Tendency to Cling to Mother

Degree of tendency	Local mother	Hong Kong mother	Total
Never showed such a tendency	2	1	3
Showed tendency to some extent	3	5	8
Went through a stage of strong tendency	11	4	15
Total	16	10	26

two persons who offered help regularly. In most cases one of these helpers turned out to be a native nurse. These native nurses are not in the same position as a traditional Chinese wet nurse who takes almost the entire responsibility of bringing up the child and to whom the child is bonded instead of to its own mother. The native nurse in a Chinese family of Papua New Guinea serves as a standby caretaker whose main duty is to give a hand when the child's mother is preoccupied at a particular moment. They are not usually given a large share of the responsibility for the child until after it is 8 or 9 months old. Bowlby (1971) believes that it is at this time that a child begins to discriminate between a mother figure and other people. Whether a native nurse affects the bond between the child and his mother is of special interest here. Chinese mothers in the majority of cases expressed reservations as to the amount of freedom in handling the baby allowed to a native nurse. First, when the child is less than 2 years old, few mothers allow the nurse to carry it out of its mother's sight or hearing. Second, none of the mothers reported that they left the child to sleep with the nurse at night. The mother invariably looks after the baby after dark. Third, I observed on many occasions at private parties or holiday gatherings that many native nurses accompanied the mother and child. The mother would seldom leave the baby or young child at home in the care of the nurse while she herself went out to attend social functions. It is thus likely that in most cases the nurse does not seriously affect the child's bond with the mother, whereas the nurse certainly becomes a substitute attachment figure (see Bowlby, 1973:22). Furthermore, Chinese children possibly develop bonds with a number of substitute attachment figures, given the fact that the number of caretakers is large. It is undeniable, however, that a few mothers did leave their children entirely in the hands of the nurse. These reports correlate with the fact that three mothers reported that their children when small showed no signs of a strong tendency to cling to them (see Table 9.3).

The amount of care mothers give to their infants can best be judged by

Table 9.4 Mother's Responsiveness to Infant's Crying

	Local mother	Hong Kong mother	Total
Unresponsive: never picks up crying baby	—	1	1
Responds only after baby has cried for a while, or allows the nurse to handle the problem	4	2	6
Conditional response: picks up baby only when she knows it is hungry or something might be wrong	6	2	8
Very responsive: picks up in most cases	3	2	5
Highly responsive: picks up crying baby immediately	3	3	6
Total	16	10	26

their response to their infants' crying. The mothers were asked to report whether or not their children cried a lot as babies. The majority of the mothers answered that their baby was a good one who seldom cried. Many of them believe that a healthy baby does not cry very much: "Only when they are sick, hungry, or wet do they cry." If a baby is reported to have cried a great deal when it was not sick, it is most likely that it was not promptly attended to when it cried.

I observed several mothers who remained "on guard" after putting their babies to sleep in a room other than the one in which they were working. Whenever she heard a faint noise that she suspected to be from the baby, any one of these mothers would rush to the baby and check. However, when they were asked how they responded to their baby's crying, many did not indicate a highly responsive attitude, perhaps because they answered my question in terms of what they thought they ought to do rather than what they actually did. The variation in individual mother's reports on their attutudes is shown in Table 9.4.

Many mothers told me that if they were certain that the baby was not hungry or sick, they would let it cry for a while. The majority of them said they were taught to do this by a doctor or a hospital nurse. As one mother said: "The Chinese habit of picking up the baby whenever it cries is a bad habit. The Western doctors have taught us the better way of letting the baby cry. Sometimes, nevertheless, I would not have the heart to let the baby cry for too long." Asked why it was good to let the baby cry, two mothers remarked specifically that it was good for the baby's lungs. Another mother believed that crying would help the baby grow faster. "The Western doctor said so," she added. In Kavieng, one local mother's answer is most interesting. She said: "We Chinese (*tong Jan*) believe that it helps the baby to exercise its lungs to let it cry once in a while." This mother apparently had mixed up the origin of this value and believed that it was a traditional Chinese cultural value to let the baby cry. It is plain from these examples that in adhering to different cultural values, the mothers made different kinds of choices on what they should do with their children. Those who had accepted the new values of the doctors and nurses in the hospital tended to respond negatively to an infant's crying, while those who had not accepted the new values were apt to pick up the baby to nurse and comfort it when it cried.

In addition to cultural values, environmental factors also play a part in determining the mother's behavior. A mother who had to work in a store and who was not able in these circumstances to respond promptly to her baby's demands had to delay her response or get somebody to act in her place, for example, a native nurse. The new cultural value of letting the baby cry for its health becomes a good excuse to justify their altered behavior.

Many Chinese mothers, some fathers too, were observed to rock their young infants a lot when holding them in their arms. This rocking of the infant seemed habitual and was done whether or not the infant was crying—indeed in most cases it was not. "Rocking a baby, it is found, is effective not only in terminating rhythmic crying but in delaying its onset" (Bowlby, 1971:353). The Chinese usually rock their infants in a rapid up and down (shaking) manner, about two cycles a second. Rocking the infant from left to right is less commonly seen. It is interesting to know that experiments have shown (Bowlby 1971:353) that to terminate a baby's crying "rocking must be at 60 cycles a minute or above." This explains why the Chinese way of rocking the infant is effective and perhaps accounts for the mothers' reports that their infants seldom cry. I cannot recall ever having heard any prolonged crying by an infant, in spite of my frequent participation in the people's activities.[3] Another evidence of Chinese mothers' frequent response to infants' need can be found in their frequent diaper changes. Two-thirds of the mothers interviewed reported changing more than two dozen diapers daily. The Chinese mothers commented on the European (Australian) mothers' negligence by accusing them of not changing their babies' diapers frequently enough to keep the babies comfortable (Wu, 1981:153).

The extent to which attachment behavior is developed between an infant or young child and its mother can also be examined with respect to sleeping arrangements. Of concern here is whether or not the child is

---

[3] Here we are reminded of Caudill and Weintein's (1969) report that, compared to American infants, Japanese infants were quieter and more passive; but Japanese mothers rocked and lulled the infants more.

Table 9.5   Sleeping Arrangements: Time of Separation from Mother

Time of separation	From mother's bed			From mother's room		
	Local mother	Hong Kong mother	Total	Local mother	Hong Kong mother	Total
From birth	10	5	15	2	1	3
Over 3 months	1	1	2	—	—	—
Over 6 months	—	—	—	1	—	1
Over 1 year	—	1	1	—	1	1
Over 2 years	1	—	1	3	—	3
Over 3 years	1	1	2	2	3	5
Not separated yet	3	2	5	8	5	13
Total	16	10	26	16	10	26

allowed to sleep in the same room as the parents with its bed placed beside the parents' bed. Only three mothers reported that from birth their child was assigned a room separate from the parents'. However, in all three cases, the infants were put into a room in which their elder siblings also slept. The various arrangements are listed in Table 9.5.

Those children who still slept in the same bed as their locally born mothers were two boys age 8 and 11 and one girl age 5. The two boys were both the last born. The girl, along with her younger siblings, slept with her mother in one bed while her father slept in another bed. Of the children of the Hong Kong mothers, the two children who did not yet sleep separately from their mothers were one boy of 3 and one girl of 9. Neither of them was the last born. While the boy slept with his parents and a younger brother in one bed, the girl slept with her mother in a room different from her father's, where he slept with her younger brother of 7. The eight children who had not been moved out of their parents' room were four boys ages 5, 6, 8, and 11 and four girls ages 3, 5, 5, and 7. The five children born of Hong Kong mothers were two boys, one 3 and one 2 and three girls ages 5, 6, and 9. It is proposed that children allowed to sleep in the same bed as their parents or in the same room have the bond between them reinforced; besides, they are likely to be less susceptible to fear. This idea is discussed further in the following section.

SITUATIONS THAT AROUSE FEAR AND THE SUSCEPTIBILITY TO FEAR

It has been demonstrated that the growth of attachment between a young child and its mother figure is well formed by the latter half of the first year (Bowlby, 1971:383); withdrawal from a fear-arousing situation is also developed at the same time (Bowlby, 1973:120). The most fearful situations for children of ages 1 to 3 are, according to experiments and clinic reports, noise, rapidly approaching objects, strange people, a strange environment, darkness and, most of all, being alone (Bowlby, 1973:101–118). It could be argued that those experiments and clinical reports cited by Bowlby are to a great extent derived only from modern European and American societies, where, in a normal family, the mother is the only attachment figure and the young child is unlikely to be very frequently exposed to novel situations or a large number of people. In such a cultural environment, the young child is fearful of novel situations and strangers, and separation from the mother usually means being left alone or being left with a nonbonded figure, whereby stress and anxiety are more likely to be aroused. In a different cultural or social environment where the child is exposed to constant noises of all kinds and a large number of people—familiar or unfamiliar—and is carried around to different places, it is likely to be used to such situations and should be less prone to fear.

Two variables, indeed, affect the condition of the degree of fear (Bowlby, 1973:97). When two or more stimulus situations are presented together, for example, being alone and in the dark, the fear may be intensified. However, the presence or absence of an attachment figure or some other companion makes an immense difference to the intensity of fear aroused.

In very few situations are the ordinary Chinese children in Papua New Guinea prone to be fearful, for they are almost always accompanied either by their parents or by other attachment figures, and they have from early childhood been familiar with a great variety of noises, people, and novel environments. An average child under the age of 4 or 5 is taken by his or her mother wherever she goes: shopping, visiting, and to social gatherings or celebrations. A European, commenting on Chinese parties, said they must be very boring, both because of the participation of a lot of children and because adults' interactions were disturbed by the children. In contrast, I also heard two young Chinese mothers say that they would not want to go to the Europeans' parties because European hosts ask the guests not to bring their children with them. No Chinese social gathering, even of an official nature (e.g., annual meetings of the associations), is without a great number of infants and children running up and down, laughing and shouting and adding to the noise, which usually does not happen in comparable European gatherings.

The extent of noise in Chinese life was best described by a European visitor to Rabaul: "One assumes the Chinese to be totally deaf. They shout to each other throughout the day and night, undauted by the blaring of gramophones, radios at top strength, the crowing of roosters, and the barking of dogs" (*Pacific Islands Monthly*, 1960:99). This statement does not greatly exaggerate the actual situation. Similar impressions of the noise accompanying Chinese life elsewhere have been reported by anthropologists. Anderson (1972:145–146), for instance, gives the following explanation of the Chinese concept of noise:

> Significantly, the Chinese phrase for desirable activity, excitement and good times is *je-nao*, "hot noise" (cognates are known in all Chinese languages; I have used the Mandarin form here). Noise in a household is the sign of life and action, and household moves in a shimmering ambience of sound from waking to sleep.

In middle-class Euro–American society it is common to find that children are forbidden to make a lot of noise at home. But Chinese children have no such restriction on making noise in the presence of adults. Several Papua New Guinea mothers said that it was all right to let the children play at home and make a noise as long as they were happy and not quarreling. One father said he had always listened to the six o'clock evening news on the radio, but the boys made such a noise that he could not concentrate. He said he had asked the children to stop but they took no notice, so he decided to tape-record the news every evening and listen to it after the children had gone to sleep.

Chinese children in Papua New Guinea do not lead a life separate from that of adults. Children fully participate in almost all of the adults' activities except productive work—and even here children are, to some extent, involved. Visitors to Chinese trade stores might find a bassinet behind the counter in which an infant or young child is sleeping or playing. Older children of about 8 or 9 help customers after school. On several occasions and in various towns, I saw a child of only 9 or 10 working the cash register and supervising the native clerks in the absence of adults. The children read or do their homework beside the register, stopping to help customers and to receive and give change to the native clerk.

When the Chinese visit each other in the evenings and on Sunday afternoons, children and elderly family members are never left out of social gatherings. Many of my interviews were carried out either in a store during the day or in the middle of a gathering of visitors at night. Because our visits were seldom differentiated from those of other friends and relatives, we were often joined by visitors.

Parents usually do not expect young children to go to bed at a specified hour. Children go to bed whenever they feel sleepy, although those of school age are encouraged by their parents to go to bed early so that they can get up in time for school. When there are visitors or when their parents are going out for a visit, children are almost always allowed to join the party and stay up late. I have frequently seen children fall asleep in their parent's laps or on a sofa and at the end of the party, have to be carried to

124

DAVID Y. H. WU

Table 9.6   Mothers' Responses to "Does Your
Child Have the Habit of Holding a Pillow?"

Response	Local mother	Hong Kong mother	Total
Yes	12	4	16
No	4	6	10
Total	16	10	26

bed or home. Eight mothers specifically mentioned that they allowed children who slept with siblings in a room separate from the parents' to have a dim light on throughout the night "because they are afraid of the darkness."

It is difficult to ascertain the origin of one habit associated with children's sleeping. As indicated in Table 9.6, many of the local mothers provide their children with a pillow, other than a head pillow, to hold while sleeping. We note with interest that in Singapore, "holding pillows" (narrow but longer than the head pillow) were sold in departmental stores.

Several mothers explained that the pillow is meant to be a security measure; when the child has a nightmare, he or she has the pillow to hold to and will not be frightened if the mother is not immediately available. Four Hong Kong mothers said that they were taught by their mothers-in-law or other older women to provide such a pillow for their children, but the other Hong Kong mothers said that their children did not need it. Several elderly women whom I consulted agreed that this habit is not found in China. The habit possibly developed when some of the mothers began to adopt the Western custom of removing the baby from the mother's bed at birth or at a very young age, and the pillow is intended as a substitute mother figure for the child to cling to at night.

Thus, there are very few occasions when Chinese children are left alone. Moreover, most parents show great concern for their children's protection and avoid all possible risks. Young children are often confined to the home or the store, although some have been entrusted to the watchful eyes of native nurses, while older children—over age 9 or 10—are not encouraged to visit their peers unless they are in the company of older siblings or other children. Not only are children not encouraged to roam about by themselves, but they are also frequently warned to keep away from possible danger—particularly cars in the street and "wild natives." Many appear to share the attitude expressed by Bowlby (1973:140) as "better to be safe than sorry." It is interesting that when the Papua New Guinea Chinese take holiday trips overseas, they almost always travel with a group of people, such as family members, relatives, and friends.

The fundamental point in Bowlby's account of fear is that its origin lies in the persistence of fear or anxiety caused by separation from the mother figure, not so much in the actual or possible fear-arousing situation in the environment. The accessibility of the mother is one of the crucial factors that intensifies the loving bond between the mother and the child, and the child's experience of confidence in the availability of the mother during childhood should remain relatively unchanged throughout the rest of his or her life.

We have shown that a large proportion of Papua New Guinea Chinese mothers keep their children in close proximity day and night, especially children under the age of 5. However, the actual behavior of each mother still needs to be scrutinized in order to be accurately assessed. Since I did not conduct fieldwork under optimum conditions, which would have included long-term systematic observations, I have to base my conclusions on interviews and less systematic observations. There were a few mothers who had occasionally left their children for various periods of time or had otherwise neglected them, and the anxiety clinging or alienating behavior towards the mother as a result of such separation was very clear.

Another area under investigation concerns the degree of dependency behavior exhibited by the child and the mother's responses to this behavior—that is, whether she is rewarding or punitive. The mothers were asked the extent to which a child could look after himself or herself, washing, dressing, bathing, and so forth, and the extent to which he or she sought attention and assistance from the mother. The answers of these mothers are given in Table 9.7. The children of the Hong Kong mothers are seen to be slightly more dependent on their mothers than children with local mothers.

Although parents expect children of school age to be able to look after themselves, they are seldom upset by a request for help. As a matter of fact, several mothers told me that they were well aware of their children's *tsa dai* behavior—the feigning of inability in order to elicit the mother's care—and approved of such behavior. Although *tsa dai* literally means "pretending," the concept fits the Japanese notions of *amaeru*—display of dependence on another person, especially that of a child on a parent (Doi, 1962). As one mother put it: "Stanley [a boy of 4] is big enough to look after himself. When I am not around, he knows to get a bottle of cold drink and open it himself with an opener. But when I am around, he insists on me getting it and opening it for him. I know he is *tsa dai*."

The age of the children is the crucial variable; the mother usually responded positively to a younger child's needs, but her response to an older child, say, of 8 or 9, depended on whether she was busy. While they expect their children to learn to do jobs for themselves, mothers seldom respond

Table 9.7   Amount of Dependency Exhibited by the Child, by Age

Dependency	Local mother		Hong Kong mother		
	5 and over	Under 5	5 and over	Under 5	Total
None; takes care of him- or herself and does not seek help from mother	6	—	1	—	7
Slight, but quite able to do most of the chores	1	1	2	—	4
Moderate; occasionally seeks help	3	2	4	—	9
Considerable; frequently seeks mother's help	1	2	—	1	4
Strong; relies on mother for everything	—	—	—	2	2
Total	11	5	7	3	26

with punitive behavior to the children's care-soliciting behavior. Two mothers who replied that they would respond negatively toward their child's request for help indicated that they would put it this way: "You are big enough; why don't you learn like the other kids do."

Young (1972) studied the socialization of Hawaiian Chinese children with particular regard to achievement motivation and behavior. She discovered that responses by Chinese mothers to the independence training questionnaire used, which was formulated by Euro–American psychologists, failed to support any expected correlations between overall independence training and the children's achievement behavior. The questionnaire was invalid in this context because certain areas of independent behavior, such as demands on the child's separation from the mother, physical mobility, and sociability, are (as with the Papua New Guinea Chinese) delayed until a much later age than is usual with other ethnic groups (mainly Euro–Americans). Young found that irrespective of whether they were immigrants or had been born in Hawaii, the Chinese children's achievement-oriented behaviors were not significantly different from those of other ethnic groups. She believes that the explanation lies in the fact that Chinese cultural values govern the Chinese mother's decision on her expectancies of her children's achievement behavior. However, following Bowlby, it can be argued that it is the theory on which Young has based her independence-achievement model that is inadequate and misleading. The model is based on European notions of psychologists who supposed that the early separation and independence of children is conducive to achievement motivation and achievement behavior. Yet this model has never been verified by behavioral studies (Bowlby, 1973).

Bowlby also emphasizes the point that a mother's threat to leave her child may be taken by the child as real and thus cause distress or anxiety. In his view, the threat of separation, which is often used by mothers as a means of discipline, may have the same effect as actual separation. Many Chinese mothers admitted that they had sometimes threatened their children when they misbehaved. Commonly used phrases are, "I don't want you any more; if you don't stop crying, I will give you away," and, "If you don't listen to Mummy this instant the highland natives will come and take you away." However, most mothers said that they would sometimes add: "If you stop this and be good, I won't do this to you." Mothers' responses to questions regarding the frequency of direct or implied threat of separation in 26 cases are as follows: One threatened frequently; 17, sometimes; 4, seldom; and 4 never.

The discussion thus far has amply documented variations in the behavior and attitudes of Chinese mothers, but it is also evident that the majority of mothers show care, concern, and protection in their treatment of their children. Most Chinese children, and those under the age of 4 or 5 in particular, are almost always gratified in their needs for attachment and security and are seldom placed to a situation where fear, or fear of separation from mother, are likely to be aroused. On the basis of observations, interviews, and general participation in the affairs of this community, there is little reason to doubt that the majority of mothers establish an affectionate and secure bond with their children. When the bond is firm and lasts throughout life, it would seldom be jeopardized by the transition from childhood to adolescence or from adolescence to adulthood. The parents continue to worry about the future of their children as they grow up, arranging their marriages and helping them to set up businesses or continuing to share a business with them. The parent's constant willingness to answer the child's call for comfort and assistance is a major reason why many Chinese in Papua New Guinea still honor the concept of filial piety (looking after elderly parents and respecting aged relatives) and of living together. Ancestor worship, which is still conducted annually at the cemetery, has little meaning in the generalized context of kinship and social organization but becomes meaningful when one considers this lifelong bond. The ceremony is a memorial, rather than worship in the religious sense (see M. Freedman, 1957:218). Although many Chinese are devoted Christians, the traditional Chinese ceremony of burning incense and candles and offering liquor, cooked rice, roast chicken, roast pork, and underworld currency to the deceased is invariably performed at the parent's and grandparent's tomb. This ceremony symbolizes the desire to continue succoring and providing support for aged parents.

It is also necessary to consider that from infancy a child is in contact with a large number of kin and other caretakers. Bowlby makes only passing reference to the fact that familiarity with a large number of caretakers helps to mediate a child's anxiety and distress in the absence of his mother figure. However, the research team of the laboratory of Human Development, Harvard University, on the basis of cross-cultural studies of child rearing, developed a hypothesis that supports Bowlby's theory. As Whiting (1963:9) asserts, "Indulgence in infancy, a large number of nurturing agents, and mild transition from infantile indulgence into childhood will produce: (1) a trustful attitude toward others, (2) general optimism, and (3) sociability."

Although the primary bond of security and affection is established through the loving care of the mother figure, it is believed that in an environment where many other caretakers as well as other familiar persons (e.g., kin in frequent contact) are present, the child's life can be said to contain many supplementary bonds. While the secure bond established with the mother figure provides the sound base from which the child can confidently explore the outside world, any supplementary bonds can be viewed as extended bases from which the child can make confident excursions into the outside social world.

In sum, a normal Chinese child establishes an interpersonal intimacy (F. Hsu, 1971) with a wide range of people during very early childhood. The Chinese child's cognitive organization and developing perception of the social world thus comprises a wide range of people, who not only provide the child with comfort and protection (and indeed give a wider range of experiences, most of which are pleasant) but who also interfere with the child's wishes and behavior. In other words, these people also serve as agents of sanction toward the child when he or she displays disapproved behavior. The mother usually expects and approves their disciplining her child—teaching and correcting the child—just as she expects them to protect and nurture her child. It was frequently observed that while the mother did not punish her child herself, she used other people with whom the child had already established an intimate relationship as agents of punishment and thus reinforced the image of these people as controlling as well as loving figures.

When a mother becomes angry and is about to slap a child, one of the close kin may take the child away for awhile (See Wu, 1981, concerning this mediating behavior in Taiwan). The child learns, on the one hand, that these other people are trustworthy and can be relied on when venturing into the outside world, and, on the other hand, that these people can exercise sanctions and are not to be offended. In my view, in the Chinese child's cognitive organization of the world, he or she is not the center of the social world but is only part of a social network of individuals who are intimate yet variously dominant. The Chinese concept of personality is very closely associated with such a world. F. Hsu (1971) maintains that the concept *personality* is culturally biased toward individualism in the West, while the Chinese equivalent *jen* is based on a different conceptual frame of reference and emphasizes the idea of psychosocial homeostasis—"the central ingredient in the human mode of existence: man's relationship with his fellow men" (p. 23).

AGGRESSION

Having isolated the possible cognitive organization of the Chinese child toward the social world, we may now consider the mother's and other adults' punitive behavior and its consequences for children. I have shown that the majority of young children can be certain of their mother's care and attention. Although few young children, especially those under the age of 4 or 5, can expect to be physically punished, they are not exempt from the threat of punishment (as discussed in the preceding section). The Cantonese word *kai*, (naughty, misbehaving, and bad) is often used by mothers to refer to their children's bad behavior that requires correction. The interviewed mothers considered the most serious *kai* to be aggression and disobedience. There is a certain amount of inconsistency between the mothers' stated ideal punishment and their reported actual behavior. The mothers, both local and Hong Kong, reported themselves to be highly intolerant of a child's antiparental aggression or disobedience and said that they were quite severe in dealing with the child for such offences. Although they almost unanimously agreed that beating is the best way to punish a child—a revelation of prevalent cultural values—the majority of mothers turned out to be very lenient toward their children in terms of the reported frequency of physical punishment actually employed (see Table 9.8). According to their own reports, the Hong Kong mothers beat their children more frequently than the local mothers. I observed, however, that in reality these reports were exaggerated: No mother severely beat her child—for most of them, one slap was regarded as serious punishment. Furthermore, many mothers admitted that they usually only put on a beating performance to scare, rather than actually hurt, the child. Indeed, I observed on many occasions that the mother simply threatened to beat the child and seldom actually did so, particularly in the case of younger chil-

Table 9.8 Frequency of Actual Physical Punishment

	Local mother	Hong Kong mother	Total
Never used	3	—	3
Only once or twice since birth or about once a year	10	3	13
About once a month	3	2	5
About once a week	—	3	3
Almost every day	—	2	2
Total	16	10	26

dren. A duster was the most commonly used symbol of punishment. Ordinarily, before the mother actually raised the duster, the child had quietened down or the mother had decided that she had taught the child a lesson sufficient to make him or her conform. It is possible that Chinese children have been conditioned to this ritual of threatened punishment in the very early stages of their cognitive development. Thus, the child reacts to this ritualized sanction of a parent's demand and also reacts to other people in similar situations. To conform in silence, instead to contend with other people, seems to be an adaptation learned in early childhood.

A further significant feature of the parents' punitive behavior that needs to be considered is the giving of love reassurance after a scolding or physical punishment. Chinese parents usually teach the child that it is because of wrong-doing that he or she is punished, not because of the adult's own distress. (Certainly, there is no guarantee that parents do not punish their children as a result of their own distress; see Wu, 1981). On many occasions after a mother had scolded a child or performed a beating ritual, she would order the child to apologize to her for the misbehavior, and she would assure the child that she would love him or her again as long as he or she was good. Mothers with young children usually held them more affectionately after contention situations, and the children seemed to quickly forget the punishment.

In the attitude toward the physical fighting of older children, either with siblings or other children, we do find some disparities between that of the local mothers and Hong Kong mothers. While in no circumstance did any of the Hong Kong mothers encourage aggressive behavior, some local mothers advised the child to use self-defense if necessary. The local mothers also would not punish the physical aggression of her child "if he [or she] is not in the wrong."

Two striking socioenvironmental factors in Papua New Guinea have affected Chinese child training with regard to physical aggression. First, the Hong Kong mothers registered their dismay when their school-age children reported that the Australian teachers expected them to fight back if attacked by other children, rather than to tell the teachers as taught by the Chinese mothers. The teachers actually discussed this matter with some Chinese parents in a PTA meeting, advising them to teach their children to defend themselves in a fight and not to run to the teachers for rescue. This presented the Hong Kong mothers with a dilemma: whether the traditional Chinese teaching of nonviolence and seeking help from an authority or the Western value of fighting for oneself was correct.

Second, we found all the local mothers in Kavieng, New Ireland, expected their children to fight back if attacked. They believe that a child should be reprimanded only if he or she is the one who started the fight. Furthermore, the local Chinese mothers taught their children to make a distinction between whom they should or should not fight: If the other child is a Chinese, they should avoid fighting; but if the other child is not a Chinese, especially if he or she is bad (*kai*) and of mixed racial descent, they should hit him back. This is a concrete example of child training regarding aggression in the context of in-group and out-group differentiation. Incidentally, the Kavieng Chinese community is small and resides among a larger mixed-descent population. Bond and Wang (1981) review aggressive behavior in Chinese culture and come to the conclusion that while Chinese parents inhibit childrens' physical aggression, Chinese adults may act violently in groups and against "outsiders (whether by kinship, residential, or class distinction)."

CONCLUSION

In this chapter, I have discussed bonding behavior through child socialization in an overseas Chinese society. My systematic investigation yielded information that enabled an understanding of the socialization process, characteristic cultural behavior, and changes that have taken place. The Chinese mothers I studied made some adjustment in their treatment of their infants and older children because of the teaching they received from authorities (doctors, nurses, mothers-in-law, and school teachers). Because of their adherence to certain cultural values or because the group mode of production changed, there were additional behavioral adjustments. How these changes affected their overall socialization towards Chinese or non-Chinese behavioral characteristics remains to be seen.

I am interested in comparative studies among Chinese communities and between Chinese and other cultures, yet information is scarce. For many years, we have received little scientific information on Chinese child rearing and child training, because scholars have been preoccupied with the formal education and moral development of children (e.g., R. W. Wilson, 1970, 1974, 1981; see also Brown, 1981, for the current situation in mainland China). Most literature available on child socialization in China is, unfortunately, based either on impressions or on brief visits to model nurseries or kindergartens (see Sidel, 1972; Stavrianos, n.d.; R. W. Wilson 1981). Yet, there are indications that child rearing has changed little in rural China but dramatically in urban centers. Parish and Whyte (1978) report that little change has taken place in child-rearing practices in the rural village family, even though China has undergone social and ideological transformation. This view is supported by individual mothers' reports from mainland China (see Brown, 1981:232-233).

Urbanization, rapid industrialization, and migration are world phenomena. When we deal with the consequential mental health problems, we must examine the fundamental child socialization process and change. After studying the question of child abuse, I warned: "With the decreasing interaction between a young couple and their older relatives, the decreasing and interrupted socialization for attachment, and changing values and life styles, more problems in child rearing for the young generation, especialy in urban situations, will arise" (Wu, 1981:163). It is high time we conduct systematic investigation into parent–child interaction in the family situation and in other social contexts so that comparative studies of Chinese culture and mental health can be carefully examined. The benefit of such studies will certainly help us to understand better and to deal with the effects of social, economic, and political developments as expressed in resulting mental health problems.

REFERENCES

Anderson, E. N., Jr.
    1972   Some Chinese methods of dealing with crowding. *Urban Anthropology, 1*(2), 141–150.
Barnouw, V.
    1973   *Culture and personality*. Homewood, IL: Dorsey.
Bond, M. H., and Wang, S. H.
    1981   *Aggressive behavior in Chinese society: The problem of maintaining order and harmony* (Occasional Paper No. 95). Hong Kong: The Chinese University of Hong Kong, Social Research Centre.
Bowlby, J.
    1971   *Attachment and loss*: Vol. 1. *Attachment*. Harmondsworth, England: Penguin. (Original work published 1969).
    1973   *Attachment and loss*: Vol. 2. *Separation: Anxiety and anger*. London: Hogarth.

Brown, L. B.
  1981   *Psychology in contemporary China.* Oxford: Pergamon.
Caudill, W., and Weinstein, H.
  1969   Maternal care and infant behavior in Japan and America. *Psychiatry, 32,* 12–24.
Doi, L. T.
  1962   *Amae: A key concept for understanding Japanese personality structure.* In R. J. Smith and R. Beardsley (Eds.), *Japanese culture: Its development and characteristics.* Chicago: Aldine.
Draguns, J. G.
  1979   Culture and personality: Old fields, new directions. In L. Eckensberger, W. J. Lonner, and Y. Poortinga (Eds.), *Cross-cultural contributions to psychology.* Lisse: Swets and Zeitlinger B. V.
Freedman, D. G.
  1971   An evolutionary approach to research on the life cycle. *Human Development,* 14, 87–99.
  1974   *Human infancy: An evolutionary perspective.* Hillsdale, NJ: Erlbaum.
Freedman, M.
  1957   *Chinese family and marriage in Singapore* (Colonial Research Studies No. 20). London: Her Majesty's Stationery Office.
Hsu, C. C.
  1963   *Xue-xao kung-ju-zheng ji ju-jue shang-xue-zheng zhi lin-chuang yen-ju* [A clinical study on "school phobia" and "refusal of going to school" among Chinese children]. *Acta Paediatrica Sinica, 4*(3), 203–213.
Hsu, F. L. K.
  1971   Psychosocial homeostasis and *jen*: Conceptual tools for advancing psychological anthropology. *American Anthropologist, 73*(1), 23-44.
Kuhn, T. S.
  1962   *The structure of scientific revolutions.* Chicago: University of Chicago Press.
Landy, D.
  1959   *Tropical childhood.* Chapel Hill: University of North Carolina Press.
LeVine, R. A.
  1982   *Culture, behavior, and personality.* Chicago: Aldine.
Lloyd, B. B.
  1970   Yoruba mothers' report of child rearing: Some theoretical and methodological considerations. In P. Mayer (Ed.), *Socialization.* London: Tavistock.
Pacific Islands Monthly.
  1960   Sydney, September.
Parish, W. L., and M. K., Whyte
  1978   *Village and family in contemporary China.* Chicago: University of Chicago Press.
Sears, R. R., E. Maccoby, and H. Levin
  1957   *Patterns of child rearing.* Evanston, IL: Row, Peterson and Co.
Sidel, R.
  1972   *Women and child care in China.* New York: Hill & Wang.
Stavrianos, B. K.
  n.d.   *Observations of pre-school children in China.* Unpublished manuscript.
Whiting, B. B. (Ed.)
  1963   *Six cultures: Studies of child rearing.* New York: Wiley.
Wilson, E. O.
  1975   *Sociobiology.* Cambridge: Harvard University Press.
  1978   *On human nature.* Cambridge: Harvard University Press.

Wilson, R. W.

1970   *Learning to be Chinese: The political socialization of children in Taiwan.* Cambridge: M.I.T. Press.

1974   *The moral state: A study of the political socialization of Chinese and American children.* New York: The Free Press.

1981   Comformity and deviance regarding moral rules in Chinese society: A socialization perspective. In A. Kleinman and T. Y. Lin (Eds.), *Normal and abnormal behavior in Chinese culture.* Boston: Reidel.

Wu, D. Y. H.

1968   Child training among the Easter Paiwan. *The Bulletin of the Institute of Ethnology, Academia Sinica, 25,* 55-107.

1981   Child abuse in Taiwan. In J. E. Korbin (Ed.), *Child abuse and neglect: Cross-cultural perspectives.* Berkeley: University of California Press.

1982   *The Chinese in Papua New Guinea: 1880–1980.* Hong Kong: The Chinese University Press.

Young, N. F.

1972   Independence training from cross-cultural perspective. *American Anthropologist, 74*(3), 629-638.

CHAPTER 10

Characteristics of Temperament in Chinese Infants and Young Children

Chen-Chin Hsu

INTRODUCTION

Temperament refers to the stylistic characteristics that are evident in early infancy and continue fairly persistently through adulthood. It is understood that inborn behavior characteristics greatly influence parent–child interaction during infancy, contribute to the development of later psychological organization, and relate to peer interaction and to adjustment in school (Thomas and Chess, 1977). It also relates to the later development of behavior disorders (Rutter, Birch, Thomas, and Chess, 1964). Thus, the study of the characteristics of temperament in infants and children is very interesting to child mental health workers, not only from the genetic and psychological points of view but also from the sociocultural point of view. It certainly provides an approach to the investigation of the pattern of genetic–environmental interaction.

135

CHINESE CULTURE
AND MENTAL HEALTH

Categories of Temperament

The first and most intensive study carried out by the New York University Medical Center—the New York Longitudinal Study (NYLS)—has accumulated rich data since 1956 indicating marked individuality in temperamental characteristics (Thomas, Birch, Herzig, and Karn, 1963; Thomas, Chess, and Birch, 1968). By an inductive content analysis, the NYLS group has demonstrated that temperamental characteristics could be identified in nine independent concrete behavior categories. The nine categories are:

1. *Activity level.* This category describes the extent to which a motor component exists in a child's functioning. Protocol data on motility during bathing, eating, playing, dressing, and handling, as well as information concerning the sleep–wake cycle, reaching, crawling and walking, are used in scoring this category. Some examples of representative behaviors that are scored as high activity are: "He moves a great deal in his sleep"; "I cannot leave her on the bed or couch because she always wiggles off"; "He kicks and splashes so in the bath that I always have to mop up the floor afterward"; "Dressing her becomes a battle, she squirms so"; "Whenever I try to feed him he grabs for the spoon." Examples for low activity behaviors are: "In the bath she lies quietly and does not kick"; "In the morning he is still in the same place he was when he fell asleep"; "She can turn over, but she doesn't much."

2. *Rhythmicity.* This category bases itself upon the degree of rhythmicity or regularity of repetitive biological functions such as sleeping and waking, eating and appetite, and elimination. A child's sleep–wake cycle is considered to be regular if the child falls asleep at approximately the same time each night and awakens at approximately the same time each morning. The child's functioning is irregular if there is a marked difference in the time of retiring and arising from day to day. The child is considered regular if he or she naps for the same length of time each day and irregular if there is no discernible time pattern of function established. Eating and appetite behavior is scored as irregular if intake fluctuates widely from day to day or if the child can be induced to eat at times that differ widely from day to day. Bowel function is scored as regular if the number and time of evacuation are constant from day to day and irregular if the time and number are not readily predictable.

3. *Approach or withdrawal.* This category describes the child's initial reaction to any new stimulus, be it food, people, places, toys, or procedures. A few examples of approach responses are: "He always smiles at a stranger"; "She loves new toys"; "The first time he had his hair cut, he sat on his father's lap and laughed through the whole thing." Withdrawal responses are illustrated by: "When I gave her her orange juice the first time, she made a face. She did not cry, but she did not suck it as eagerly as she

does milk"; "Whenever he sees a stranger, he cries"; "When we went to the doctor for the first time, she started to cry in the waiting room and did not stop until she got home again"; and, "It takes a long time to warm up to a new toy; he pushes it away and plays with something more familiar."

4. *Adaptability*. In contrast to the previous category, it is not with the initial response that one is concerned here. Rather, emphasis is on the ease or difficulty with which the initial pattern of response can be modified in socially desirable directions. Examples of adaptive behavior are: "She used to spit out cereal whenever I gave it to her, but now she takes it fairly well, although still not as well as fruit"; "Now when we go to the doctor, he does not start to cry till we undress him"; "At first she used to hold herself perfectly stiff in the bath, but now she kicks a little and pats the water with her hand"; "Every day for a week he'd go over to the stuffed lion someone gave him and say, 'I do not like it'; but today he started playing with it and now you'd think it was his best friend." Nonadaptive behavior can be illustrated by the following examples: "During the summer she used to nap in the carriage outside, and now that it's cold I have tried to put her in the crib, but she screams so I have to take her out and wheel her up and down the hall before she falls asleep"; "Every time he sees the scissors he starts to scream and pull his hand away, so now I cut his nails when he's sleeping"; "Whenever I put her snowsuit and hat on, she screams and struggles and she does not stop crying till we are outside"; "He does not like eggs and makes a face and turns his head away no matter how I cook them."

5. *Intensity of reaction*. In this category the interest is in the energy content of the response, irrespective of its direction. Examples of intense reactions are the following: "When he is hungry he starts to cry, and this builds up to a scream"; "When she hears music she begins to laugh and to jump up and down in time to it"; "When he's full he spits the food out of his mouth and knocks the spoon away." Examples of mild responses are: "She squints at a bright light but does not cry"; "To a loud noise, he jumps and startles a little, but he does not cry"; "If she's hungry, she starts to whimper a bit"; "When she's had enough, she turns her head away and I know it is time to stop"; "If he does not like a new food he just holds it in his mouth without swallowing and then lets it drool out."

6. *Quality of mood*. This category describes the amount of pleasant, joyful, friendly behavior as contrasted with unpleasant, crying, unfriendly behavior. Examples of behaviors scored as negative mood are: "Whenever we put him to bed he cries until he falls asleep"; "She cries at almost every stranger, and those that she does not cry at, she hits"; "I have tried to teach him not to knock down little girls and sit on them on the playground, so now he knocks them down and does not sit on them"; and "Everytime she sees food she does not like, she starts to fuss and whine until I take it off the table." Examples of positive mood statements are: "Whenever he sees me

begin to warm his bottle, he begins to smile and coo"; "She loves to look out of the window. She jumps up and down and laughs"; "He always smiles at a stranger"; and "If she is not laughing and smiling I know she's getting sick."

7. *Distractibility.* This category refers to the effectiveness of extraneous environmental stimuli in interfering with, or in altering the direction of, the ongoing behavior. If the course of a child who is crawling toward an electric light plug can be altered by presenting him with a toy truck, he would be considered distractible. If such efforts to alter his behavior are unsuccessful, he would be considered nondistractible. A child who is crying because of hunger but stops when she is picked up is distractible, as opposed to the nondistractible child who continues to cry until she is fed.

8. *Persistence.* This category refers to the definition of a direction of functioning and to the difficulty with which such an established direction of functioning can be altered. In other words, it is the maintaining of an activity by a child in the face of obstacles to the continuation of the activity. If a child is playing with water and continues to do so while his mother is saying "no," he would be considered persistent. The obstacles may be much more directly related to the child's abilities. For example, the child who continually attempts to stand up although she always falls down would be scored as persistent, as would the child who struggles with a toy she cannot make perform properly without asking for help. This category, therefore, is an omnibus one that includes selectivity, persistence, and, at a later age level, frustration tolerance.

9. *Threshold.* This refers to the intensity level of stimulation that is necessary to evoke a discernible response irrespective of the specific form that response may take or the sensory modality affected. "You can shine a bright light in her eyes and she does not even blink, but if a door closes she startles and looks up" would be scored as high threshold for visual stimulation and low threshold for auditory stimuli. "He loves fruit, but if I put even a little cereal in with it he won't eat it at all" is scored as low threshold for taste. "She does not pay attention to new people; she does not cry, but she does not really respond to them either" is an example of a high threshold in the area of social relations, as contrasted with, "He laughs and smiles at a stranger, and starts to cry if they do not play with him," which is scored as low threshold.

Temperamental Constellations: Subgroup Classification

The following three temperamental constellations of functional significance are defined using qualitative analysis and factor analysis by Thomas and Chess (1977) in the NYLS:

1. *Easy child.* This group is characterized by regularity, positive approach responses to new stimuli, high adaptability to change, and mild to moderately intense mood that is preponderantly positive. These children quickly develop regular sleeping and feeding schedules, take to most new foods easily, smile at strangers, adapt easily to a new school, accept most frustration with little fuss, and accept the rules of new games with little trouble. Such a youngster is aptly called an easy child and is usually a joy to his parents, pediatricians, and teachers. This group comprises about 40% of the NYLS sample.

2. *Difficult child.* At the opposite end of the temperamental spectrum is the group with irregularity in biological functioning, negative withdrawal reactions to new stimuli, nonadaptability or slow adaptability to change, and intense mood expressions that are mostly negative. These children show irregular sleep and feeding schedules, slow acceptance of new foods, prolonged adjustment periods to new routines, people, or situations, and relatively frequent and loud periods of crying. Laughter also is characteristically loud. Frustration typically produces a violent tantrum. This is the difficult child, and mothers and pediatricians find such youngsters difficult indeed, while teachers feel these children are unteachable. This group comprises about 10% of the NYLS sample.

3. *Slow-to-warm-up child.* The third noteworthy temperamental constellation is marked by a combination of negative responses of mild intensity to new stimuli with slow adaptability after repeated contacts. This type of child is referred to as the slow-to-warm-up child. About 15% of the NYLS sample falls into this category.

Not all children fall into these three groups. Carey (1970) added two other groups: *"Intermediate High"* and *"Intermediate Low"* to include the infants who are not classified in the three groups. Carey's criteria for classifying infants are as follows:

1. *Easy.* Scores greater than the mean in no more than two of the difficult-child categories (rhythmicity, approach versus withdrawal, adaptability, intensity, and mood), and with no greater than one standard deviation.

2. *Difficult.* Four or 5 scores greater than the mean in the difficult versus easy categories. These have to include intensity, and two of the scores must be greater than 1 standard deviation.

3. *Slow-to-warm-up.* The same as difficult, but if either approach versus withdrawal or slow adaptability is greater than 1 standard deviation, activity may vary up to one half a standard deviation, and mood may vary down to one half a standard deviation.

4. *Intermediate.* All others. Intermediate high: 4 or 5 difficult versus easy categories above the mean, with one score greater than 1 standard

deviation, or 2 or 3 scores above mean, with 2 or 3 scores greater than 1 standard deviation. Intermediate Low: all other intermediate.

Temperament and Behavior Disorders

In the course of the first 5 years, the NYLS was able to accumulate detailed parents' reports and interviewing and observational information about the behaviors of 136 out of the original sample of 141 children. Of these, 42 clinical cases (30%) who developed behavior problems severe enough for psychiatric intervention of some sort or another were identified during the 5-year period.

The clinical cases were divided into those with active versus passive symptoms. The passive children were largely nonparticipators. Typically, they stood on the sidelines of a group, taking no part in the group's ongoing activity. If this nonparticipation included overt evidence of anxiety or was accompanied by active tension symptoms such as crying, nausea, stomachache, dizziness, or active complaints that nobody liked him or her, the child was included in the group with the active rather than the passive symptoms. The active symptoms included these or other overt expressions of anxiety: sleep problems, tantrums, aggressive behavior, stuttering. Both before and after the development of symptoms of behavior disorder, the total active clinical group differed from the nonclinical group in their temperamental characteristics. The former were characterized by an excessive frequency of high activity, irregularity, low threshold, nonadaptability, intensity, persistence, and distractibility. The clinical cases with passive symptoms differed significantly in their temperament scores from the nonclinical group only in the fourth and fifth years of life. Mood was different in years 4 and 5, and activity level, approach versus withdrawal, and persistence only in the fifth year.

On the other hand, many nonclinical children had temperamental traits similar to those that characterized the clinical cases. These findings are not surprising considering of the current view that neither temperament nor environment alone determines the course of psychological development. Both normal and pathological development are determined by the dynamic interaction between the child's individual temperament and the environmental experiences, expectations, and demands that the child encounters. In analyzing the nature of the temperament–environment interactive process, the NYLS group found the evolutionary concept of *goodness of fit* as elaborated by Henderson (1913) and the related ideas of *consonance* and *dissonance* to be very useful. Goodness of fit results when the properties of the environment and its expectations and demands are in accord with the organism's own capacities, characteristics, and style of behaving, that is, temperamental individuality. When this consonance between organism and environment is present, optimal development in a progressive direction is possible. Conversely, poorness of fit involves discrepancies and dissonance between environmental opportunities and demands and the capacities and characteristics of the organism, so that distorted development and maladaptive functioning occur. Goodness of fit does not imply an absence of stress and conflict. Quite the contrary. They are inevitable concomitants of the developmental process, in which new expectations and demands for change and progressively higher levels of functioning occur continuously as the child grows older. The longitudinal, qualitative analysis of the cumulative data of both clinical and nonclinical NYLS cases indicates that demands, stresses, and conflicts, when consonant with the child's developmental potential, capacities for mastery, and temperamental characteristics, are constructive in their consequences and should not be considered an inevitable cause of behavior disturbance. The issue involved in disturbed behavioral functioning is rather one of excessive stress resulting from poorness of fit and dissonance between environmental expectation and demands and the capacities of the child and his or her temperamental constellation at a particular level of development. Thus, it was confirmed that features of temperament played significant roles in the development of childhood behavior disorders and that children with certain temperamental attributes and constellations are more at risk for behavior disorder. Beyond this, it became clear that any temperamental trait or pattern in any individual child could significantly enter into the development of a behavior disorder if the environmental demands and expectations were sufficiently dissonant with the child's behavior style.

The child's temperament influences his or her responses to parental practices and attitudes and helps to shape the parents' judgments and feelings toward the child. Sibling and peer-group relationships, school functioning and academic achievement, behavioral responses to illness or other special stress—all can be significantly affected by specific temperamental traits.

It is, therefore, logical to conclude that in the understanding, management, and, more actively, prevention of the development of behavior disorders and malfunctioning, it is vital to assess the temperamental individuality of each child under question and then proceed to inspect its dynamic interaction with the environment.

Short Rating Scales for Measurement

Unfortunately, the NYLS work in developing methods for the identification and rating of temperamental characteristics necessarily involved rather elaborate data collection and data analysis that have practical unfeasibility for those professionals who are in daily contact with the children. Shorter methods of measuring and rating temperament, especially if put in the form of short questionnaires, would make the determination of temperament economically feasible for research workers in normal and deviant child development, for child psychiatrists and pediatricians dealing with problems of parental practice and behavior disorders in children, and for educators working with nursery, kindergarten, and elementary school children. Because of this need for short rating scales and other methods for measuring temperament, a great deal of attention and effort have been given to this issue by a number of workers in the past several years. A short questionnaire for rating temperament in infancy was developed by Carey (1970, 1973) in Philadelphia and was later revised by Carey and McDevitt (1978). The reliability and validity of the questionnaire were assessed against the NYLS method and proved to be satisfactory. Sameroff and Kelly (1977) administered the Carey questionnaire to a Rochester, New York, sample of 300 women with 4-month-old infants. Their data were almost identical with Carey's norms. Wilhoit (1976) administered the questionnaire and the NYLS interview to the mothers of 24 white middle-class children at ages 3–9 months. The comparison of the ratings obtained by the two methods supports the conclusion that the questionnaire is a reliable and valid method of measuring infant temperament as defined by the NYLS interview protocol. The NYLS group has completed the development of a questionnaire for the 3- to 7-year-old period.

Cross-Ethnic Study of Temperament

The NYLS team conducted the first cross-ethnic study of temperamental characteristics, in which the temperamental data of infants of Puerto Rican mothers were obtained and scored by the same team member in the same manner as in the NYLS sample. The results showed that there existed ethnic difference in the temperamental characteristics of infants (Thomas and Chess, 1977). The differences between the two ethnic groups were markedly significant for rhythmicity and intensity, of borderline significance for activity level, mood, and threshold, and not significant for the other four categories. DeVries and Sameroff (1977) report temperament data from an African sample of infants in three East African tribes. The Carey questionnaire was translated and administered by DeVries. Compared to the American norms, there was only one category in which the African sample was in congruence: threshold. In every other category there were significant differences between the African and American sample, as well as among the three tribes. In a comparison of white and black children, Sameroff and Kelly (1977) found that black infants were rated as less rhythmic, less adaptable, less approaching, and more negative in mood. In the first study of Chinese infants' temperamental characteristics using the unrevised Carey's questionnaire, Hong (1978) found that, compared with the Carey's norms, the Chinese infants scored significantly differently from the American infants in eight of the nine temperamental categories. The only category that showed no difference was threshold.

The findings reveal that there exist significant ethnic differences in temperamental characteristics. There is strong indication that regardless of the possible reasons that caused the differences in temperamental scores obtained by questionnaires—even within the same ethnic group—such scores should be compared to subgroup norms rather than to total population norms. The findings further suggest that each ethnic or cultural group should develop its own norms.

REPORT OF CHINESE STUDIES

The study of temperamental characteristics of Chinese infants and young children was carried out in Taipei by using the Chinese language version of the questionnaire. The Chinese data are presented here and comparison is made with those from other ethnic groups to illustrate the importance of collaborative cross-cultural research work on this important issue in child development and mental health.

Temperamental Characteristics of Chinese Infants

SUBJECTS AND METHODS

In order to study the temperamental characteristics of Chinese infants, 349 normal babies who were brought to the well-baby clinic of five general hospitals in the Taipei area were sampled as subjects for the study. The babies were ages 4–8 months, with a mean age of 179 days (about 6 months). All subjects had to fulfill the following criteria of normal babies:

1. Normal gestation without any severe maternal complication during pregnancy and an absence of maternal ataraxics at delivery.
2. Normal spontaneous delivery, excluding Cesarean section and forceps delivery. Gestation period of 37–43 weeks and birth weight no less than 2500 gm.
3. No fetal distress prior to delivery and AGAR scores no less than 8 at 1 minute after delivery.
4. Absence of central nervous system infection or seizure disorder in early life.

There were 182 boys and 167 girls; 238 infants were the firstborn in their families and 111 were later-born. The socioeconomic status of each infant was classified on the basis of the occupational status and educational attainment of the parents, and it was found that the sample was predominantly upper-middle class (37.6% were upper class, 47.3% middle class, and 14.1% lower class).

The Chinese version of the revised Carey and McDevitt Infant Temperament Questionnaire was used for this study. The questionnaire administered to the mothers of infants is composed of 95 concrete behavior descriptions of infants, each of which is scorable on a 7-point rating scale. The questionnaire was translated carefully and completely from English to Chinese, was checked and then translated back into English, and the result was compared with the original questionnaire by a native English-speaking colleague who could read and speak Chinese fluently (Hsu, Soon, Stigler, 1981). Pretesting of the Chinese version was carried out on 52 mothers of healthy infants. The mothers were able to answer the questions in the Chinese version easily, and none of them complained that they could not understand any of the questions. The test–retest reliability of the instrument was also established during the pretesting, with 2-week interval correlation coefficients ranging from .74 for intensity to .86 for approach.

RESULTS

Temperamental Scores.   Means and standard deviations were calculated for each of the nine categories for 349 subjects studied. The data were compared with the American norms as reported by Carey and McDevitt (1978) (Table 10.1). The mean differences between the Chinese and American norms were highly significant ($P < .01$) on all categories except the category of persistence.

Subgroup Classification.   Using Carey's criteria, the subjects were subdivided into five groups according to the pattern of scores among the nine categories: 8.3% of the subjects were classified as difficult, 2.9% as slow-to-warm-up, 15.5% as intermediate high, 21.5% as intermediate low, and 51.9% as easy.

Table 10.2 presents the breakdown into subgroups obtained in the present study and in the study of Carey and McDevitt. A chi-square test showed the breakdown across the five groups to be significantly different in the two samples ($X^2 = 11.80$, $df = 4$, $p < .02$). The most outstanding finding is that the number of Chinese infants classified as slow-to-warm-up is much smaller than in the American sample.

Table 10.1   Comparison of Infant Temperament Scores for Chinese and American Norms

Category	Chinese norms (N = 349)		Carey– McDevitt norms (N = 203)		t value
	Mean	SD	Mean	SD	
Activity	3.96	.64	4.40	.56	−8.15*
Rhythmicity	3.09	.63	2.36	.68	12.75*
Approach and withdrawal	2.91	.83	2.27	.78	8.94*
Adaptability	2.56	.65	2.02	.59	9.74*
Intensity	3.78	.72	3.42	.71	5.97*
Mood	3.44	.64	2.81	.68	10.90*
Persistence	3.00	.85	3.03	.82	−0.41
Distractibility	2.73	.64	2.23	.60	9.06*
Threshold	4.13	.71	3.79	.76	5.29*

* $p < .01$.

Gender and Temperament Scores.   Most of the studies reported by scholars of other countries either did not consider the gender difference or found no gender difference in the scores of temperamental categories. In our study only the category of approach versus withdrawal showed a reliable gender difference, with males being more willing to approach the new than females. This may be due to the relatively small size of the sample; or, at this stage of infancy, gender differences in temperament still may not be evident enough to be scorable by the mothers.

Gender and Temperamental Subgroups.   With regard to the five temperamental subgroups, there was also no significant difference between males

Table 10.2   Comparison of Subgroup Classifications of Temperament from Chinese Study and Carey–McDevitt Study

Subgroup	Chinese study		Carey– McDevitt study	
	%	N	%	N
Difficult	8.3	29	9.4	19
Slow-to-warm-up	2.9	10	5.9	12
Intermediate high	15.5	54	11.3	23
Intermediate low	21.5	75	31.0	63
Easy	51.9	181	42.4	86
	100.0	349	100.0	203

and females. This finding is understandable as can be judged from what was revealed regarding gender and temperament scores.

Correlation with Global Judgment. In addition to the more objective ratings on the questionnaire, mothers were asked subjectively to rate globally in each of the nine categories and to classify their child as easier than average, average, or more difficult than average. The mothers' global ratings correlated with the questionnaire for eight of the nine categories ($r =$ .14 to .45, $p < .01$); only in distractibility was the correlation not significant ($r = .03$, $p < .10$). Though the tendency is consistent with what is expected, the mothers tended to minimize the difficulty of the temperament of their children in the overall estimates. This is consistent with the finding of Carey and McDevitt (1978).

Temperamental Characteristics of Chinese Young Children

SUBJECTS AND METHODS

For the study of young children, the NYLS Temperamental Questionnaire for Children ages 3–7 was translated, checked, retranslated and pretested following the same procedures as for the Chinese version of the revised Infant Temperament Questionnaire of Carey and McDevitt. This questionnaire contains 72 concrete behavior descriptions scorable with a 6-point rating scale. The test–retest reliability at the 2-week interval, based on 53 mothers of children, resulted in correlation coefficients ranging from .79 for activity to .92 for mood. Even the interrater reliability of the two kindergarten teachers taking care of a single class of 32 children yielded correlation coefficients ranging from .38 for persistence to .70 for activity level. Interrater reliability of this degree could be said to be rather satisfactory considering the fact that one teacher was the main teacher and the other was an assistant who was not in constant contact with the children.

One group of the sample was chosen from a district of Taipei City to represent young children living in an urban area, and the other group from Tai-shan Village, about 10 miles from Taipei City, to represent children of a rural area. From a population list of all children ages 3–7 years, the sample was chosen at random. Each child had to fulfill the healthy child criteria as described in the study of infants and also had to be living with the mother. Putting the young children from the two districts together, the distribution of the sample according to the socioeconomic status of the family, indicated that 18.3% belonged to upper, 48.7% to middle, and 33.0% to lower socioeconomic groups.

Table 10.3   Temperament Scores of Young Chinese Children

Category	Boys (N = 995)		Girls (N = 936)		t value
	Mean	SD	Mean	SD	
Activity	4.06	.83	3.74	.87	8.27**
Rhythmicity	4.47	.79	4.45	.78	.57
Approach and withdrawal	4.50	.86	4.44	.83	1.56
Adaptability	4.84	.78	4.80	.76	1.14
Intensity	3.87	.75	3.78	.80	2.55*
Mood	4.76	.62	4.83	.64	−2.44*
Distractibility	4.20	.71	4.28	.69	−2.51*
Persistence	3.98	.62	3.92	.59	2.18*
Threshold	3.30	.77	3.25	.78	1.42

$* p < .05. ** P < .01.$

RESULTS

Temperamental Scores and District Difference.   Two of the nine temperamental categories—approach versus withdrawal and threshold—showed a small district difference, with the young urban children being scored as more positive in their approach to the new and as lower in threshold. Since the temperamental scores on each category for the two districts showed little difference, the following presentations lump the two groups together.

Gender and Temperamental Scores.   In contrast to the results obtained through the Infant Temperamental Questionnaire, the scores for the questionnaire of the young children showed gender differences on more categories. As can be seen in Table 10.3, boys tended to be relatively higher in motor activity, showing intense reaction and being persistent, while girls were higher in pleasant mood and being distractible. The fact that there are significant gender differences on more categories may be due to a larger sample in the study of young children. The other possible reason may be that the gender differences in temperament tend to become more apparent as the children grow older, and the criteria of cultural expectation on behavioral attitudes for different gender may also have influenced the rating attitudes of the mothers at this stage in the development of children.

Gender and Temperamental Subgroups.   As with infants, no significant gender difference was found in the composition of the five temperamental subgroups for the young Chinese children as defined by Carey and McDevitt.

Table 10.4   The Relation between Mothers' Overall Rating and Temperamental Subgroup Classification

| | Mothers' global rating | | | | | | | |
| | Easier than average | | Average | | More difficult than average | | Total | |
Subgroup	N	%	N	%	N	%	N	%
Difficult	1	0.9	27	26.2	75	72.8	103	100
Slow-to-warm-up	0	0.0	2	11.7	15	88.2	17	100
Intermediate high	23	5.3	189	43.8	219	50.8	431	100
Intermediate low	107	14.3	446	59.9	191	23.6	744	100
Easy	389	16.1	240	37.7	7	1.1	636	100
	520	26.9	904	46.8	507	26.2	1,931	100

Correlation with Mothers' Global Judgment.   The mothers' global judgement of the young children in terms of the easy versus difficult classification as shown in Table 10.4 became more consistent with the ratings on the questionnaire and subgroup classification according to the scoring. This differs from the situation when mothers estimate about their infants, tending to minimize the difficulty of temperament.

Cross-Ethnic Comparison.   Comparison with the NYLS Provisional Norms (A. Thomas, personal communication, 1982) obtained from 148 cases yielded a result that except for quality of mood and threshold there existed highly significant differences in the scores on the other seven temperamental items as rated by Chinese and American parents. Chinese children were less active, more regular, more approaching toward the new, more adaptive, more intense in reaction, more distractible, and less persistent. The implication of this ethnic difference, as for the infants, awaits exploration through a more sophisticated cross-cultural study of a larger sample.

DISCUSSION

The revised version of the Carey–McDevitt Questionnaire and the NYLS 3–7 Years Temperamental Questionnaire appear to be handy, reliable, and valid tools for assessing the temperamental characteristics of Chinese infants and young children, respectively. The distribution of scores on the nine temperamental categories of the two questionnaires used in our study closely approached normality. In addition, mothers found the two Chinese versions of the questionnaire easy to answer, which lends face validity to the temperamental questionnaires within the different cultural context.

The comparison of our data on infants with the results of the Carey and McDevitt study reveal striking ethnic differences, which are also reported by some other cross-racial comparisons (Thomas and Chess, 1977). These ethnic differences in the temperamental scores as obtained by the questionnaire deserve careful interpretation that includes cultural perspectives.

The first explanation that comes to mind is that the differences reflect some kind of response bias on the part of the raters (mothers). However, there is some evidence that tends not to support the presence of a simple numerical bias in the different culture, that is, the tendency to choose the higher or lower number on the scale or to favor the middle over the extremes of the scale or vice versa. An examination of Table 10.1 reveals that in one category—persistence, the mean is almost exactly the same for the two ethnic groups, and, in general, the standard deviations are quite similar for the two samples.

The other possibility is that the findings really do represent ethnic differences in the temperamental characteristics of different ethnic groups. Clearly, standardized observational studies by investigators from different countries trained in a single institute like the NYLS laboratory will have to complement mothers' ratings if the root of such ethnic and cultural differences are to be determined.

Instead of merely comparing the temperament scores, there are many issues that could be further investigated cross-ethnically and cross-culturally. For example, McDevitt and Carey (1981), report that even though all nine categories of temperaments were observed as significantly stable in early infancy and at 1–3 years, maternal impression on degree of difficulty changed over time; that is, in infancy, perception of difficulty was significantly correlated with negative mood, high activity level, and low distractibility, while at 1–3 years, they were related to withdrawal, low adaptability, high intensity, and negative moods. It will be interesting to study whether the Chinese mother changes her perception of the difficult child over time in the same way as the American mother, and if she does, why?

Torgersen (1981), after studying same-gender twins from 2 months to 6 years of age, points out that the three temperamental traits with the least evidence for a genetic factor at 6 years—regularity, adaptability, and mood—have been identified by other investigators (Thomas, Chess, and Birch, 1968) as risk factors for the development of behavior disorder. Again, it will be very interesting to study whether this is the same for Chinese children.

It has been clearly pointed out by Thomas and Chess (personal communication, 1981) that different character temperaments may have different adaptation value in different cultural settings. For example, in the study of Puerto Rican children in New York City, it was observed that children with high psychomotor activity would have difficulty adjusting in the crowded ghetto street neighborhood, while the same characteristic may be a desirable temperament for children raised in a setting with wide recreational facilities. Another interesting example is that during the follow-up of temperament carried out in Kenya, Africa by DeVries (1984), it was found that after a natural disaster of drought, the difficult child, not the easy child, had a higher survival rate.

It is apparent that there is a great need to investigate the cross-ethnic and cross-cultural aspects of temperamental characteristics. Even within the Chinese ethnic groups, many collaborative projects could be developed for exploration. For instance, if temperament is determined mostly by genetics, data gathered on infants from Taiwan should be similar to that gathered on infants born to parents of corresponding provincial origins, such as Fu-chen and Kuan-Tong, in mainland China. If there is a response bias caused by cultural differences, the belief about normative behaviors of infants and young children held by the mothers in Taiwan and mainland China can be compared. The more rewarding and academically important contribution that this sort of collaborative research endeavor can yield is to clarify how the same temperamental characteristics may be responded to by mothers, child caretakers, teachers, and the community as a whole with completely different value systems, child-rearing practices, goals, and purposes of education. By looking at the interaction between individuals of the same ethnic origin in completely different social contexts, we can proceed toward a realistic understanding of the role of culture in human development and mental health.

REFERENCES

Carey, W. B.
    1970   A simplified method of measuring infant temperament. *Journal of Pediatrics, 77,* 188–194.
    1973   Measurement of infant temperament in pediatrics. In Westman (Ed.), *Individual difference in children.* New York: Wiley.
Carey, W. B., and McDevitt, S. C.
    1978   Revision of the temperament questionnaire. *Pediatrics, 61,* 735-739.
DeVries, M. W.
    1984   Temperament and infant mortality among the Masai of East Africa. *American Journal of Psychiatry, 141,* 1189–1194.
DeVries, M. W., and Sameroff, A. J.
    1977   Influences on infant temperament in three East African Cultures. In A. Thomas and S. Chess (Eds.), *Temperament and development.* New York: Brunner/Mazel.

Henderson, L. J.
   1913   *The fitness of the environment.* New York: Macmillan.
Hong, C. C.
   1978   *Assessment of Chinese infants' temperamental characteristics.* Unpublished Master's Thesis, Institute of Public Health, National Taiwan University Medical College.
Hsu, C. C., Soon, W. T., and Stigler, J. W.
   1981   The temperamental characteristics of Chinese babies. *Child Development, 52,* 1337–1340.
McDevitt, S. C., and Carey, W. B.
   1981   Stability of ratings vs. perceptions of temperament from early infancy to 1–3 years. *American Journal of Orthopsychiatry 51(2),* 342–345.
Rutter, M., Birch, H. G., Thomas, A., and Chess, S.
   1964   Temperamental characteristics in infancy and the later development of behavioral disorders. *British Journal of Psychiatry, 110,* 651–661.
Sameroff, A. J., and Kelly, P.
   1977   Socio-economic status, racial and mental health factors in infant temperament. In A. Thomas and S. Chess (Eds.), *Temperament and development.* New York: Brunner/Mazel.
Thomas, A., Chess, S., and Birch, H. G.
   1968   *Temperament and behavior disorder.* New York: New York University Press.
Thomas, A., and Chess, S.
   1977   *Temperament and development.* New York: Brunner/Mazel.
Thomas, A. S., Birch, H. G., Herzig, H., and Karn, S.
   1963   *Behavioral individuality in early childhood.* New York: New York University Press.
Torgersen, A. M.
   1981   Genetic factors in temperamental individuality—A longitudinal study of same-sexed twins from two months to six years of age. *American Academy of Child Psychiatry, 20,* 702–711.
Wilhoit, P. D.
   1976   *Assessment of temperament during the first months of life.* Unpublished Ph.D. dissertation, Florida State University.

CHAPTER 11

The One-Child-per-Family Policy: A Psychological Perspective

Tao Kuotai
Chiu Jing-Hwa

INTRODUCTION

China is the most populous country in the world, with a population of close to one billion at the end of 1980, that is, 22.7% of the world's total. A growing number of people now recognize that population growth must keep in step with material production. For this purpose, great effort in planned control of population growth has been made since 1956. The spectacular success that has been achieved is shown by the fact that the rate of natural increase of population fell from 26 per 1000 in 1970 to 12 per 1000 in 1980. However, the population is still growing faster than production.

A NEED FOR BETTER FAMILY PLANNING

In pre-1949 China, there was a consciousness characterized by commitments to a feudal doctrine; that is, a large family meant prosperity, but

153

CHINESE CULTURE
AND MENTAL HEALTH

there was also deeply rooted gender inequality that saw a boy as more valuable than a girl. At that time, economic and public health conditions were serious drawbacks. According to data from 1936, the birthrate was 38 per 1000 and the mortality rate was 28 per 1000, so the rate of natural increase was 10 per 1000. The large population brought disaster to the country and suffering to the people.

Since 1956, China has come a long way in planned control of population growth. In that year, the government gave a general call for family planning, but because no strong measures were adopted, there was little success in fulfilling the plan. At the same time, medical facilities were being expanded, and many infectious diseases were brought under control. The general health conditions of the people were markedly improved, and the Chinese people could finally discard the designation of "the sick man of East Asia." The birthrate, however, from 1949 to 1970 was approximately 33–38 per 1000. At the same time, the mortality rate dropped from 18 to 7.64 per 1000. So the rate of natural increase was kept at the high level of 19–28.5 per 1000. The natural consequence was a rapid growth of population from 500 million in 1947 to 800 million in 1970. This means the rate of increase was 2% of the total population every year ("A Need," 1981; "Questions and Answers," 1981; "Single-Child," 1981).

It was not until 1970 that the Chinese government took effective measures to push the planned regulation of population growth forward. There has been broad publicity about a need for better family planning. School curricula include an explanation of how controlled population growth through encouraging single-child families would not only improve population quality but also improve the general living standard. The government dispensed free supplies of birth-control pills and devices and gave awards to couples who pledged to have only one child. It is highly important that China advocate population planning and encourage people to delay marriage and childbearing. Such policies have been incorporated into the constitution of the nation and the body of marriage law. These measures have been proved to be successful. ("Population Control," 1982). The rate of population growth decreased to 12 per 1000 in 1980. Grain and other agricultural production, however, still cannot keep up with the rate of population growth.

China has announced that it plans to hold its population to 1.2 billion by the end of this century, based on the following factors:

1. The projection for the next 20 years is that if 90% of the families in the country have only one child, the annual rate of natural increase will be only 0.2 per thousand, close to parity between birth and death.

2. China has the world's youngest population. More than half the nation's population is under 20, with those 65 and over constituting less than 5% of the total population ("China Plans," 1981).
3. The productive force is still low. Economic development cannot keep pace with the rate of population growth. Thus, related requirements, such as an adequate school system, sufficient employment opportunities, as well as housing, transportation, and other needs, are increasing and following the rapid growth of the population. The multisibling family imposes a heavy burden, particularly inasmuch as the household chores are left to women: Two children could make a mother a slave to the household.

With all these considerations, the country realized that it must take further steps to limit population growth. It has therefore adopted the single-child policy.

Millions of people now have responded to the call by volunteering to have only one child: At present, over 90% of the couples in urban areas have only one child. However, in rural areas, where peasants feel they need more than one child to help with the work and where there is a tradition of gender inequality, only about 50% of the rural area families had a single child prior to 1982. However, since 1982, owing to the adoption of new Rural Responsibility Systems and other measures, most provinces have succeeded in bringing their birthrate down, and the number of only-child families has markedly increased (*China Daily*, 1982a).

RECENT DEVELOPMENTS IN FAMILY PLANNING

Family planning demands a gigantic effort to change customs and habits. It also involves the vital interest of every family. Patient and meticulous political and ideological work, public education concerning modern methods of contraception, eugenics, and maternal and child care are emphasized. But awards to parents for following government policy are also very important because of existing economic conditions. In some cities and provinces, the single-child family draws a monthly award of 5 *yuan* ($2.50; 5–6% of a worker's monthly wage) until the child is 14 years old. In other places, the only child enjoys free nursery care, free medical care, and free primary school tuition. In some areas, maternity leave is extended to a half year or longer. In rural communes, provisions are made in accordance with local conditions and income distribution policies.

To take a long view of the matter, we have to insure the healthy growth of these only children. It is not only that the single-child policy benefits all, but this policy is considered extremely important for future economic and social development. There is a slogan with that meaning: "One born, one well nurtured, and one well educated." For purposes of this long-range plan, the only-child study, including the general survey and the psychological perspective has particularly important significance at the present.

In recent years, this study has been carried out in Shanghai, Taiyu, Nanjing, and many other places. Now, we report what was done in Dai-Dai Hong Kindergarten in Gu Lou district, Nanjing.

First, more and more parents have responded to the government's call to adopt the one-child family plan, as shown by the increasing proportion of only children in the general population. According to a report of the Tai-Ping Shan Kindergarten in the Bai-Shua urban district, Nanjing, of 90 children who entered the kindergarten in 1979, there were 57 only children (63.5%). Fifty-two children entered the kindergarten in 1980, of whom 51 were only children (98%). In 1981, those who entered were 100% children of one-child families (Nanjing Tai-ping Shan Kindergarten, 1982).

In 1979, 40 children entered Dai-Dai Hong Kindergarten in Gu Lou urban district, Nanjing, of which only children constituted 42.5%. In 1980, of 34 children who entered, 70.6% were only children. In 1981, the proportion had increased to 97%.

Figure 11.1 shows the rapidly increasing proportion of only children in these two kindergartens from 1979 to 1981.

Second, the living conditions and nutrition of the only children are significantly better. Parents who send their children to Dai-Dai Hong Kindergarten are predominantly primary (equivalent to U.S. grades 1–6) and middle school (equivalent to U.S. grades 7–12) teachers, members of district government cadres, and factory workers. They usually have the means

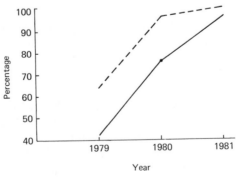

Figure 11.1   Percentage of only children in Tai-Ping Shan Kindergarten (dashed line) and Dai-Dai Hong Kindergarten (solid line).

to provide their children with highly nourishing food. The parents who send their children to Tai-Ping Shan Kindergarten are factory workers, shop assistants, members of common cadres, and so forth. Although the family budgets are not large, about 80% of only children consume milk, eggs, extract of malt and milk, and cake at breakfast. They have even more varieties of food of high quality at supper and always have fruits. In contrast, only one out of eight 3–4-year-old multisibling children drink milk at breakfast.

ADVANTAGES AND DISADVANTAGES OF ONLY CHILDREN

According to the reports of the Shanghai Kindergarten Normal School and Shansi Con-Lo Kindergarten, the average body weight and height of only children were greater than that of multisibling children. In addition to nourishing food, the only child usually has a clean bedroom with furniture and storage space for personal use.

Under the parents' intensely focused attention, the only child is helped to learn. Toys are provided, as well as books and other materials that are necessary for promoting intellectual development. Parents devote more time to playing with and telling stories to the only child. They also use weekends and vacations to take the only child to visit the zoo, botanical gardens, parks, and similar recreational areas, thus encouraging their children to enjoy nature and society. Parents provide a variety of kinds of opportunity for the only child to increase his or her other knowledge and experience. These activities have definite advantages in cultivating the desire to learn and in promoting intellectual development and emotional health.

The Draw a Person Test, an instrument for measuring the child's intelligence formulated by Aranaka and Ueda (1978), was administered to 40 children without siblings and 33 children with siblings between 4 and 6 years of age at the Dai-Dai Hong Kindergarten. On the basis of the test results, it was determined that the average IQ was 127.4 and 120.7, respectively.

According to observations made by parents and teachers, most of the 67 only children and the 33 multisibling children 3–6 years of age have common preferences and interests in activities such as hearing stories, looking at picture books, reading and music, talking, singing, and interacting with parents. While all were fond of gymnastic activity, only children seem less interested than multisibling children. Only children display the

Table 11.1 Selected Characteristics of 67 Only Children and 33 Multisibling Children

	Only children		Multisibling children	
Characteristic	Number	%	Number	%
Preferred activities				
Storytelling	65	97	33	94.3
Playing games	61	91	33	94.3
Reading picture books	59	88.1	31	88.6
Talking	58	88.6	30	85.7
Watching television	58	88.6	30	85.7
Enjoying music	53	79.1	29	82.9
Gymnastic activities[a]	52	77.6	35	100
Drawing	46	68.7	26	74.3
Seeing films	46	68.7	28	80.0
Dancing	37	55.2	24	68.6
Positive attitudes				
Imagination[b]	55	82.9	15	42.9
Warmth	53	79.1	29	82.9
Initiative	49	73.1	21	60.0
Broad interest	49	73.1	22	62.9
Optimism	48	71.6	24	68.6
Cheerfulness	42	62.7	21	60.0
Self-confidence	35	52.5	17	48.6

[a] $\chi^2 = 9.18$, $p < 0.01$.
[b] $\chi^2 = 16.2$, $p < 0.01$.

character trait of imagination to a higher degree than do the multisibling children. This finding is shown in Table 11.1.

The deficiencies of only children are worthy of note and must be emphasized. According to the recent study of only children undertaken at Dai-Dai Hong Kindergarten, most only children display negative character traits and behavior problems, such as marked food preferences, short attention span, obstinacy, demand for immediate gratification, disrespect for their elders, bossiness, timidity, lack of initiative, and so forth. However, these character traits and behavior problems also occurred in multisibling children, particularly in the second-born, considered the ideal child by some parents. These second-born children sometimes displayed more negative behavior problems than did the only child.

Statistically, among the 67 only children in Dai-Dai Hong Kindergarten, strong preferences for and refusals of certain foods, obstinacy, timidity, bad temper, and nail-biting or thumb-sucking occurred at significantly higher rates than in multisibling children (see Table 11.2).

Marked Food Preference and Refusal. Forty-nine only children (73.1%) and 15 multisibling children (42.9%) displayed this behavior. Most parents give particular attention to the only child's food consumption and make every effort to have the only child eat well and eat more. Some parents even prepare special foods or provide expensive, highly nutritional foods for these children. Some children display strong food dislikes—they do not like fat meat, vegetables, bean cake, or other foods and may refuse to take even a single bite. Some of them show no interest in food supplied by the kindergarten. Owing to preferences and dislikes of certain foods, such children may lack certain required nutrients, and their general health condition may as a result, deteriorate.

Short Attention Span and Obstinacy. Forty-seven only children (70.5%) and 21 multisibling children (60%), and 26 only-children (38.8%) and 6 multisibling children (17.1%), respectively, displayed such negative be-

Table 11.2 Comparison of Negative Behavior Patterns between 67 Only Children and 35 Multisibling Children

Behavior	Only children		Multisibling children	
	Number	%	Number	%
Food preference and refusal	49	73.1	15	42.9
Dress preference and refusal[a]	26	38.8	13	37.1
Short attention span	47	70.5	21	60.0
Obstinacy[b]	26	38.8	6	17.1
Stubbornness	36	53.7	16	45.7
Demand for immediate gratification	47	70.5	22	62.9
Destructiveness	44	65.7	22	62.9
Timidity[c]	39	58.2	12	34.3
Temper outbursts[d]	34	50.7	10	28.6
Lack of initiative	38	56.7	17	48.6
Loud and frequent crying	36	53.7	14	40.0
Suppressiveness	34	50.7	15	42.9
Demand for attention, self-centeredness	25	37.3	11	31.4
Over-dependence	24	35.8	9	25.7
Disrespect to elders	29	43.3	9	25.7
Resistance to discipline	29	43.3	14	40.0
Nail-biting or other biting[e]	11	16.4		
Over-sensitivity	28	41.8	11	31.4

[a] $\chi^2 = 9.06, p < 0.01.$
[b] $\chi^2 = 4.59, p < 0.05.$
[c] $\chi^2 = 5.26, p < 0.05.$
[d] $\chi^2 = 4.6, p < 0.05.$
[e] $\chi^2 = 6.54, p < 0.05.$

havior. These related behavioral patterns are encouraged by parents spoiling the only child, that is, trying to do everything the child requests or demands. In some families, the child may act as a dictator, prevailing upon the parents to respond to his or her every whim on the threat of a temper tantrum.

Timidity and Lack of Initiative.   Thirty-nine only children (58.2%) and 12 multisibling children (34.4%), and 38 only children (56.7%) and 17 multisibling children (48.6%), respectively, displayed these behaviors. A considerable number of parents do not know how to rear their children. By threatening children with such traditional warnings as, "The wolf will come to get you," and, "A criminal will take you away," such parents try to frighten children into obeying. However, these same parents are overprotective. The effect of these parental behaviors has a detrimental effect: The child becomes overly timid, unable to care for himself or herself, and overly dependent. We have even observed a few such only children who although 5 years old or older, were still unable to feed themselves. Overdependence is a common characteristic in the only child.

Disrespect to Elders and Resistance to Discipline.   Twenty-nine only children (43.3%) and 9 multisibling children (25.7%), and 29 only children (43.3%) and 14 multisibling children, respectively, (40%) displayed these patterns. These children are spoiled. At home, parents look upon them as dolls to play with. Even in the face of markedly naughty and willful behavior by these children, parents cater to them. Frequently, parents reinforce these negative behaviors through their own undisciplined actions in the family setting. Contentiousness and arguing in the presence of the child trains the child to behave as the parents do.

CAUSES OF NEGATIVE BEHAVIOR PATTERNS IN ONLY CHILDREN

According to some investigators, certain undesirable behavior that is found predominantly among only children results partly from the influence of the home environment (Shanghai Preschool Educational Research Department, 1980). The parents of some only children neglect character development in early childhood, which also causes undesirable behavior. The following examples illustrate these causes of negative behavior patterns.

1. Parents tend to spoil their only son or daughter. Because the only child tends to be the focus of attention in the family, parents frequently

become overly worried when the child is ill. This concern makes the child feel worse or may even create imaginary illness. Parents tend to provide foods that are too rich, clothing that is too expensive, and too many books and toys. Whatever the child demands is provided. The only child becomes the center of the family. Character development is neglected. There is little demand for the child to mind the parents. When the child shows strong preference for or refuses certain food, throws objects, or shows disrespect for older people, the parents usually ignore the behavior, as they are afraid the child will have a temper tantrum. Spoiling and lack of discipline are the most common weaknesses of the only child's parents.

2. Parents' negative behavior influences the child. Parents of the only child are most often approximately 30 years of age when the child is born. Usually they do not have enough life experience to realize the importance of moral development nor do they realize the harm in spoiling the child. They also do not know the importance of providing a good example and lack suitable ways to help the child form desirable habits and patterns of behavior. Some parents overprotect the child even when he or she misbehaves, and some do not encourage the only child to share books and toys with friends. Thus, such parents encourage selfishness in the child (Gao, 1980).

3. There is inconsistency among family members in handling the child. In some cases, the father demands discipline, but the mother spoils the child. In other cases, the mother demands that the child behave properly while the grandmother indulges the child. When the child is overly demanding or disobedient, the father does not give in, but the mother takes the side of the child. Thus, the child gets whatever he or she demands, even when misbehaving, because there is always somebody to back him or her up. The only child often tends to be the cause of family conflict. According to the Nanjing Tai-ping Shan kindergarten (1982) study, 45.4% of the only children live in a three-generation family where they are very much spoiled by the grandparents. There is usually inconsistent disciplinary behavior exhibited by the parents and grandparents, and this inconsistency causes much family dispute and conflict. Thus, the only child becomes the authority or center of the family, and his or her undesirable behavior is indulged.

SPECIAL ASPECTS OF EARLY CHILDHOOD EDUCATION

In accordance with the psychological characteristics of the only child, special aspects of early education should be taken into consideration (Gao,

1981; Shanghai Preschool Educational Research Department, 1980). Early childhood is a stage of physical and intellectual development as well as a period wherein the personality is formed. Children of preschool age begin to regulate themselves through the functioning of language; More consciousness appears in their psychological development. For children at this age, psychosocial development is very plastic and is subject to many influences. The psychological receptivity to training education is developed during this period. According to the special psychological characteristics of only children; their early childhood education is especially important, and we feel that the following points should be taken into consideration:

1. Parents are the child's first teachers, and the home is the first school. The way in which the child is educated by the parents and affected by the home environment is highly influential and last for a long time. Usually, parents are given more information about the physical care of their children than about the mental hygiene that is essential in child rearing. It is particularly important to study the psychological condition of the parents of the only child. Many parents look upon their only child as their great treasure and place all their hope on him or her. They try their best to provide the best nutrition so that the child will be healthy. They do their best to grant the child's various demands (including unreasonable ones) in order to make him or her happy. They try to protect the child from difficulty or danger. They have all sorts of fears and are overly anxious about whatever concerns their child. Thus, they spoil and indulge the child for fear of losing their only treasure. The child senses this and takes advantage of it and will threaten parents in order to fulfill unreasonable demands. For example, a little girl was very fussy about her food and refused to eat. Her parents urged her: "Oh come, eat your food! Tomorrow we'll make something delicious for you!" She still refused to eat. Her parents tried to persuade her: "You will starve to death if you don't eat!" The little girl answered: "When I'm starved to death, you would have no daughter." If the parents' unhealthy attitudes are not changed, they cannot discipline their child and thus enable the child to face difficulties. Therefore, it is essential to study the psychological condition of such parents and to give them help such as guidance in mental hygiene.

2. Imitation is one of the characteristics of young children. Before children enter kindergarten, parents are the models: They are the child's first teachers. Parents' behavior has a great influence on the child. If the parents are fussy about food, how could they expect their child to be otherwise? When the parents love and respect each other and live in harmony, they create a harmonious and joyful family atmosphere, which is essential for

the child to develop healthily; this kind of family surrounding is essential for early childhood education. Inconsistency between parents is harmful to the child's psychosocial development. After the child goes to kindergarten, consistency between teachers and parents in handling the child is most important. Parents and teachers demonstrating exemplary behavior is a fundamental basis of early childhood education.

3. Parents can invite other children to come to the house and play with their only child so that the only child can have experience in building relationships. Parents can help the children to share toys and books with each other or arrange for them to have meals together. In this way, the parents have the chance to broaden their perspective concerning their own child. It would be helpful both to the parents and to the child by ameliorating attitudes of anxiety and self-centeredness.

Children learn more about group life when they enter kindergarten. There, every child is a member of the group. They learn to be friendly to each other, learn to give and take, and learn group routine and behavior. Teachers help children to distinguish right from wrong, especially through activities such as "doing something good for the group" or acting out the roles of policeman, shop attendant, or soldier in a play. In this way, they can learn to do good for others. Visits to factories, stores, and communes are also helpful to young children in accordance with their cognitive abilities.

4. Only children have the desire to improve just as other children do. Adults should respect them and cherish this desire. When we criticize their weak points, we should encourage their strong points and make stronger demands on them. Comparing and appraising each other's behavior is one way to encourage their desire to improve. The standard for comparing and appraising may be set according to the objectives of education, such as manners and graces, doing good for the group, and so on. Through comparing and appraising children learn to accept praise and criticism. We should make higher demands on those who improve as we praise them. And we should trust those who fail to make much improvement and be cautious not to hurt their feelings when we criticize them. Activities such as comparing and appraising carried out with children should attract their interest in order to be beneficial. Reward and punishment is one of the principles of early childhood education.

5. Some of the only child's weaknesses and behavior problems are formed by unfavorable home environment and lack of early education. Unacceptable behavior is a conditioned reflex in response to certain behavior of the parents. According to the law of conditioned reflex, such patterns may disappear when not intensified. But if they are not corrected in time,

they may be formed as a self-centered habit with a selfish motive that may then become selfishness. Undesireable behavior and habits in young children are not fixed at the beginning of their development, and they can be corrected quite easily when early childhood education is emphasized.

CONCLUSION

Advocating only one child for each married couple suits the economic condition of China, where the aim is for every child to be healthy and well educated. The only child has many assets, such as better environmental and health conditions, broader interests, better cognitive development, and higher intellectual ability, in spite of the fact that he or she may have some weaknesses. Some Western scholars have held that lack of siblings leads to certain types of experiences, which, in turn, mold character formation along specific lines and may result in typical pathological tendencies and vulnerabilities. In 1907, G. Stanley Hall even considered being an only child a disease in itself (Hagenauer and Tucker, 1979). These older view points have no scientific basis. According to studies of the only child in certain Western countries, there are many desirable qualities in the only child. As a result, one child per couple has become the desire of numerous families and has, in fact, turned out to be a general trend (Moore, 1981). So it is advocated not only in China but in other countries as well. In China, children are looked upon as flowers of the nation and seedlings of the society. To care for the younger generation is to be concerned with the future of the country and the hope of the people. It is essential to study the mental health aspects of an only child systematically and throughly in different sociocultural contexts. It is very important to investigate the potential merits and demerits of an only child and to learn how to minimize potential demerits, such as by enforcing early socialization through the participation of an institutional program or by educating the parents in the proper parenting of an only child. It is hoped that with the devoted care of parents, teachers, caretakers, mental hygiene workers, and the whole of society, all the only children as well as the entire new generation will grow up with high ideals, sound moral standards, solid educational backgrounds, and good health, as well as readiness to make contributions to the progress of their country and to humanity as a whole. We are planning further studies of the character traits of the only child in relationship to family environment and family training methods in particular cultural backgrounds. We believe that to make such a survey and follow-up will provide scientific knowledge that will be helpful to better family planning and to better single-child nurturing.

REFERENCES

Aranaka, S., and Ueda, L.
1978   *Ningen-hattatsu* [Human development]. In *Japan Medical Encyclopedia*, Volume 4.

China plans for people
1981   *China Daily*, October 27.

Gao, Z.
1980   *Xue-ling-quan du-sheng-zi zi-si xing-wei de xin-li-xue fen-xi* [The psychological analysis of selfish behavior by only-child at preschool age]. Abstracts in *Shang hai shi fan da xue xin li ke xue* [Psychological science of Shanghai Teacher's University], *3*, 21.

1981   *Du-sheng zi-nu de zao-qi jiao-yu wen-ti* [The problems of early childhood education for the only child]. *Jiao Yu Yan Jiu* [Education Research], *6*, 37.

Hangenauer, F., and Tucker, H.
1979   The only child. In J. D. Noshpite (Ed.), *Basic handbook of child psychiatry* (Vol. 1). New York: Basic Books.

Moore, D. D.
1981   *Guan-yu mei-guo du-sheng-zi-nu de diao-cha* [The investigation of only-children in the U.S.A.] *New York Times*, (B. May, Trans.). *Huan Qiu* [Globe], April 4:39. (Original work published January 18, 1981)

Nanjing Tai-ping Shan Kindergarten
1982   *Guan-yu du-sheng-zi-nu de diao-cha he jiao-yu* [The investigation and education about the only child]. Internal Reference Material.

A need for better family planning
1981   *China Daily*, October 7.

One child in family is better
1982   *China Daily*, January 7.

Population control is vital to China's development
1982   *China Daily*, November 1.

Questions and answers on family planning policy
1981   *China Daily*, October 27.

Shanghai Preschool Educational Research Department
1980   *Si zhi liu sui du-sheng zi-nu de xing-wei yu jiao-yu de diao-cha* [Study on the behavior and education of 4–6-year-old children]. *Shang-hai xin-li ke-xue tong-xun* [Shanghai Information on Psychological Science], May.

Single-child policy benefits all
1981   *China Daily*, October 27.

CHAPTER 12

Child Mental Health and Elementary Schools in Shanghai

Xu Taoyuan

INTRODUCTION

Childhood is an important period of life, since it is the time that determines a person's mental attitude. During this period, children receive their life education, mainly in the home, nursery, kindergarten, and elementary school. Elementary school lasts for a long period of time; therefore, it has a great impact on the child. It is very important for the mental health worker to be concerned with the elementary school and its relation to child mental health. This is especially true in China because of the large number of children in elementary school. According to the official report of 1980, there are 982,550,000 people in mainland China, of whom 14% are school-age children. Thus, there are 146,270,000 children in elementary school; approximately 11,510,000 children, about 1.2% of the total population, are in kindergarten.[1] In China, nursery school and kindergarten are

[1] According to the educational system in mainland China, preschool children from ages 2–5 go to nursery school and kindergarten. At age 6, children enter elementary school (grade school). Elementary school was a 5-year system during the 1950s and 1960s, but it is currently a 6-year system. After elementary school, students enter middle school, which is composed of junior middle school (intermediate school—the first 3 years) and senior middle school (high school—the second 3 years). Senior middle school graduates become eligible for college.

167

relatively easily available in the city, but this is not so on farms in rural areas. Because the majority of the people in rural areas (about 80%) live on farms, most of the preschool children in rural areas are cared for in their homes. However, most school-age children, both in the city and in rural areas, attend school.

Since 1949, the population of China has doubled. During this period there have been several peaks in the growth rate. As the result of one peak in the 1950s, there was a remarkable increase in the number of school-age children in the early 1960s, about one decade later, resulting in a shortage of schools. In order to meet that situation, in Shanghai as well as in other areas, the two-shift school system was adopted: Half of the students attended school in the morning and studied by themselves at home in the afternoon; the other half attended school in the afternoon and studied at home in the morning. This system was used only as a temporary measure. However, the students who went through school with this system went to middle school during the Cultural Revolution, or Ten-Year Turmoil (1966–1976) and graduated from school with a generally low educational level. This fact was perhaps related to the influence of the Cultural Revolution as well as to the two-shift school system during their elementary school period. There is no way for retrospective systematic study to validate the speculation of such influence, since it happened in the past.

THE ELEMENTARY SCHOOL SYSTEM IN CHINA

The educational system in China is more or less unified. However, it is allowed to have some variation in accordance with local conditions. If there is a need for major change, a pilot study is always carried out in some selected school to prove its usefulness before broad application. Unfortunately, during the Great Leap Forward in the late 1950s and the ten-year turmoil in the 1960s, the method of spreading over a whole area from one point, or making experiments first then popularizing the successful experiment, was not well carried out. Changes were frequently made so impulsively that often the results were not useful. Based on such past experience, we are careful nowadays to respect the traditional system of the past and to change the educational system gradually, after having made the necessary pilot study, before making any radical reforms in the school system.

The School System in General

In the 1950s, the elementary school was changed into a five-year system. Because the length of time was shortened, although the number of subjects and courses was not reduced accordingly, it was quite a burden on the students. Since 1981, most of the schools have been changed back to the six-year system, and it is expected that within a few years, all of the schools will be changed back to the six-year system.

All children of age 6 are considered to have reached the appropriate age to attend school. Unless there is a negative indication, such as the presence of serious mental illness, all children are expected to attend school. There is no written examination for entrance; however, teachers administer an oral basic cognitive examination, such as recognition of colors or figures, which serves to screen for mental retardation.

Such student is expected to enter the school in the area near his or her home. Thus, each school accommodates students from its designated catchment area. In Shanghai, the average number of students is about 700 per school, with 40 to 50 in each class; and there is a teacher who is responsible for all the students in the class.

China's schools, including elementary schools, middle schools, and colleges are divided into ordinary schools and key schools. A key school is a school with both strong administrative and teaching staff, with high levels of moral, political, and ideological, as well as intellectual, education. There are few key schools, and they are often selected to be key schools for historical reasons. For example, the well-known Beijing University and Qinghua University in Beijing were selected for their unique past background and reputation as institutions of high academic quality. Many key schools are selected or established by the Minister of Education and Administration according to established national education planning. In the past, there was some tendency in the key schools to overemphasize the intellectual aspect of the curriculum while neglecting physical education. This tendency has been noticed by the departments concerned and corrections have been made.

Generally speaking, graduates from the key middle schools have higher rates for passing the college entrance examination, and graduates from the key universities are the most welcomed workers by employing institutions because of their higher academic level.

There is a division of key and ordinary schools at the elementary level. However, the question of continuance of such divisions is currently under debate. Some believe that the purpose of the elementary school is to provide basic education, not to prepare students for higher education; therefore, it is felt that elementary schools should not be divided into different levels. Others, who believe that a key elementary school could serve as a model for other schools, argue for preserving the present system. In Shanghai, such divisions were, in theory, eliminated. However, in practice, some schools are better organized than others, and distinctions, therefore, are still being made.

Curriculum and School-Year Division

School entrance registration takes place in the summer. The children reaching school age are notified by the neighborhood committee and brought to school by their parents for registration. The academic term starts in the fall, and there are two semesters in a school year. The first semester runs from early September to January and is followed by a 1-month winter vacation. The second semester begins in February, ends in July, and is followed by a summer vacation that lasts for $1\frac{1}{2}$ months. The elementary school, middle school, and college all follow the this 2-semester system.

In the elementary school, the curriculum is divided into junior classes and senior classes. For the junior class, there are classes in national language, mathematics, music, physical exercise, art, and handwork. For the senior class, in addition to the above classes, there are foreign languages (mainly English), history, geography, and natural science. There are about 30 sessions per week for the junior class, while the senior class has slightly more than that. Among the classes, the language class is given relatively more sessions.

Prior to and during the Cultural Revolution, political and ideological education for the elementary school were centered around the theme of Five Loves—love of country, love for people, love of labor, love of science, and love of community, environment, and public property. In practice, this theme was carried out in the school through the activities of the Young Pioneers, an organization similar to the Boy Scouts, which promoted identification of and learning about heroic persons and doing good for others. The Young Pioneers is organized by the children. In the past, it was organized by the better students from the class; nowadays, almost all of the students participate in the organizing.

After the Cultural Revolution, political and ideological education for elementary school children has centered around the moral regulations for primary school students. (There are regulations for middle school students as well.) After these regulations were given a pilot utilization, it was formally announced by the Ministry of Education in 1981 that they would be applied in all elementary schools. The regulations for elementary school students contain the following ten points:

1. Love of country, love for people, love for the Chinese Communist party, and studying hard and improving every day.
2. Punctual and consistent class attendance; attention to instruction, and application to academic work.
3. Active participation in physical training and extracurricular activities.

4. Concern for good physical hygiene, dressing neatly, and cultivating good personal habits such as not spitting in public places.
5. Love of physical labor, extending oneself to the maximum, and self-reliance.
6. Living a simple life, conserving food, refraining from fussiness concerning food and dress, and concern for wise spending.
7. Observing school discipline and regulations and observing public regulations.
8. Respect for teachers, working with classmates as a group, politeness to others, maintaining a good temperament, and avoiding quarreling with others.
9. Concern about the collective group, protection and care of the community environment, and returning lost items to police or teachers.
10. Striving for honesty and courage and willingness to take responsibility for one's actions.

These ten regulations include the ideas from the Five Loves but cover broader areas in more practical terms and are, therefore, easier for school children to understand and to follow.

AN EXAMPLE OF THE SCHOOL MENTAL HEALTH SITUATION IN SHANGHAI

Having described the general picture of school systems in China and provided some concrete information about schools in Shanghai, I now discuss examples of the situation of mental health in schools in the Shanghai area. In order to carry out child mental health work, the Shanghai Psychiatric Institute has developed working relations with an elementary school, Dong An San Cun (East-Peace Third Village) Elementary School, which is located near the institute. We carried out a discussion with the principal and the teachers of the school and conducted psychological examinations of a portion of the students in order to understand the mental health situation of children in the school.

Dong An San Cun Elementary School is and has always been one of the ordinary schools. It accommodates all the residential school-age children in Dong An San Cun as well as children staying in that village temporarily. Each apartment-house residential area in Shanghai is known as "such-and-such new village." Each new village or residential quarters, contains several blocks of 3- to 6-floor apartments. Each block apartment house may accommodate a dozen to several dozen households. In general, in each new village, there is a neighborhood committee. As the institute is located on the margin of Shanghai City and is surrounded by vacant land, many residential apartments have been built, which now form five or six new villages. Dong An San Cun is one of these new villages.

Dong An San Cun Elementary School has approximately 730 students. This school is still in the process of changing from a 5-year curriculum, although the junior class has already changed to the 6-year curriculum. There are several classes per grade, and the number of students in each class varies according to the number of school-age children needing to be accommodated each year—on the average about 50 students. There are about 40 teachers, of which the majority are female and in their 40s. (Most schoolteachers in Shanghai are females.) The majority, very few of whom are older than 45, graduated from normal school in the 1960s and went through the period of the Cultural Revolution in the early part of their careers. As a result, they have had little opportunity to improve their experience and level of professional ability. Because the 1960s was a time when China greatly expanded the elementary school system and because there was a shortage in the availability of teaching staff, some youths were recruited to be school teachers without having graduated from normal school. These persons felt the influence of the Ten-Year Turmoil period and need to update their professional training. This is, to one degree or another, a phenomenon observed in other schools in Shanghai. Because the pay for teachers in the elementary school, as well as in the middle school, is low, work efficiency has been affected. The government has given attention to this matter: In 1983, it increased the salaries of teachers and has been making an attempt to improve their living conditions. Based on discussions with school teachers, the mental health–related situations at Dong An San Cun Elementary School can be summarized as follows.

Age of School Entrance.   Some teachers prefer children to enter school at the age of 6. According to the opinion of these teachers, 6-year-olds, in comparison to 7-year-olds, are more pliable and are more easily educated, while the seven-year-olds "know the ropes" and do not respect the teacher's discipline.

Intellectual Subnormality.   There are not too many children assessed as having severe mental retardation and susequently screened out at the time of the entrance examination. It is usually 1 or 2 years later, that they are found to have academic difficulty and have failed to advance to the next class. There are about 10 such students in Dong An San Cun Elementary School, and they continue to stay at the school because there are only a few schools in Shanghai that provide special classes for the mentally retarded and these few schools are unable to accommodate all of the subnormal students.

Running Away from School or from Home.   This situation is very rare. Only a few students—less than 1% run away from school occasionally. There is only one student in this school who frequently runs away from the school, and this student shows some difficulty in academic performance. The student's father is a ship's crewman, which means he is gone frequently, and there is a stepmother. However, the relation with the stepmother is not bad. The main reason for the truancy of this student is not yet clear.

Reading and Writing Disability.   There are very few of these cases also. There is one student who makes mistakes in spelling when writing Latin, such as confusing *b* and *d*, which he corrects later. Another student makes mistakes in writing Chinese calligraphy by missing some strokes, and he has difficulty in correcting such errors. This student has a history of high fever during childhood, indicating the possibility of brain damage.

Hyperactive Syndrome or Minimal Brain Disorder.   In Shanghai, many elementary school students are diagnosed as having this kind of dysfunction. Teachers in Dong An San Cun Elementary School maintain conservative attitudes concerning this kind of dysfunction. Most of them consider that a child manifesting hyperactive behavior has an inherited tendency, rather than a disorder. Even though medication could help calm the hyperactive child, making it easier for the teacher to regulate the child's behavior, teachers feel that it is not the best way to handle such a child. They believe that the proper way is to modify the hyperactive child's behavior through education and discipline. The teachers feel that the reason for many students having recently been diagnosed as having this dysfunction may be related to the fact that in the past several years, there have been many articles about the hyperactive syndrome in children, which disseminate theories of the existence of such a disorder and the possibility of medical treatment for it. Parents and teachers have become sensitive about this subject and tend to refer the child to a pediatric or psychiatric clinic for assessment; consequently, there is an increased tendency for the child to be diagnosed as having the disorder.

Students' Attitudes toward Subjects.   Generally speaking, students are not much interested in the subjects of language and literature. Perhaps there are too many sessions for such subjects, more homework, and more exercises in composing sentences and essays, which students find difficult—as a result, they are not particularly fond of the subjects. However, if such material were taught in a more stimulating way, students might show more interest. Nowadays, students do not pay much attention to studying Chinese brush calligraphy. As for studying a foreign language—English, in particular—some students show interest. The majority are uncertain about memorizing the vocabulary and are, therefore, not very enthusiastic about language study. However, students are interested in subjects that allow more activity, such as physical exercise, or handwork and are very interested in mathematics. (The middle school students show this enthusiasm in studying physics and chemistry as well.) There is a saying: "Once science and technology are mastered, you can get a job anywhere in the world." Perhaps such thinking still affects people in this society.

Attitude toward Learning.   The teachers in this school feel that prior to the Cultural Revolution, the students in the senior classes were more serious about studying for higher academic performance than the present students. The reason for this feeling may be that in the past, there was a need to compete to enter middle school, while at present, there is no such competition. However, there are still some students, particularly children of intellectuals, who are interested in entering a key middle school and, therefore, study hard because competition is very keen.

Parents' Expectations of Children.   As most of the parents have only one or two children, they have high expectations of their children. They have placed high demands on the school and teachers by expecting their children to attain academic distinction in hope of entering them in key middle schools. With only one or two children, parents frequently indulge in pampering their children, which results in the tendency for the children to be spoiled and not show respect for parental authority. Therefore, some parents may leave the discipline of their children to the teachers. There are some parents with lower educational levels who do not have much concern about their childrens' studies and who do not care strongly about the moral character of their children.

Moral Education.   Moral education is centered around the regulations for elementary school students issued by the Ministry of Education. It is the teachers' general impression that if the parents have a higher educational level, their children are more interested in intellectual pursuits, more likely to obey rules, more polite, but less favorable toward physical activities. With parents of lower educational levels, children show the reverse phenomenon. In Dong An San Cun, there are some households in which the parents have university or scientific institution educational backgrounds. School teachers comparing children of these families with others sustain the general impression described above.

The Issue of Students' Study Load.   Teachers all recognize that students nowadays have a heavy study load and that this situation has an unfavorable effect on their health. However, as the curriculum is determined by the education authorities, the school teachers cannot do anything about it.

Although the change in length of the school program from 5 years to 6 years has helped to relieve some of the study load, there is still a problem. An additional pressure comes from society, which includes the school and its administrators, who evaluate and criticize the achievement and status of the school according to the rate of entrance to middle school. A school has more prestige if it has a higher middle school entrance rate; a teacher feels prouder if the students obtains high academic scores. As a result, the school expects students to study harder in order to obtain a higher entrance rate. Now, educational authorities have requested schools not to be concerned with entrance rates but to be more concerned with the integrated development of moral, intellectual, and physical preparation. In some areas, limits have been imposed on the hours of study in school and the amount of homework permitted. However, it will take quite some time to change the habits and attitudes of society.

Concerning the question of what school teachers expect from psychiatrists or psychologists working collaboratively with them to improve teaching and mental health, most of the teachers from Dong An San Cun school do not yet have specific suggestions. This reluctance is based on the fact that we as psychiatrists are just beginning to contact them. Therefore, they are not familiar with the function and role of psychiatrists in the area of school mental health.

PSYCHIATRIC DISORDERS AMONG STUDENTS

Major Psychoses

No case of psychosis has been found in the Dong An San Cun Elementary School nor in another elementary school investigated—a school which has about 700 students also. In fact, it is not common to find school children suffering from major psychoses. This is supported by the statistical finding from our outpatient clinic that child psychosis is a rare disorder. A report from the West (Fish and Ritvo, 1979) shows that the prevalence of child psychoses is about 4 per 10,000, with half of them being infantile autism. As infantile autism is rarely found in China, the rate of child psychoses is low for Chinese children.

Mental Retardation

In Dong An San Cun School and another school investigated, there were 10 cases of mental retardation in one school and 2 cases in the other. The average prevalence is less than 1%. This figure is small, but it is an issue difficult for the schools to manage. In the past, teachers have made an attempt to pair students with good academic performance with students of poor academic performance, with the intention of having the former assist the latter. This has worked well for those students who have poor academic performance because of bad study habits, but it has not significantly helped those who are mentally retarded. When the teacher discovers that a student has a defect in intellectual endowment, they refer the child's parents to medical treatment or to a special class. However, there is a limited number of special classes available for such students. Because in most families, both parents work and cannot take care of retarded children during the day, such students are kept in the school year after year, just so they will be cared for while the parents are at work.

Hyperactive Syndrome

The majority of the cases (more than 95%) have visited child psychiatric clinics in Shanghai or other cities and have been diagnosed as having hyperactive syndrome, thus having a need for special attention and investigation. In early 1981, our institute carried out a survey at an ordinary elementary school, asking teachers and parents to respond to a questionnaire regarding their children's behavior. As a result, children suspected of having this syndrome, as described by both parents and teachers, reach 15% of the total student enrollment (112 cases per 733 students). This survey was followed by clinical assessment, which confirmed that 5% of the total number of students could be diagnosed as having this dysfunction. Among all the grades investigated, the syndrome is found predominantly (9.4%) among third grade children (average age, 9). Later in 1981, our institute and other hospitals jointly studied six elementary schools with a total of about 4000 students. The result indicates that the prevalence rate varies between 3 and 14%, which is similar to the rate reported by Western countries (Eisenberg, 1979).

The living environment and educational level of the residents varies in different parts of Shanghai City. The preliminary data indicate that the prevalence rate of hyperactive syndrome is higher in the area where the living conditions and educational level of the residents are lower, showing that the syndrome is related to the economic and educational background of the family. We speculate that the dysfunction has no direct relation to the educational system itself.

However, from the historical point of view, we are aware that at least in the case of Shanghai, it is closely related to the sociocultural and educational system. In 1978, the issue of hyperactive syndrome was introduced in the popular scientific magazine, *Ke Xue Hua Bao* (*Science Pictorial*). As a result, great interest and concern was engendered among school teachers, who asked parents of problem children to take their children to see child psychiatrists. It happened that some of these children were diagnosed as suffering from hyperactive syndrome, were treated by medication, and showed remarkable improvement. The news of this matter was so broadly reported in the newspapers and communicated by the school teachers that society began to pay attention to the issue, and it has become one of the subjects of highest concern in the field of child mental health.

In addition to the previously described event, which was influenced by the news media, there is a basic social issue relating to the phenomenon of school entrance competition. At present, in China, only 5% of high school graduates can enter college. It is generally believed that preparation for college should begin as early as the elementary school level. Therefore, many parents as well as teachers expect elementary school children to concentrate on their academic performance. Active children, who are in the normal range but less able to control and restrict their behavior, are seen as being unable to sit still while engaged in study and suspected of being hyperactive. Now, as the educational authorities are becoming aware of the overemphasis on studying, they are placing more emphasis on the need for physical activity, as well as moral education, for school children. This policy should diminish the overemphasis on hyperactive syndrome among school children in the near future.

Neurotic Disorders

Neurotic disorders, such as separation anxiety among small children, are frequently described by Westerners (e.g., Allen, 1955; Coolidge, 1979). However, such problems among school children in China are seldom observed. In Shanghai, most of the children enter kindergarten after nursery school and elementary school after kindergarten. Therefore, most of them are already used to going to school and being separated from their parents. Even if they don't attend nursery school or kindergarten prior to elementary school, children go to the school with neighborhood children, and it is relatively easy for them to adjust to the new life in school when they enter.

CLOSING COMMENT

Even though the concept of school mental health is a new field for child psychiatry in China, there is no doubt of the great role child psychiatry will play in promoting the mental health of school children in addition to providing psychiatric care for mentally ill children. Child psychiatrists will provide consultation, education, and research for special mental health problems such as the presently popular issue of the hyperactive syndrome. Currently in China, there is an emphasis on the one child family policy to address the population problem. The concern on how to improve the mental health of the only child is an urgent task for the government and the people. Child psychiatrists must share in coping with this new challenge.

REFERENCES

Allen, F. H.
   1955   Mother–child separation—Process or event? In G. Caplan (Ed.), *Emotional problems of early childhood.* New York: Basic Books.
Coolidge, J. C.
   1979   School phobia. In J. D. Noshpitz (Ed.), *Basic handbook of child psychiatry: Vol. 2. Disturbances in development.* New York: Basic Books.
Eisenberg, L.
   1979   Hyperkinetic reactions. In J. D. Noshpitz (Ed.), *Basic handbook of child psychiatry: Vol. 2. Disturbances in development.* New York: Basic Books.
Fish, B., and Ritvo, E. R.
   1979   Psychoses of childhood. In J. D. Noshpitz (Ed.), *Basic handbook of child psychiatry: Vol. 2. Disturbances in development.* New York: Basic Books.

PART III

ADJUSTMENT IN DIFFERENT SETTINGS

Cultural aspects of behavior, stress, and coping patterns can be high-lighted for study if we cross-compare life experiences and adjustments in different sociocultural settings or examine the migration situation in which transcultural adjustments occur. Part III explores Chinese adjustment in different locales: Singapore, Hong Kong, and Hawaii.

Kuo (Chapter 13) examines the complicated issue of language and iden-tity among Chinese in the multiethnic, multilingual social setting of Singa-pore. He views language as a cognitive system, a communication instru-ment, and a social function that is closely related to personal and ethnic identity and analyzes how language affects identity in Singapore.

This is followed by Lee's (Chapter 14) discussion of social stress and coping behavior in Hong Kong. He describes the special circumstance of Hong Kong—one of the most populated industrialized cities in Asia, where people face the stresses of high-density living and the great need for achievement. In his review of the mental health situation, he notes that certain traditional ways of adjustment exist. These include following the cultural norms that govern interpersonal relations in overcrowded situa-tions and using religious–mythical beliefs to explain and manipulate life's vicissitudes. Use of these time-honored adjustment methods tends to mini-mize possible emotional damage.

179

CHINESE CULTURE
AND MENTAL HEALTH

In conclusion, Lum and Char (Chapter 15) report on Chinese adaptation in Hawaii. They note that the majority of Chinese in Hawaii have utilized some of their Chinese cultural heritage to make relatively successful adaptations in a short period of time. To demonstrate both this positive adaptation and how ethnic identity of different generations change, they present results of interviews with two successful father–son pairs.

CHAPTER 13

Language and Identity: The Case of Chinese In Singapore

Eddie C. Y. Kuo

INTRODUCTION

Language is essential in human communication. Individuals who come into contact with one another have to share the same system of symbols to make meaningful interaction possible. It is therefore obvious that language plays an important function in communication.

What is less obvious is the function of identification of language; that is, language also serves as a rallying point for group identification among those who speak the same mother tongue. Feelings of language group identity, primordial as they often are, can be highly emotionally charged when contacts with members of other language groups are involved. This is especially so since there is often a close association between language identity and cultural identity. The sense of identification is thus strengthened by common experiences based on language, ethnicity, religion, and culture.

While the mother tongue and the mother tongue group may provide the strongest basis for the development and emergence of a language group identity for an individual, it should be noted that languages other than the mother tongue with which a person is associated in other forms may also be another anchorage of identification for the individual. One important example is the sense of identification developed as a result of common educational experiences. In Singapore, for instance, the older generation Chinese who went through the Chinese-medium educational system (using Mandarin as the major language of instruction) are known to be associated with or identified as the Chinese-educated, and are differentiated from the vaguely defined English-educated.

This chapter starts off with the assumption that language is an important (albeit not the only) element in group identification. To the extent that the sense of group or cultural identity of an individual is threatened as a result of changes in the environment (due to, for instance, migration or political forces), the language experience may be an important and crucial factor underlying such changes and an initiator leading to further changes in group- and self-identity. In the case of the Chinese in Singapore, the changing sociolinguistic conditions and language policy measures have resulted in some confusion or even in some crisis in identification among at least some of the Chinese in this young independent state.

THE SOCIOLINGUISTIC SITUATION IN SINGAPORE

Singapore is a multiethnic society whose population is about 77% Chinese, 15% Malay, 6% Indian and 2% other smaller ethnic groups, according to the 1980 census (Saw, 1982). It is therefore justifiable to classify Singapore as an ethnically plural society with a predominantly Chinese population.

The Chinese in Singapore, however, do not form a homogeneous group as far as language-dialect background is concerned. Singaporean Chinese today are immigrants or children of immigrants originating from different places in mainland China, speaking dialects different from and often unintelligible to one another. The latest census (1980) reveals the complexity of the dialect group composition of the Chinese population as the following percentage distribution shows:

Hokkien	43.1
Teochew	22.0
Cantonese	16.5
Hakka	7.4

Hainanese	7.1
Foochow	1.7
Henghua	0.7
"Shanghainese"	0.8
Other	0.7

In order to interpret the above statistics, it should be noted first that these categories reflect quite strictly dialect group *identification* and need not indicate actual language-dialect proficiency of persons identified. In other words, a Hokkien so identified may not be able to speak Hokkien either as a mother tongue or even as a second language at all. Second, the category "Shanghainese" used as a census label in Singapore does not refer to the Wu-speaking Chinese originating in Shanghai and its vicinity. Rather, the label is used, for reasons yet to be explored, to refer to those originating in places other than the southern provinces of Fujian, Guangdong, and Guangxi. It is therefore best to combine this group with the Other category. The case of Shanghainese in the Singapore context therefore represent an interesting situation whereby a person may be identified by a new label that has little to do with his or her true identity—dialect group identity in this case.

The complexity of the sociolinguistic situation in Singapore is thus reflected in the presence of three major ethnic groups and more than a handful of Chinese dialect groups in this island-state of 2.4 million population. Furthermore, there are four official languages in Singapore, not including any of the Chinese dialects listed above.

At the time of independence, the leaders of Singapore decided that there would be four official languages in the Republic: Malay, Chinese (Mandarin), and Tamil to represent the three ethnic-cultural traditions in Singapore, and English because of its international status and Singapore's colonial background.

Of the four official languages, Malay was designated the national language, reflecting both the historical and geographical position of the island-state. The role of the national language, however, is almost exclusively symbolic at the official level, used in the national anthem and military commands. As a national language, Malay is not taught as a compulsory subject for non-Malays, and a person need not pass a national language test to become a naturalized citizen of Singapore. However, at the informal level, a pidginized form of Malay—Bazaar Malay—is commonly used for interethnic group communication. This function of Bazaar Malay, however, is declining, and its place is likely to be taken over by English of an indigenized variety in the future.

English, as the nonethnic and, thus, neutral official language, has, over the years, evolved to become the de facto dominant working language in Singapore. It is the high language for all formal official functions and the only language taught in all schools at all levels. As more and more of the younger generation Singaporeans are going through the formal educational system, the trend toward the increasing use of English in all domains seems sure to continue.

The other official language, Tamil, which was chosen to represent the Indian population in Singapore, is in a rather weak position. The Indian community in Singapore is not only small but also diversified in language and religion. As more and more Indian families are shifting to using English as the home language, the position of Tamil appears to be weakening. Its official status may be seen as predominantly token and symbolic, and its future deserves close observation.

Mandarin Chinese is not the mother tongue of the majority of the Chinese. Yet historically, the national language of China has long been accepted by the Chinese in Singapore (and, indeed, Southeast Asia) as the language to officially represent the ethnic Chinese. It is therefore the language taught as a subject and used as the medium of instruction in Chinese schools. It is also used among the Chinese-educated as the high language for official and formal functions. For informal occasions, Hokkien, the mother tongue of the major dialect group, has long been the lingua franca, highly functional in many social domains. Since 1979, a campaign to promote the learning and use of Mandarin in place of Chinese dialects has been launched. The implications of the Mandarin campaign in relation to the identity problem of the Chinese in Singapore are discussed later.

From the preceding discussion, it is clear that Singapore society is characterized by the coexistence of several competitive great traditions. There is, at the same time, the lack of a strong indigenous host culture and host language. It is quite unlikely, therefore, that there can be rapid cultural and linguistic assimilation, with the Singapore society as the melting pot, among the heterogenous population. Cultural and linguistic pluralism has been adopted by the leadership and accepted by the majority of the population as the guiding policy in this multiethnic society.

THE POLICY OF MULTILINGUALISM

The guiding sociolinguistic policy in Singapore is best described and expressed as multilingualism, which officially prescribes that all four official languages are to be treated as equals. Thus, all official languages can be used in parliamentary debates with instant interpretation provided. Signs

in government offices and on certain forms for official purposes are provided in all four languages. The official languages are also taught as subjects and used as mediums of instruction in schools, either as the first or
second language. In public communications (television, radio broadcast-
ing, and the press), messages in all four official languages are available for
the multiethnic population.

In actual practice, however, few would argue that the four official languages can be treated as precisely equal, and it is known that some are
"more equal" than others. As indicated above, English is clearly becoming
the dominant working language. Signs in the new Changi airport and in
new housing estates are given only in English. Income tax forms are
printed with instructions given in English and Chinese, and the counseling
sessions offered by the family planning authority are available in English,
Mandarin, and Malay. For efficiency in communication and for economy,
the trend seems to be moving toward the increasing parallel use of English
and Mandarin Chinese, to the extent that bilingualism in Singapore is
coming to mean English and Mandarin Chinese rather than other combi-
nations.

During the colonial time and the early period after independence in
1965, there were in Singapore four distinct educational systems, each using one of the official languages as the major medium of instruction. In
1965, 62.3% of the pupils in the first grade of primary school were registered in English-medium schools, 28.6% in Chinese-medium schools,
8.9% in Malay schools, and only 0.2% in Indian (Tamil-medium) schools
(*Straits Times*, 1977). The trend since independence (in fact, since long
before independence) has been for more and more parents to send their
children to English-medium schools. Thus, in 1981, as many as 89.2% of
the Primary 1 pupils were enrolled in schools using English as the major
medium of instruction; the rest (10.8%) were in Chinese schools (Ministry
of Education, 1982:10).

It must be noted, however, that the educational system in Singapore
puts much emphasis on bilingual education. All pupils are required to
learn two official languages, both in language classes and as teaching languages for certain subjects from Primary 1 onward. The two languages are
English and one of the three ethnic languages. Thus, all Chinese students,
whether they are enrolled in English or Chinese schools, are required to
learn Chinese and English. The difference between so-called English-medium and Chinese-medium schools is only in the ratio of teaching hours
allocated to the two languages. It is no longer legitimate to talk about the
coexistence of four language streams in Singapore's educational system. A
common Singapore-type school is emerging with up to 90% of pupils in
the English-medium schools. The distinction between the Chinese-edu-

cated and the English-educated Chinese is becoming meaningless among young Singaporeans.

The teaching of two official languages—which often means two new languages for the majority of Chinese pupils, since most families do not use either English or Mandarin at home—is a demanding task for both teachers and pupils. Language teaching has long been a major and difficult educational issue for the Ministry of Education in Singapore. While proficiency in both the first and second school languages are important criteria for promotion at all educational levels, the emphasis is no doubt stronger in English than in the other language, especially at the higher educational levels, that is, preuniversity (high-school juniors and seniors) and university. (The National University of Singapore, the only university in the republic, uses English as the medium of instruction except in language courses.) It is a common concern among the older generation Chinese with Chinese educational backgrounds that the standard of Chinese among young Singaporeans will be far too low to sustain a viable literacy tradition.

The mass media in Singapore are also characterized by multilingualism (Kuo, 1978a). For newspaper readership, Chinese and English language papers attract about the same number of readers. But the trend appears to be favoring English. As far as Chinese language dailies are concerned, although circulation has been increasing in recent years, there is serious concern that it may begin to decline soon as older readers are replaced by the basically English-educated younger generation who are more proficient in English and who tend to choose the English newspaper as the major source of information.

As far as television broadcasts and movies are concerned, Mandarin programs have been highly popular among the Chinese. Recent ratings of TV viewership showed that all of the 10 most popular TV programs are in Mandarin. It may be argued that mandarin is being sustained and promoted through the active working of a popular culture. This is an interesting contrast to the promotion of English supported by official and formal channels such as schools and government functions.

In Singapore, the policy of multilingualism at the societal level is translated into the policy of bilingualism at the individual level. Each student and, in fact, each responsible citizen, is expected to be proficient in English and his or her ethnic language. The English language is expected to provide an access to Western technology for economic and social progress, and moreover, it is to become the common means of communication (lingua franca) for the whole population and for the development of a supraethnic identity. At the same time, learning ethnic languages assures that emotional attachments to cultural roots and traditions can be maintained and the virtues of Asian values can be retained.

The language policy articulated and implemented in Singapore is based on the assumption that English is functional for technological advancement and Mandarin for the maintenance of cultural roots and traditional values. However, the rhetorical arguments presented to promote the policy often go beyond the simple functional distinction between the two languages. It is at times argued that English can be an effective medium in the teaching of Asian values, such as Confucian ethics; meanwhile, since the advent of the Speak Mandarin Campaign, Mandarin has been promoted not only for its cultural values but also for its potential economic utility in the anticipated expansion of trade relations with mainland China.

THE TREND OF LANGUAGE SHIFT

The Chinese in Singapore are heterogeneous in dialect background. They identify themselves and are identified by others as belonging to different dialect groups. The maintenance of dialects is supported by the home environment and institutions such as clan associations and traditional occupational organizations. However, increasingly, the trend of social change has been such that Mandarin and English are gaining institutional support from schools, mass media, and formal working environments. At the same time, interdialect and interethnic mixes in residence (public housing), education, occupation, and marriage are exerting pressure for language shift and threatening the strength of dialect group identity.

In Singapore, all Chinese are identified as belonging to one of the dialect groups. Yet some of the Chinese belonging to a certain dialect group may no longer retain that dialect as their mother tongue. In the 1957 census, when the detailed information on both dialect group background and mother tongue was gathered, it was reported that various dialect groups demonstrated a different degree of mother tongue retention (Kuo, 1978b). For instance, 99.1% of those who identified themselves as belonging to the Cantonese group reported that they had learned Cantonese as their mother tongue. This is in contrast to the Foochows and the Hokchias, of whom only 83.7% and 83.4%, respectively, said they had retained their own dialect as the mother tongue. In other words, more than 16% of the Foochows and Hokchias has shifted to having other dialects or languages as their mother tongue.

The type of mother tongue transition reported in the 1957 census could have been the result of a number of factors. For instance, the change in language use might have occurred several generations ago. Generally, Chinese people in Singapore tend to retain their dialect group identity, as a label at least, even after they have ceased to speak the given dialect as a mother tongue at home. This is the case for the Baba Hokkiens, for instance, who still retain their Hokkien identity but who, many generations ago, shifted to using Baba Malay as the language learned and used at home (Png, 1969).

A second possibility is that the language shift occurred as a result of interdialect group marriage when, for example, a Cantonese woman married a Hakka man and continued to use Cantonese to her husband and later to her children, making Cantonese the principal language at home. In such a case, as far as the husband is concerned, a generational language shift has happened between his mother tongue and that of his children. The children, who are by definition Hakkas, have actually acquired their mother's mother tongue, Cantonese in this case, as their mother tongue.

Since 1965, a more distinct pattern of language shift seems to have emerged with government policy support (especially in education) for the official languages, suggesting a trend toward the increasing acceptance of English and/or Mandarin among the Chinese.

In the 1980 census, while no mother tongue data similar to those in the 1957 census were gathered, statistics were obtained with regard to the principal language used at home. According to the census statistics (Khoo, 1981), 10.2% of the Chinese reported Mandarin as the major language used among the family members at home; another 7.9% reported that English was the principal language used. In other words, of all the Chinese who have come from various dialect group backgrounds, almost 20% had adopted either Mandarin or English as the principal home language; many more are using either of these two official languages in addition to one of the Chinese dialects at home. It can be suggested that a large proportion of the Chinese in Singapore, especially among the better educated, are shifting to using either Mandarin or English, not only as the major home language but also as a mother tongue for the younger generation. The pattern and the trend appear to be consistent with Fishman's observation: "Ultimately, the language of school and government replaces the language of home and neighborhood, precisely because it comes to provide status in the latter domains as well as in the former, due to the extensive social change to which home and neighborhood have been exposed" (Fishman, 1972:102).

Such a language shift in the home domain is not only indicative of a general pattern of language shift at the societal level; what is far more significant is the impact of such a trend to changes in the identity orientation among the Chinese in Singapore. In this connection, the Speak Mandarin Campaign underway since 1979 deserves careful assessment.

THE CHINESE DILEMMA

The Speak Mandarin campaign was launched in 1979 with the full support of Chinese community leaders and endorsed by the political leadership represented by none other than the Prime Minister himself. The Prime Minister spoke in Mandarin, English, and Hokkien at the opening ceremony. In his English speech, he began by saying, "Chinese Singaporeans face a dilemma." (*Straits Times*, 1979:1). In his analysis of the language trend in Singapore, Lee Kuan Yew pointed out that English is to be accepted by all as the "common language between different ethnic Singaporeans." He continued, "And if we continue to use dialects, then English will become the common language between Chinese of different groups." The choice is therefore between English-plus-dialect and English-plus-Mandarin for the Chinese. And he concluded, "Logically, the decision is obvious. Emotionally, the choice is painful" (*Straits Times*, 1979:1).

The objective of the Speak Mandarin Campaign, therefore, is to promote the use of Mandarin to replace Chinese dialects among the Chinese. It strengthens the position of Mandarin as a symbol of Chinese identity at a time when the status of Chinese education is being threatened. As such, it has aroused some suspicion not only among the other groups in Singapore but also from neighboring countries. To dispel such feelings, government leaders have had to reassure the population repeatedly that the campaign was meant only for the Chinese Singaporeans and purely for instrumental (communication and education) objectives.

The campaign has also caused some resistance from both the dialect-speaking (mostly older generation) and the English-educated (mostly younger generation) Chinese. What has been carefully designed for the promotion of Mandarin to replace dialects turns out to have become a tug of war among the three languages. While many dialect speakers struggle to resist any change in language habits, some are obviously persuaded or are under pressure to make a shift. For those making the shift, however, there is no guarantee that they are shifting to Mandarin, as planned, and not to English. Judging from the trend in education and the overall emphasis on English, it is clear that English is in a strong position to compete with Mandarin to become the common language among the Chinese in the future.

To analyze the situation from the point of view of language policy, several dilemmas are confronted by the policy maker. First, the continued use of dialects is seen to be a divisive force in the Chinese community and is thus considered undesirable. But due to the strong tradition and mass basis of dialects in Singapore, a great part of Chinese cultural traditions and values are closely associated with and transmitted through dialects and not through Mandarin. As a result, the weakening of dialects may, in fact, mean the weakening of the cultural base.

Second, when Mandarin is stressed as providing a common ground for the retention and promotion of Chinese traditions and values, the emphasis often arouses the worry that the use of Mandarin may unduly encourage strong chauvinistic feelings. The policy of multilingualism and multiethnicism leads to the danger of cultural involution, as Benjamin (1976) puts it. When each ethnic group looks inward and highlights its cultural distinctiveness, the cultivation of a national identity beyond the ethnic level tends to be thwarted.

Finally, among the Chinese, the functional importance of English as the language for educational advancement and occupational mobility is accepted by most and is well reflected in the increasing percentage of parents sending their children to English-medium schools. It is also understood that English has to become the language for wider communication across ethnic boundaries. Yet, the Chinese in Singapore are warned that the use of English must not mean blind adoption of Western values. The learning of Mandarin is thus promoted to provide a cultural ballast to guard against undesirable Western influences. The Speak Mandarin Campaign has again reminded the Chinese of their common ethnic and cultural identity and inevitably leads to a stronger consciousness of ethnic distinctiveness. It satisfies the need for sentimental attachments to the ethnic culture; it also arouses some uneasiness among the non-Chinese in Singapore.

LANGUAGE AND IDENTITY: SOME CONSIDERATIONS

The sociolinguistic pattern of the Chinese community today is such that dialects are retained as the ingroup language used at home and with members of the same dialect group. Mandarin is encouraged for interdialect group communication and is thus an outgroup language. But, from the perspective of the Chinese as an ethnic group, Mandarin is also an ingroup language, wheras English is an outgroup language for interethnic group communication, although it is also used neutrally as the working language for many functions.

It appears, therefore, that dialects are associated with dialect group identity and Mandarin with Chinese identity. What remains to be seen is the ascending status of English as it is accepted and associated with the emerging Singapore national identity. The English language has the advantage of being neutral and supra-ethnic; it is an international language serving important instrumental functions. The major unsolved problem is the question of authenticity in a young nation whereby sentimental attachments of the population to the ethnic identity remain strong.

The Chinese in Singapore can thus be described as having multiple and overlapping identities: A Hokkien is not only a Hokkien but also a Chinese and a Singaporean. Different situations then call for the display of different identities. The three distinctive identities may also be seen to be associated with different cultural traditions. To the extent that cultural traditions of the Singaporean Chinese as manifested in folk beliefs and practices are transmitted over the generations through the use of dialects and the activities of dialect groups, the dialect group identity may be said to be attached to the more mundane (Little) traditions of Chinese culture. However, Mandarin, as the official language (of China and Singapore), has a closer association with the Great tradition of Chinese literature, philosophy, and value systems. Chinese ethnic identity, because it is associated with Chinese education and competence in the use of Mandarin, is thus reinforced by its attachment to the great tradition of Chinese culture.

The case of the Singapore national identity and its presumed association with the competence and use of English is more ambiguous. Since the promotion of English in Singapore is often articulated in reference to its functions in modern technology and development, it can perhaps be argued that the English language is associated with modern culture and is thus conducive to the emergence of Singapore as a modern state.

The strength of attachment to each of the three identities appears to vary from individual to individual. In this sense, the Chinese population is heterogeneous even though all of its members are Chinese and Singaporeans. Traditionally, the dialect group identity was the most important; in fact, it remains so today for some Chinese of the older generation. The ethnic (Chinese) identity, however, is often associated with the experience of Chinese education and the ability to appreciate Chinese literary tradition, especially for those who went through the educational system before indepenence. At the same time, the new Singapore national identity is being actively cultivated through a variety of mass campaigns and public policy measures. There have been some encouraging signs of its success.

The problem is complicated because both dialect group and ethnic group identities tend to extend beyond the state boundaries. Dialect group-based associations in Singapore, for instance, keep close contact with their counterparts in Malaysia. Common identity as Hokkiens, for example, tends to supersede differences in nationality (i.e., being Singaporeans and Malaysians). Similarly, Chinese identity becomes salient when the Chinese from Singapore come into contact with Chinese from other parts of the world. As a contrast, the Singapore national identity does not find this type of reinforcement, and its development tends to be hindered by the short history of the Republic, the small but heterogeneous population, and the lack of an integrated cultural tradition. All these factors have made the development of the national identity a very challenging task for the political leadership of Singapore.

REFERENCES

Benjamin, G.
    1976   The Cultural Logic of "Multiracialism." In R. Hassan (Ed.), *Singapore: A society in transition*. Kuala Lumpur: Oxford University Press.
Fishman, J.
    1972   *The sociology of language*. New York: Newbury.
Khoo, C. K.
    1981   *Language spoken at home* (Release No. 8, Census of population 1980). Singapore: Department of Statistics.
Kuo, E. C. Y.
    1978a   Multilingualism and mass media communications in Singapore. *Asian Survey, 18*(10), 1067–1083.
    1978b   Population ratio, intermarriage and mother tongue retention. *Anthropological Linguistics, 20*(2), 85–93.
Ministry of Education
    1982   *Key education statistics 1982*. Singapore: Education Statistics Section.
Png, P. S.
    1969   The Straits Chinese in Singapore: A case of local identity and socio-cultural accommodation. *Journal of Southeastern Asian History, 10*(1), 95–114.
Saw, S. H.
    1982   *Demographic trends in Singapore* (Census Monograph No. 1). Singapore: Department of Statistics.
Straits Times (Singapore)
    1977   February 26, p. 1.
    1979   September 8, p. 1.

CHAPTER 14

Social Stress and Coping Behavior in Hong Kong

Rance P. L. Lee

INTRODUCTION

Among the central features of Hong Kong society since 1950 are rapid population growth coupled with phenomenal economic progress in a relatively stable social and political environment.

It has been estimated that Hong Kong had a total population of about a quarter of a million at the end of the nineteenth century and about 2 million at the middle of the twentieth. In 1981, there were over 5.1 million people. The surplus of births over deaths was a dominant factor in the population growth (Ng, 1981); nevertheless, it should be noted that the natural increase rate declined from 2.4% in 1951 to 1.2% in 1981. Another important component of population growth is the increase in net immigration, particularly during certain periods of time (Chan, 1981). Two large-scale immigration waves during the approximate periods of 1945–1947 and 1949–1952, for instance, brought over 1 million people from mainland China to Hong Kong. In more recent years, a new surge of immigration has taken place, accounting for about one-fifth of the population growth.

CHINESE CULTURE
AND MENTAL HEALTH

Concomitant with the rapid population growth has been the miraculous economic progress in Hong Kong since 1950 (Lin, Lee, and Simonis, 1979). As of 1981, the per capita gross domestic product was HK$26,260 (about U.S.$4,600). In terms of constant market prices, this represents a five-fold increase. This economic progress is due primarily to industrial and commercial developments. At present, only 2% of the working population is engaged in the primary sector.

Another striking feature of Hong Kong is the remarkable stability in social and political order (Kuan, 1979), which is obviously a favorable condition for economic and population growth. Since 1950, Hong Kong has not experienced any enduring, large-scale revolution or political upheaval (although there were riots in the late 1960s); nor has it experienced industrial disputes in more recent years.

Economic growth, together with social and political stability, has helped upgrade the living standard of the general population. For instance, it is now rare to find a household without a television set, there are nearly 40 private cars per 1000 people and over 347 telephones per 1000 people, and there is approximately one registered doctor for every 1400 people and four hospital beds per 1000 people. The general health of the people has also improved. From 1951 to 1981, the crude death rate per 1000 dropped from 10.2 to 5.0, while the infant mortality rate per 1000 live births declined from 91.8 to 10.0. The life expectancy at birth is now 72 years for men and 78 years for women.

Nevertheless, the foregoing does not mean that the people of Hong Kong have no worries. Among the social problems that are often regarded by many people in Hong Kong as serious are the housing shortage, violent crime and juvenile delinquency, traffic congestion, illegal immigration, narcotic addiction, environmental pollution, family disorganization, inadequate care for the aged, industrial accidents, and occupational diseases. Since around 1970, emotional distress and mental illness have also emerged as problems of important concern to the people.

According to the annual reports of the government's Department of Medicine and Health (Hong Kong Government, 1966, 1967, 1979, 1980), total outpatient attendance at government and government-assisted psychiatric centers increased more than five times over the past 15 years (from 31,462 in 1965–1966 to 162,176 in 1979–1980), while new outpatient attendance at these centers more than doubled over the same period (from 1728 to 3973). These statistics reveal only the tip of the iceberg, as there were, and still are, numerous cases treated at hospitals, government psychiatric day centers, and private psychiatric clinics. No less importantly, there is a high incidence of people with relatively minor psychiatric problems in the community who do not seek help from psychiatric resources or seek no medical help at all (Chen, 1981).

PREVALENCE OF PSYCHIATRIC STRESS

There have been several psychiatric epidemiological studies in Hong Kong (see Cheung, Chapter 19, this volume). Most of them have dealt with psychiatric patients rather than with general populations. A community-wide study that deserves special attention is the Biosocial Survey undertaken in the mid-1970s (Millar, 1979).

A major feature of the Biosocial Survey was the detection of the true prevalence of psychiatric problems in the urban sector (90% of the total population) of Hong Kong. A stratified random sample of 3983 household heads between the ages of 20 and 59, of whom approximately 98.5% were Chinese in origin, was interviewed in the summer of 1974. In this chapter, I focus on only these Chinese household heads.

One of the key measures of psychiatric stress in the Biosocial Survey was the 22-item screening scale developed by Langner (1962). The scale deals mainly with relatively mild forms of self-reported psychoneurotic and physiological symptoms. Its Chinese version was found to have an acceptable degree of reliability and validity in the context of Hong Kong (Millar, 1979). It was discovered that about 31.8% (25.0% male and 36.8% female) of the Chinese respondents expressed four or more symptoms. Differences in stress among the various age groups were very small for both male and female repondents (see Table 14.1).

In this connection, it should be reported that Mitchell (1969) and his staff conducted a Family Life Survey in the urban areas of Hong Kong in 1967, interviewing a total of 3966 individuals ages 18 and over. One of the topics under study was emotional illness that was measured by 11 items from Langner's (1962) scale. Respondents reporting four or more symptoms were labeled as "emotionally ill." In 1967–1968, Mitchell and his staff also conducted similar studies in urban Bangkok–Thon Buri ($N = 2000$), in Singapore ($N = 2001$), in Taipei ($N = 1000$), and in six major cities of western Malaysia ($n = 1995$). It was found that the comparative prevalence rate of emotional illness in Hong Kong (38%) was higher than that in Taipei (30%) but was lower than that in Malaysia (39%), in Singapore (43%), and in Bangkok (49%). If we take ethnic origin into consideration, the rate among the Hong Kong Chinese (38%) was lower than among the Bangkok Thai (53%), the Singapore Malay (51%), the Singapore Indians (49%), the Bangkok Chinese (43%), the Malaysian Malay (43%) and the Malaysian Indians (40%), and was about the same as among the Malaysian Chinese (38%). The rate among the Hong Kong Chinese, however, was slightly higher than that among the Singapore Chinese (36%) and was substantially higher than that among the Taipei Chinese (30%). These findings suggest that in the late 1960s, emotional problems among the Chinese in the urban sector of Hong Kong were

Table 14.1   Percentage of Males and Females Reporting Four or
More Symptoms among Different Social–Demographic Groups[a]

Groups	Male %	Male n	Female %	Female n
Age				
20–29	26.1	529	36.6	563
30–39	23.8	311	29.4	524
40–49	24.0	411	40.5	692
50–59	25.6	394	39.9	471
Population density				
High	27.4	898	39.9	346
Medium	21.7	471	35.9	577
Low	23.8	235	28.6	1242
Economic level				
Low	29.6	260	47.0	338
Low-middle	27.5	403	39.6	560
High-middle	24.9	482	36.6	658
High	19.3	488	29.1	619
Education				
No schooling	21.8	101	40.4	684
Primary or tutoring	25.7	794	35.4	1011
Secondary	26.0	595	36.4	448
Postsecondary	18.6	183	29.0	107
Status inconsistency				
Underachievers	29.6	385	46.0	263
Consistents	24.9	610	37.6	646
Overachievers	21.7	612	34.6	1237

[a] From Millar (1979).

generally not as serious as those among the people in some other Asian cities but that the Hong Kong Chinese suffered from greater stress than did the Chinese in at least two other cities: Singapore and Taipei.

We may then ask, What are the major sources of emotional distress among Hong Kong Chinese? Of course, many factors might have contributed to the relatively high level of psychiatric stress in Hong Kong. In this chapter, I focus on two social factors: the high level of population density and the high level of material aspiration.

HIGH-DENSITY LIVING AND ADJUSTMENT

Hong Kong has a total land area of 1037 square kilometers. The overall population density is thus over 5000 persons per square kilometer. In some districts, the population density even exceeds 160,000 per square kilometer.

It is widely believed by people in Hong Kong and in many other societies that high-density living is a major source of stress. Arguments in support of this belief include that it produces excessive stimulation, restricts behavioral freedom, and causes imbalance between supply and demand of resources (J. Freedman, 1975). Since the density of population in Hong Kong is exceedingly high, whether or not it actually results in psychiatric stress deserves careful, systematic study.

A central concern of the Biosocial Survey was to examine the relationship between population density and psychiatric stress in urban Hong Kong. In the study, both neighborhood density (number of persons per hectare in the residential Tertiary Planning Unit) and household density (amount of effective floor space per person in the dwelling unit) were considered and were combined into a composite index of population density with three levels.

It was found that 34.9% of those living in high-density situations suffered from stress, as compared to 29.5% of those living in medium-density situations and to 26.7% of those living in low-density situations. The relationship was statistically significant (chi-square test), although it was relatively mild ($\gamma = +0.17, p < .001$). The relationship remained positive and weak among both male ($\gamma = +0.02$; not significant at the .05 level) and female ($\gamma = +0.15, p < .001$) respondents (Millar, 1979; Table 14.1).

These findings indicate that high-density living does produce stress on the Chinese adults in Hong Kong. The question is, Why was the effect so mild? Millar (1979) proposes that this might be due to the attitude of density tolerance. She found, in fact, that over two-thirds of the respondents were tolerant of high-density living. They made few complaints either about the shortage of space or about being surrounded by a great number of people. Millar also found that the intolerance of high density, rather than high density itself, was clearly a major source of stress in Hong Kong.

The tolerance of high density was found to be particularly prevalent among certain kinds of Chinese people in Hong Kong: the older, the less educated, the poorer, and the immigrants from mainland China. These findings suggest that certain traditional ways of living among the Chinese population may be conducive to the development of density tolerance. In other words, for many generations, the Chinese people may have had special ways of coping with high-density situations and thus could short-circuit the feelings of being overcrowded. But what are the coping mechanisms?

In her study of child socialization in a Hong Kong fishing village, Ward

(1970) suggests that the early habituation to frustration and interference and the inculcation of self-control of aggressive behavior and of emotional self-reliance during childhood are some of the possible factors that contribute significantly to the success with which Chinese adapt to conditions of overcrowding. From his observation of a few traditional Chinese households in Hong Kong and Penang, Anderson (1972) discovered several coping mechanisms in Chinese culture, such as positive value given to several generations sharing the same dwelling unit, a definition of privacy in terms of primary groups (e.g., family and close friends) rather than of individuals, a conformity to a hierarchy of seniority (e.g., the rule of "elders first"), and an avoidance of social or emotional interactions among nonrelated persons in public places.

The observations of Ward (1970) and Anderson (1972) result primarily from studies of rural populations. The extent to which their observations are applicable to the urban dwellers has yet to be determined. As a Chinese growing up in the urban context of Hong Kong, I have gained the impression that the following social customs may be helping the urban Chinese to cope with the pressure of high-density living:

1. Many ordinary Chinese families are accustomed to using space within their dwelling units for multiple purposes, such as sleeping, dining, reading, chatting, and playing games. They are also used to equipping their dwelling units with compact furniture, such as double-deck or sofa beds, folding chairs, and folding tables. All these customs allow the family to continue normal life without feeling a lack of space.

2. In the private housing sector of Hong Kong, it is not unusual to find several nonrelated families sharing the same apartment. Under such circumstances, the families usually develop conventions about who can use which facilities (e.g., kitchen, bathroom) at what time. Such a practice of scheduling their activities helps the dwellers avoid competing for use of the limited spatial resources. Moreover, because of the social sanctions against peeping and eavesdropping, each family can usually preserve privacy by setting up wooden or other temporary partitions.

3. It has been a custom of many Chinese families to meet with and to entertain friends in restaurants rather than homes. Such a widely accepted practice reduces the need for more space within the dwelling unit.

4. It is difficult for couples living in a congested setting to engage in sexual relationships. To meet this basic need, an increasing number of hourly rate hotels and apartments in the city areas have developed. As the rents are relatively inexpensive, people can use these facilities at least once a while.

5. Playing *majong* and watching television have become exceedingly

popular in Hong Kong. Such types of leisure activity, which make intensive use of the limited space, allow people to enjoy themselves for long hours without feeling the spatial constraint.

6. The first-come-first-served principle has been increasingly enforced in many realms of public service, such as lining up for the bus, for the canteen, and for the purchase of lottery or cinema tickets. People in a crowded setting can thus be structured to meet their needs in an ordered fashion.

7. Many Chinese individuals accept a relatively close physical distance between themselves and others. As a result, they may not find it unpleasant to walk, sit, or talk in a congested situation.

The preceding observations have yet to be elaborated and confirmed by systematic studies in a more controlled setting or with more representative samples. Nevertheless, they suggest that the Hong Kong Chinese may have special ways of coping with the strain of enormous density. Consequently, the effect of high-density living on their mental health is less adverse than might be expected.

MATERIAL ASPIRATION AND ADJUSTMENT

In addition to high-density living, another factor that may contribute to emotional distress among the Hong Kong Chinese is the great need for material success coupled with its discrepancies with actual achievement.

The Hong Kong Chinese are typically achievement oriented. One of the most popular sayings in Hong Kong is, *Wu hao zhi shu* (Never fall behind others). It appears that striving for greater success than others has become a dominant cultural value in the society. The traditional Chinese value of *zhi zu* (contentment with one's lot) has been abandoned by many of the Hong Kong Chinese. From a stratified random sample of 1065 Chinese household heads in an urban district, for instance, Shively (1972) found that achievement was considered not important at all by a very small portion (5.2%) of the respondents. It should be underscored that an overwhelming majority of Shively's respondents were working-class individuals. Most likely, middle- and upper-class Chinese would have a greater need for achievement.

The great need for achievement has a double-edged significance to the individuals in society. It can be a source of social and economic progress, but it can also be a source of emotional distress. Failing to fulfill the need for achievement would lead to feelings of frustration and symptoms of stress (Merton, 1959). This postulate has been supported by a number of studies in the West (see, e.g., Hollingshead, Ellis, and Kirby, 1954; Kleiner and Parker, 1963; Dunham, 1964; Rinehart, 1968). The question is whether or not this is the case among the Hong Kong Chinese. The Biosocial Survey hypothesized that those Hong Kong Chinese who have achieved a lower level of social–economic success are more likely to suffer from stress symptoms. This is so because individuals in lower social–economic strata are less able to achieve their aspirations.

In the Biosocial Survey, the social–economic factor was divided into two components: (1) the educational level of the individual, and (2) the economic condition of the individual's household.

It was found that of respondents with four or more symptoms, 38.0% were in the no schooling category, 31.1% in the elementary school or private tutoring category, 30.9% in the secondary school category, and 22.4% in the postsecondary school category. It is clear that the less-educated individuals were more likely to suffer from stress ($\gamma = -0.12$; $p < .001$). Based on the data in Table 14.1, the relationship remained negative among both male ($\gamma = -0.03$; not significant) and female ($\gamma = -0.08$; insignificant) respondents, although it became weaker.

The household's economic level was indicated by housing quality, total income per month, and material possessions (for details, see Lee, 1981b). These indicators were combined into a composite index with four levels: low, low-middle, high-middle, and high. Respondents with four or more symptoms in these levels were 39.5%, 34.6%, 31.6%, and 24.9%, respectively. This inverse relationship between stress symptoms and economic condition is relatively mild ($\gamma = -0.17$) but is statistically significant ($p < .001$). The inverse was true among both male ($\gamma = -0.15$, $p < 0.001$) and female ($\gamma = -0.19$, $p < 0.001$) respondents. These findings indicate that the economic level of a household is associated with stress: The worse the economic situation, the more likely it is that the individual will suffer from emotional distress.

These findings about the adverse effects of educational and economic disadvantages lend support to the postulate that aspiration–achievement discrepancies may be a source of emotional distress in Hong Kong. Nevertheless, it should be noted that the effects were relatively mild.

Another way to study the effects of social–economic conditions is to delineate the extent to which, and the ways in which, the different types of status of a single individual are consistent or inconsistent with one another (Martin, 1965). Studies in the West have shown that status inconsistency produces stress on the individuals concerned (e.g., Jackson, 1962; Meile and Haese, 1969; House, 1975; Hornung, 1977).

In a reanalysis that focused on the inconsistency between educational level and economic status in the Biosocial Survey data, it was found that the difference between consistents and inconsistents in stress symptoms was negligible and that this was the case among both male and female respondents. Moreover, neither the magnitude of inconsistency or consistency (1 point versus 2 or 3 points difference) was sufficient to cause a difference in stress (Lee, 1979). However, the direction of status inconsistency did affect the prevalence of stress symptoms: 36.1% of the underachievers (high education and low economic status) reported four or more symptoms, as compared to 30.3% of the overachievers (low education and high economic status). The percentage difference (36.3 − 30.3 = 6.0) was statistically significant (Z-test, $p < 0.01$). The overachievers did not differ significantly from the consistents in stress symptoms (30.3% − 31.4% = 1.1%; insignificant), but the underachievers differed significantly from the consistents (36.3% − 31.4% = 4.9%; $p < 0.05$). Moreover, Table 14.1 shows that among both males and females, underachievers were more likely than overachievers and consistents to suffer ($p < 0.050$). These findings indicate that status inconsistency in the direction of underachievement (i.e., economic status lower than educational level relative to other persons) is conducive to stress in urban Hong Kong.

It should be explained that in Hong Kong, educational attainment is often regarded as an investment, while economic success is a reward. When economic status is lower than educational status, statuses are inconsistent in an undesirable direction because achievement fails coincide with expectation. Individuals in this category are considered to be underachievers and are likely to suffer from stress. On the contrary, if material reward is relatively higher than educational investment, the individual is likely to be content. Despite the status inconsistency, overachievers are less likely than underachievers to develop stress symptoms. These findings about the effects of status inconsistency suggest that the high need for achievement, coupled with its discrepancies with actual achievement, is a source of emotional distress in Hong Kong.

The statement that in Hong Kong, education is regarded as a means to economic gain is not meant to deny the long-standing traditional emphasis on the moral value of education in Chinese culture, reflected in the saying, "Study is superior to all other walks of life" (*Wan ban jie xia pin, wei you du shu gao.*) However, other Chinese maxims say "good education leads to official positions" (*xue er you ze shi*), and "golden houses and beautiful wives will come through study" (*Shu zhong zi you huang jin Wu, Shu zhong zi you yan ru yu*). Hence, it cannot be overstated that in traditional Chinese society, education was considered important not only for its moral value but also for its pragmatic value.

The dual value of education is, in fact, shared by the Hong Kong Chinese (Lau, 1981a; Ward, 1980). Probably because of this dual value, Hong

Kong Chinese parents place a great deal of emphasis on schooling. This great enthusiasm has led to the great intensity of academic competition and examination pressures in the schools, from kindergarten to the university (Tu, 1981). The extent to which the striving for better education has placed emotional stress on students and parents has yet to be systematically studied. However, one thing is sure: The number of parents and students making hotline telephone calls to voluntary service centers for advice about their worries and anxieties in relation to educational pressures is increasing. (*Hong Kong Standard,* 1981; Tu, 1981).

As mentioned previously, the need for educational achievement is partly, if not largely, a result of material concern. To my knowledge, the kind of achievement that is most highly valued by the Hong Kong Chinese is material success. It is often said, "With money, [one is] a dragon; without it, a worm" (*You qian yi tiao long, Wu qian yi tiao chong*) and, "Men die for wealth; birds for food" (*Ren wei cai si, niao wei shi wang*). The Hong Kong Chinese are so concerned with wealth that when they meet during the Chinese Lunar New Year festival, the first thing they usually do is bless each other: *Gong xi fa cai* (May you make a fortune). It should be noted that until the 1960s, the popular New Year blessing was, *Tian ding fa cai* (May you have more children and more wealth). Apparently the first half of the blessing has been discarded, which reflects a material concern: In the present social–economic structure, it is easier for a small family than for a larger family to accumulate wealth and have a better standard of living (Ng, 1981).

The preceding observations about the Hong Kong Chinese preoccupation with wealth are supported by at least two empirical studies. Lau (1981a) studied a random sample of 550 adults from the urban population and found that even if the respondents were already well fed and well clothed, a majority (58.9%) still expressed yearnings for more money, while a minority (29.6%) did not. Moreover, Lee, Cheung, and Cheung (1979) reanalyzed the Biosocial Survey data and found that material success was indeed an important source of life satisfaction among adult respondents and that this was the case for both males and females and for people in all age categories.

Despite the great need for material achievement, the Biosocial Survey findings indicate that social–economic disadvantages were mildly associated with psychiatric stress. Why is this so? It cannot be adequately explained by the role of the government or by the role of intermediate voluntary organizations. In Hong Kong, neither the government nor the voluntary organizations have given the socially and economically disadvantaged a sufficient quantity of resources to relieve their stress.

From 1950 to 1970, the government maintained not only an economically, but also a socially, noninterventionist policy. It is only since the 1970s that the government has begun to expand its scope of welfare services, moving from the mere prevention of starvation toward community care and mutual help (Hodge, 1981). Even so, the social security system is still relatively underdeveloped compared to those in many Western industrial societies (Chow, 1981). Moreover, most Hong Kong Chinese, particularly those in the lower social–economic strata, do not perceive that the government has been a significant channel for need satisfaction (Lau, 1981a; Lau and Ho, 1980).

The Chinese people are well known for their practices of establishing voluntary organizations for material aid and for mediating between the government and the governed. In Hong Kong, there are a substantial number of such organizations as clan associations, district associations, chambers of commerce, and *kaifong* (neighborhood) associations. Since the late 1960s, however, these organizations have ceased to function in an effective way. They are limited in the range of services provided and are also quite small in size (Lau, 1981b).

Since neither the social policy of the government nor the functioning of the intermediate organizations can adequately explain the mild relationship between social–economic disadvantage and emotional stress, let us turn to some other possible mechanisms. From a sample survey in urban Hong Kong, Shively and Shively (1972) found that individuals with lower social–economic status were more oriented to traditional Chinese values. Hence, it may be that some traditional Chinese cultural elements provide mechanisms for the people to cope with the stress resulting from excessive economic striving. In this chapter, I suggest two possible mechanisms: (1) the practice of constructing personal primary networks for the satisfaction of material needs, and (2) the belief in the mythical explanation and manipulation of life's vicissitudes.

Like the situations in many societies elsewhere, industrialization has led to the rise of individualism (Lau, 1981a) and of the nuclear family system in Hong Kong (Wong, 1975). This, however, does not mean that the Hong Kong Chinese are losing their social ties with friends and relatives. On the contrary, primary networks are formed frequently, and these personal relations are particularly strong among nuclear family members. Apparently, this is also the case in many other contemporary societies (Firth, Hubert, and Forge, 1969; Schimdt, Guasti, Landé, and Scott, 1977; Wolf, 1966).

Because of its emphasis on personal concern and mutual support, the primary network can help satisfy the expressive, or emotional, needs of the individual. And, no less importantly, the relations are often so enduring and so dependable that they can be used by the individual as valuable channels for achieving instrumental or material aims. Hence, for both expressive and instrumental reasons, informal primary ties can be found in any society.

In traditional, preindustrial societies the formation of the primary network may be based mainly on expressive considerations. Nevertheless, it is unlikely that the instrumental implication of primary ties would be overlooked by the individuals involved. There were, for instance, many cases of using personal relations for accomplishing things in traditional China (Lau and Lee, 1981; Yang, 1959). In contemporary industrial societies, the rise of instrumentalism has made many people place a greater emphasis upon material considerations in the formation of primary networks. The personal relations are needed and are even deliberately developed, largely because of their pragmatic rather than moral value. As argued previously, the personal bonds are often so enduring that they can be depended upon to achieve one's instrumental needs. Hence, to maintain and also to widen the personal primary networks is an important strategy for increasing one's capabilities of adaptation and advancement; and such a strategy is particularly essential for the individual struggling in a highly competitive and ever-changing, complex society (for related arguments in the context of Chinese society, see King and Bond, Chapter 3, this volume).

The kinds of primary networks that are deliberately constructed for the purpose of achieving material needs can be called *instrumental primary networks*. The composition of each network may include a variety of people, such as relatives, neighbors, friends, and coworkers. What is of importance is that these people have close ties, largely, though not exclusively, on the basis of material considerations. Thus, there is usually a strong emphasis on the norm of mutual protection and obligation, particularly in relation to economic matters.

The construction of instrumental primary networks is a widespread practice in Hong Kong, a society in which material success is of overriding concern to the people. For instance, from empirical studies and extensive review of the research literature, Lau (1981a) found that an essential feature of contemporary Hong Kong society is what he calls "utilitarianistic familism" a kind of instrumental primary network. At the core of each network are members of a nuclear family who recruit other individuals or groups (both relatives and nonrelatives) into the network. The recruitment, however, is largely based on material rather than nonmaterial consideration, and, as a result, there is usually a great emphasis on economic interdependence among members of the network. The composition of the network is always fluid and undefined, which permits the core members to meet their various economic requirements in a changing environment.

Lau's empirical studies reveal that the Hong Kong Chinese do care about their families, as well as about their friends and their rather remote relatives. But what should be noted is that many of them do not seem to value these ties merely for the sake of the ties themselves: It is not uncommon for them to bear in mind their material interests in the course of constructing and maintaining the larger personal networks. It should be added that many tactics can be employed to create and maintain this kind of personal tie. One of the most popular tactics is the formation of pseudokinship bonds (see also King and Bond, Chapter 3, this volume). As I describe in Lee (1981a: 79–80):

> In letters or conversations, friends usually address each other in kinship terms, such as 'elder brother', 'younger sister', or 'uncle'. Employer and employees in the same firm often perceive themselves as a team of 'brothers' [xiong di ban] Government officials are often called 'parent officials' [fu mu gong] whereas the people are 'children-people' [zi min]. Persons who are not blood-related may go through a ceremony of a sacred nature and become 'sworn' [jie bai] brothers or sisters. With the use of a sacred ritual, two individuals may, by mutual consent, form a 'sworn' father–son [qi fu zi] or mother–daughter [qi mu nu] relationship.

In the context of Hong Kong, these various forms of pseudokinship relationship are often constructed on the basis of instrumental considerations (King and Leung, 1975; Lau, 1979; Lee, 1981a). This may also be a common practice in other contemporary Chinese societies (Gallin and Gallin, 1977).

The practice of constructing instrumental primary networks is particularly widespread in the lower social–economic strata of Hong Kong (Lau, 1981a), and this may have important implications for the people's mental health. As argued previously, each of the networks is so rationally constructed and its membership so fluidly composed that the persons or families involved can depend on it as an effective channel for the satisfaction of their material needs, such as the pooling of human and material resources for business ventures and for the rendering or receiving of financial and other forms of aids in time of need. Because of laissez-faire economic attitudes, the Hong Kong Chinese have to undertake fierce economic competition in order to promote their material interests and to overcome their economic uncertainties. It is the instrumental primary network that has given them and their families, particularly those in the lower social–economic strata, a sense of economic security and also a chance for economic advancement, thus reducing the likelihood of emotional stress in the process of struggling for success. Of course, this assertion about the relationship between instrumental primary network and stress should, for the time being, be treated as a hypothesis because it requires further empirical verification.

Besides the deliberate construction of instrumental primary networks, another factor that may help reduce emotional stress in the process of struggling for economic success is the use of mythical ideas for explaining and manipulating the environment. It has been commonly assumed that industrialization and urbanization lead to the decline of the influence of supernatural beliefs. However, this may not be the case in an industrial–urban society in which people are repeatedly confronted with social or economic uncertainties. Such is the situation in Hong Kong today: The influence of traditional Chinese religious beliefs and practices remains pervasive.

There are over 350 Chinese temples in Hong Kong, some of which are impressive new buildings. Countless people worship in these temples, particularly during the festivals. During the Tin Hau (Tian Hou) festival, often as many as 250,000 people worship in the approximately 20 Tin Hau temples. The third day of the Lunar New Year is the birthday of the Che Kung (Che Gong) god, and on that day, the Che Kung temple is visited by roughly 100,000 worshippers. Yet, neither the Tin Hau temples nor the Che Kung temple are as popular as the Wong Tai Sin (Huang Da Xian) temple, which is located in the heart of the city and is crowded by worshippers almost every day.

In addition to the temples, there are many households and shops with an ancestral shrine and/or a god shelf. From a survey of 818 households in an urban district, Ng (1975) found ancestral shrines in 64% of the households, the Earth God (Tu Di Shen) in 60%, and the Kitchen God (Zao Jun) in 44%.

There are two forms of supernatural beliefs and practices—*feng-shui* (*feng shui*; geomancy) and *yuan-fen* (*yuan fen*; predestined affinity)—that deserve special mention because, to my knowledge, they are no less popular than the worship of ancestors and deities and yet their possible contributions to mental health have not been explored. Strictly speaking, *feng-shui* and *yuan-fen* are mythical rather than scientific beliefs (M. Freedman, 1979). However, neither is involved with deities, and, in this sense, they differ from the other forms of Chinese religion.

The faith in *feng-shui* is well-known in Chinese society (M. Freedman, 1979). What should be noted is that it has not been driven out by the forces of industrialization and urbanization. It remains widespread at least in the context of the Hong Kong Chinese community. Of course, living in high-density situations, the Hong Kong Chinese can hardly practice *feng-shui* as regards the choice burial site, but they can do so in many other ways. Walking through the streets of Hong Kong, one can easily observe that many shops, factories, and residential buildings have an object—the Eight Diagrams (ba gua, or a pan, a gong, a knife, etc.)—hanging on the outside wall. The display of the object is meant to manipulate the *feng-shui* in such a way that the persons concerned can maintain or achieve a good life. In talking to the Hong Kong Chinese, one finds that many of them still bear in mind the Chinese saying: "One's life is determined first by destiny, second by luck, third by *feng-shui*, fourth by moral conduct, and fifth by education" (*Yi ming, er yun, san feng shui, si ji yin de, wu du shu*). Accordingly, a person's misfortune and success are often explained away in *feng-shui* terms. In order to manipulate *feng-shui* so as to change one's life, people often invite geomancers to advise on the siting, orientation, and arrangement of furniture, and opening dates of domestic and other buildings.

It should be emphasized that in Hong Kong, *feng-shui* appears to be more popular than other forms of Chinese religious practice (M. Freedman, 1979). This is so because *feng-shui* is a preoccupation with success. A person who wishes to ensure continuing success, or to achieve greater success, for self and family cannot afford to ignore the geomantical considerations. And it is the pursuit of success that is of overriding concern to the Hong Kong Chinese.

In addition to *feng-shui*, the Hong Kong Chinese also tend to believe in *yuan-fen* (Lee, in press), in which it is assumed that one's relationships with other people and also with certain objects are predestined. *Yuan-fen*, a key concept of Buddism, has a rich philosophical meaning. As it has been part of daily life in Chinese culture for many centuries, its original meaning has been inevitably modified. In Hong Kong nowadays, the term *yuan-fen* frequently appears in mass media and in daily conversations. Like *feng-shui*, however, *yuan-fen* is largely used as a retrospective explanation of success or failure in interpersonal or person–object relationships. It is widely believed that a man marries a woman simply because the *yuan-fen* exists; if they are divorced subsequently, it is because their *yuan-fen* is over. Similarly, *yuan-fen* is employed to explain one's friendship with some people but not with others, one's seeking treatment from one doctor but not from others, one's love or hate of a particular kind of animal, and one's possession or loss of a valuable product (such as a painting, jade, or antique). According to a Chinese saying, "Where *yuan-fen* exists, a thousand miles puts not asunder; where *yuan-fen* does not exist, nearness cannot unite" (*You yuan qian li neng xiang hui, wu yuan dui men bu xiang feng*). Even economic success or failure can be attributed to one's *yuan-fen* with money or with certain kinds of business undertakings.

Yuan-fen is employed, not merely for retrospective explanation, but, like *feng-shui*, to bring good fortune. This is so because to the Chinese people, *yuan-fen* is not static but is subject to change within one's generation or from one generation to the next. It is believed that to behave morally or to be benevolent to others can help achieve and accumulate *yuan-fen* for oneself as well as for one's family or descendants (*xing shan yi hua yuan*). Moreover, since it is impossible to know one's *yuan-fen* with a particular person or object before testing the relationship, it is necessary to engage actively in relationships in order to search out those with whom one has *yuan-fen*. And since *yuan-fen* may change over time, one should not be discouraged by failure; there is always a second chance. Hence, *yuan-fen* gives people hope: Although at present, one may not have the desired *yuan-fen*, it is obtainable either by moral conduct or by trial and error.

To sum up, Hong Kong has become a highly industrialized urban society, but many of the Chinese residents retain belief in the worship of ancestors and deities and particularly in such concepts as *feng-shui* and *yuan-fen*. It should be emphasized that these beliefs have been found to be more widespread in the lower social–economic strata of Hong Kong (Lee, 1982; Myers, 1981b). Since the beliefs are mythical in nature, many Hong Kong Chinese may not actually believe in them but are nevertheless opportunistic enough to cling to the long-standing wisdom: "Rather believe it to be true than not" (*Ning ke xin qi you, bu ke xin qi wu*). After all, they reason, there is little to lose by worshipping the deities or by observing the *feng-shui* or *yuan-fen*.

An important point about the worship of deities and about the practice of *feng-shui* or *yuan-fen* is that they are often used by believers as meaningful tools for explaining and manipulating life's vicissitudes. They give the believers a sense of comfort, as these people are then able to explain and comprehend what is going on around them. No less importantly, they give believers a sense of security and also a sense of hope in their struggles for success in the highly competitive and ever-changing environment of Hong Kong. As mentioned previously, the need for success is shared by many of the Hong Kong Chinese, and it is the members of the lower social–economic segments who are least likely to achieve their aspirations. However, it is individuals with lower social–economic status who are most likely to worship deities and to observe *feng-shui* and *yuan-fen*. As a result, they may not suffer greatly from the stress of failing to satisfy their achievement needs. In other words, these forms of mythical–religious practice may serve as mechanisms for coping with stressful events.

Of course, whether or not mythical beliefs are actually associated with emotional stress has yet to be directly verified by empirical studies. But it is my hypothesis that when people have to face social–economic uncertainties or risks in a highly competitive industrial–urban environment, they develop mythical beliefs about life's vicissitudes, and that these mythical beliefs can serve as mechanisms for reducing stress resulting from the struggle for success.

CONCLUDING REMARKS: THE FADING OF IMMIGRANT CULTURE

It has been shown that a high-density level of living and a great need for material achievement are characteristic of the Hong Kong Chinese. The Biosocial Survey findings indicate that high-density living and social-economic disadvantage are associated with emotional distress but that the relationship is relatively mild. This mild relationship could be due to the existence of certain coping mechanisms in the Chinese culture, such as cultural norms governing interpersonal adjustments in high-density situations, the deliberate construction of primary networks for need satisfaction, and the adoption of certain supernatural beliefs for the explanation and manipulation of life's vicissitudes. Because people in high-density areas and in lower social–economic strata are more likely to be tradition-oriented, they are more likely to hold to these traditional Chinese methods of coping with stressful events. The question is, Can these coping mechanisms be maintained in the years ahead?

It should be noted that the various sample surveys mentioned in this chapter dealt largely with adults in the mid-1970s. At that time, most of the Chinese adults were first-generation immigrants from mainland China. (The 1976 By-Census Survey estimated that about 66% of Chinese adults ages 20 and over were not born in Hong Kong.) A great majority of them came to Hong Kong before the early 1950s. They had long lived in overcrowded conditions and had long suffered from the social–political turmoil in their homeland. No less importantly, these immigrants were the primary carriers of Chinese cultural traditions. Before coming to Hong Kong, they had acquired a variety of traditional Chinese habits and beliefs.

When the immigrants came to Hong Kong, they met with a highly competitive laissez-faire economy. In view of the hardships they had gone through in their homeland and in view of the fierce economic competition they had to face in the new environment of Hong Kong, they had no choice but to occupy themselves with materialistic interests (Lau, 1981a). As newcomers, many of them drifted to the high-density areas and to the lower social–economic sectors. Nevertheless, they carried with them traditional cultural habits and beliefs that proved appropriate to their adjustment. These cultural habits and beliefs enabled them to tolerate the pressure of high-density living, to form primary networks for need satisfaction, and, no less importantly, to explain away life's vicissitudes in mythical terms so that they could always be hopeful of better times to come. As a result, the ill effects of high-density living and economic struggles were not as strong as they might have been.

The future of Hong Kong, however, does not appear to be this rosy, as the children of the other immigrants seem not to share the habits and attitudes of their parents. Most people in the younger generation were born and brought up in Hong Kong. (According to the 1976 By-Census Survey, about 95% of the Hong Kong Chinese under the age of 20 were born in Hong Kong.) Compared with their immigrant parents, they are less tradition oriented, better educated, and more secure about their lives (Lau and Ho, 1980; Lee, 1981a; Shively and Shively, 1972). Consequently, they have become more demanding than their parents: What they want is not simply a place to live, but the comfort of a spacious and attractive living environment (Myers, 1981a), and not just the satisfaction of material needs, but also the fulfillment of nonmaterial desires (Lee, Cheung, and Cheung, 1979). Failure to achieve these aspirations could lead to emotional disturbance and even political unrest. Since the young do not hold the traditional habits and beliefs of their parents, one wonders what kinds of coping mechanisms they have for dealing with the stress resulting from their extensive demands. This is a topic that deserves serious study. Recent years have already witnessed a growing number of youths who express their uneasiness with their present life situations. It should be noted that the rise of pressure groups and the increasing influence of mass media in the community are likely to make the situation worse. This is so because the pressure groups and the mass media have made the ordinary (i.e., the poor and powerless) people increasingly aware of their misfortunes.

Since the 1970s, the government has tried hard to expand the scope of social services, particularly those (e.g., recreational facilities and educational opportunities) for the young. The government's total expenditure on social services (including education, medical care, housing, welfare, and labor service) in fiscal 1979–1980 was over 5.7 billion Hong Kong dollars, which was 169 times the expenditure in 1950. The government has also made many attempts to decentralize its administrative system so as to understand and meet people's needs in different localities (Lau, 1981b). However, because people's traditional ways of meeting their own needs appear to be disappearing, it is questionable whether or not the government's strategies can effectively accommodate the ever-expanding needs of the generations to come. Perhaps, in addition to the government's administrative accommodation of needs, we should also begin to think of revitalizing and/or inventing mechanisms for the ordinary Chinese to make their own social accommodation of needs (Lau, 1981b). People can rely on the government but should also rely on themselves for coping with life's stressful events. It is the social scientists, together with the psychiatrists, who can and should help people to identify and to design appropriate methods of adjustment.

REFERENCES

Anderson, E. N., Jr.
1972   Some Chinese methods of dealing with crowding. *Urban Anthropology, 1,* 146–151.

Chan, Y. K.
1981   The development of new towns. In A. Y. C. King and R. P. L. Lee (Eds.), *Social life and development in Hong Kong.* Hong Kong: The Chinese University Press.

Chen, C. N.
1981   Mental health and education. In T. P. Khoo (Ed.), *Aspects of mental health care, Hong Kong.* Hong Kong: Mental Health Association of Hong Kong.

Chow, W. S. N.
1981   Social security provision in Singapore and Hong Kong. *Journal of Social Policy, 10*(3), 353–366.

Dunham, H. W.
1964   Anomie and mental disorder. In B. Clinard (Ed.), *Anomie and deviant behavior.* New York: Free Press.

Firth, R. W., Hubert, J., and Forge, A.
1969   *Families and their relatives: Kinship in a middle-class sector of London.* London: Routledge and Kegan Paul.

Freedman, J. L.
1975   *Crowding and behavior.* San Francisco: Freeman.

Freedman, M.
1979   Chinese geomancy: Some observations in Hong Kong. In G. W. Skinner (Ed.), *The study of Chinese society: Essays by Maurice Freedman.* Stanford: Stanford University Press.

Gallin, B., and Gallin, R. S.
1977   Sociopolitical power and sworn brother groups in Chinese society: A Taiwanese case. In R. D. Fogelson and R. N. Adams (Eds.), *The anthropology of power: ethnographic studies from Asia, Oceania, and the New World.* New York: Academic Press.

Hodge, Peter
1981   Social policy for a caring society. In T. P. Khoo (Ed.), *Aspects of mental health care, Hong Kong.* Hong Kong: Mental Health Association of Hong Kong.

Hollingshead, A. B., Ellis, R. A., and Kirby, E. L.
1954   Social mobility and mental illness. *American Sociological Review, 19,* 511–520.

Hong Kong Government
Various   *Hong Kong, report for the year.* (1966, 1967, 1979, 1980.) Hong Kong: Hong Kong Government Press.

Hong Kong Standard July 29.
1981

Hornung, C.
1977   Social status inconsistency and psychological stress. *American Sociological Review, 42,* 623–638.

House, J. S.
1975   Why and when is status inconsistency stressful? *American Journal of Sociology, 81,* 395–412.

Jackson, E. F.
1962   Status consistency and symptoms of stress. *American Sociological Review, 27,* 469–480.

King, A. Y. C., and Leung, H. K.
    1975   *The Chinese touch in small industrial organizations* (occasional paper). Hong Kong: The Chinese University of Hong Kong, Social Research Centre.
Kleiner, R. J., and Parker, S.
    1963   Goal-striving, social status, and mental disorder: A research review. *American Sociological Review, 28,* 162–203.
Kuan, H. C.
    1979   Political stability and change in Hong Kong. In T. B. Lin, R. P. L. Lee, and U. E. Simonis, (Eds.), *Hong Kong: Economic, social and political studies in development.* New York: Sharpe.
Langner, T. S.
    1962   A twenty-two items screening score of psychiatric symptoms indicating impairment. *Journal of Health and Human Behavior, 3,* 269–276.
Lau, C. C., and Lee, R. P. L.
    1981   Bureaucratic corruption and political instability in 19th century China. In R. P. L. Lee (Ed.), *Corruption and its control in Hong Kong.* Hong Kong: The Chinese University Press.
Lau, S. K.
    1979   Employment relations in Hong Kong: Traditional or modern? In T. B. Lin, R. P. L. Lee and U. E. Simonis (Eds.), *Hong Kong: Economic, social and political studies in development.* New York: Sharpe.
    1981a   Chinese familism in an urban-industrial setting: The case of Hong Kong. *Journal of Marriage and the Family, 43,* 181–196.
    1981b   The government, intermediate organizations, and grass-roots politics in Hong Kong. *Asian Survey, 21,* 865–884.
Lau, S. K., and Ho, K. F.
    1980   *Social accommodation of politics: The case of the young Hong Kong workers* (occasional paper). Hong Kong: The Chinese University of Hong Kong, Social Research Centre.
Lee, Rance P. L.
    1979   Stress as a function of the inconsistency between educational and economic status. *Hong Kong Journal of Mental Health, 8*(3), 1–5.
    1981a   Incongruence of legal codes and folk norms. In R. P. L. Lee (Ed.), *Corruption and its control in Hong Kong.* Hong Kong: The Chinese University Press.
    1981b   Sex roles, social status, and psychiatric symptoms in urban Hong Kong. In A. Kleinman and T. Y. Lin (Eds.), *Normal and abnormal behavior in Chinese culture.* Dordrecht, Holland: Reidel.
    1982   She-hui ke-xue yu Ben-tu guan-nian: yi yi-yuan wei li [Social science and indigenous concepts: With "yuan" in medical care as an example]. In K. S. Yang and C. I. Wen (Eds.), *She-hui ji xing-wei ke-xue yan-ju de chung-guo-hua* [The sinicization of social and behavioral science research in China]. Taipei: Institute of Ethnology, Academia Sinica. Monograph Series B, No. 10. pp. 361–380.
Lee, R. P. L., Cheung, T. S. and Cheung, Y. W.
    1979   Material and non-material conditions and life satisfaction of urban residence in Hong Kong. In T. B. Lin, R. P. L. Lee and U. E. Simonis (Eds.), *Hong Kong: Economic, social and political studies in development.* New York: Sharpe.
Lin, T. B., Lee, R. P. L., and Simonis, U. E. (Eds.)
    1979   *Hong Kong: Economic, social and political studies in development.* New York: Sharpe.

Martin, W. T.
    1965   Socially induced stress: Some converging theories. *Pacific Sociological Review,*
              8(Fall), 63–69.

Meile, R. L., and Haese, P. N.
    1969   Social status, status incongruence and symptoms of stress. *Journal of Health and
              Social Behavior,* 10, 237–244.

Merton, R.
    1959   Social theory and social structure (rev. Ed.) New York: Free Press.

Millar, S. E.
    1979   *The biosocial survey in Hong Kong.* Canberra: The Australian National University,
              Centre for Resource & Environmental Studies.

Mitchell, R. E.
    1969   *Levels of emotional strain in Southeast Asian cities* (Vol. 1). A Project of the Urban
              Family Life Survey. Taipei: Orient Cultural Service.

Myers, J. T.
    1981a   Residents' images of a Hong Kong resettlement Estate: A view from the chicken
              coop. In A. Y. C. King and R. P. L. Lee (Eds.), *Social life and development in Hong
              Kong.* Hong Kong: The Chinese University Press.
    1981b   Traditional Chinese religious practice in an urban–industrial setting: The ex-
              ample of Kwun Tong. In A. Y. C. King and R. P. L. Lee (Eds.), *Social life and
              development in Hong Kong.* Hong Kong: The Chinese University Press.

Ng, P. P. T.
    1975   *The people of Kwun Tong survey: Data Book* (occasional paper of the Social Re-
              search Centre). Hong Kong: The Chinese University of Hong Kong.
    1981   Social factors contributing to fertility decline. In A. Y. C. King and R. P. L. Lee
              (Eds.), *Social life and development in Hong Kong.* Hong Kong: The Chinese Uni-
              versity Press.

Rinehart, J. W.
    1968   Mobility aspiration-achievement discrepancies and mental illness. *Social Prob-
              lems, 15,* 478–488.

Schmidt, S. W., Guasti, L., Landé, C. H., and Scott, J. C. (Eds.)
    1977   Friends, followers, and factions: A reader in political clientelism. Berkeley:
              University of California Press.

Shively, S.
    1972   *Kwun Tong life quality study: Data book.* Unpublished manuscript, The Chinese
              University of Hong Kong, Social Research Centre.

Shively, A. M., and Shively, S.
    1972   *Value change during a period of modernization: The case of Hong Kong* (occasional
              paper) Hong Kong: The Chinese University of Hong Kong, Social Research
              Centre.

Tu, A.
    1981   Examination pressure. In T. P. Khoo (Ed.), *Aspects of mental health care, Hong
              Kong.* Hong Kong: Mental Health Association of Hong Kong.

Ward, B. E.
    1970   Temper tantrums in Kau Sai: Some speculations upon their effects. In P. Mayer
              (Ed.), *Socialization: The approach from social anthropology.* London: Tavistock.
    1980   The integration of children into a Chinese social world: A preliminary explora-
              tion of some non-literate village concepts. *Bulletin of the Hong Kong Psychological
              Society, 4,* 7–17.

Wolf, E. R.
    1966   Kinship, friendship, and patron-client relations in complex societies. In M.
              Banton (Ed.), *The social anthropology of complex societies*. London: Tavistock.
Wong, F. M.
    1975   Industrialization and family structure in Hong Kong. *Journal of Marriage and the
              Family*, 37, 958–1000.
Yang, C. K.
    1959   Some characteristics of Chinese bureaucratic behavior. In A. Wright (Ed.),
              Confucianism in action. Stanford: Stanford University Press.

CHAPTER 15

Chinese Adaptation in Hawaii: Some Examples

Kwong-yen Lum
Walter F. Char

INTRODUCTION

This chapter discusses the adaptation of Chinese in Hawaii. Based on a study of specific cases, it demonstrates the general pattern of how the majority of the Chinese in Hawaii have utilized some of their Chinese cultural heritage to make appreciably successful adaptations within several generations, a relatively short period of time. It serves also to illustrate how the ethnic identity of different generations have been changing. The Chinese population in Hawaii consists of two groups: the descendants of Chinese who came largely prior to 1900 and Chinese who migrated to Hawaii since the end of World War II (Zuckerman, 1978). This chapter deals with the experiences of those who belong to families that have been in the islands for almost 100 years.

Like other clinicians, the authors, who are psychiatrists, spend most of their efforts studying psychopathology and do not often pay attention to the *patterns* of successful adaptation. In the present study, positive adaptation was deliberately chosen for illustration through interviewing two suc-

CHINESE CULTURE
AND MENTAL HEALTH

cessful father–son pairs. Although these two cases are extraordinarily successful ones, in many ways they epitomize the general pattern of successful adaptation to the host society among the Chinese descendents of early immigrants in Hawaii.

Compared to other Asian immigrants to the islands, the Chinese have done well. Their general level of family income is the highest among ethnic groups on the islands, and the average educational attainments are among the highest of any group. They constitute one of the smallest ethnic groups on the islands, roughly 5% of the population. Yet, due to certain cultural traits and fortuitous circumstances, they wield influence far out of proportion to their numbers in nearly every field of endeavor: business, education, government, law, politics, medicine, and art (Char, Tseng, Lum, and Hsu, 1980).

Some generalizations can be made regarding the stages that immigrant groups go through after arriving in the United States. Most original immigrants make an *adjustment* to the culture. They often come sojourners, people who do not usually plan to stay: The first-generation Chinese came to Hawaii between 1852 and 1898 to make their fortunes and to return to China wealthy. For one reason or another, many of them did not return, but became settlers and formed families in Hawaii. The thoughts and feelings of the first generation of immigrants, however, were generally turned toward the homeland; and even most Chinese who formed families in Hawaii stayed within their own ethnic group and entertained some idea of going back to mainland China to retire or at least to be buried there (Glick, 1980, Zukerman, 1978).

The second generation makes an *adaptation* to the host country. Chinese born to the original immigrants adapted to the environment they found themselves in. Although they did not wholly view themselves as full members of the host culture, they felt that they had a legitimate place in Hawaii and fought for what they considered their rightful place in the scheme of things. The third, fourth, and subsequent generations became generally assimilated into the host culture. By *assimilation,* we mean that the descendents of the earlier settlers and immigrants take on many of the characteristics and values of the host culture; and in many ways, their basic value systems cannot be distinguished from those of the host culture.

We believe that assimilation has taken place to a large degree in Hawaii among the third- and fourth-generation Chinese, and we illustrate this by interviews of two father–son pairs in which both the fathers and the sons have been eminently successful in their career endeavors in Hawaii. We use materials from the interviews to illustrate our ideas concerning adaptation and assimilation and, at the same time, to identify the traits that remain distinctly Chinese through the generations.

BACKGROUND: THE CHINESE IN HAWAII

The Hawaiian islands were first discovered in 1778 by Captain James Cook; and shortly thereafter, Europeans began making the Hawaiian Islands a regular stopping place for replenishing supplies for whaling ships and the like. The native Polynesian people numbered about 300,000 at the time of Captain Cook and were scattered throughout the islands, with the largest group—approximately 80,000—living on what is now the Kona coast of the island of Hawaii.

Foreign, largely Caucasian, migration to the islands increased rapidly after 1820, when the first missionaries were sent to the islands from New England. Advanced technology and the greater complexity of the Caucasian social structure quickly gave Caucasians dominance that lasted until the end of the nineteenth century, climaxing in the annexation of the Hawaiian Islands by the United States in 1898. From then to 1959, Hawaii was a territory of the United States; and in 1959, it became a state, enjoying equal status with the other states.

The first Chinese came to the Hawaiian Islands as early as 1789 and developed the first commercial sugar mill in the islands in 1802. The number of Chinese immigrating to the Hawaiian Islands during the first part of the nineteenth century remained small, probably approximately 100. It was not until Caucasian businessmen became interested in developing sugar plantations that a sizable need for laborers in the sugar plantations became necessary. Because native Hawaiians did not take well to the idea of working long hours in the sun and because the Chinese were known to be good fieldworkers, 175 fieldhands and 20 houseboys from Amoy, China, were imported in 1852. The influx of Chinese to Hawaii remained low, however, until a 1876 reciprocal trade agreement between the United States and Hawaii was passed and Hawaiian sugar and rice were allowed to be exported on a duty-free basis to the United States. This necessitated a tremendous increase in plantation labor, so a great many more Chinese were imported to the islands from the late 1870s through the mid-1880s. After that, however, concern that there were too many Chinese already in Hawaii caused a decrease in the rate of importation of Chinese laborers, and Japanese laborers began to be imported instead. A few Europeans, including Portuguese, Scottish, and Germans, were brought in to work on the plantations, usually as *lunas* (overseers) of the work of the oriental laborers. With the passage of the Oriental Exclusion Act of 1924, which excluded the Japanese, a large number of Filipino immigrants were brought in to fill the need for plantation labor.

Hawaii is now populated by many different ethnic groups, with no group forming a majority of the population (Char, 1975). The major groups are the part-Hawaiian, Caucasian, Japanese, and Filipino. In 1884, there were 18,254 Chinese, forming 22.6% of the population. By 1900, there were 25,000 Chinese, but with the population growth, the Chinese proportion dropped to 16.7%. With the increasing growth of all other ethnic groups, the Chinese population remained almost static through 1950, when roughly 32,000 were present, forming 6.5% of the population; however, by 1980, there was a growth in actual numbers of Chinese from 32,000 to 56,000 (5.8% of the population) largely because of less restrictive laws regarding Asian migration (Glick, 1980). This figure may not be quite accurate in terms of fully ethnic Chinese since the 1980 figures were based on self-identification (U.S. Bureau of Census, 1980). In fact, the Chinese probably form only 6–7% of the state population, and most reside in Honolulu.

Many of the original Chinese who came to Hawaii returned to China. Those who remained in Hawaii often sent for wives from China or married native Hawaiians. Most of them eventually left the plantations and became involved in small retailing businesses, in crafts such as carpentry, or in farming taro and rice. They started clan associations and rapidly became a part of the commercial scene in Hawaii. Because a strong emphasis was placed on education as a means of gaining opportunity in a foreign land, education was highly stressed among the immigrant Chinese. In the two generations born after 1890, 6 out of every 10 Chinese entered the preferred occupations: professional, proprietary, clerical, and skilled. According to the census of 1971, 20% went to college and 10.4% went to graduate school. The advent of World War II brought about powerful political, social, and economic changes in Hawaii; and the Chinese made tremendous economic gains. After World War II, large real estate holdings were acquired and large business enterprises were established by the Chinese of Hawaii.

Although small in number, the Chinese have achieved a significant place for themselves in Hawaii, not only in the business community but in almost all other areas—the arts, politics, education, the professions, and government.

The majority of Chinese who originally migrated to Hawaii came from the Chung Shan district near Canton in the province of Kwang Tung. Many of them were Hakka and Punti people, who share a long-standard hatred, and they brought their strife with them. It was not too long ago that a marriage between a Hakka and a Punti was considered a problem. However, as the years have passed, the Hakka and Punti dichotomy is no longer an issue, and, in fact, many current Chinese descendants do not even know whether they are Hakka or Punti (Char, 1975; Char et al., 1980; Zuckerman 1978).

SUCCESSFUL EXAMPLES: THE SUBJECTS OF THE INTERVIEWS

We chose two father–son pairs to illustrate the kinds of issues faced by the Chinese in Hawaii and to show how they have coped with their environment. Before discussing the interviews, we present brief histories of the four men interviewed.

Chinn Ho and Stuart Ho

Chinn Ho, one of the most successful Chinese businessman in Hawaii, was born in 1904. His grandfather, Ho Tin Yee, arrived in Hawaii in 1875 at the age of 25. His grandfather, who worked as farm laborer, remained in the islands and raised a family of four sons and four daughters. One of these sons, Ho Tin Yen, was born in Honolulu in 1879 and spent his life in the islands, working as a clerk and bartender at the Pacific Club. He also owned a store in Chinatown. His son, Chinn Ho, was born in 1904.

In 1924, Chinn graduated from McKinley High School, the only public high school in Honolulu at that time, but because of lack of funds in his family, he was not able to attend the university although he wished to. He began working at one of the local banks and then with a stock brokerage firm. He married in 1934 and became the father of six children—three sons and three daughters. Through his own efforts, he became a very prominent businessman: He is Chairman of the Executive Committee of his own company, Capital Investment of Hawaii, Inc.; the developer of the large Makaha land development; and Chairman of the Board of the *Honolulu Star Bulletin,* the largest daily paper in the islands. He serves on the boards of numerous estates and trusts, is a managing trustee of the Mark A. Robinson Trust, and is Director of the Victoria Ward, Limited (Buker, 1972). He has won numerous personal awards and is highly regarded throughout the islands, the United States, and the Pacific as an astute and formidable businessman and a civic leader.

Although Chinn Ho is not actually second-generation, but rather third-generation, Chinese, his story parallels that of many second-generation men. Although his grandfather was the first to arrive, his own father remained strongly tied to the Chinese community in many ways. However, Chinn Ho branched out and has been highly successful in the corporate world of American business.

Stuart Ho, the son of Chinn, was born in 1935, the eldest of Chinn's six children. Stuart was educated in Hawaii at Punahou School, a prestigious private school, and graduated from Claremont McKenna College, a prestigious private college, in 1957. He attended the University of Michigan Law

School and received a doctor of law degree in 1963. In addition to practicing law in Hawaii since 1965, he was elected to the State House of Representatives in 1966 and was Majority Floor Leader from 1968 to 1970. He belongs to numerous civic organizations and, in addition, was a member of the Board of Regents of the University of Hawaii, a group that is traditionally composed of civic leaders from various walks of life. He was named the State Junior Chambers of Commerce's Outstanding Young Man in 1966 and at the present time, is Chairman of the Board of the Capital Investment of Hawaii, Incorporated, the company of which his father is Chairman of the Executive Committee (Buker, 1972).

Hiram Fong, Sr., and Hiram Fong, Jr.

Hiram Fong, Sr., a prominent politician, was born in Honolulu in 1907. His father and mother migrated from China in the late nineteenth century. The father worked first as an indentured sugercane plantation laborer, and later as a laborer in a fertilizer factory. Hiram was a classmate of Chinn Ho at McKinley High School and graduated in 1924. He worked his way through the University of Hawaii and graduated Phi Beta Kappa in three years with honors in 1930. He went to Harvard University, where he received his law degree in 1935. He then returned to the islands and rose gradually but steadily both in the political and economic fields. He spent 14 years in the Territorial House of Representatives, 6 years of which was Speaker of the House. He practiced law and was one of the group of founders of Finance Factors, Limited, a financial conglomerate that has spawned a host of other companies including a life insurance company, an industrial loan company, and a real estate and investment company. In 1959, following statehood, he was the first of two senators—and the first U.S. Senator of Asian ancestry—elected to the United States Senate, and he retired from the Senate in 1977 after 17 years of service. He remains vigorous and is still active in business and community affairs (Buker, 1972; see also Chou, 1979). He is recipient of 11 honorary doctor of law degrees and two decorations, one from Taiwan, China and the other from Korea.

Hiram Fong, Jr., the oldest of Hiram Fong, Sr.'s four children, was born in 1939. He attended local schools, went to the University of Hawaii Laboratory School, graduated from LaFayette University, and subsequently went to law school. After a tour of duty with the Army in Vietnam, he returned to Honolulu and began practicing law. He, too, followed his father's footsteps and has been active in politics, first as a member of the State House of Representatives and, at the present time is serving as a councilman for the City and County of Honolulu.

RESULTS OF THE INTERVIEWS

All four of the interviewees were seen individually in their offices. The data presented in this chapter are only a small part of the information gathered during the interviews.

The general results of the interviews show that both fathers, like most second-generation Chinese, although feeling very Chinese, give no thought to returning to China. Their roots, they feel, are in Hawaii; and although they have taken trips to China on numerous occasions after their successful careers, their home is Hawaii. Both talked of tremendous struggles overcoming discrimination from the Caucasian oligarchy as well as from the political hegemony that existed in Hawaii. As a result of their own intelligence, drive, and persistence, each was able to rise to the highest ranks of the socioeconomic ladder.

In contrast to this, the strong sense of struggle against discrimination appears to be missing in the sons, who are third-generation Chinese. Favored by the successes of their fathers, the sons appear to have had no trouble settling into the community as high-status members.

Education is important to the fathers. Chinn Ho had wanted a college education, but could not afford one. Hiram Fong, Sr., had to work 3 years before he could begin to think of college, and 2 years after college before going to law school. He was, in fact, the only member of his family to graduate from college until he sent his youngest sister through. He had tremendous individual drive for education. To quote Fong, "I always wanted to have more education. I always felt that I wanted to be a lawyer. Actually, as I say in my biographical studies, my biggest achievement was to secure a college education. That was the biggest achievement I had in my life. Everything that came afterwards was anticlimatic. I regard going to college and finishing college as the greatest achievement in my life." This is from a man who was a U.S. Senator for 17 years.

The importance of education is shown in that the three sons of Hiram Fong all became attorneys and all the sons of Chinn Ho received college educations. The sons had little trouble obtaining the finest educations available and accepted a good education almost as a birthright.

A series of questions regarding the issue of Chinese identity were explored specifically during the interview. These are summarized next.

How do you feel about being Chinese? The two fathers, as members of the second generation, were much surer of their identities as Chinese. There was no question in their minds that they were Chinese and that their closest friends and associates remained Chinese. Although each has made a significant mark in the non-Chinese community, their intimates remain Chinese. The two sons are not as strongly tied to their Chinese background.

Though they recognize their ethnicity, their friends and associates are a multiethnic group. Although the fathers belong to a number of Chinese clubs and societies, neither of the sons belongs to any specifically Chinese organization.

Although Stuart Ho did not voice his "Hawaiianness" as strongly as Hiram Fong, Jr., did, Hiram Fong, Jr. probably epitomizes what many third- and fourth-generation Chinese in the islands feel. To quote him: "I think my dad's generation, even though he was born and raised here in Hawaii, considers [itself] Chinese first, perhaps Hawaiian second, and American third. I have the order mixed up a little bit, but I'm almost certain that he feels himself Chinese first. I have always felt myself Hawaiian first, American second, and Chinese third." By Hawaiian, Hiram Fong, Jr., means someone who was born locally, not necessarily of Hawaiian ethnic stock.

Although all four have gone to mainland China and remain quite aware of their ethnic identity as Chinese, they have few actual cultural ties with China. Although both of the older men speak Chinese, the language is lost to the younger two.

What factors in your upbringing that you consider uniquely Chinese have influenced your life and career? None answered this specifically. At the time Chinn Ho and Hiram Fong, Sr., were growing up, the influence of American culture was pervasive; and, except for Chinese food and some Chinese ritual celebrations, the interviewees could not come up with anything that they felt was uniquely Chinese. However, it was clear to the interviewers that all four men had a strong sense of family, a sense of pride in Chinese culture, and the feeling of belonging to an ancient race; these all probably exerted subtle but strong influences on their behavior and growth.

Hiram Fong, Jr., stated that during his adolescence he rebelled against his father and, in fact, left home several times during his high school years. He went to a school where individual ideas and autonomy were stressed, and he rebelled against his father to the extent that he spent a good deal of his time away from his nuclear family. This overt rebelliousness in adolescents is a common American cultural phenomenon and, indeed, is expected to a certain extent as part of individual development in the highly competitive American social scheme.

Which of these factors do you consider unique to Chinese in general, and which of these appear to you to be unique to Chinese in Hawaii? This question might have been too difficult for nonspecialists in the field to answer; however, here, as in the previous questions, what was implied was perhaps more germane to the issue. For example, Chinese are generally seen as a practical, hard-working, family-oriented people; and traditionally among Chinese, there is great pride in being Chinese. This is reflected in the older generation as in this quote from Hiram Fong, Sr.: "Being Chinese, you represent a very, very ancient race. You represent a very smart group of people. In my practice of the law, there [are] a lot of immigration cases that come through. These young kids, 8 to 9 years old, having to use false papers to come in, are trained to represent a certain family which they are not a member of, and when they come in and you listen and talk to them, you find they have a terrific mind. The Chinese mind is a terrific mind. . . . Take, for example, my father and mother. They were not learned people and yet they were deeply philosophical people. They would analyze things very logically and were thrifty. They were hard workers. These are the things that you admire in people. When they give you their word, you can respect it. You would respect that they would live by it."

What was different about the Chinese experience in Hawaii? Fong had this to say: "Our community is not segregated. Chinese were spread all over the place. Because in this community there is not a predominant group, every ethnic group is a minority. From that standpoint, we were very lucky."

All four mentioned the fact that Chinese food was their favorite kind of food.

Do you feel that you have values that differ from your peers of other ethnic groups? All seemed to feel that the Confucian values of family, stability, and responsibility remained a part of their value system. They did not see this as necessarily very different from other ethnic groups such as the Japanese.

Our general assessment of the interviewees, though, was that they value business success highly. For none of them did formal religion play an overwhelmingly important part in their lives. All seemed to have made extremely successful adaptations to what is essentially a secular culture.

Do you feel that your experience in growing up in Hawaii and living in Hawaii has made you different in a significant way from Chinese in other overseas areas such as the continental United States or in places such as Malaysia, Singapore, or the Philippines? All four felt that there was much less ethnic segregation and discriminatory pressure on Chinese in Hawaii than in some of the other overseas areas. By the 1920s and 1930s, many Chinese were able to disperse from Chinatown and moved to outlying multiethnic areas in Honolulu (Zuckerman, 1978). Because of this, they had greater opportunities to mingle with other peoples on the islands and have not remained as culturally centripetal as other Chinese groups appear to have done in other places. As a result of this, they feel that their experience of growing up in Hawaii and living in Hawaii was significantly different from Chinese living elsewhere.

The fact that Hawaii is part of the United States gives the Hawaiian Chinese a democratic society to live in. Each interviewee stressed the multiethnic quality of the islands, the lack of any particular majority, and something that was not quite defined but is called the "Aloha spirit," or, according to Hiram Fong, Jr., "Hawaiianness," which provided a relatively benign base for Chinese to settle and prosper. Stuart Ho felt that the survival instinct was much more finely honed in the Chinese in other overseas areas such as Malaysia than in the Chinese in the United States. He felt that the attitude of the host country toward overseas Chinese has never been very friendly except where they happen to dominate, as in Singapore or Hong Kong; but even in those countries, economic competition and survival tend to rule their lives. He felt that the Chinese appear to have done extremely well for themselves when they have "been allowed to operate under the protection of laws which are predictable and enforceable". He also noted that overseas Chinese have much in common with the Jews inasmuch as the struggle to survive was a predominant need in both groups. He felt that struggle was much more prominant on the United States mainland, since the Chinese groups in mainland U.S. cities feel generally much less secure when dealing with non-Chinese groups.

How close do you feel toward China as the "mother" country? Again, none felt particularly close in terms of wanting to go back to China to live. None refuted their Chinese heritage, but none felt particularly close to China as a culture or civilization except in the ways previously noted. They have lost the language, and none of them expects that his children will ever go back to China and be part of that country. Although Hiram Fong, Sr., Chinn Ho, and Stuart Ho married Chinese women, Hiram Fong, Jr., married a woman of Japanese ancestry, and siblings of both Stuart and Hiram, Jr., have married into Caucasian and other ethnic groups. They see China as a country from which they are proud to have come, but of which they no longer really feel an integral part in any way. This is a far cry from the view of their grandfathers, who probably had hoped at some point in their lives to return to China to retire or at least to have their bones interred in their village.

Regarding the future of the Chinese in Hawaii, there probably will be a distinctive Chinese community in the islands for a long time to come because of the steady influence of Asian Chinese from other parts of the Pacific. However, the group of Chinese who belong to families who have lived in Hawaii for a long time, may become smaller and smaller. To quote Hiram Fong, Jr.: "I think that the Chinese in Hawaii have become a smaller and smaller group—through intermarriage, basically. I think we'll assimilate more and will get away more from our Chinese identity. . . . What is it like to be Chinese? What is my culture? Where do I come from? What I [want] to do is to have my 12-year-old build a family tree, both from the Japanese and the Chinese side, so she can understand her heritage and have an appreciation of what she is and where she comes from." When asked whether he would have any preferences regarding the choice of spouses for Chinese offspring, he responded, "I would like them to marry a Hawaiian, a citizen of Hawaii first. And that's first, and that's my only response. . . . That's my only desire, but the way we're bringing them up, we're not going to have any say at all."

DISCUSSION

These interviews involved only two example pairs, but they serve the purpose of providing some of the flavor of the Chinese experience of adaptation and assimilation in the Hawaiian islands. Generally speaking, the Chinese settlers found a relatively benign host culture in which to adapt and grow; and Hawaii, with its unique blend of multiethnic peoples, without any one group having a clear majority, provided an atmosphere and an environment that allowed the Chinese to progress.

In order to advance in what was a primarily Caucasian-dominated society in the first half of the century, the Chinese had to overcome the discrimination and hostility of the Caucasian oligrachy. But with intelligence and persistence, and aided by the stable and essential fairness of the laws of the United States and by the "Aloha spirit," the Chinese were able to make great gains.

Although the early Chinese immigrants were poor, they held together as a family for mutual support. Cohesive family ties is one of the significant assets they utilized, along with the Chinese cultural emphasis on personal industry, adaptability, education, and achievement. Traditionally, Chinese stress the importance of education. For overcoming discrimination against the minority and gaining opportunity in a foreign land, Chinese parents highly stress children's education. Many second- and third-generation Chinese in Hawaii owe their success to the sacrifices their semiilliterate parents made to give them better educations.

From a sociohistorical point of view, the Chinese, predominantly farmers, place a high premium on land ownership. It is probably this goal that has led to a greater percentage of Chinese owning their own homes and land in contrast to other ethnic groups in Hawaii. In addition, many of the Chinese fortunes in Hawaii have been gained from making more and more wise investments in real estate or other types of land-related business.

Ethnic identity involves a sense of social belonging and ultimate loyalty. It is a form of role attribution, both internal and external (De Vos and Romanucci-Ross, 1975). The formation and manifestation of ethnic identity are subject to variable factors, including the following: (1) ethnic identity develops only after an ethnic group recognizes the existence of others who do not belong to the group; (2) there is often a tendency to exaggerate, in the presence of foreigners, an ethnic identity trait that is less obvious in intraethnic relations; and (3) behavior expressing ethnic identity tends to disappear when a strong upheaval brings about a state of affairs incompatible with the ethnic-identity model (Devereux, 1975).

It is interesting to observe how the Chinese in Hawaii, as illustrated by the cases reported, demonstrate the shift of ethnic identity from one generation to the next. Hawaii is a living laboratory for studying the meeting of different cultures, and the blending and conflicts of the cultures form a unique society in which the Chinese have played an important part.

REFERENCES

Buker, B. F. (Ed.)
    1972   *Men and women of Hawaii.* Honolulu: Star Bulletin.
Char, T. Y.
    1975   *The sandalwood mountains.* Honolulu: University Press of Hawaii.
Char, W. F., Tseng, W. S., Lum, K. Y., and Hsu, J.
    1980   The Chinese. In J. F. McDermott, Jr., W.-S. Tseng, and T. M. Maretzki (Eds),
            People and cultures of Hawaii: A psychocultural profile. Honolulu: University Press
            of Hawaii.
Chou, M.
    1979   *Memories of Hiram L. Fong, United States Senator from Hawaii, 1959–1977.* Unpublished manuscript.
Devereux, G.
    1975   Ethnic identity: Its logical foundations and its dysfunctions. In G. De Vos and L.
            Romanucci-Ross (Eds.), *Ethnic identity: Cultural continuities and change.* Palo
            Alto, CA: Mayfield.
De Vos, G., and Romanucci-Ross, L. (Eds).
    1975   *Ethnic identity: Cultural continuities and change.* Palo Alto, CA: Mayfield.
Glick, C. R.
    1980   *Sojourners and settlers.* Honolulu: Chinese History Center and University Press of
            Hawaii.
U.S. Bureau of Census
    1980   *Census of Population, Supplementary Report: Age, Sex, Race, and Spanish Origin of
            the Population by Regions, Divisions, and State.* Washington, DC: U.S. Government Printing Office.
Zukerman, S. R.
    1978   Pake in paradise: A synthetic study of Chinese immigration to Hawaii. *Bulletin
            of the Institute of Ethnology Academia Sinica, 45,* 39–80.

PART **IV**

MENTAL HEALTH PROBLEMS

Part IV concentrates on mental health problems in various Chinese societies. Chapters 16–18 review the general picture of mental disorders among three groups of Chinese: those in Singapore, Taiwan, and—a special group—Chinese migrants in Australia.

Tsoi (Chapter 16) comprehensively presents the sociocultural–demographic background of Singapore, describing family planning, mass public housing, and rapid economic development as the major social changes. With that as background, he comprehensively reviews the various kinds of mental disorders observed among Singapore's Chinese. The details and findings about suicide and homosexuality are especially interesting.

E. Chiu and Tan (Chapter 17) describe the sociohistorical background of Chinese immigration to Australia and describe the psychiatric disorders observed in that group. Case illustrations of psychological stress associated with migration are given.

Yeh (Chapter 18), after describing the general social and health background of Taiwan, reviews epidemiological findings about mental disorders as reported since the early 1940s. An attempt is made to understand how sociocultural change effects mental health as reflected in changes in the frequency and nature of disorders such as neurosis, suicide, juvenile delinquency, and alcohol abuse. Finally, he makes methodological sugges-

227

tions for more valid cross-comparisons for future epidemiological investigation.

Special issues in mental health problems are addressed in the Chapters 19–22. Cheung (Chapter 19) reviews psychopathology observed in Hong Kong and focuses on the issue of somatic presentation among Chinese patients. She explores in detail the implications of this patient behavior in the process of help-seeking, interprets its possible relationship to culture factors, and suggests directions for future study.

Yu's (Chapter 20) presentation, based on the results of a school survey in mainland China, reports valuable findings about mental health problems observed among elementary school students in Nanjing area. The survey results demonstrate how age, gender, family, and geographical location—rural versus urban—affect differences in emotional dysfunctions.

Yang (Chapter 21) describes the results of an epidemiological study of minimal brain dysfunction among school students in the Beijing area. She explores how the school system, teacher–student relations, expected classroom behavior, and parents' expectations of the child's academic achievement may contribute to the increased recognition of such minor psychiatric disorders among school children.

In Yan's (Chapter 22) focus on neurotic patients, informative case material is used to demonstrate the common psychological problems observed. Yan uses analyses of the psychological problems manifested by patients to study the reflected cultural and psychological background of the society.

CHAPTER 16

Mental Health In Singapore and Its Relation to Chinese Culture

Wing Foo Tsoi

THE SINGAPORE CHINESE

Singapore is an island-city republic situated 137 km north of the equator at the southern end of the Malay Peninsula in Southeast Asia. In 1980, it had an area of 616 km² and a population of 2,413,495, of which 76.9% were Chinese, 14.6% Malay, 6.4% Indian, and 2.1% other races (Singapore National Census, 1980). The Chinese originated mainly from the southeastern Chinese provinces of Guangdong and Fujian. To understand the cultural characteristics of the Singapore Chinese, it is necessary to trace their migration to and settlement in this region over the past two centuries.

Early Chinese in Malaya–Singapore

Male Chinese probably started to settle in large numbers in Malacca (a state of Malaya) in the sixteenth century. These early Chinese settlers married native women and, over several generations, there emerged a new

229

ethnic subgroup, the Straits Chinese, who spoke Malay at home and Hokkien Chinese for trading purposes (Purcell, 1967). They practiced and observed modified forms of Chinese customs and traditions (Song, 1923).

Modern Singapore was founded in 1819 by Sir Thomas Stamford Raffles. At that time, there were only 150 inhabitants, of whom 30 were Chinese. In 1822, Raffles allotted different areas to the various ethnic groups, with the Chinese occupying all of the town southwest of Singapore River (Buckley, 1965).

The Chinese immigrants did not come to Singapore as a community: They were drawn individually from various parts of the southeastern provinces of China and comprised five main groups—Hokkien, Teochew, Cantonese, Hainanese and Hakka—speaking more than 10 different dialects, with each group often regarding the others as foreigners (Purcell, 1967). In addition to these ethnic subgroups were the Malacca-born Straits Chinese, who spoke Malay. Thus, the Chinese were, at the onset, not a homogenous people, and for the next 100 years, they remained by segregated dialect group. They came to Singapore mainly as laborers and merchants to seek a better life, and their ambition was to return to China as soon as they had made a fortune. However, many remained either because they married Malaccan women or because they were addicted to opium and gambling and became too poor to return home.

Period of Rapid Growth through Immigration

The Chinese population in Singapore grew very rapidly mainly because of immigration from southeastern China. During the period 1850–1914, large numbers of Chinese were brought to Singapore as indentured laborers, increasing the Chinese population by more than 11-fold, from 27,988 in 1850 to 315,100 in 1921. Many others came over as merchants and traders. Some were very successful and became community leaders. Because of the economic depression of 1933, the immigration of adult male Chinese was restricted. This was followed by a rise in female Chinese immigrants, who helped to balance the sex ratio, which increased the marriage rate and resulted in a healthier family and social life. However, their presence also contributed to later population growth because of the high birth rate. After 1960, immigration from mainland China was almost nonexistent.

Influence of Education

The Chinese were exposed to two main languages of education: Chinese and English. Early Chinese education was based on the curriculum of schools in China and was taught in dialects. The curriculum began to be modernized when China was exposed to Western influences. The two most important changes were the introduction of *Baihua* (plain speech or written vernacular) in 1917 and of *Guoyu* (national language, or Mandarin) as the medium of instruction, in 1920.

From this time onward, politics heavily influenced Chinese schools, and in 1923 the British introduced the Education Ordinance, which aimed to bring Chinese education under control (Gopinathan 1976). However, these political activities continued until about 1965, when Singapore gained independence. English education did not attract many Chinese in the early years, but after the second World War, in 1946, enrollment in English schools began to increase and overtook enrollment in Chinese schools by 1954.

English education during the Colonial period exposed the children to the English language as well as to British-European culture. It caused the majority of the Chinese to be divided into one of two linguistic groups—the English-educated and the Chinese-educated. The English-educated tended to be British-oriented and many became British subjects. Their education prepared them for recruitment into the civil service, mainly as clerks. The Chinese-educated had a different experience. They were exposed to the political developments in China during the first half of the twentieth century. Chinese schools were often used as breeding groups for political activities (Doraisamy, 1969). After Singapore's independence in 1965, there was a rapid shift toward the English stream of education, mainly because of better prospects and opportunities for employment and further education. With the revisions in curricula and the introduction of bilingualism, which increased exposure time to Chinese (the second language), the difference between the English and Chinese streams of education was lessened.

Cultural Changes in Recent Years

The early Singapore Chinese individuals resembled working class natives of southeastern China in their social and cultural characteristics. This trend continued for about 100 years, until several important events transformed them over the next 50 years, a relatively short period, into the present Singapore Chinese, many of whom have lost their contacts with China. These events include:

1. *The shift toward an English medium of education.* This caused the Chinese, especially those who also converted to Christianity, to change some of their old values, customs, and traditions.

2. *The Japanese invasions and occupation from 1942 to 1945.* This relatively short period helped to unite the Singapore Chinese as one group, whereas previously they had existed as different rival dialect tribes, each residing in a different part of the town.
3. *The Communist Chinese revolution in 1949.* This isolated the Singapore Chinese from mainland China. As a result, most Singapore Chinese became indifferent to or ignorant of the cultural developments in China, thus alienating themselves culturally from the mainland Chinese.
4. *The political struggle for self-government and independence,* which was achieved in 1965. This was followed by the promotion of a "Singapore Culture" and the Mandarin language as the lingua franca for the Chinese. This influence combined with that of English educational background causes many Singapore Chinese now to regard themselves as Singaporeans rather than overseas Chinese.

Important Changes after Independence

Many events that occurred after Singapore's independence have had an influence on the cultural development of its people. Among them, all the following events probably had the most profound effect on the life of the Singaporeans, of whom the majority (78%) are Chinese.

Family Planning and the Two-Child Family Concept.   Family planning became a government movement in 1960, and by 1970, the two-child norm was gaining acceptance. By 1980, the gross reproduction rate was reduced to 840 per 1000. The mean number of children born alive to Chinese women in 1980 was 3.3 children.

Massive Public Housing Program and Urban Renewal.   Singapore suffered from severe housing problems after World War II. Most of its people lived in overcrowded shophouses, often 10 to a cubicle the size of two double beds, in the slums of old Chinatown (Josey 1979). In 1950, less than 3% of the population lived in low-cost public flats built by the Housing and Development Board of Singapore, (Known as HDB flats). Over the next 30 years, the proportion of people living in HDB flats rose rapidly from 9% in 1960 to 39% in 1970 and 70% in 1980. Many of these flats are at present located in newly created towns of 70,000 to 250,000 population. This massive redistribution of population tended to break up larger extended families into smaller nuclear units and uproot and sever most of the social relationships of the former community. It narrowed the physical distance between the dwellers while it widened their social distance (Chen, 1976).

However, it helped to further integrate the various dialect and ethnic groups.

Economic Development. Industrialization started soon after independence. This resulted in the eradication of unemployment and in a demand for skilled workers. It was also accompanied by rapid growth in other economic sectors mainly reflected in the rapidly rising volume of external trade, the increasing number of tourists (exposing the Chinese to foreign life-styles), and a steady rise in the per capita income. All these raised the standard of living and expectation of most people.

The Singapore Chinese in 1980

According to the 1980 Singapore Census (*Census of Population, 1980*), there were 1,856,237 Chinese (76.9% of the population), with a ratio of 1.015 male to 1.000 female. The majority (69%) were locally born. They were divided into more than nine dialect groups. About 83% were literate (defined as the ability to read a newspaper). The four main religious groupings were Taoism (including ancestor worship and Shenism), Buddhism, Christianity, and no religion. About 70% lived in HDB flats, 76% lived in nuclear families, and only 10% lived with their parents. They were employed mainly (53%) in manufacturing or trading activities. By occupation, they were mostly (79%) production, clerical, or sales workers. Fourteen percent were professional, technical, managerial, or administrative workers. The average number of children in a family was 3.3, and the fertility rate was 0.8 per person. Recreational activities usually included watching television, seeing movies and window-shopping. Eating out was regarded as a natural way of spending spare time.

At present, for descriptive purposes, the Singapore Chinese can be divided culturally into two overlapping populations according to age:

1. *The older generation, born mostly before the war.* Members of the older generation are culturally more closely related to their ancestors in China. They belong to large families with many children, and some are polygamous. They speak their own dialects and often conduct their business in Chinese. Many have little or no formal education and practice modified forms of Chinese religions (a mixture of personal habits, rituals, superstitions, and idol worship). When they are ill, they may still seek treatment from traditional Chinese physicians and spirit mediums. They observe most of the Chinese religious and cultural festivals, practice Chinese customs in a traditional way, and may believe in geomancy and reincarnation. Many are unmarried or widowed, and they still regard China as the homeland to which they wish to return on retirement.

2. *The younger generation born after the war.* The younger group can be further differentiated into two ill-defined subgroups—the English-educated and the Chinese-educated. These groups are not clearly demarcated, as there may be many similarities between members of different groups, and, at the same time, there may be differences in cultural values and practices among members of the same group. This complex situation is the result of the changes described previously.

The younger generation, especially the English-educated, are more Westernized and less attached to Chinese customs. They have adopted English as their main medium of communication and are constantly exposed to Western influence through the mass media or through their social and business contacts. Their main link with their Chinese cultural background is through their parents (if the parents happened to be traditional Chinese). If they marry and live separately, this link may weaken and slowly disappear. The Chinese-educated are less Westernized, but they are exposed to the same Western influence and technology prevailing in Singapore. Many are adopting Western norms out of practical necessity. With the promotion of bilingualism and the use of Mandarin as the common Chinese lingua franca, the distinction between the Chinese- and the English-educated is slowly disappearing. From a survey on the life values of youth in Singapore in 1980, Tai (1980) found that the majority of Singapore youths have successfully adapted themselves to the environment. Their personalities are described as "self-centered, materialistic, impersonal, apolitical" but "optimistic, pragmatic, forward-looking, appreciating the value of education and hard work". They consider education, money, and occupation to be the three most important symbols of success in life.

MENTAL HEALTH SERVICES IN SINGAPORE

Mental health services in Singapore had their beginning in 1841 when a 30-bed "insane hospital" was erected. By 1847, there were 35 patients. Treatment consisted of purgatives given once a month, tartar antimony, and counterirritation. Belladonna and morphia were administered as stimulants. The number of patients increased to 131 (including one female) in 1860, when the hospital was transferred to a new locality and enlarged to 100 beds (Lee, 1978). It was shifted further away from the town and enlarged to 300 beds in 1887, and finally, the present Woodbridge Hospital was commissioned in 1928 to accomodate 1030 patients. Some of the treatments introduced were malaria fever for general paralysis of the insane in 1931, electroconvulsive therapy and insulin shock treatment in 1947, carbon dioxide therapy and prefrontal lobotomy in 1953, and psychotropic drugs in 1955. Outpatient services were started in 1953 and the Child Psychiatric Service in 1970. (Woodbridge Hospital, 1978).

Early treatment at Woodbridge Hospital involved mainly custodial care. From early 1960, active intervention with psychotropic drugs, physical therapy, and outpatient treatment resulted in a rapid turnover and a reduction in the length of hospital stay to a few weeks for most cases. Rehabilitation of long-term patients was intensified from 1970. In 1980, a total of 2280 beds were divided into the following types: short-term (510), long-term (1210), special, for example, forensic, mental defective (500), and residential (60) (Woodbridge Hospital, 1980). The forms of treatment included chemotherapy, electroconvulsive therapy, psychotherapy, occupational therapy, social casework, and rehabilitation. The hospital has about 5000 admissions (or which 1000 are new cases) and 5000 discharges a year. Its staff also looks after a 250-bed psychiatric rehabilitation hospital, a forensic ward in Changi Prison, a day-care center and six outpatient clinics—one at the hospital and five in various parts of Singapore. The total outpatient attendance was 78,000 in 1980 (Woodbridge, 1980).

All the psychiatrists in Singapore received their postgraduate training in Britain, with one exception, who was trained in Australia. Singapore psychiatric practice is very much influenced by this British experience. It is eclectic and medically oriented. Treatment usually includes psychotropic drugs. Electroconvulsive therapy is used for severe depression and acute psychosis. Psychological treatment is usually in the form of behavior therapy or supportive psychotherapy. Formal psychotherapy is rarely carried out and classical psychoanalysis not practiced.

An analysis of the patients treated at Woodbridge Hospital and its outpatient clinic is shown in Table 16.1. Of the patients seeking psychiatric treatment from Woodbridge Hospital and its outpatient clinics, about 50% are diagnosed as schizophrenic (which includes paranoid psychosis) and 28% as neurotic.

Schizophrenia among Singapore Chinese

Although all but one of the psychiatrists in Woodbridge Hospital were trained in England and their practice is influenced by the British schools, they do not adopt the narrow British concept of schizophrenia; their diagnostic methods are similar to those of American psychiatrists.

An analysis of all the first admissions to Woodbridge Hospital in 1975 shows that 78.8% of the patients were Chinese and 61.8% were schizophrenic (Tsoi and Chen, 1979). The diagnosis of schizophrenia was not based on British criteria, such as disorders of thinking, emotion, conation, and motor behavior, nor on the presence of Schneider's first-rank symptoms. If these criteria were used, there would be many undiagnosed psychotic disorders. Diagnosis was based mainly on the presence of a cluster of abnormalities usually elicited in the history given by relatives. Most of the Chinese schizophrenic patients admitted to Woodbridge Hospital were unable to express their abnormal thoughts verbally. They tended to deny their abnormal thoughts and feelings and to express them rather in the form of behavioral abnormalities. The 15 most common symptoms in 660 schizophrenic patients admitted to Woodbridge Hospital for the first time in 1975 are shown in Table 16.2.

Formal thought disorder, which is regarded as a very important symptom in schizophrenia, occurred infrequently. If it was present, it was usually elicited from English-speaking patients. Catatonia was also uncommon, being observed in only seven cases. Spontaneous exhibition of Schneider's first-rank symptom was recorded at the time of admission in only one patient, who complained of his thoughts being controlled. The treatment for the acute phase consisted of antipsychotic drugs like chlorpromazine (average daily dose 200 mg) or trifluoperazine (average daily dose 15 mg). Electroconvulsive therapy was given to 26% of the cases during their first month of treatment in hospital (Tsoi and Chen, 1979).

Table 16.1 Percentage Distribution by Diagnosis: Woodbridge Hospital[a]

Diagnosis and code according to ICD-8[b]	New outpatients, 1975 ($N = 911$)	First admissions, 1975 ($N = 1032$)	Inpatients, December 31, 1976 ($N = 2032$)
Dementia (290)	1.6	3.8	8.0
Schizophrenia (295)	29.4	60.2 }	74.8
Paranoid psychosis (297)	2.5	3.1 }	
Affective disorder (296)	2.7	2.7	3.8
Other psychoses	4.2	7.0	—
Neuroses (300)	45.7	9.1	0.6
Personality disorders (301)	1.5	3.8	—
Others (302–309)	3.5	5.0	4.3
Mental retardation (310–315)	4.6	5.3	8.4
No psychiatric illness	4.3	—	—

[a] From Tsoi and Tan (1978).
[b] International Classification of Diseases, 8th ed. (1968).

Table 16.2 The 15 Most Common Abnormalities Recorded[a]

Abnormality	Number	Frequency (%)
Paranoid ideas	187	28.3
Hearing voices	184	27.9
Talking to oneself	135	20.4
Insomnia	132	20.0
Aggressiveness	122	18.5
Abnormal behavior	117	17.7
Laughing to oneself	99	15.0
Disturbed behavior	99	15.0
Crying to oneself	68	10.3
Withdrawnness	64	9.7
Suicidal ideas	63	9.5
Blunting of affect	62	9.4
Ideas relating to charms	60	9.1
Violence	59	8.9
Talking nonsense	59	8.9

[a] From Tsoi and Chen (1979).

The Influence of Chinese Culture on Schizophrenia

A study of the patients' delusional ideas brings out some of the cultural influences on the patients' illness. A 1975 analysis by the author of 555 Chinese patients under age 60 years consecutively admitted to the hospital showed that 166 (30.1%) had delusional ideas of harm and influence. There was no significant difference between Chinese and non-Chinese in the frequency of these paranoid symptoms. Among the Chinese, these paranoid ideas can be divided into three groups: harmed (54%), charmed (33%), disturbed by spirit (13%). These types of delusions are described next.

Most patients experienced a vague feeling of someone trying to harm them (beating, poisoning, arresting) but were unable to elaborate further. In about 50% of the cases, these feelings were accompanied by hallucinatory voices. Among males, delusions tended to be connected with outsiders—foreigners, members of other ethnic groups, gangsters, police, fellow workers, and, in two cases, the Prime Minister. The females tended to direct their paranoid ideas toward family members—husbands, parents, sisters, and their neighbors. Nine male and six female patients made suicide attempts because of their paranoid ideas. A special, culture-related form of delusion, probably peculiar to the Chinese in this region, is one of being charmed or affected by a special type of black magic or being possessed or disturbed by spirits (gods or devils). Most patients were again rather vague about these phenomena and were unable to elaborate on them. But there appears to be a belief pervading the minds of many Singapore Chinese that it is possible for a person to use black magic to cast a spell on a victim; for example, a woman may use a charm to make a married man fall in love with her. This type of black magic is known by the Singapore Chinese as *kongtow*. Its origin is obscure. It is believed to come from Siam (Thailand) where the *knogtow* is more powerful. Some of the ways in which a person can be affected by *kongtow* are as follows:

1. stepping on objects or places on which *kongtow* spells have been cast ("dirty things");
2. taking in food or drinks containing *kongtow* (e.g., used on any unwilling love partner or make him or her fall in love); and
3. having *kongtow* performed on one's clothes or photograph.

Occasionally, a patient may have delusions of being charmed by *kongtow*. More commonly, it is the relatives who believe that the patient's mental illness or abnormal behavior is the result of being charmed by *kongtow*.

Apart from delusions of *knogtow*, 13 males and 4 females had symptoms connected with spirits. About 75% of these patients had auditory hallucinations usually in the form of voices coming from gods or devils. A few patients were disturbed or possessed by spirits but none of the cases were severe enough to be diagnosed as a spirit possession syndrome. Such a syndrome is a rare manifestation of schizophrenia, but is occasionally found in cases of hysteria or personality disorders. Patients presenting cultural symptoms such as delusions of *kongtow* (spirits) are usually taken to seek help from spiritual healers prior to hospitalization. About 50% of all the first admissions to Woodbridge Hospital were found to have consulted traditional healers prior to hospitalization. (Tan, Chee, and Long, 1981)

Traditional Healers and Chinese Religions

It is necessary to digress a bit in order to introduce other systems of healing in Singapore. Chinese traditional medicine has been popular since as early as the second decade of Singapore's history (1829–1839), as early reference is made to several retail druggists doing good business and to Chinese physicians coming from mainland China (Song, 1923). In 1956, a survey showed that at least 90% of patients in an acute medical unit had received traditional Chinese medical treatment (Gwee, Lee, and Tham, 1969). In a morbidity survey in Singapore in 1977, less than 10% of persons who had been ill during the previous 2 weeks had sought treatment from traditional healers (Ministry of Health, 1978). In survey in 1979, 12 of the patients who had more than four neurotic symptoms—as measured by Langner's scale—consulted Chinese physicians (7.2%) or temple mediums (4.5%).

The system of traditional Chinese medicine in relation to psychiatry was reviewed by Liu (1981). It is based on the teaching of the first Chinese medical book *Neijing* (The Canon of Internal Medicine) compiled between 300 and 100 B.C. A study of Chinese medical practice in Singapore showed that diagnosis was based on symptoms and that some diseases were classified according to organs involved (Gwee et al., 1969). Treatment is by acupuncture and the use of a great variety of herbs imported from China. Some Chinese physicians also make use of Western medicines like antibiotics, steroids, and hypnotics (all illegally). Although not many Singapore Chinese have consulted traditional physicians for their illnesses in recent years, self-medication with Chinese medicine (herbs) is still popular. Some of the herbs have become food items.

Patients with mental illness are more likely to consult a Chinese spiritual healer than a Chinese physician. A study of 153 consecutive first admissions to a psychiatric unit in Woodbridge Hospital showed that 75 (51%) had been to spiritual healers prior to hospitalization. There were 66 Chinese (88%), suffering from either schizophrenia or depression with suicidal intent, and all except one of them had been to temple mediums (Tan et al., 1981). The Chinese spirit medium is a type of shaman. A comprehensive study of the Chinese spirit-medium cult, which is closely related to the Chinese religions, was carried out in Singapore during the period 1950–1954 (Elliot, 1964). In these phenomena, a *shen* (spirit or god) possesses the body of the medium (a person), and through the medium's body the *shen* can speak to his or her worshippers and followers, giving them advice or prescribing treatment for their illnesses. Most mediums can voluntarily called on the *shen* when their services are needed. They then assume the personality and speak the language of the *shens* (T. M. Chong, 1970). Some can be possessed only at certain times of the day or on certain days.

Spirit mediumship is based on the Chinese religious systems in Singapore. Apart from 11% Christians and 17% without religion, the Singapore Chinese, mostly the older and less educated, are Buddhists or Taoists. The majority of the Chinese who call themselves Buddhists or Taoists do not follow or practice the teaching of Buddha or Lao Zi (founder of Taoism). According to Wee (1976), Buddhism in Singapore can be divided into two general categories:

1. those which refer directly to specific Buddhist canonical traditions: the Theravada and the Mahayana schools (these have only a very small following in Singapore); and

2. those which have no canonical references: the Chinese syncretic religion to which the great majority of the Buddhist and Taoist Singapore Chinese belong.

Spirit mediumship is based on this Chinese syncretic religion. Apart from worshipping the Buddha and his images, the Chinese also pray to many other lesser known *shens*. The four *shens* most commonly connected with spirit mediumship in Singapore are the Monkey God, Third Prince, General Guan, and the Goddess of Mercy, Guanyin (see Elliot, 1964 for details).

In Singapore, spirit mediumship is practiced in the approximately 30 temples (mostly small ones) and in many private homes, some of which may be decorated, usually internally, like small temples. The spirit mediums, who can be of either gender, range in age from adolescent to elderly, and are very often children or grandchildren of mediums (T. M. Chong, 1970). Besides mental illness, they treat a variety of medical conditions, including some for which Western medicine does not provide relief. The treatment usually takes the form of a *fu*, a yellow paper on which the medium may make some scribblings, sometimes with his blood. The *fu* may be burnt and its ashes used as medicine, or it may be wrapped up and carried as a talisman, hung around the neck to protect against evil. In spite of rapid modernization and increased literacy in recent years, spirit mediumship continues to attract worshippers. However, the impact of traditional healers on the mental health delivery system in Singapore has been minimal compared to other countries in this region.

Neurosis among Singapore Chinese

The next most common psychiatric syndrome referred to the psychiatrist is neurosis, and it is difficult to estimate its prevalence among the Singapore Chinese. A mental health survey (General Health Survey, 1978) showed that 7.9% of the Chinese (6.7% for males and 8.9% for females) showed four or more symptoms (the cut-off point for neurosis on the Langner scale, which is a 22-item questionnaire that measures psychosomatic and neurotic symptoms; Langner, 1962). About 55% of this group sought treatment, 80% from Western doctors and only 10% from native healers—Chinese physicians (5.2%) and temple mediums (4.7%); 10% treated themselves by medication.

Neurosis, at its best, is an ill-defined condition. Its prevalence and classification depends very much on the criteria used and on the attitude and training of the psychiatrist and his or her subjective impression. It constituted about 46% of the cases referred to the psychiatric outpatient clinics in

Table 16.3 Presenting Symptoms of Anxiety Neurosis in Singapore Chinese

Presenting symptom	Male	Female	Total
Discomfort	7	17	24
Headache or giddiness	6	15	21
Pain (stomach, back)	5	10	15
Anxiety (including palpitation)	7	8	15
Depression	5	7	12
Other	2	4	6
	32	61	93

Singapore, and anxiety neurosis and neurotic depression formed 88% of all the neuroses. In a review of 103 consecutive Chinese patients diagnosed as neurotic by the author, there were 93 cases of anxiety-depressive neurosis (91%), the 4 of hysteria, 2 of phobia, 2 of obsessive–compulsive neurosis, and 2 of anorexia nervosa. These exclude all parasuicide (attempted suicide).

Anxiety–depressive neurosis, which forms the bulk of the diagnosed neuroses, is the typical neurosis seen among Singapore Chinese. In this group of 93, there were 32 males and 61 females. Instead of presenting free floating of phobic anxiety or depression, the majority presented somatic complaints. The Singapore Chinese, like their counterparts in China (Tseng and Hsu, 1969–1970) somatize their emotional problems. Their presenting symptoms (excluding insomnia) are shown in Table 16.3.

Culture-Related Neurotic Syndromes

Latah (startle reaction), which previously afflicted mainly the Straits Chinese, has become extinct. *Koro* (impotence panic), a well-known condition affecting southern Chinese, has become uncommon since the last epidemic in October 1967. *Koro* is a state of acute anxiety caused by the belief, among males, that the penis is retracting into the abdomen or, among females that the nipples are retracting. It is found mainly in southern mainland and southeast Asian Chinese (Rin, 1965). During the 1967 outbreak, which lasted one week, 454 males and 15 females were affected (Gwee, 1969). Ninety-six percent were Chinese, and 60% were in the age range 16–30 (Ngui, 1969). The fact that *koro* has become very uncommon is probably due to better sex and health education and a high literacy rate among the younger Chinese. In general, many so-called cultural-related neurotic syndromes have become rare in recent years.

Suicide

The annual suicide rate in Singapore has fluctuated around 10–11% per 100,000 since 1906. It was high during the depression of 1939–1940 (15.5 per 100,000) and during the Japanese occupation of 1941–1945 (13.1 per 100,000; Chia, 1981). The first review on suicide covering the period 1925–1952 was by Murphy (1954), who noted that the rate was high among the immigrant Chinese, a statistic he believed was due to the success-motivated and superambitious nature of the immigrant population. Subsequent study for the period 1970–1974 (Chia, 1981) and a review of the statistics for 1980 by the author shows that the same cohort of immigrant Chinese continues to register a high suicide rate, as reflected in the Table 16.4.

The suicide rate among Singapore Chinese shows a parallel relation to the percentage of immigrants. There are many reasons for this trend. The most important is probably the aging immigrant Chinese who could not adapt to the rapidly developing and changing Singapore environment. Suicide is often presented as an honorable form of death in Chinese history and literature: Men of distinction often killed themselves to defend righteous causes or following defeats, and women often committed suicide to defend their honor and chasity.

A comprehensive study by Chia (1978) shows that the method of suicide changed according to its availability. During the earlier period (1921–1923), suicide by hanging was the most common method for both genders (94% for male Chinese and 88% for female Chinese). Corrosive poisoning by caustic soda was also a common method amongst Chinese females. From 1960 onward, jumping from high buildings became the leading method: In 1980, this was the method used by 63% of the Chinese, with hanging (21%) and other methods (16%) being less popular.

Jumping from high buildings is unique to Singapore, and the percentage of such cases roughly parallels the number of such buildings in Singapore.

Table 16.4   Age-Specific Suicide Rates for Chinese in Singapore, 1980

Age group	Chinese suicide rate per 100,000	Percentage of immigrant Chinese from mainland China
16–19	3.3	0.3
20–49	7.8	4.2
50–59	17.5	32.0
50–69	22.4	67.2
70 and above	47.6	80.8

Table 16.5   Records of Suicide by Jumping

Year	Suicide by jumping (%)	Population in HDB flats (%)
1932	1.9	0.0
1947	4.6	1.5
1960	16.6	9.1
1965	23.0	23.2
1970	39.7	34.6
1974	47.5	42.7
1980	60.0	69.7

It rose steadily from 2% in 1933 to 20% in 1942, to 40% in 1970, and to 60% in 1980 (see Table 16.5). However, repeated studies have not shown other serious adverse physical or psychological ill effects from living in low-cost high-rise HDB flats. A sociological survey showed that the residents were satisfied with the changes brought about by moving into HDB flats. The change was for the better in terms of public security, health of household members, environment for bringing up children, and cleanliness of the neighborhood. There were also better employment opportunities for women (Yeh, 1975). However, another survey showed that those who lived on the upper floors tended to be less sociable and were more concerned about the safety of their children, who were mostly confined indoors. The rates for parasuicide were also lower among those staying in HDB flats (41.4 per 100,000) than those staying in other types of houses (62.8 per 100,000; Chia and Tsoi, 1974).

The causative factors of suicide in Singapore Chinese were physical illness (31%), mental illness (31%), interpersonal problems (18%), financial problems (11%), and other (7%; Chia, 1981). Of the mental illnesses, schizophrenia accounted for 63% and depression for 27%. However, in a study covering 1969–1972, psychotic depression continued to have the highest suicide risk, and psychiatric patients had a greater tendency to jump from heights (55%), compared with nonpsychiatric cases (39%; Tsoi and Chia, 1974). Some of the common reasons for suicide were fear of business failure, the fear of an aged mother of surviving her oldest son, inability to bear a son, inability to return to China during old age, belief in life after death, and opium addiction (Chia, 1978). Many of these reasons have a cultural basis.

Parasuicide

A statistical study of suicidal behavior in 1980 showed that parasuicide was 7 times more frequent than suicide. The sex ratio was 1 male to 2.2

Table 16.6 Parasuicides by Age Group

Age group	Cases		Rate per 100,000 population
	N	%	
10–19	292	17.2	56
20–29	841	49.5	153
30–39	301	17.7	87
40–49	109	6.4	46
50–59	36	2.1	22
60–69	34	2.0	31
70–99	26	1.5	40
Unknown	59	3.5	—
	1698	99.9	

females. The most susceptible age group was 20–29 years, which accounted for 50% of the cases (Tsoi and Kok, 1982; see Table 16.6).

Parasuicide is a disorder of young people in Singapore as in other places, and its investigation may reveal some of the cultural aspects of the younger generation. The most common method is the ingestion of some form of "poison"—either a liquid detergent, insecticide, lotion, or psychotropic drugs or analgesics, usually in tablet form.

Unlike suicide, about which statistics were kept for many years, there is much less hard information regarding parasuicide. Comparison of studies over a 12-year period (1967–1980) shows that the incidence of self-poisoning continued to be high but that the type of poison used has changed. There has been a slight shift to the use of tablets—mainly hypnotic and psychotropic drugs—reflecting the greater exposure of the young people to the drug culture. A survey of the pharmaceutical industry showed that Singapore has the highest per capita consumption of medicinal preparations in the Asian region—about $40 per person per year, which is about half the rate for Europe and the United States (*Straits Times*, 1982).

The causes of suicide attempts have not changed significantly since 1967 (Tsoi, 1970). The most common precipitating event continues to be interpersonal problems, which increased from 52% in 1967–1969 to 58% in 1980–1981. Among these, the most frequent problem for women is an unhappy relationship with either husband or boyfriend, which usually took the form of rejection (Tsoi and Kok, 1981). The selection of life partner among Singapore Chinese is left to individual free choice. Arranged marriage, as practiced by older generations of Chinese, is a thing of the past. This trend probably contributes to parasuicide. Other changes are the reduction of physical illness and financial problems (see Table 16.7).

Table 16.7 Comparison of Main Causative Factors for Parasuicide

Cause	1967–1969 (N = 192) %	1980–1981[a] (N = 100) %
Interpersonal	51	58
Physical illness	19	13
Mental illness	13	14
Financial	13	7
Other	4	8
	100	100
$\chi^2 = 4.745$; $df = 4$; N.S.		

[a] Self-poisoning only

Other Psychiatric Problems and Alcoholism

Apart from psychoses and neuroses, Singapore psychiatrists do not frequently encounter other psychiatric disorders. The prevalence of chronic alcoholism and its psychiatric complications is usually low among Singapore Chinese. A survey in 1977 showed that among Chinese ages 15 and above, 27% drank socially, 2% drank regularly, and 1% drank daily. (Ministry of Health, 1978). These percentages are the same for the Singapore Indians, and yet the rate of alcoholism for the Chinese is only about 5% that of the Indians. A study by Khoo and Fernandez (1971) showed that 1 in 10 Chinese and Indians above the age of 12 drank but that in a 6-month survey in a Medical Unit, there were only 16 Chinese compared to 27 Indians admitted for alcoholism, although the Chinese population was about twelve times that of the Indians. The common alcoholic beverages consumed by the Chinese are beer and stout, Chinese wine, and brandy. Beer and stout are usually consumed by regular drinkers during meals, and brandy usually during formal Chinese dinners. The low prevalence of alcoholic psychiatric disorders among Chinese is believed to be due to the manner in which alcohol is consumed—usually with food and in the company of other people.

Psychosexual Problems in General

The sexual behavior of the Singapore Chinese is largely unknown. It is difficult to do a survey because the Singapore Chinese do not speak a common language, and it is difficult to obtain a representative sample because the Singapore Chinese ethnic group can be divided into many small subgroups according to various criteria such as age, dialects spoken, religion, education, and occupation. In addition, most Chinese do not freely express themselves to interviewers on matters relating to their sexual behavior, and there is no single cultural norm for sexual behavior that can be applied to all Singapore Chinese. Sexual inadequacy is not a problem that is commonly referred to the psychiatrists. A survey by a general practitioner showed that of 220 patients ages 35–72, fewer than 4% confessed impotence when leading questions regarding erection were asked. The majority had erection failure, and only about 20% of the cases had premature ejaculation (P. K. G. Chong, 1980). These are probably minor sexual problems, as many are treated with the injection of vitamins. Over a period of 1 year (1981), of 903 cases referred to the psychiatric outpatient clinics, 20 were diagnosed as impotent. Sexual deviations, apart from transsexualism, were seldom brought to the attention of the psychiatrists.

TRANSSEXUALISM

The first sex reassignment operation was performed on a 24-year-old Singapore Chinese male in February 1971, and this story was given some publicity. Following this, there was a steady flow of people, some coming from neighboring countries, requesting this sex change operation. Table 16.8 shows a breakdown of the cases for Singapore residents only. The figures do not represent all cases, as some that were assessed by psychiatrists other than the author are not included. In spite of this, they are about four times higher than figures given for the United States and Sweden.

A psychiatric investigation was carried out on 56 male transsexuals in Singapore during the period 1971–1976 (Tsoi, Kok, and Long, 1977). Their age range was from 18 to 34, with a mean at 24 years. Most of them took up female occupations including prostitution. Eighty percent were English educated compared to 42% for the Singapore population in 1970.

Table 16.8   Number of Requests for Sex Reassignment Surgery: Singapore Residents

Year	Male to female		Female to male	
	Chinese	Others	Chinese	Others
1971–1975	70	13	10	1
1976–1980	22	5	14	2
1980	11	4	10	3
	103	22	34	6
Rate per 100,000	11.0	7.4	3.7	2.3

None were married, but 61% had steady boyfriends and 34% were cohabitating with their boyfriends. Ninety-one percent had started to have transsexual feelings before the age of 9 years, and their transsexualism continued to develop as they grew older. By age 24, 80% were completely dressed as, and living the life of, women. By 1976, 34 had undergone the sex reassignment operation.

During the period 1972–1978, 20 females were assessed for sex reassignment surgery (Tsoi and Kok, 1980). Eighteen of them (90%) were Chinese. Their ages ranged from 18 to 31, with a mean of 25. Eighteen started to develop the transsexual syndrome during childhood and as they grew older, became more masculine in their behavior. Eighteen had girlfriends and 10 indulged in sexual activities with their girlfriends. Ten were undergoing the multistage sex reassignment operation in 1979.

Male transsexuals have been known to congregate in certain places in Singapore for many years, and, until recently, these areas were tourist attractions. Behavioral characteristics of transsexuals were largely unknown to the medical profession until the sex reassignment operation was available. The etiology of this condition is unknown; it does not appear to be related to upbringing or to relationship with parents. English education seems to have an influence. The apparently high prevalence of transsexualism in Singapore is probably due to the availability of the sex reassignment operation, which usually draws these people to the attention of the medical profession.

CONCLUSION

Singapore is one of the main centers of overseas Chinese concentration. It began as a deserted island 163 years ago and is presently populated mainly by Chinese from southern China. The majority of the Chinese settlers were from the working class; they came to become laborers and brought folk culture practices with them.

During the first 100 years, the Chinese were culturally an extension of the Chinese community of southern China. With the march of progress and modernization and the subsequent restriction of Chinese immigration, the original group of Chinese is aging and dwindling in number. They are slowly being replaced by an emerging group of younger Chinese who are educated bilingually or in English alone.

Singapore's psychiatric therapy is based mainly on the British school. The two most common conditions treated by psychiatrists are schizophrenia and neurosis. Schizophrenics present mainly behavioral abnormalities rather than mood and thought disorders, and neurotics present mainly somatic complaints. This could be due to the reluctance of the Singapore Chinese to express their thoughts and feelings freely.

Because of modernization and the increasing influence of English education and exposure to Western culture, symptoms and syndromes with Chinese cultural connections are becoming less common. However, mental illness is still linked with spirit possession and black magic, and traditional Chinese healers exist side-by-side with modern medical practitioners. The traditional healers are made up of two groups: the Chinese physicians who deal mainly with minor illnesses and the temple mediums who deal with mental abnormalities. The temple mediums do not belong to any school nor do they have a unified system of practices. Each healer seems to act according to his or her own faith and beliefs, but treatment normally involves the prescription of a *fu*.

Another problem related to Singapore's modernization is the increasing number of multistory buildings. This has led to a high incidence of suicide by jumping. The impact of modern medicine has given rise to a high incidence of parasuicide by drug poisoning. The main causes for suicidal behavior are physical illness, mental illness, and interpersonal problems, rather than financial difficulties. This is related to Singapore's modernization and its attending psychosocial stresses. However, the suicide rate has not changed for the past 30 years.

REFERENCES

Buckley, C. B.
    1965   *An anecdotal history of old times in Singapore*. Kuala Lumpur: University of Malaya Press.
Chen, P. S. J.
    1976   *Asian values in a modernizing society: A sociological perspective*. Singapore: Chopmen Enterprises.
Chia, B. H.
    1978   *Suicide in Singapore*. Unpublished M.D. Thesis. University of Singapore, Faculty of Medicine, Singapore.
    1981   *Suicidal behavior in Singapore*. Tokyo: SEAMIC.
Chia, B. H., and Tsoi, W. F.
    1974   Statistical study of attempted suicide in Singapore. *Singapore Medical Journal, 15,* 253–256.
Chong, P. K. G.
    1980   Impotence in general practice. *The Family Physician, 6,* 21–25.
Chong, T. M.
    1970   Trance states in Singapore and their role in the community for healing. *Proceedings, Fifth Malaysia–Singapore Congress,* pp. 138–145.
Doraisamy, T. R.
    1969   *150 years of education in Singapore*. Singapore: Stamford College Press.

Elliot, A. J. A.
   1964   *Chinese spirit medium cults in Singapore.* Singapore: Donald Moore Books.
General health survey
   1978   Unpublished report, Ministry of Health, Singapore.
Gopinathan, S.
   1976   Towards a national educational system in Singapore. In R. Hassan (Ed.), *Society
             in transition.* Knalalumpur: Oxford University Press.
Gwee, A. L.
   1969   The koro "epidemic" in Singapore. *Singapore Medical Journal, 10,* 234–242.
Gwee, A. L., Lee, Y. K., and Tham, N. B.
   1969   Study of Chinese medical practice in Singapore. *Singapore Medical Journal, 10,*
             1–7.
Josey, A.
   1979   *Singapore: Its past, present and future.* Eastern Universities Press. Sdn Bhd.
Khoo, O. T., and Fernandez, P.
   1971   The problem of alcoholism in Singapore. *Singapore Medical Journal, 12,* 154–
             160.
Langner, T. S.
   1962   A twenty-two item screening score of psychiatric symptoms indicating impair-
             ment. *Journal of Health and Social Behavior, 3,* 269–276.
Lee, Y. K.
   1958   *The medical history of early Singapore.* Tokyo: Southeast Asian Medical Informa-
             tion Center.
Liu, X. H.
   1981   Psychiatry in traditional Chinese medicine. *British Journal of Psychiatry, 138,*
             429–433.
Ministry of Health
   1978   *Report of the first national survey on morbidity in Singapore 1976–77.* Singapore.
Murphy, H. B. M.
   1954   Mental health in Singapore: Suicide. *Medical Journal of Malaya, 9,* 1–45.
Ngui, P. W.
   1969   The koro epidemic in Singapore. *Australia and New Zealand Journal of Psychia-
             try, 3,* 263–266.
Purcell, V.
   1967   *The Chinese in Malaya.* London: Oxford University Press.
Rin, H.
   1965   A study of the aetiology of koro in respect to the Chinese concept of illness.
             International Journal of Social Psychiatry, 11, 7–13.
Singapore National Census
   1980   *Census of Population.* Singapore: Singapore National Printers.
Singapore yearbook
   1980   Singapore: Singapore National Printers.
Song, O. S.
   1923   *One hundred years' history of the Chinese in Singapore.* London: John Murray.
Straits Times (Singapore)
   1982   February 18, p. 1.
Tai, C. L.
   1980   *Life value of youth in Singapore* (Research project series). Singapore: Nanyang
             University.

Tan, C. T., Chee, K. T., and Long, F. Y.
  1981   Psychiatric patients who seek traditional healers in Singapore. *Singapore Medical Journal, 22,* 643–647.
Tseng, W. S., and Hsu, J.
  1969–   Chinese culture, personality formation and mental illness. *International Journal*
  1970   *of Social Psychiatry, 16,* 4–5.
Tsoi, W. F.
  1970   Attempted suicide. *Singapore Medical Journal, 11,* 258–63.
Tsoi, W. F., and Chen, A. J.
  1979   New admissions to Woodbridge Hospital 1975 with special reference to schizo-
          phrenia. *Annals of the Academy of Medicine, Singapore, 8,* 275–279.
Tsoi, W. F., and Chia, B. H.
  1974   Suicide and mental illness in Singapore. *Singapore Medical Journal, 15,* 191–
          196.
Tsoi, W. F., and Kok, L. P.
  1980   Female transsexualism in Singapore. *Australia and New Zealand Journal of Psy-
          chiatry, 14,* 141–143.
  1981   Self-poisoning in Singapore: Main causative factors. *Singapore Medical Journal,
          22,* 284–287.
  1982   Suicidal behaviour in Singapore for the year 1980. *Singapore Medical Journal,
          23,* (b), 299–305.
Tsoi, W. F., Kok, L. P., and Long, F. Y.
  1977   Male transsexualism in Singapore. *British Journal of Psychiatry, 131,* 405–409.
Tsoi, W. F., and Tan, C. T.
  1978   *Mental health services in Singapore.* Paper presented at the First ASEAN Teaching
          Workshop on Culture and Mental Health, Jakarta, Indonesia.
Wee, V.
  1976   "Buddhism" in Singapore. In R. Hassan (Ed.), *Society in transition.* Kuala Lum-
          pur: Oxford University Press.
Woodbridge Hospital
  1978   *Woodbridge Hospital newsletter* [Special Issue], *2*(9).
  1980   Woodbridge Hospital annual report. Singapore.
World Health Organization
  1968   *International classification of diseases* (8th ed.).
Yeh, H. K.
  1975   Summary and discussion. In H. K. Yeh (Ed.), *Public housing in Singapore.* Singa-
          pore: Singapore University Press.

CHAPTER 17

Psychiatric Pathology among Chinese Immigrants in Victoria, Australia

Edmond Chiu
Eng-Seong Tan

DEMOGRAPHIC SKETCH

Australia, situated at the south-most point of the Pacific rim, is an island continent with a land area of about 1.11 million km² and a population in 1980 of about 14.5 million people. Australia has about 80% of the land area of the United States with only about 7% of the population.

The state of Victoria is located in the southeastern corner of the continent and has a population of about 4 million, of whom 2.5 million live in the metropolitan area of the capital city of Melbourne. Like the United States, a large proportion of the population is of immigrant stock, who come from all over the world, initially from Great Britain, Ireland, and other parts of western Europe before the Second World War. After 1945, there was a large wave of immigrants from southern and eastern Europe.

251

From the late 1960s, with the abrogation of the so-called white Australia policy on immigration, increasing numbers of immigrants from Asia started to arrive in Australia. Beginning in the mid-1970s there has been a major wave of immigration in the form of refugees from Vietnam, Laos, and Cambodia. A large proportion of these refugees are ethnic Chinese.

In Victoria, of an estimated population of about 35,000 people of Asian origin in 1976, approximately 15,000 are believed to be of ethnic Chinese origin, most of whom lived in metropolitan Melbourne. The exact number is not known because, for political and administrative purposes, official statistics do not record people by ethnic origin, but rather by country of birth. Further, the influx of refugees from the Indo–Asian countries— Vietnam, Cambodia and Laos—reached a peak in 1978, and the effect of this immigration on the population structure in the state of Victoria is still unknown.

HISTORICAL BACKGROUND

Human migration to Australia from Asia and Europe has contributed to an evolving multicultural society, which is a sociopolitical reality becoming accepted as the new direction for the 1980s in Australia. Historically, the Chinese have been in Australia since as early as the fourteenth century, when a group arrived accidentally on Australian shores (the first "boat-people"). It is likely that certain Chinese fishermen landed in Australia long before the arrival of Captain James Cook.

In the nineteenth century, a few Chinese seamen jumped ship in Sydney Harbor and settled in the colony. Some of them worked as agricultural laborers, doing the most menial tasks. The first numerically significant influx of Chinese was probably in the 1830s, when they were employed in agriculture. In 1846, Lieutenant Charles Mundy recorded that there was a sizeable number operating stores, restaurants, and traditional market gardens.

When gold was discovered in 1852, there was a massive deluge of Chinese who flocked to the "new gold mountain" (California, where gold was discovered in 1849, was the "old gold mountain.") In 1852, there were an estimated 2000 Chinese in the gold fields of Victoria. By 1855, there were 8000 in one camp north of Ballarat in central Victoria, and the press of the day began to refer to the "plague of grasshoppers, which had once descended upon Egypt."

Such a massive immigration of Chinese gave the Victoria legislature considerable anxiety, and an attempt to have all Chinese repatriated was narrowly defeated, but a poll tax of "10 pounds per Chinaman" landing in

Table 17.1   Perceived Social Characteristics

Chinese	Australian
Upwardly socially mobile	Increasingly middle class ("implosion" of class structure)
Low profile stance	Preferring a low profile
Nonghetto—"centrifugal"	Suburban
Conformist, middle class	Conformist, conservative
Materialistic orientation	Hedonistic orientation, self-absorbed
Strongly driven toward personal success	Preferring personal satisfaction to success
Avoiding partisan politics ("middle-of-the-road")	Politically polarized
Noncontroversial, nonprovocative, noninvolved, uncommitted	Do-it-yourself attitude
Family centered	
Quietly competitive	Easy-going and noncompetitive

the colony was introduced. However, the Chinese shrewdly sidestepped this piece of legislation by landing in Guichen Bay, near Robe just over the border in South Australia, the neighboring state. There is a cairn commemorating this event standing in Robe today.

How did the Chinese interact with their hosts? Until the late 1960s, the legislation on administrative discrimination was well known. At present, the white Australia policy no longer exists, although some of the more conservative elements in Australian society are trying desperately to restore this restrictive immigration policy. Generally, in the spirit of the new multiculturalism, the Chinese are seen in the 1980s as valued members of the Australian community.

As the legislative and administrative bars are removed, the social characteristics of the Chinese in Australia have become more important determinants of adaptation. Table 17.1 compares the perceived social characteristics of the Chinese and the "average" white Australian.

CURRENT PSYCHIATRIC SURVEY

The ethnic Chinese population in Australia has gone through the stages of suffering, persecution, discrimination, and, more recently, acceptance and integration into the wider Australian community. It would be interesting to see how well this integration is taking place by examining the psychiatric morbidity of the ethnic Chinese residents in Victoria, Australia.

There have been a number of studies of the mental health status of overseas Chinese communities living in different parts of the world. With a few exceptions, it would appear that the consensus from most of these studies is that the rate of psychiatric hospital admission among Chinese communities is much lower than those of other ethnic groups living in the same geographical areas (Kinzie, 1974; Lin, Kleinman, and Lin, 1980; Sue and McKinney, 1975).

Background of the Study

In 1981, the Department of Psychiatry, University of Melbourne, in partnership with the Mental Health Research Institute of Victoria, obtained funding to conduct a longitudinal research project on the mental health adjustment of Indo–Asian refugees in Melbourne. Because the predominant ethnic groups of refugees from Indo–Asia are of Chinese origin, a basic study of the mental health of ethnic Chinese became relevant and necessary.

As population data by ethnic origin are not available in Australia and because the sample of this study is not large enough for any meaningful epidemiological deductions, this might be considered a preliminary report that serves to provide some understanding of the mental health of ethnic Chinese in Melbourne.

Methodology

The data presented here are drawn from three sources: (1) the authors' part-time private practice; (2) the psychiatric unit of St. Vincent's Hospital; and (3) state-run facilities. St. Vincent's is a general hospital that is one of the teaching hospitals of the University of Melbourne medical school and one of the larger and more prestigious teaching general hospitals in the city of Melbourne. This hospital has a 25-bed psychiatric unit and sees about 1800 new patients annually. The data from the first two sources were collected over 3 years, from 1979 to 1981 inclusive.

For comparison, data from the third source were collected from contacts made by ethnic Chinese patients with the clinical facilities of the Mental Health Division of the Health Commission, which has a total of 4172 beds in its facilities in Victoria and consists of 8 acute psychiatric hospitals within the metropolitan area, 2 general hospital psychiatric units, about 14 psychiatric clinics in various parts of the metropolitan area, and about 7 psychiatric hospitals or general hospital psychiatric units in rural towns. These data also include the admission of any Chinese patient to any of the specialized facilities, such as the Alcohol and Drug-Dependence Services and the Mental Retardation and Forensic Psychiatry Services throughout the state. J. Krupinski, Director of Research of Mental Health Research

Institute the (M. H. R. I.), coordinates the collection of the data from these state facilities. (Unfortunately, the data available from the state source are only for the year 1978. Therefore, for purposes of comparison, one would need to divide each of the figures from the private practice and general hospital sources by 3 to make the figures more comparable with those of the Mental Health Division).

All the patients included in this study can be classified as belonging to one of four categories: (1) immigrants to Australia, (2) refugees either from the Indo–Chinese countries or Timor, which is now officially Indonesia, (3) overseas students coming to study in Australia, or (4) tourists visiting for very short periods of time. (Very few tourists are included in this sample, and, indeed, we believe that very few of them require psychiatric treatment during their short stay in the country.)

We can say with a fair degree of confidence that the data presented here cover almost all the psychiatric cases among the students and refugees and 95% of the other ethnic Chinese patients who seek private or general hospital psychiatric treatment.

FINDINGS

DEMOGRAPHIC DATA OF PATIENTS

In the interpretation of our data, it is to be remembered that basic demographic information for ethnic Chinese cannot be directly obtained from the National Census, because the data base does not specify ethnic origin. For each person, the country of birth is recorded, but this does not equate with ethnic origin. For example, Chinese born in Malaysia are listed as Malaysians, Greeks born in Egypt are listed as Egyptians, and Russians born in Shanghai are considered to be Chinese. Therefore, statistical comparison should be avoided and care should be exercised when interpretations are being attempted.

A total of 106 Chinese cases were collected in this study: 43 cases from private practice; 35 from the general hospital; and 28 from psychiatric hospitals (Table 17.2). The utilization rate for patients with all types of psychiatric disorders in the State Mental Health facilities is 10 per 100,000 population (Krupinski, 1980). Assuming that the ethnic Chinese population of Victoria is 15,000, the figures in this study indicate the current utilization rate of psychiatric facilities is only 5.3 per 100,000, which contrasts markedly with the 25.7 per 10,000 population prevalence rate in 1870 (Chiu, 1977); it is difficult to be certain about the reason for this discrepancy. Because there does not appear to be a predominance of male ethnic Chinese in the general population in Victoria, one is curious about

Table 17.2   Demographic Data of Patients by Facility

| | Number treated in | | | |
Categories	Private practice	General hospital	Psychiatric hospitals	Total
Total number per year	43	35	28	106
Gender				
Male	26	20	16	62
Female	17	15	12	44
Age				
19 years and under	7	9	4	20
20–29 years	18	15	12	45
30–39 years	9	5	6	20
40 years and over	9	6	6	21
Marital status				
Single	24	25	20	69
Married	15	8	7	30
Separated or divorced	2	1	1	4
Widowed	2	1	—	3
Residential status				
Immigrants	24	6	18	48
Refugees	4	16	5	25
Overseas students	13	13	4	2
Tourists	2	—	1	—
Country of origin[a]				
Malaysia and Singapore	20	15	7	42
Indo–China	4	14	5	23
Hong Kong	16	1	14	31
China	2	3	2	7
Indonesia	1	2	—	3

[a] Estimated 1976 population in Victoria: from Malaysia and Singapore, 7000; Indo–China, 600; Hong Kong, 2100; China, 4200; Indonesia, 360.

the reason for the male predominance of ethnic Chinese seeking psychiatric treatment shown in Table 17.2.

There is an overwhelming predominance (45% of the sample) of patients who are ages 20–29 years. The explanation for this is that 30 of the 106 patients are overseas students. Most of the refugees from the Indo–Chinese countries fall within this age group as well. The large number of overseas students and the refugees from the Indo–Chinese countries account for a predominance (nearly 70%) of single persons in the sample. Many of the students are in their early 20s; and the young refugees are single, which explains why they were able to escape either in boats to Malaysia, Thailand, or Indonesia or overland to Thailand before being resettled in Australia.

COUNTRY OF ORIGIN

Table 17.2 also shows the distribution of patients with respect to their countries of origin and the 1976 estimated population of ethnic Chinese in Victoria, based on country of origin. The number of people from Indo–China is low because these data were gathered before the influx of the Indo–Asian refugees to Australia that began in late 1976 and is still going on, although not in such large numbers as in 1979 and 1980. The figure for Indonesia (600) represents mostly those ethnic Chinese who came as refugees from Portuguese Timor after the Portuguese colony was taken over by the Indonesians.

The majority of ethnic Chinese patients in this sample come from Malaysia and Singapore. However, there is a disproportionately large number of patients from Hong Kong, and most of these are treated in psychiatric hospitals. There is no ready explanation for this discrepancy. This finding contrasts markedly with the report of Lee (1981) that the Chinese in Hong Kong, despite having to live in highly overcrowded conditions, make a generally good adaptation and do not have a strikingly high psychiatric morbidity. The population pressure in Australia is very low compared to that in Hong Kong. It may be the change from very high density to very low density living, which makes for difficulty in adjustment, that these Chinese from Hong Kong are reacting to. This social decompression phenomenon as a hypothesis needs further research to test its validity.

SERVICE UTILIZATION AND DIAGNOSIS

About one-third of the patients in this sample were seen within the first year of their arrival. There is a tendency for the patients to seek psychiatric treatment either as private patients or as general hospital patients. They seldom go to the psychiatric hospital facilities of the Mental Health Division, even though these are widely scattered throughout the metropolitan area of Melbourne and—perhaps more significantly—even though at the time of this study there were five ethnic Chinese psychiatrists, two consultants, and three trainees in the service of the Mental Health Division. The majority of the cases (82%) are seen as outpatients, with few seen as inpatients (18%). This ratio is more pronounced in private practice.

Schizophrenia is the most common diagnosis made among these ethnic Chinese patients, neurotic disorders are the next most common, and situational reactions are third (see Table 17.3). What is perhaps more noteworthy and consistent with other reported studies, such as that of Lin et al. (1980) in Taiwan, is the infrequency of alcoholism and drug abuse among the ethnic Chinese. There was only one patient for whom alcoholism was the principal diagnosis and only one for whom it was a secondary diagnosis; one patient seen in the psychiatric hospital had a problem of drug

Table 17.3 Clinical Diagnosis by Facility

Diagnosis	Number treated in			
	Private practice	General hospital	Psychiatric hospitals	Total
Schizophrenia	9[a]	15	13	37
Affective disorders	3[b]	5	1	9
Neurotic disorders	12	8	3	23
Situational reactions	10	3	5	18
Personality disorders	3	3	2[c]	8
Alcoholism	1	—	—	1
Organic status	1	—	—	2
Childhood behavior disorders	2	—	2	4
Epilepsy	1	—	—	1
Mental retardation	—	—	2	2
Others[d]	—	1	—	1
Total	43	35	28	106

[a] 1 case of concomitant mental retardation.
[b] 1 case of concomitant alcoholism.
[c] 1 case of concomitant drug abuse.
[d] 1 case diagnosed as deaf mutism.

abuse. This contrasts rather starkly with the general picture in Australia, especially among University students, where the frequency of drug abuse is relatively high; although there were 30 students in the sample, there is only one case of drug abuse among the ethnic Chinese patients.

MODALITY OF TREATMENT

Although there is a general tendency for patients to be treated mainly with medication, many of them may also be treated with psychotherapy, either alone or in conjunction with medication, by the private practitioners or in the general hospital. This is true even for refugees and new immigrants who are not well-established economically. (This is in contrast with the findings of Hollingshead and Redlich (1958) in New Haven, Connecticut.) The general availability of psychotherapy is largely due to the universal health insurance coverage in the Australian health care system. It is also a measure of the availability of Chinese-speaking psychiatrists in the community to provide this service. In our opinion, the choice of medication over psychotherapy as the chief modality treatment in the psychiatric hospitals merely reflects the clinical style and time constraints of the psychiatrists.

AVAILABILITY OF SOCIAL SUPPORT NETWORKS

For the purpose of this study, we operationally classified the availability of the social support network systems into three categories: family, friends, and social services. If a patient has support from more than one of these categories, he or she is rated "good" in terms of support networks; if only one categories is available, the rating is "fair" and the rating is "poor" if none of them is present. Most of the ethnic Chinese patients had only fair social support networks. Although the patients going to private practitioners tended to have better support networks than those going to the general and psychiatric hospital, they tended also to be the more affluent migrants from Malaysia or Singapore who came with their families and who, because of their relative fluency in the English language, made new friends and were more aware of, and had better access to, the social services available within the community.

OCCUPATIONAL STATUS

In this sample as a whole, there is no greater tendency for patients in professional or skilled occupations to be seen in private practice than in the general hospital and in the psychiatric hospitals. It is noteworthy that there is a predominance of the unemployed who were treated in the general hospital psychiatric unit.

What is more interesting, however, is the small number of changes of occupational status after arrival in Australia. Of the 66 patients who are either immigrants or refugees (106 minus the 40 who are either overseas students or tourists), 41 (62%) had more or less the same occupational status that they had before coming to Australia. Four (8%) reported being in occupations of a higher status than those they had before they came. These were persons who had come to Australia to complete either their education or their training. On completion of their education or training, they were, of course, able to move on to higher occupational levels than they had before. Only 21 subjects (32%) were in occupations of lower status than before their arrival. These included two medical practitioners who, because of illnesses, were not able to continue in their profession and had to accept lower-level jobs. Seven were students who came to Australia as immigrants or refugees.

PROBLEMS OF IMMIGRATION AND ADJUSTMENT
IN A NEW SETTING

Almost half of the psychiatric cases share the problems of adjusting to a new environment and of dealing with the effects of past tramatic experiences because they are either overseas students or refugees. Case examples are described to illustrate these problems.

Adjustment to a New Environment. E. J. is a 20-year-old student from Malaysia who was financed by his parents, who are school teachers, to study for a business degree in Australia, although he would have preferred a degree in science. He was assigned by the Australian Department of Education to study in a small coastal resort town about 200 miles from Melbourne.

He found lodgings with a middle-aged Australian widow who became a mother figure to him, but he made very few friends among his peers. He soon developed a neurodermatitis and began to feel that the other 20 or so Malaysian students on the campus were agents of the Malaysian government watching his every move. This paranoid feeling quickly became very intense, and he was referred by a local psychiatrist to St. Vincent's Hospital, where he was diagnosed as schizophrenic. The paranoid feelings, which were of delusional intensity, were brought under control with moderate doses of chlorpromazine and his skin problem cleared up.

After discharge, he did not continue his studies for the year but managed to be transferred to a university in Melbourne where he registered for a bachelor of arts degree. There are more Malaysian students on this larger campus, and he has been able to make a few friends among them, though not among the Australian students. Thus he was able to make a reasonable adjustment. His concern now, apart from passing his exams, is what employment he will find and what discrimination he will face when he returns to Malaysia.

The Effect of Past Experiences. T. S. is a 32-year-old ethnic Chinese housewife from Saigon. Her family and her husband's family left Vietnam at great expense in two boats in 1978. Before they cleared the Vietnamese coastline, the first boat, which carried her husband's parents, siblings, and their families, was spotted by the Vietnamese coastal patrol, which opened fire. That boat was sunk, with all on board, in the sight of the boat that T. S. and her family were in. They managed to evade the coastal patrol and arrive in Malaysia. They were in a refugee camp for about 9 months.

T. S. was pregnant when she left Vietnam, and at term, she developed complications during labor and had to be moved to Kuala Lumpur for 6 weeks of treatment. In the meantime, her husband developed pulmonary tuberculosis in the refugee camp and had to be sent to a tuberculosis hospital for isolation for 4 months.

Finally, T. S., her husband, and their four children were selected by the Australian immigration team for settlement; but her parents, her siblings, and their families were not and had to wait in Malaysia. On arrival in Melbourne in 1979, her husband found a factory job within a few weeks but had to stop work because of a relapse of his tuberculosis, for which he again needed hospitalization. While in Melbourne, the patient received no news from her parents and siblings. She became anxious, sleepless, and slightly depressed. Associated with the insomnia were frequent nightmares of death and of seeing her in-laws being shot out of the water. She was diagnosed as having a case of situational reaction. The insomnia was resistant to all forms of treatment, including psychotherapy, relaxation exercises, medication, and a short course of electroconvulsive therapy. It persisted long after her husband was discharged from the hospital and was back at work, and even after she heard that her family was comfortably settled in Montreal. She eventually improved after 20 months of drug treatment and started work in a factory.

SUMMARY

From the foregoing discussion, it appears that, notwithstanding the non-availability of base-line demographic information, there is a suggestion that the population of ethnic Chinese in Victoria, Australia shows the same pattern of utilization of psychiatric services as overseas Chinese in other parts of the world; that is, there is an underutilization (Lau, 1981; Kinzie, 1974). There is a predominance of male patients over female, although because of the lack of base-line demongraphic data it is unclear whether this is due to a predominance of males in the ethnic Chinese population in Victoria. From personal impressions, this does not seem to be the case. A large proportion of these patients were seen as outpatients, and only a small proportion (less than 20%) were admitted to hospitals as inpatients.

The people in this study are classified as immigrants, refugees, overseas students, and tourists. Because of a lack of base-line demographic data, there has previously been no indication as to which of these four major categories tends to make greater use of psychiatric services. The biggest proportion of this sample are ethnic Chinese from Malaysia and Singapore, which is understandable because the largest proportion of ethnic Chinese coming to Australia are from these countries. In terms of utilization of services, however, the ethnic Chinese from Hong Kong show a striking predominance. We cannot be sure of the reason for this; more work is needed to test our social decompression hypothesis. It appears that most of the contacts with psychiatric services are made within the first year after arrival, with the chances of contact decreasing with each year the person is a resident in Australia.

There is no difference in the modality of treatment given to the patient whether he or she is seen as a patient in the general hospital or as a patient in private practice. There are almost equal chances for a patient to be given medication, psychotherapy, or a combination of medication and psychotherapy. The patients in the psychiatric hospital tend to be treated with medication, but a sizeable proportion were treated with psychotherapy.

Schizophrenia is the most common principal diagnosis made of these patients, with a group of neurotic disorders being the next most frequent. In contrast to findings for patients of European origin, affective disorders are only the fourth most frequent diagnosis. Alcoholism was diagnosed only in two cases, in one as a principal diagnosis and in the other as a secondary diagnosis; drug abuse was reported in only one case.

There does not appear to be any increased tendency for patients in professional or skilled occupations to be seen in private practice, although this tendency is suggested when one compares the private practice with the general hospital, since many of the general hospital patients are unemployed.

Despite the general observation that most immigrants suffer a lowering of occupational status in their host country, few subjects in this sample show this tendency. More than two-thirds of patients who are immigrants or refugees enjoy the same or better occupational status after arrival in Australia. Perhaps this reflects the immigration policies of the Australian government, which selects only those ethnic Chinese immigrants, and to some extent, refugees, who have occupational skills that are acceptable in Australia and for whom employment is likely to be available. The infrequency of patients with criminal charges is to be noted among this sample of ethnic Chinese patients.

This is essentially an impressionistic study, although we were able to collect some figures relating to the types of patients and problems we encountered. One purpose of the study is to highlight the sort of psychiatric problems encountered by the ethnic Chinese population in Victoria in the process of their adjustment to life in Australia. Another purpose is to provide some data to compare with those reported for the ethnic Chinese living in other parts of the world outside mainland China. But for this to be done effectively, a better planned study will have to be done, and the figures obtained will have to be converted into various rates against a known population base that could be derived from the 1981 Australian census.

REFERENCES

Chiu, E.
    1977   "Fart Din" 1 and 2. *Medical Journal of Australia, 1,* 541–544; *2,* 594–597.
Hollingshead, A., and Redlich, F. C.
    1958   *Social class and mental illness,* New York, Wiley.

Kinzie, J. D.
    1974   A summary of literature of epidemiology of mental illness in Hawaii. In W. S.
            Tseng, J. F. McDermott, and T. W. Maretzki (Eds.), *Peoples and cultures in
            Hawaii.* Honolulu, University of Hawaii School of Medicine.
Krupinski, J.
    1980   *Statistical bulletin No. 14: Admissions, discharges and deaths, 1977–78.* Melbourne,
            Australia: Mental Health Research Institute, Health Commission of Victoria.
Lau, L.
    1981   *The delivery of mental health services to an immigrant population: A report of the first
            year of operations of the Chinese Clinic.* Honolulu, Hawaii: State Department of
            Health, Mental Health Division.
Lee, R. P. Y.
    1981   *Social stress and adjustment in Hong Kong: Problem of high density living.* Paper
            presented at the 18th Annual Congress of the Royal Australian and New
            Zealand College of Psychiatrists, Hong Kong, 12–16 October.
Lin, K. M., Kleinman, A., and Lin, T. Y.
    1980   Overview of mental disorders in Chinese cultures: A review of epidemiological
            and clinical studies. In A. Kleinman and T. Y. Lin (Eds.), *Normal and abnormal
            behavior in Chinese culture.* Dordrecht, Holland: Reidel.
Sue, S., and Mckinney, H.
    1975   Asian-Americans in the community mental health care system. *American Jour-
            nal of Orthopsychiatry, 45,* 111–118.

CHAPTER 18

Sociocultural Changes and Prevalence of Mental Disorders in Taiwan

Eng-Kung Yeh

GENERAL SOCIAL AND HEALTH BACKGROUND

Approximately 160 km southeast of the coast of the Chinese mainland is the leaf-shaped island of Taiwan. This island of (36,000 km^2) was a province of the Chinese Empire for centries until it was taken by Japan in the peace settlement ending the first Sino–Japanese War of 1894–1895. With the defeat of Japan in World War II 50 years later, in 1945 Taiwan was restored to China. Because of changes in the political situation, it was once again separated from mainland China in 1949.

Since 1950, Taiwan has undergone tremendous social changes associated with rapid industrialization, modernization, and the increase of population. Owing to the promotion of family planning since 1964, the birthrate has dropped sharply from 50.0‰ in 1951 to 23.4‰ in 1980. However, the marked decline of the annual death rate, from 18.1‰ in 1947 to 4.8‰ in 1980, has resulted in a net natural increase rate of around 19‰ (*Health Statistics, 1946–1970; Health Statistics: 2. Vital Statistics, 1970–1980*). In

265

1980, a population of 17,805,067 occupied the island at a density of 494.6 per km², giving Taiwan the second highest population density in the world. There were, however, changes in population composition: a gradual decrease of the dependent age group (under age 15) and an increase in the productive age group (15–64). There have also been changes in family constellation in terms of a gradual increase of nuclear families and a decrease of large extended families, a situation evident in larger cities. This has resulted in a gradual decrease in the size of the average family—to 4.0 in Taipei City and 4.9 in other areas—according to 1980 figures. Average life expectancy has been extended from 52.9 for males and 56.3 for females in 1950 to 68.6 for males and 74.1 for females in 1980. The improvements in medical care, industrialization, and modernization have also resulted in changes in the main causes of death. Infectious disease, which was the primary cause of death two decades ago, has been replaced by cerebral vascular disease, malignant neoplasm, cardiovascular disease, and accidents during the past several years (*Health Statistics*, 1946–1970; *Health Statistics: 1. General Statistics*, 1970–1980). The sharp increase in accidental death deserves special attention. In 1959, the rate of death by accident was only 1.4 per 100,000 population, ranking as the thirty-second most prevalant cause of death. In 1972, accidental death increased to 10.2 per 100,000, sevenfold in 13 years, ranking fourth main cause of death. This rate increased to 54.1 in 1975, further increased to 64.0 in 1980, and has, since 1975, ranked as the third main cause of death.

Rapid modernization and industrialization have brought about economic prosperity and an improvement in the standard of living, but, at the same time, these changes have increased the occurrence of stressful situations created by conflicts between modern and traditional, Western and Chinese value orientation and have demanded constant adaptation by the population to continuously changing life-styles and arrangements in the social structure.

In addition to the previously mentioned social changes, Taiwan has the following interesting ethnic groups, which are frequently referred to as different subcultural groups in psychiatric epidemiological and clinical studies.

1. *Aborigines* are Malayo–Polynesian in origin and constitute 2% of the total population. This group is organized into nine tribes, which exhibit varying degrees of acculturation to Chinese culture.

2. *Native Taiwanese Chinese* refers to the descendants of Chinese who migrated to the islands primarily from Fukien and, to a lesser extent, from Kwangton province of China during the seventeenth and eighteenth centuries. This group, which constitutes approximately 70% of the current

population, has lived on the island for generations and was influenced to some extent by Japanese culture during the 50 years of Japanese administration.

3. *Mainland Chinese* refers to those who migrated to Taiwan after World War II, and to their descendants as well as, a group that includes approximately 28% of Taiwan's inhabitants. A massive influx of migrants took place between 1947 and 1953, immediately following political changes in mainland China. The members of first generation of this group that migrated from all parts of China went through similar refugee experiences and have maintained subcultures different from that of the native Taiwanese. This group of inhabitants is of special research interest in terms of the impact of migration and refugee experience on mental health.

With this ethnic and subcultural composition combined with the rapid social and cultural changes since 1945, Taiwan provides investigators concerned with culture and mental disorders with a variety of interesting subjects and rich opportunities for comparative study.

This chapter reviews some important findings on the prevalence and clinical manifestation of mental disorders, based on certain major studies carried out in Taiwan. The findings are discussed in relation to social and cultural changes, and topics are proposed for future studies.

PREVALENCE OF MENTAL DISORDERS

A series of communitywide psychiatric epidemiological studies has been conducted by a team of psychiatrists at the National Taiwan University Hospital since 1946. The studies provide information about the prevalence of mental disorders in Taiwan and serve as the basic data for planning in mental health services, as well as for cross-cultural comparison (T. Y. Lin, 1961).

Overall Prevalence Rates of Mental Disorders

During the period 1946–1948, the first psychiatric survey was carried out in three communities representing village, small town, and a section of an urban area in Taiwan (T. Y. Lin, 1953). A total population of 19,931 was studied in these three communitywide census surveys. Three steps were undertaken: (1) the survey of census registers regarding each inhabitant's basic data and the gathering of information from key figures in the community, which served to identify psychiatric cases; (2) visits to every household for interviews and brief psychiatric examinations of all family

Table 18.1   Prevalence of Mental Disorders in Three
Communities in Taiwan, 1946–1948

Disorder	Number	‰ of population[a]
Psychotic	76	3.8
Schizophrenia	43	2.2
Manic-depressive psychosis	13	0.6
Senile psychoses	6	0.3
Other psychoses	14	0.7
Nonpsychotic	112	5.6
Psychoneurosis	24	1.2
Alcoholism	2	0.1
Psychopathic personality	18	0.9
Mental deficiency	68	3.4
All disorders	188	9.4

[a] Population investigated, 19,931; Taiwanese only.

members to ensure the completeness of the survey; and (3) detailed and careful examination of the reported and identified cases to confirm the final diagnoses. The generally well-established and reliable census registration system in Taiwan and the cooperation of officials and community leaders greatly facilitated the success of the surveys.

The results of the surveys (see Table 18.1) revealed that the prevalence rate for schizophrenia was 2.2‰, and the rate for manic–depressive psychosis was 0.6‰. These rates are roughly comparable with these found in other cultures. The rates for nonpsychotic disorders, such as neuroses and personality disorders, were unreliable for cross-cultural comparison due to the variation in diagnostic criteria adapted by different investigators. However, the survey revealed an extremely low rate for alcoholism among Chinese (T. Y. Lin, 1953).

From the demographic and ecological points of view, schizophrenia, personality disorders, and neurosis were more prevalent in urban than in rural communities and were more concentrated in the central part of each community. In contrast, mental retardation and senile psychosis were more prevalent in rural communities and also more evident in peripheral parts of each community. As to the gender factor, the rates for manic–depressive psychosis and neurosis were higher in females, while that for personality disorder was higher in males. The rates for schizophrenia, manic–depressive psychosis, and neurosis were highest in the working age group (20–59). Mental disorders in general were more prevalent in unemployed, unskilled, and lower-status occupations. The rates for schizophrenia, organic psychosis, and alcoholism were inversely related to socioeconomic status.

Changes in Prevalence Rates 15 Years Later

In order to understand the impact of social and cultural changes on prevalences and manifestations of mental disorders, a longitudinal follow-up study was carried out 15 years later in 1961–1963 in the same three communities by the same group of investigators (T. Y. Lin, Rin, Yeh, Hsu, and Chu, 1969)

The most significant finding in the follow-up survey was that while there was essentially no change in the rate for psychoses, the rate for neurosis had sharply risen from 1.2 to 7.8‰ among the Taiwanese Chinese population (Table 18.2).

Since the mass of mainland Chinese had not yet migrated to Taiwan at the time of the first survey, there were no data for follow-up comparison. However, the influence of migration on mental health was inferred from two sources of data: The prevalence rate of neuroses for mainland Chinese (16.1‰) and for native Taiwanese Chinese (7.8‰), the former being considerably higher than the latter. Even among the native Taiwanese Chinese group, when divided into the group of original inhabitants of the communities surveyed and the group of recently settled inhabitants, the prevalence rates of neuroses shows 6.9‰ and 12.1‰, respectively, with significant differences. The marked difference in rate of neurosis between migrants and nonmigrants indicates the impact of migration on the individual's adaptation and mental health. This difference was not observed in the rate of psychosis.

These findings seem to support the generally accepted theory that, etiologically, psychosis is more associated with the genetically determined predisposition than with sociocultural environmental factors and that neurosis is more associated with the latter factors than the former.

Mental Retardation

The rate of mental retardation was 3.4‰ in the 1946–1948 survey and 4.4‰ in the 1961–1963 survey. The rate was higher among the native Taiwanese Chinese group than the mainland Chinese group. This is understandable because the mentally retarded would have found migration from the mainland to Taiwan relatively difficult.

In the native Taiwanese Chinese group, a slight increase in the rate was seen in the age group under 10. This is assumed to be due to an improvement in medical care, resulting in a decrease in the death rate and an

Table 18.2 Comparison of Mental Disorders in Two Studies

| | 1946–1948 | | 1961–1963 | | | |
| | Taiwanese | | Taiwanese | | Mainland Chinese | |
Disorder	Number	‰ of population[a]	Number	‰ of population[a]	Number	‰ of population[a]
Psychotic	76	3.8	92	3.1	29	2.9
Schizophrenia	43	2.2	41	1.4	19	1.9
Manic-depressive psychosis	13	0.6	16	0.5	1	0.1
Senile psychoses	6	0.3	11	0.4	0	0.0
Other psychoses	14	0.7	24	0.8	9	0.9
Nonpsychotic	112	5.6	410	14.1	206	20.9
Psychoneurosis	24	1.2	227	7.8	158	16.1
Psychopathic personality	20	1.0	40	1.4	19	1.9
Mental retardation	68	3.4	143	4.9	29	2.9
All disorders	188	9.4	502	17.2	235	23.9

[a] Population investigated: 1946–1948, 19,931; 1961–1963, 29,184 Taiwanese and 9,840 mainland Chinese.

increase in survival rates of young children with brain-related illness in this age group.

The overall rate of mental retardation found in these two surveys relates to clinically diagnosable cases, with the great majority of cases including cases with moderate and severe mental retardation and not including cases of minor mental retardation.

The degree to which modernization and the resultant social and cultural changes in the society affect the prevalence, clinical manifestations, and rehabilitation of mental retardation deserves careful longitudinal study. It can be hypothesized that cases caused by postnatal biological and environmental factors will decrease owing to the improvement in health care and living standard, while cases due to genetic factors will increase slightly owing to advances in the skill of diagnosis and care associated with the increased opportunity for survival.

Cross-Ethnic Comparison with Aborigines

By applying the same methodology, a psychiatric survey was carried out for aborigines in 1949–1953 for cross-ethnic comparison. Most of the Taiwan aborigines were living in mountain areas. For aboriginal tribes, with a total population of 11,442, were studied (Rin and Lin, 1962). The results of the survey show that the prevalence rate for schizophrenia was significantly lower among the aborigines, while the rates for alcoholism, personality disorders, and organic psychosis were much higher than those for Taiwanese Chinese. The higher prevalence of organic psychosis among the aborigines can be understood in terms of their poor environmental hygiene and the endemic condition of various infectious diseases including malaria.

Another significant finding was the benign course of the majority of schizophrenic cases: Among the 10 identified cases, there were no relapses, and only one showed chronic deterioration. This may be further clarified by noting the clinical manifestations. Out of 10 cases of schizophrenia, 4 were catatonic, 4 unclassified, and 1 case each hebephrenic and paranoid. While the hebephrenic and paranoid cases still evidenced active psychotic symptoms, most of the catatonic and unclassified cases (6 out of 8) were free from active symptoms at the time of the study. These cases were characterized by acute onset, short duration of illness, and favorable outcome and thus, diagnostically, may be considered atypical rather than typical schizophrenia. There are two hypotheses that can be considered for interpreting the benign course of schizophrenia among the aborigines. First, poor environmental hygiene, nutrition, and treatment opportunities may diminish the chance for survival of the chronic cases. Second, the relatively simple sociocultural environment of these tribes may be more favorable for the recovery of schizophrenia. The second hypothesis seems to be in accord with the World Health Organization report from the International Pilot Study of Schizophrenia: that recovery from schizophrenia varies inversely with the level of technological development among the nine societies studied (Cooper and Satorius, 1977).

Community Survey of Psychophysiological Disorders

In order to investigate the prevalence of psychophysiological disorders and their relationship to various social, cultural, and demographic factors, a community epidemiological survey was carried out on Baksa, a subrural area of Taipei City, one of the three communities previously studied (Rin, Chu, and Lin, 1966). Methodologically, this survey showed several important advancements in comparison to previous epidemiological studies in terms of (1) utilizing age- and sex-stratified random sampling, (2) using well-defined criteria for diagnosis, and (3) applying a specifically designed health questionnaire in order to cross-validate the clinical diagnosis.

The overall prevalence rate for diagnosable psychophysiological disorders was 42% among the community population. The rate for such disorders was generally lowest in the 15–24 age group (27%), tended to parallel the increase in age, reached its peak in the 45–54 age group (64%), and declined in the age group over 55. Marriage and socioeconomic status were related to the rate of psychophysiological disorder. Significantly higher rates were found in (1) younger married males and females (more males than females), (2) lower class males, (3) upper class females, and (4) oldest sons and youngest daughters. It can be speculated from these findings that while lower class males and those who marry young are subject to greater financial stresses, the upper class females may be more hampered by cultural restrictions. While oldest sons are subject to higher expectation from the parents and may, thus, be exposed to more psychological pressure, the youngest daughters are often neglected or even overtly rejected in Chinese families.

The other two important factors associated with the prevalence rate of such disorders were (1) modernity–traditional value identification and (2) migration. Those who had more contact with modern life-styles together with strong traditional value identification had lower rates than those who had less contact with modern life-styles and weak traditional value identification. Taiwanese Chinese who had recently migrated and mainland Chinese with refugee experience showed higher rates of the disorders. The impact of migration seemed to be most severe in older females and in those of lower socioeconomic status.

Distribution of Neuroses among Outpatient Population

Although the statistical data of the outpatient clinic do not reflect the actual prevalence of disorder in the community, such data may serve as a clue for understanding the pattern of distribution of disorders. According to the statistical data of the Psychiatric Clinic, National Taiwan University Hospital (1969–1979), one of the major psychiatric treatment centers located in the center of the Taipei City, about one-third (36.3%) of the outpatients in 1978–1979 were categorized as having disorders of neurosis.

Of all the neurotic cases, more than half (55.4%) were diagnosed as having anxiety disorder, the top-ranking condition of neuroses. Approximately one-fifth were diagnosed as having depressive neurosis, which ranked as the second largest group. In contrast to evidence found in earlier studies, depressive neurosis was more frequently diagnosed, while the typical form of conversion hysteria declined in frequency between 1969 and 1979. Symptomatology, diagnosis, and biochemical aspects of depression and its treatment were increasingly emphasized in medical school undergraduate teaching, psychiatric residency training, and clinical research during the 10-year study. The increased rates of depression in psychiatric clinics may be due, therefore, to the increased professional attention given to this disorder, not only among psychiatrists, but also by nonpsychiatric professionals, whose awareness resulted in an increased referral rate.

Though the tendency to present somatic complaints among neurotic patients is still evident in Taiwan, hysteria in the form of conversion or dissociation has become less effective as a defense mechanism, so that the prevalence of the classic and exaggerated form of hysteria is becoming less frequently observed in the psychiatric clinic. Instead, there is an increasing tendency for neurotic patients to present more psychological problems such as anxiety or depression. That the increased rates of anxiety and depressive disorders in Taiwan are in accord with findings from technologically developed Western societies, can, thus, be speculated to be associated with the changes in the society.

Another interesting finding derived from the psychiatric clinic data is that approximately 5% of neurotic outpatients are diagnosed as having obsessive–compulsive disorder—the same rate as reported from Western societies (Nemiah, 1975). These data are certainly contradictory to the previous impression drawn from the findings of the census surveys in three communities—that the obsessive–compulsive neurosis is rare among the Chinese (T. Y. Lin, 1953). This observation deserves future investigation in order to clarify whether the evidence is due to methodological error in case findings or whether there has been an actual change in the disorder in Taiwan.

Student Mental Health

A 4-year longitudinal follow-up study of mental health was carried out in a university in Taipei during 1963–1967 (Yeh, Chu, Ko, Lin, and Lee, 1972). All freshmen, including three different subcultural groups, Taiwanese Chinese, mainland Chinese and overseas Chinese (mainly from Southeast Asian regions), were studied at the time of entrance to the university and were followed up every academic year up to graduation by means of specifically designed mental health questionnaires and individual interviews. Using a list of well-defined criteria for symptom manifestation and diagnosis, nearly one-third of the freshmen (30.7%) were found to be ratable as psychiatric cases, out of which 5.1% were definite cases and 25.6% were highly probable cases. These rates are fairly comparable to studies reported from other cultures (Kidd, 1965).

The great majority of symptoms manifested were psychophysiological disorders and neuroses. On the whole, the rate of psychophysiological disorders was significantly higher among female students than among male students. In female students, this rate was highest among the overseas Chinese and lowest in the Taiwanese Chinese group. This difference was, however, not seen in male students. These findings clearly indicate that overseas Chinese female students tend to manifest psychophysiological disorder more than males and other domicile groups do in the early phase of adjustment to a new living and study environment. The overall rate of psychophysiological disorder was, however, significantly lower than in the corresponding age group (16–25) of the general population in males, yet showed no significant difference in females. The rate of neurosis appears to be higher among male students than among females. This rate was also higher in male student group compared to the corresponding age group of the general population, while there was no difference noted in the female student group. The rate of psychosis was around 1.7‰ and was apparently much lower than that of the general population.

The overall rate of psychiatric disorders in the senior year was found to be essentially the same as those of the freshman year when the same cohort of students was studied. There was, however, a significant increase in neurotic symptoms that replaced psychophysiological symptoms. Four years of college experience seem to have affected the students' coping methods for stress.

There have been no systematic epidemiological studies yet carried out in Taiwan on mental health problems of senior high school students. Still, from observation in school and clinical experiences, it can be speculated that the prevalences of symptom manifestations in senior high school students are comparable to those of college students. This speculation is based on the fact that there exist tremendous psychological pressures on the majority of senior high school students to undertake the highly competitive, nationwide joint entrance examination for colleges. In the previously described study on mental health of college students, it was found that only 37.5% of the psychiatric cases had their onset of symptoms during college years, while the remaining 62.5% of the cases had onset of symptoms as early as the senior or even junior high school years and these symptoms had been carried over to college years.

A series of studies using ratings by class teachers on students' behavior revealed that the prevalence rate of behavior problems among junior high school students was 10–12%, while among primary school pupils, the rate was 10–13%. (C. C. Hsu 1970, 1973, Shen, Wang, Chen, and Yang, 1978.) The rates of behavior problems were higher in males in both junior high school and elementary school.

Suicides

Suicide is a highly disturbing, life-threatening behavior that often serves as one of the indications of the psychopathology of an individual as well as of the society, although the prevalence rate of suicide in the general population is generally underestimated due to difficulties in case finding and reporting.

Annual government health statistics (*Health Statistics: 1. General Statistics,* 1970–1980) show that in Taiwan, the suicide rates between 1946 and 1976 were 12–14 per 100,000 population. The committed suicide rate was generally higher among males than females, at a ratio of about 2:1. As a whole, with fluctuations, the gradually increased after 1946—during and after the crisis periods of turmoil or transition from the Japanese administration to the Chinese after World War II, which was followed by massive influx of migration from mainland China to Taiwan around 1949, reaching a peak in 1964. In 1964, the highest rate of 19.1 per 100,000 population was recorded. Subsequently, associated with the growing stability of society and economic prosperity, the rate steadily declined reaching the lowest rate of 8.7 per 100,000 population in 1976 (see Figure 18.1). Since 1977, the rates have increased slightly, but until 1980, they were all below 10 per 100,000 population.

Though the rate of suicides in the general population has been declining, death by suicide has jumped to tenth rank among the main causes of death in Taiwan during the past several years (*Health Statistics: 1. General Health*

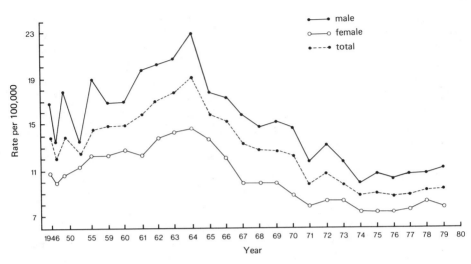

Figure 18.1 Suicide death rate in Taiwan, 1946–1979.

Statistics, 1970–1980). There are some age-related characteristics. The suicide rate increases after age 15, with the first peak appearing in the 20–24 age group, declines in age group 34–49, and increases again in persons over 50 years of age, showing the second peak (higher than the 20–24 age group) in the age group over 65. Due to the smaller proportion of the age group over 65 in the total population in Taiwan compared with Western developed countries, the actual number of suicidal deaths in this older age group is, however, small. The relatively high rate of suicidal deaths in the younger age group in Taiwan is different from that of Western developed countries and seems to be related to rapid social changes, to which these young people have difficulty in adjusting.

In contrast to the number of committed suicides, attempted suicides have shown a different picture that is associated with a different psychopathology, requiring separate treatment. A survey of three major newspapers in Taiwan revealed that among a total of 364 reported suicide cases, 248 cases (68.1%) died, and 116 cases (31.9%) were attempted suicides (Rin, Tsen, and Chen, 1974).

The statistics of the Suicide Prevention Center in Taipei show that 74% of the total attempted suicide cases were under age 30, with 36% in the 21–25 age group, 23% in the under 20 age group, and 15% in the 26–30 age group. There were only 4% of cases in the age group over 50. In all age groups, the females significantly outnumbered males by as many as 2.5–3.5 times (Mackay Memorial Hospital, 1969–1971). The most frequently reported precipitating factors for suicides were family conflicts, marital discord, and frustration or failure in love affairs. This finding supports the clinical impression that this group of young females were particularly subject to psychosocial stress relating to family affairs in Chinese society.

Juvenile Delinquency

The rate of juvenile delinquency in a society is a rather arbitrary one, depending largely upon such factors as the attitudes of community, human resources and effectiveness in action taking on the part of security authorities, and the existing legislation against the crimes. Therefore, careful interpretation of its implications needs to be made.

The rate of juvenile delinquency in Taiwan, both in comparison with the crimes of all age groups and with the population of corresponding age groups, increased every year between 1953 and 1973. Thereafter, the rate has been fairly stable (Hwang, 1978). However, what is noteworthy is not the changes in the rates, but the changes in the types of crimes and the manners in which they are committed. Until 1974, the top-ranking crime among youngsters was stealing. The 70% rate was nearly 10-fold the rate of the second ranking crime, bodily injury. There had been very few violent crimes, such as robbery, homicide, and crimes associated with sex.

The picture has changed since 1975, and there have been two noteworthy findings in juvenile delinquency. One is the relative decline in stealing (though the rate is still high—approximately 60%) and the gradual increase of violent crimes, such as bodily injury, robbery, homicide, blackmail, and sexual crimes, and the abuse of substances such as penthazocine, hypnotics, tranquilizers, and, less popularly, stimulants and glue sniffing (Cho, 1981). The other change is in the increasing number of female offenders. These findings are much more observable in urban areas than in rural.

In general, violent crimes were often committed under the effect of psychedelic drugs or hypnotics. The sniffing of glue and paint thinner were popular among young offenders for some time, but for the past several years, these substances have been replaced by pentazocine. Pentazocine, also known as Sosaigon, is a synthetic analgetic, equivalent to morphine in its effect but without the chemical properties of morphine. Because of its rapidly increasing abuse by young people, the health authorities classified and controlled this drug as a narcotic in 1978. Statistics of the Taipei Municipal Narcotic Treatment and Prevention Center show that in the past 7 years, there has been a markedly increasing number of patients who are admitted either by court order or on a voluntary basis for treatment of glue sniffing and the abuse of pentazocine and hypnotics. These changes in the nature and severity of juvenile delinquency seem to indicate adjustment difficulties and the related drastic changes in coping methods among these youngsters in the rapidly changing society of present-day Taiwan.

Alcoholism

Alcoholism is rarely reported in a Chinese population in the literature. In the first community survey in Taiwan, as discussed previously, there were only two cases of alcoholism identified—0.1‰ of the total population studied.

The rate of alcoholism among Taiwan aborigines was 1.1‰—10 times as high as that for Taiwanese Chinese. The rarity of alcoholism in the Chinese population has been explained from the biological point of view: that Chinese are highly sensitive to alcohol and have low tolerance (Ewing, Rouse, and Pellizziri, 1974; Wolff, 1972). Additionally, from a sociocultural point of view, Chinese generally drink only with meals and on ceremonial occasions, alcohol-induced behavior is rejected by most Chinese, and the absence of popular drinking places (such as taverns or bars) discourages the regular and excessive comsumption of alcohol (F. L. K. Hsu, 1955, T. Y. Lin, 1953, Singer, 1974, Wang, 1968). In a communitywide survey in Taiwan, it was found that a great majority of the Chinese saw alcohol as being harmful to health and were opposed to excessive drinking (Rin, 1978). An earlier survey conducted in San Francisco on Chinese subjects in Chinatown showed similar findings (Chu, 1972). The increasing rate of alcoholism with severe impairment in social functioning has been observed in Taipei among psychiatric outpatients during recent years. For example, there were 6 male alcoholic patients identified at the Taipei City Psychiatric Center out of 100 randomly selected outpatients during a 3-month period in 1980. Although the number was considerably smaller than the counterpart in Los Angeles (16 men and 9 women) during the same period of time, the Chinese alcoholic patients showed a higher average score on the alcohol-drinking behavior scale, thus indicating greater social problems with alcohol than the American patients in Los Angeles had (Yeh et al., 1980).

Wu, Wang, Hwang, and Liu (1983) report a clinical study in Taiwan on 57 alcoholic patients with severly disturbed social functions admitted to a medium-sized general hospital during a 1-year period. All the patients were males, and a large majority (80.7%) of them sought treatment primarily for surgical and physical diseases. Only about one-fifth (19.3%) of the patients consulted psychiatrists primarily for drinking-related psychiatric symptoms.

It can, thus, be concluded that the Chinese alcoholic patients do not seek psychiatric treatment primarily for drinking problems unless their symptoms become severely disturbed. This is similar to the help-seeking behavior that has been popularly observed in all other psychiatric disorders among the Chinese. It can be also speculated that the rate of alcoholism in Chinese community is not as low as has been reported previously and that the low rate of alcoholism in psychiatric settings depends largely on the attitudes of the patients, their families, and the public in general toward drinking problems.

In a community survey covering the total population over age 18 by means of the Chinese-modified version of the Diagnostic Interview Schedule (DIS-CM-II) during 1982–1983; it was found, according to DSM-III criteria, that among an age- and sex-stratified sample of 5000 individuals, the lifetime prevalence of alcohol abuse was 3.4‰ (6.4‰ for males and 0.4‰ for females) and alcohol dependence was 1.5‰ (2.8‰ for males and 0.1‰ for females), with 4.9‰ total prevalence for both genders (Yeh and Hwu, 1983). It will be highly revealing to study whether the rate of alcoholism in Taiwan has actually increased since 1946 under the influence of rapid social changes since 1946 or the changes of the rates were simply due to the different criteria used in the respective studies.

DISCUSSION

Integration of Findings

Social and cultural changes may theoretically be expected to affect the incidence and prevalence of mental disorders in a number of ways (Wallace, 1970). Social change involves shifts in the hierarchical rankings within the social structure, geographic mobility, urbanization, and a host of political and economic processes, including the redistribution of occupations and other patterns. With cultural change, effects are noted in modifications and variations in life-styles, values, and beliefs as they pertain to patterns of human interaction and to the utilization of objects of material culture, particularly technological (Schwab and Schwab, 1978). In evaluating the impact of rapid cultural change on mental disorders, it has been suggested that two dimensions, namely, traditional–changing culture, and social integration–disintegration, should be considered together. It has been speculated that social and cultural changes do not lead to higher risk when the social system itself does not become disintegrated (Leighton et al., 1963). The impact of migration on mental health has been reviewed by many investigators around the world. In general, it was considered that migration, as a unitary variable, is not necessarily directly related to increased mental disorders but that there are many factors that combine to produce the hardships of magration and then may contribute to the occurrence of certain psychopathology. For example, the motive of migration, the host environment for migration, the relationships between the migrants and the host population, and the cultural differences between the migrants and host country are some of the factors that may affect the process of migration and adjustment (Murphy, 1965).

A series of psychiatric epidemiological studies had been carried out in Taiwan since 1946 while tremendous sociocultural changes and migration were taking place. These studies provide information for studying the possible impact of social and cultural change on mental disorders in Chinese culture settings within a chronological framework.

It is a salient fact that there was tremendous sociopolitical-cultural turmoil during the first decade of the post-World War II period in Taiwan. This turmoil occurred as the aftermath of war, a period which also required recovery from massive destruction and the transformation of the political system from Japanese to Chinese, which was associated with the radical changes in the language and educational system. Superimposed upon this situation was the massive influx of migrants from mainland China. The dramatic political changes in mainland China, combined with changes in the community of 6 million native Taiwanese Chinese, occurred in a period of time characterized by socioeconomic turmoil, cultural confusion, and subgroup conflict and was gradually followed by socioeconomic recovery, sociocultural adjustment, and reintegration.

During this period, two successive psychiatric epidemiological studies were carried out on three communities in Taiwan at an interval of 15 years: 1946–1948 and 1961–1963. The follow-up surveys provided information about psychiatric conditions among Chinese people during that period of sociocultural change. The basic findings are that there was essentially no change in the prevalence of psychoses, there was a significant increase in the rate of minor psychiatric disorders such as neuroses, and the prevalence of neuroses was higher among the migrant groups than among the nonmigrant groups.

From the evidence indicating that there was no significant change in the prevalence rate of psychoses, the inference is made that either psychotic disorders are less affected by sociocultural and environmental changes or that the span of 15 years is too short a period for environmental factors to provoke a psychotic process (T. Y. Lin et al., 1969). The interpretation that psychotic disorders are less affected by sociocultural change is in accord with other investigations from other cultures and lead to the conclusion that there is no evidence to indicate that psychoses are generated by a disintegrated environment (Schwab and Schwab, 1978).

Although the impact of the environmental factor on the genesis of psychoses is denied, there is some evidence to support the fact that the sociocultural environment may affect the course of schizophrenia. A 2-year follow-up of the patients included in the World Health Organization International Pilot Study of Schizophrenia, conducted in nine research centers around the world, including Taipei, revealed that patients in developing areas, such as Taiwan, had a more favorable course and outcome than those in developed areas (Sartorius, Jablensky, and Shapiro, 1977). It is speculated that the sociocultural variables, such as size of family, nature of interaction among its members, social attitude toward and acceptance of such disorders, opportunity of social rehabilitation, and the medical and social welfare services system are some factors that may influence the prognosis of such a disorder.

In contrast to psychoses, neuroses was found to have shown significant increase during the 15-year period before the follow-up study, namely, that the prevalence rate increased from 1.2 per 1,000 population in 1946–1948 to 7.8 per 1,000 population in 1961-63 (T. Y. Lin et al., 1969). The increase was found among: (1) all adult age groups (ages 21 to 70); (2) upper, middle, and lower social classes; and (3) different occupations, including salaried workers, merchants, farmers and fishermen, laborers, and the unemployed, but not professionals. This increase indicates that all the people in the society were affected by sociocultural environmental changes and that there was significant increase of neuroses during this period among various groups of people with regard to age, occupation, and social class.

Although there has been no further communitywide follow-up epidemiological survey carried out since 1963, there are some epidemiological data that provide us with the possibility of taking a glance at the vicissitude of sociocultural change and its effect on mental disorders in Taiwan. Suicide, as a frustration-related self-destructive behavior, may serve as one of the indices of psychosociopathology. Available government data indicate that there was a steady increase in the suicide death rate between 1946 and 1964. During the first several years of this period, there was tremendous sociocultural turmoil. Later, when society was more stable and there was economic prosperity associated with the rapid modernization and industrialization during the 1950s, the suicide death rate gradually declined and has maintained its low rate since the early 1970s.

A similar pattern was noted for juvenile delinquency, another psychosociopathological index, for it increased steadily between 1953 and 1973 and has been stable since that time, although the nature of delinquency has been gradually changing, with an increase of severity in the form of violent crimes and association with substance abuse.

Although drug abuse among youths was found sporadically as early as the late 1960s, when it was popular among youths in many Western countries, Chinese society generally reacted with an attitude of prohibition. The government, the community, and parents took a strong stance in discouraging the infusion of related influences such as the "youth culture" or "hippie movement" from the outside. However, as previously described, the recent data indicate that, even though it has not become as serious as in many Western societies, there has been a marked increase in the number of cases of problems with glue sniffing and abuse of drugs such as pentazocine since the early 1970s. This increase, in a way, is shared by the abuse of alcohol. In spite of the fact that alcoholism is rare in Chinese society, there is now some clinical evidence that the disorder is slightly increasing, at least in the city of Taipei (Yeh et al., 1980). It is speculated that, even though there has been steady progress in the society in Taiwan since the 1970s, particularly in terms of increased modernization and industrialization associated with economic persperity, there are also social changes in increased population density, changes in family structure, an increase of competition among youth in the educational systems, all of which affect the mental health of the population, particularly the youth.

Methodological Considerations for Future Investigations

Significant findings regarding prevalences of mental disorders in Taiwan that appear to be relevant to the issues of social and cultural changes and their relationships to mental disorders have been reviewed. The findings reported are drawn from some major epidemiological and clinical studies that have been conducted in Taiwan. The first psychiatric epidemiological study on three communities was carried out in 1946, when the profession of psychiatry was not yet regarded as a branch of modern medicine in Taiwan and there was no standard diagnostic classification system nor a known and tested set of research methodology. In reviewing these studies in the 1980s, when psychiatry has undergone remarkable changes in theory and practice, it is appropriate to note here some methodological issues for discussion.

Diagnostic classification has long been a major obstacle, not only in cross-cultural comparison of mental disorders, but also in the development of psychiatry itself. International Classification of Diseases (ICD) 7, 8, and 9, on which the Diagnostic and Statistical Manual of Mental Disorders (DSM) I and II of American Psychiatric Association are based, were introduced into practice in the 1950s, 1960s, and 1970s, respectively. Traditionally, psychiatry in Taiwan has followed DSM-I and -II in clinical practice and ICD-7, -8, and -9 for official statistics. All of these diagnostic classifications are, unfortunately, lacking in objectivity and in clearly defined criteria for diagnosis, and thus, disagreements between diagnoses have been numerous.

The World Health Organization's research project of the International Psychiatric Study of Schizophrenia (IPSS), in which Taipei was one of the nine centers studied, claimed that it was possible to make cross-cultural comparisons of schizophrenia on mutually accepted criteria for diagnosis. However, when the new DSM-III classification system was used for reassessment 10 years later, only 65 of the 85 project cases originally diagnosed could still be diagnosed as schizophrenia; the remaining cases received other diagnoses, such as major affective disorders or schizophreniform psychosis (Hwu, Chen, and Chen, 1982). This means that the project cases studied as schizophrenia were not schizophrenia at all according to the DSM-III classification system.

The diagnostic classification of DSM-III is claimed by the designers to be a very useful system in clinical practice and epidemiological studies. The DIS, developed by the National Institute of Mental Health (U.S.), is a set of highly structured questionnaires designed to match the criteria for DSM-III for computer diagnosis based on data collected from structured and objective clinical interviews; it is claimed to be very useful for epidemiological community studies (Robins, Helzer, Croughan, and Ratcliff, 1981). A new epidemiological study using the Chinese version of the DIS as the main research tool on 5000 individuals representing all inhabitants over age 18 of Taipei City is being currently undertaken by the writer (Yeh and Hwu, 1982). This study will have more significance than the previous census survey in that it systematically covers the whole range of mental disorders, particularly nonpsychotic disorders such as neuroses, psychophysiological disorders, personality disorders, and substance abuse problems. This study deals with the period prevalence, life prevalence, help-seeking behavior, help received for manifested problems, course and prognosis of psychiatric treatment, level of adjustment before and after treatment, and relationship of all these to the sociocultural and demographic background and other factors. It is expected that the findings obtained from this investigation will provide more detailed and objective information on which more useful and accurate cross-comparison can be made.

In summary, this chapter has described different stages and types of sociocultural change in Taiwan since 1945. As the impact of such sociocultural change, there have been related changes in the mental disorders observed among Chinese in Taiwan, which can serve as examples for comparison with populations in other cultural settings. There is a need to improve our method of epidemiological study so that more accurate and objective data can be obtained for cross-cultural comparison. Such efforts will increase our understanding of culture and mental health.

REFERENCES

Cho, C. O.
  1981   *Shao-nian fan-zui yu guan-fu zh-du* [Juvenile delinquency and probation system] (6th ed.). Shan-Wu Press, Taipei.
Chu, G.
  1972   Drinking patterns and attitudes of rooming-house Chinese in San Francisco. *Quarterly Journal, Study of Alcoholics* (Suppl. 6), pp. 58–68.
Cooper, J., and Sartorius, N.
  1977   Culture and temporal variations in schizophrenia: A speculation on the importance of industrialization. *British Journal of Psychiatry, 130,* 50–55.
Ewing, J. A., Rouse, B., and Pellizziri, E. D.
  1974   Alcohol sensitivity and ethnic background. *American Journal of Psychiatry, 131,* 206–207.
Health statistics
1946–1970   Taipei: Provincial Taiwan Government, Department of Health.
Health statistics: 1. General statistics
1970–1980   Taipei: Department of Health, Executive Yuan.
Health statistics: 2. Vital statistics
1970–1980   Taipei: Department of Health, Executive Yuan.
Hsu, C. C.
  1970   *Zen yang zao-qi fa-xian shi-ying qian-jia xue-sheng* [Early identification of maladjusted students]. Taipei: Ioushi Publication.
  1973   Dui shi-ying qian-jia yu shi-ying liang-hao guo-zhong nan-shen zh bi-jiao [A comparative study of well-adjusted and maladjusted junior high school students]. *Journal of the Formosan Medical Association, 72,* 167–183.
Hsu, F. L. K.
  1955   *Americans and Chinese.* London: Cresset Press.
Hwang, T. C.
  1978   Qing-shao-nian fan-zui xin wei de shi-zhen yan-jiu. [A study on juvenile delinquent behavior]. In: She-hui bian-qian zhong de qing-shao-nian wen-ti yan-tao-hui lun-wen-ji [The proceedings of the Conference on Youth Problems in a Changing Society]. Taipei: Academia Sinica.
Hwu, H. G., Chen, C. C., and Chen, K. L.
  1982   Diagnostic reappraisal of the 137 Taipei IPSS cases at the 7-year follow-up. *Chinese Society of Neurology and Psychiatry Bulletin, 8*(1), 32–33.
Kidd, C. B.
  1965   Psychiatric morbidity among students. *British Journal of Preventive and Social Medicine, 19,* 143–150.
Leighton, A. H., and Hughes, J. M.
  1961   Culture as a causative of mental illness. *Millbank Memorial Foundation Quarterly, 39,* 446.
Leighton, A. H., Lambo, T. A., Hughes, C. C., Leighton, D. C., Murphy, J. M., and Macklin, D. B.
  1963   Psychiatric Disorder in West Africa. *American Journal of Psychiatry, 120,* 523–527.
Lin, K. M., Kleinman, A., and Lin, T. Y.
  1980   Overview of mental disorders in Chinese cultures: Review of epidemiological and clinical studies. In A. Kleinman and T. Y. Lin (Eds.), *Normal and abnormal behavior in Chinese culture.* Dordrecht, Holland: Reidel.

Lin, T. Y.
1953   A study of the incidence of mental disorders in Chinese and other cultures. *Psychiatry 16*, 313–336.
1961   Evolution of mental health program in Taiwan. *American Journal of Psychiatry, 117*, 961–071.

Lin, T. Y., Rin, H., Yeh, E. K., Hsu, C. C., and Chu, H. M.
1969   Mental disorders in Taiwan, fifteen years later. In W. Caudill and T. Y. Lin (Eds.), *Mental health research in Asia and the Pacific*. Honolulu: East-West Center Press.

Murphy, H. B. M.
1965   Migration and the major mental disorders: A reappraisal. In Kanter, M. B. (Ed.), *Mobility and mobile health*. Springfield, IL: Thomas.

Mackay Memorial Hospital
1969–1971   *Ma-gai-i-yuan zi-sha-yu-fang-zhong-xin tong-ji* [Report from the Suicide Prevention Center]. Taipei.

National Taiwan University Hospital
1969–1979   *Statistics of the Department of Psychiatry*, Taipei. Unpublished report.

Nemiah, J.
1975   Obsessive-compulsive neurosis. In Freedman, A. M., Kaplan, H. I., and Sadock, B. J. (Eds.), *Comprehensive textbook of psychiatry/II* (Vol. 1). Baltimore: Williams & Wilkins.

Rin, H.
1978   *Jing-shen-yi-xue yu she-hui* [Psychiatry and society]. Taipei: Medicine and Today Press.

Rin, H., Chu, H. M., and Lin, T. Y.
1966   Psychophysiological reactions of a rural and suburban population in Taiwan. *Acta Psychiatrica Scandinavica, 42*, 410–473.

Rin, H., and Lin, T. Y.
1962   Mental illness among Formosan aborigines as compared with the Chinese in Taiwan. *Journal of Mental Science, 108*, 133–146.

Rin, H., Tsen, L. T., and Chen, T.
1974   Bao-zhi suo bao-dao de zi-sha xing-wei fen-xi [Analysis of suicidal behavior reported on papers]. *Acta Psychological Taiwanica, 16*, 7–24.

Robins, L. N., Helzer, J. E., Croughan, J., and Ratcliff, K. S.
1981   NIMH diagnostic interview schedule. *Archives of General Psychiatry 38*, 381–399.

Sartorius, N., Jablensky, A., and Shapiro, R.
1977   Two-year follow-up of the patients included in the WHO International Pilot Study of Schizophrenia. *Psychological Medicine, 7*, 529–541.

Schwab, J., and Schwab, M. E.
1978   *Sociocultural roots of mental illness: An epidemiological survey*. New York: Plenum Medical Book Company.

Shen, C., Wang, S. C., Chen, K. W., and Yang, R. W.
1978   Du-shi guo-xiao yu quo-zhong shi-ying-qian jia xue-sheng de chu-xian iü yan-jiu [A study of prevalences of maladjusted primary school children and junior high school students]. In *She-hui bian-qian zhong de qing-shao-nian wen-ti yan-tao hui lun-wen-ji* [Proceedings of the Conference on Youth Problems in a Changing Society]. Taipei: Academia Sinica.

Singer, K.
1974   The choices of intoxicant among the Chinese. *British Journal of Psychiatry, 69*, 257–268.

Wallace, A.
    1970   *Culture and personality* (2nd ed.). New York: Random House.
Wang, R. P.
    1968   A study of alcoholism in Chinatown. *International Journal of Social Psychiatry,*
            14, 260–267.
Wolff, P. H.
    1972   Ethnic difference in alcohol sensitivity. *Science, 175,* 449–450.
Wu, C. T., Wang, M. J., Hwang, B. J., and Liu, H. J.
    1983   Zong-he-yi-yuan li jiu-ying-huan-zhe zhi lin-chuang yan-jiu [Alcoholism in a
            general hospital]. *Chinese Society of Neurology and Psychiatry Bulletin, 9*(2), 56–
            62.
Yeh, E. K., Chu, H. M., Ko, Y. H., Lin, T. Y., and Lee, S. P.
    1972   Student mental health: An epidemiological study in Taiwan. *Acta Psychologica*
            Taiwanica, 14, 1–26.
Yeh, E. K., and Hwu, H. G.
    1982   *Epidemiological studies of mental disorders in Taiwan: Part I. Taipei City.* Unpub-
            lished research supported by the Department of Health, Executive Yuan. Taipei.
    1983   [Prevalence of mental disorders in Taipei City: Some preliminary findings].
            Unpublished data from the research project supported by the Department of
            Health, Executive Yuan. Taipei.
Yeh, E. K., Yamamoto, J., Wu, E. C., Slavson, P., Loya, F., Chen, Y. S., Goldstein, W. X., and
Hurwicz, M.
    1980   *Symptoms and diagnoses in Taipei and Los Angeles.* Paper presented on the Sympo-
            sium on Transcultural Psychiatry, 2nd Pacific Congress of Psychiatry, Manila,
            May.

CHAPTER 19

An Overview of Psychopathology in Hong Kong with Special Reference to Somatic Presentation

Fanny M. Cheung

INTRODUCTION

In this chapter, I present an overview of psychopathology in Hong Kong by examining the forms of manifestation of mental problems, especially that of somatization. Several psychological and cultural explanations for somatization are offered. *Somatization,* as used here, refers broadly to the presentation, complaint, or manifestation of somatic symptoms that relate to psychological or emotional problems, rather than to the strict psychoanalytic meaning of the organic expression of mental process. To provide the context to the discussion of these phenomena, I briefly introduce the existing treatment resources for mental illness and raise some methodological questions encountered in the examination of these issues. The

287

aspects of psychopathology covered are restricted to the usual forms of psychiatric disorders treated at the mental health services in Hong Kong, namely; psychotic and neurotic disorders.

MANIFESTATION OF MENTAL DISORDERS

In Hong Kong, there is not yet any community-wide epidemiological study on the rates and types of mental disorders. Statistics on psychiatric disorders are available mainly from patient attendance and admissions at the Government Mental Health Service, which provides the bulk of psychiatric treatment facilities. According to such service statistics (Lo, 1981b), the total number of patients attending psychiatric outpatient services in 1980 was 25,454, including 4263 new cases and 21,191 old cases. There were 1788 new admissions and 3496 readmissions to psychiatric hospitals and units, making a total of 5284 admissions. The majority of inpatients admitted were schizophrenic (Lo, 1981a). In 1978, 63.5% of all psychiatric admissions to the Mental Health Service were schizophrenics, 6.3% were cases of organic psychoses or dementia, 4.3% were cases of affective psychoses, 2.5% were neurotics, and 1.7% bore diagnoses of acute brain syndrome. The pattern of diagnoses at an outpatient and day-treatment center was different. In 1979, 43.5% of the patients attending one of the major psychiatric centers were neurotics. Only 21.8% were schizophrenics, 10.1% were cases of affective psychosis, with 3.9% cases of organic psychosis or dementia and 1.1% of acute brain syndrome. Among the affective cases, manics were reported to be less common than depressives (less than 10% of the total number of cases of affective psychoses).

While these figures do not represent the prevalence rates of psychiatric illness in Hong Kong, they provide an overall picture of the population of patients on which most studies and reports on psychopathology in Hong Kong have been based. The Hong Kong literature has focused on cases of psychosis, neurosis, depression, and psychosomatic disorder among identified patients attending various psychiatric services.

Most of the studies on psychiatric patients in Hong Kong have suggested overall similarities in the symptomatology and the course of illness to patients encountered in Western psychiatry. In their 10-year follow-up study of Chinese schizophrenics, W. H. Lo and T. Lo (1977) found that the relationship between acute onset of illness and better prognosis established in Western psychiatric texts also holds true for Chinese patients in Hong Kong. In a similar follow-up study of obsessional neurotics, W. H. Lo (1967) concluded that the course and the prognosis of obsessional neurosis are comparable to those obtained in European studies. The impact of general sociocultural influences and child-rearing practices on child psychiatric disorders in Hong Kong was examined by Singer, Ney, and Lieh-Mak (1978). They concluded that despite the influence of culture, the psychogenic factors and the forms of psychopathological manifestation in most of their cases are similar to those found in Caucasians. In two studies concerning biological variables, relating physique, personality, and mental illness in southern Chinese men and women in Hong Kong, Singer and his colleagues (Singer, Chang, and Hsu, 1972; Singer, Lieh-Mak, and Ng, 1976) again found that the intercorrelations they obtained for these variables were in agreement with those reported for Caucasians.

The discussion on cultural variations in the manifestations of affective disorders has been more diversified. In a study on affective illness among Chinese inpatients, Yap (1965b) found that most of the clinical features paralleled those reported in Western psychiatry, except for the absence of delusions of sin and the low frequency of guilt and unworthiness feelings. However, in a later paper, Yap (1971) reversed his position on these latter cultural differences. After a detailed review of the literature, Singer (1975) also concluded that given the methodological problem of the reported studies, there is insufficient evidence to support the view that depressive disorders among Chinese have outstanding deviant features compared to those found in Western psychiatry. Yap (1965b) acknowledges that there may be cultural variations in affective disorders, but these are more differences of degree, such as in the ratio of mania to depression, than of kind.

Cultural differences in the baseline of normal and pathological behavior may be found in studies of psychological testing. Cross-cultural test comparisons show that Hong Kong subjects differ from their Western counterparts in their scale scores and item endorsement patterns. Studies based on the Chinese Minnesota Multiphasic Personality Inventory (MMPI) in Hong Kong (Cheung, 1979, 1981a) showed that even among normals, Hong Kong Chinese scored higher than Americans, especially on the Depression (D) and the Schizophrenia (Sc) scales. These scale evaluations may not be directly interpreted as indications of psychopathology among the Hong Kong subjects: Detailed analyses on the differential rates of endorsement on these scales showed that items on which the Hong Kong subjects scored higher were mostly related to the characteristics of being reserved, constrained, resigned to life, and modest about one's ability. These characteristics may be considered desirable in the Hong Kong culture. However, endorsement of items related to more florid psychiatric symptoms was more similar across cultures. Within Hong Kong, the Chinese MMPI was able to discriminate between psychiatric patients and normals.

Similarly, a comparative study of Hong Kong and British adults on the Eysenck Personality Questionnaire (EPQ) showed that Hong Kong subjects scored higher on the Psychotism scale and the Social Desirability aspect of the Lie scale but lower on the Extraversion scale than the British (Eysenck and Chan, 1982). However, the basic factor structure of the measured personality dimensions of the Hong Kong subjects was comparable to that found among British subjects as well as in several other cultures. These test results point to cultural differences in the baseline of adjustment behavior and the need to adapt interpretations of psychopathology accordingly.

Some cases of culture-bound psychiatric syndromes have been reported; however, their incidences are rare among Chinese. The diagnostic group most often associated with Chinese was *koro (suo-yang)*, an acute panic state related to the belief that the penis is shrinking (Yap, 1965a; 1967a). *Koro* is ocassionally found among young men in Hong Kong who have been exposed to the folk belief that penile shrinkage leads to death. In his discussion on folk beliefs about mental illness, Yap (1965a, 1965b, 1967a) refers to the Chinese tendency to ascribe the cause of mental illness to supernatural forces, though, of course, belief in spiritual possession is not peculiar to the Chinese culture. Even though such superstitious beliefs have been reported in clinical presentations of both adults and children (Yap, 1967b; Singer, Ney, and Lieh-Mak, 1978), these forms of symptom manifestation are in the minority among psychiatric patients in Hong Kong.

The mode of symptom manifestation most often ascribed to Chinese psychiatric patients is the presentation of psychological distress in the form of bodily symptoms (Tseng, 1975). Kleinman (1977) observed that Chinese patients tended to have a heightened awareness of their bodies and present somatic complaints in place of psychological complaints. Among patients attending psychiatric facilities, Chinese are noted for their lack of psychological awareness. Affective features are presented less frequently than neurasthenic, hypochondriacal, and psychosomatic complaints (B. Kwong and S. W. Wong, 1981; Lau, Cheung, and Waldmann, 1981; Lo, 1978; S. W. Wong, 1979; Singer, 1976; Wong, 1976).

Mental health professionals working with Chinese have further noted a relatively low rate of attendance at psychiatric and other mental health facilities. In Lee's (1976, 1980b) community survey of mental stress symptoms among urban Hong Kong residents using the Langner scale, almost one-third of the representative sample was found to be suffering from psychological disturbance. However, in 1974, the same year in which the biosocial survey was conducted, statistics on the utilization of mental health services showed that only 3019 new cases and 14,606 old cases were seen at government psychiatric outpatient clinics (Lo, 1981b). The total number of psychiatric inpatients treated in psychiatric hospitals and units was 4428. The number of psychiatrists in private practice in that year was fewer than 10, serving only a small sector of the psychiatric population. Against a population of 5 million, the rate of psychiatric treatment reported was extremely low.

Patients afflicted with psychiatric disorders often seek help from nonpsychiatric medical settings, especially the general practitioner or the Chinese herbalist (Cheung and Lau, 1982; Cheung, Lau, and Waldmann, 1980–1981; B. Kwong and S. W. Wong, 1981; Lee, 1975; 1980a, Singer, 1976). Only a small proportion of those who could benefit from psychological services attend and persist in these services.

In the study of cases attending a general medical clinic in urban Hong Kong, Lau, Cheung, and Waldmann (1981) found that depressive disorders were found among 8–20% of the daily intake of medical patients. These depressed patients complained initially of bodily symptoms, especially those related to the central nervous system (e.g., headache and dizziness), general ill health (e.g., malaise and weakness), and the gastrointestinal system (e.g., disrupted eating habits, gastric trouble, and abdominal pain). However, when the doctor inquired about specific psychological symptoms such as feelings of sadness, nervousness, restlessness, or suicidal ideation, patients would admit the presence of affective features. Cheung, Lau, and Waldmann (1980–1981) suggest that the expression mode be distinquished from the recognition mode of symptom manifestation. While patients often express somatic complaints initially, they may be aware of their affective experience without complaining overtly about them. These features may not be expressed if the attending doctor does not inquire about them.

Another distinction to make about the concept of somatization is whether somatization and psychologization are dichotomized or parallel processes. In Kleinman's (1977) definition of somatization, psychological complaints are said to be replaced by somatic complaints. A dichotomy between somatization and psychologization is assumed. This artificial dichotomy has been disputed by White (1980, 1981), who found that Hong Kong-born students in Hawaii made greater use of personality constructs when explaining interpersonal problems than when explaining psychosomatic problems. Further support that the nonpsychiatric general population in Hong Kong do admit to psychological symptoms together with somatic symptoms may be found in Cheung's (1982b) reanalysis of the biosocial survey data. She studied subscale endorsement patterns of the Langner scale in Lee's (1976) study and found that among a representative sample of the general public in Hong Kong, the number of psychological symptoms reported was higher on the Langner scale than that of psychophysiological, physiological, and ambiguous symptoms. Studies of patients' clinical presentations also showed that psychological features were frequently found alongside somatic symptoms (Cheung and Lau, 1982; Cheung, Lau, and Waldmann, 1980–1981; S. W. Wong and B. Kwong, 1981; Yap, 1965b).

Although the dichotomy between somatization and psychologization is artificial, the content of specific somatic complaints made in relation to psychological states may be of cultural interest. Some of these expressions reflect the Chinese concept of health: Vague references to *feng (feng,* wind), *gan (kan,* dryness) and *qi (ch'i,* air) may be found in descriptions of symptoms by psychiatric patients (Singer, 1976; S. W. Wong and B. Kwong, 1981). Symptoms described in association with the heart, liver, and kidney, three of the five major internal organs in traditional Chinese medicine, are common. Expressions such as *xin yu (hsin yu,* something pressing on the heart) may refer to depressed moods, *qi ding (ch'i ting,* blocking of air) to frustration and irritation, *shen kui, (shen kúei,* weak kidney) to psychosexual difficulties, and *gan huo, (kan huo,* fire in the liver) to rage. An understanding of these physical metaphors would help the therapist to identify and to interpret the emotional state of the patient.

PSYCHOLOGICAL AND CULTURAL EXPLANATIONS

The relatively low rate of consultation in psychiatric settings and the tendency among Chinese to somatize have been attributed to several aspects of the Chinese culture. Cultural explanations are often cited to account for the observed cultural differences between Chinese psychiatric patients and their Western counterparts. Singer (1976) describes the relationship between culture and mental health, referring to the belief and value system, sociocultural changes, childhood and family dynamics, psychodynamics, and the concept of illness and mental illness in Hong Kong. In particular, he points to the somatic notion of the sick role among Chinese patients; thus, Chinese patients expect to receive physical treatments from the doctor and do not regard psychotherapy as treatment for which they should have to pay. Singer attributes this sick role to "self selection, consequent upon a somatic orientation of disease and interpretation of the sick role" (p. 52).

Patients in Hong Kong seldom have a clear understanding of mental illness. Folk beliefs about mental illness are vague and stereotypic. Images of the mentally ill are associated with craziness and insanity. According to an informal street poll conducted in Hong Kong (Better Mental Health Promoters, 1980), most of the urban respondents conceived of the mentally ill as dangerous maniacs, people who act bizarrely, or people who have "gone haywire." They attributed the cause of mental illness to vague ideas of psychological trauma, irregular lifestyle, or mixed-up nerves. Mental illness is still a myth-ridden social stigma. The respondents were generally ignorant about methods of treatment. They expected doctors to know how to give medical treatment to those afflicted.

Such vagueness in the folk concept of mental health may be traced to lack of public education on physical and mental health in Hong Kong. The topics of mental health and illness have not yet been incorporated into the school curriculum (Chen, 1981). Individual efforts in community mental health education have been sporadic (Cheung, 1981c). The mass media have tended to sensationalize the bizarre and dangerous images of the mental patient. Furthermore, folk concepts of mental illness among Chinese may be influenced by the undifferentiated global descriptions of mental illness used in traditional Chinese medicine. Ethnomedical studies on Chinese concepts of health point out that Chinese medical texts have long emphasized the interactive relationship between the mind and the body in both psychological and physical disorders (Lee, 1975, 1980a; Wu, 1980). The mind and the body work hand-in-hand to maintain the homeostasis of one's life in the Chinese holistic view of health. In traditional Chinese medicine, mental illness is described in the same nomenclature as physical illness (Chang, 1980).

The integrative relationship between the soma and the psyche may be reflected in the physical metaphors often used to describe psychological states in the Chinese language. The somatic orientation of Cantonese the major Chinese dialect spoken in Hong Kong, has been examined by W. S. Wong and B. Kwong (1981). In a study of hypochondriacal concerns of mental patients and secondary school students in Hong Kong, subjects were asked to produce as many words or phrases as they could describing physical and emotional discomforts. Researchers found that a significantly higher percentage of words relating to physical discomfort was produced by both patients and normals. Among the vocabulary used for emotional discomfort, about 14% was associated with descriptions of bodily symptoms or ascriptions of the emotion to a body organ. The somatic orientation in the subjects' vocabulary was correlated with high scores on the hypochondriasis (Hs) scale of the Chinese MMPI and the tendency to choose more medically oriented forms of treatment. S. W. Wong and B. Kwong conclude that the physical bias in the Cantonese dialect draws the attention of the speaker as well as of the listener to the physiological concomitants of emotions. Data from this study and an earlier study by B. Kwong and S. W. Wong (1981) show, however, that written words describing emotional discomfort were by no means lacking. While a total of 1539 words or phrases describing physical discomfort were also produced in the B. Kwong and S. W. Wong (1981) study, 1340 words or phrases describing emotional discomfort were also produced, representing a ratio of 1.15 to 1. Despite the bias toward physical connotations in the Cantonese dialect, and contrary to what some authors claim to be the lack of an everyday spoken vocabulary or semantic network in the Chinese language for expressing depressive affective states (Kleinman, 1977; Tseng, 1975; Tseng and Hsu, 1970), a substantial proportion of the remaining words described pure emotions.

Corroborating support may be found in Cheung and Lau's (1982) study on the content of patients' statements regarding their reasons for consultation. They observed that among psychiatric outpatients, somatic symptoms were cited most often when statements of symptoms were the response. However, only half of those stating their symptoms as reasons cited somatic symptoms *alone*. In other cases, somatic symptoms were cited in conjunction with other affective, cognitive, behavioral, or vague symptoms. Clinical examinations of these cases also showed that while somatic symptoms were present in 64% of the psychiatric outpatients, the majority of these symptoms were presented with psychological concomitants. On one hand, in only 27% of the cases were somatic symptoms manifested *alone*. On the other hand, psychological symptoms *without* somatic concomitants were found in 32% of the cases. Such discrepancies between complaints and symptom presentation suggest that the perception of the sick role affects the somatic orientation in the manifestation of psychopathology.

The bias toward the somatic orientation may be encouraged by both the patient and the doctor. Physicians in Hong Kong tend to focus on somatic symptoms and ignore psychological, especially affective, features. Patients consulting in medical settings also hold preconceived expectations of Western-style doctors, including psychiatrists, who are supposed to treat their physical illness only. A comparison of the consultation behavior of psychiatric patients seen in different settings showed that the reason patients gave for the consultation varied among settings (Cheung and Lau, 1982). The psychiatric settings included a psychiatric outpatient clinic and a prison psychiatric observation unit. For comparison, nonpsychiatric patients at the prison unit and outpatients at a general medical clinic were included. Psychiatric patients attending the psychiatric outpatient clinic complained mostly about their symptoms (55%), especially those of a somatic nature (45%), as reasons for their consultation. At the prison psychiatric observation unit, both psychiatric and nonpsychiatric offenders tended to recall the events that led to their arraignment or to cite the court order on their examination as reasons for their consultation. Among the prison group of psychiatric cases, only 6% made references to somatic complaints. In the general outpatient clinic, the majority of the medical patients cited somatic symptoms (78%) or made direct requests for medical investigation or treatment (19%).

The difference in the patterns of consultation among the three medical settings illustrates the role played by *situationism* (Bowers, 1973) in eliciting expectations and behaviors from patients. Situational variations in help-seeking behavior challenge the simple generalization that the tendency of somatic presentation is a unique Chinese trait. Chinese culture has been described as situation centered (Hsieh, Shybut, and Lotsof, 1969). Behaviors of the Chinese were often determined by their concern with interpersonal transactions (Hsu, 1971).

Consultation behavior of Chinese patients is likewise shaped by the way they conceptualize their problems and the kind of help they expect to receive from the doctor in the context of the situation. Studies of health attitudes and medical consultation behaviors among Hong Kong Chinese show that both traditional and Western medical services are expected to be concerned with the treatment or the prevention of illness (Lee, 1974, 1975, 1980a). In medical settings where patients expect medical treatment for their physical symptoms, they may believe that the citation of somatic complaints is the most appropriate behavior. These expectations may in turn be perpetuated by medical doctors who inquire about the patients' somatic complaints only and focus their attention primarily on physical treatment.

Psychiatric patients tend to associate somatic complaints with their illnesses throughout their experiences with medical consultation. An examination of the consultation history of patients attending a psychiatric outpatient clinic for the first time showed that over half of the patients had symptoms for more than a year prior to their psychiatric consultation (Cheung and Lau, 1982). Almost 10% had suffered their symptoms for over 9 years. During this time, most of these patients (73%) had consulted Western-style doctors and more than a quarter (29%) had consulted Chinese herbalists. Their history of help-seeking at these medical settings shows that their concerns were attuned to their physical conditions.

Similarly, the expression of emotions is dependent upon the situational context. Wu (1980) notes that in ordinary life, Chinese have rich and subtle ways of displaying inner feelings, which depend on the circumstances under which open expression of feelings is considered appropriate. Expressions of emotional difficulties are found more frequently in nonmedical settings. Reports on counseling resources in Hong Kong show that emotional problems were among the most frequently cited problems brought in for counseling (Cheung, 1980; Samaritan Befrienders, 1981). Nevertheless, counselors at these settings commonly observed that their clients were often unfamiliar with the goals and the format of counseling, which is still a relatively new form of service to the public. In contrast, friends, peers, family, and other informal resources are more frequently used as major sources of help and support for emotional problems (Ng, 1980, S. W. Wong and B. Kwong, 1981).

The choice of help-seeking resources for psychological disturbance is determined by several factors. Some authors refer to the Chinese tradition of keeping feelings to themselves or within a close-knit circle of their family and friends (B. Kwong and S. W. Wong, 1981; Singer, 1976). This tendency is emphasized in cases of mental illness, which is still a social stigma (Ma, 1974; C. L. Wong, 1976). Patients and their relatives generally hide the fact that they have been admitted to a mental hospital. Castle Peak, the name of the district in the New Territories where the major mental hospital is situated, has been associated with the mentally ill since it was constructed and is often used in derogatory jokes and teasing. Many relatives are reluctant to send patients to the Castle Peak Hospital for fear of the life-long stigma. The fear of stigmatization and the preference for asking members of the primary social network for psychological support are not exclusive to Chinese in Hong Kong. Similar dynamics of seeking psychosocial support are also found in Western culture in general (Carney and Barak, 1976; Carney, Savitz, and Weiskott, 1979; Friedlander, 1978; Gelso and McKenzie, 1973).

In addition to conceptual and attitudinal components, objective conditions also play an important part in shaping the sick role. Help-seeking behavior may be determined by the availability and accessibility of treatment resources. The general public in Hong Kong is mostly ignorant about the facilities and the means for obtaining psychiatric and psychological help. Even if the people were more knowledgeable, the present treatment resources are still limited.

TREATMENT RESOURCES

In Hong Kong, psychological counseling and psychiatric treatment are limited with regard to facilities and staff. In terms of psychological services, there are about 10 departments or agencies at present that offer professional counseling. In some of the settings, the service is staffed by one psychologist alone. Professional psychological counseling in a relatively new social service. Much confusion about the roles and functions served by counselors has been admitted by professionals themselves (Briers, 1981; Cheung, 1981b; E. Kwong, 1981), and clients and the general public find this form of service even more confusing and inaccessible. They are often unaware of the availability of psychological services or the means of utilizing such services (Cheung et al., 1980). It is quite understandable that only 3% of the patients in the B. Kwong and S. W. Wong (1981) study said that they would seek help of the clinical psychologist.

Similarly, psychiatric facilities are serving only an unknown proportion of those in need of treatment. Psychiatric treatment in Hong Kong is a medical specialty requiring medical referral. Because of the staff shortage, services are restricted in scope and depth with regard to psychotherapy.

The history of psychiatry in Hong Kong is relatively short. Lo (1981b) gives a comprehensive account of the development of the Mental Health Service, which provides the majority of psychiatric facilities in Hong Kong. The first modern psychiatric hospital, Castle Peak Hospital, was opened in 1961. Including the recently completed Kwai Chung Hospital, there are three major psychiatric hospitals providing a total of 4225 beds. In addition, there are three psychiatric units within general hospitals that provide outpatient and day-center treatment services as well as a total of 190 inpatient beds. Four psychiatric centers offer regular outpatient and day-center services including follow-up for cases discharged from the psychiatric hospitals. Another psychiatric clinic provides a part-time outpatient treatment. Professional personnel working in the Mental Health Service in 1981 included 55 psychiatrists (15 of whom hold psychiatric qualifications), five psychologists, 23 social workers, 9 occupational therapists, and 759 nurses (including student nurses). Apart from those working in the government services, there are 25 psychiatrists in private practice and non-government psychiatric units. A shortage of staff exists in almost all the posts. Given the heavy workload of the professional personnel, little can be done in terms of more time-consuming services such as counseling and psychotherapy. Outreach into the community for early detection and after-care services is not feasible. Under these circumstances, the mental health services are dependent upon the frontline health care system to make the appropriate referral. However, even many of the allied professionals, such as general practitioners, social workers, and teachers, are not familiar with the signs and symptoms of mental disorders or how to deal with such cases.

Furthermore, many of those who need psychiatric help do not fall into this catchment network. A group of such cases that has caught public attention is the long-hair beggars (Khoo, 1980). *Beggar* may be a misnomer for these vagrants because they seldom beg. Characteristically, they are all shabbily dressed and do not attend to their grooming or personal hygiene. Most of them carry with them bundles of rubbish or their belongings and are often seen to be muttering or gesturing to themselves. In 1974, an urban survey done by college students counted 205 such long-hair types whom they suspected to be suffering from some form of mental illness. However, under the existing law and mental health ordinance, these vagrants cannot be detained for treatment. Even if they are willing, there are not enough beds available for their long-term care. Because they do not pose any imminent danger, no government department, including the Medical and Health Department, the Social Welfare Department, and the police, is willing to take any positive action. Khoo concludes that without a suitable joint effort, the authorities will continue to turn a blind eye. These long-hair beggers "will continue to publicly exhibit their symptoms, going their own way, minding their own business, remaining uncommunicative and seeking some below-subsistence existence" (p. 4).

The problem of the long-hair beggars is just one indication of the inaccessibility of mental health services for those afflicted with mental illness. Even for such an overt problem that has been present and has prompted public outcry for almost 10 years, nothing has yet been done.

Lam (1981) describes other cases of psychiatric patients who are reluctant to seek treatment and would require more active and out-reaching forms of intervention than those presently available. He suggests the inclusion of new forms of services such as walk-in clinics, emergency services, psychiatric hotline services, and home visits by psychiatrists and psychiatric nurses. Until these have been implemented, many cases of psychiatric disorders may not be brought to appropriate attention.

Meanwhile, the population of individuals whose problems have not yet been indentified is largely unknown. Help for mental disorders and psychological distress are often sought from nonpsychiatric settings, especially the general practitioner, Chinese herbalist, and religious institutions (Cheung and Lau, 1982; Cheung et al., 1980–1981; Lee, 1974, 1975, 1980a; Lieh-Mak et al., 1979; Topley, 1967). Many may not seek help at all, thinking that their emotional problems are transient and will pass away given time or can be controlled through willpower.

METHODOLOGICAL ISSUES

Given the context of the present system of treatment resources, conclusions about the study of psychopathology in Hong Kong are hampered by several methodological limitations. One major question is the reliability of the classification system used for psychopathology in Hong Kong. Basically, the ICD-9 and the system laid out in the standard text in clinical psychiatry by Mayer-Gross, Slater, and Roth (Lo and Lo, 1977) are used. This scheme is not adhered to tightly. Individual psychiatrists have also adopted the DSM-III or a combination of several classification systems. The lack of uniformity and precise terminology in diagnosis hinders the degree of accuracy and comparability in research. This unreliability impedes the development of a data base that draws upon different studies of psychopathology in Hong Kong.

At this stage, the empirical data base for describing and explaining psychopathology in Hong Kong is weak. Studies that have been reported are based primarily on known cases attending psychiatric settings. There is a lack of data on cases seen by psychiatrists in private practice, on cases seeking nonpsychiatric services, and on cases not seeking help at all, all of whom may differ from psychiatric patients in terms of their problem conceptualization, their symptom manifestation, their awareness of and access to psychiatric resources, and the extent to which they are tolerated by their families and significant others. Without a community-wide epidemiological study, these cases will remain unknown.

Given the observation that help-seeking behavior varies across situations, caution should be observed with regard to conclusions about psychopathology among Chinese based only on patient behavior in medical settings. Situationists in personality studies express their doubts as to the generalized consistency of personality dispositions and, instead, emphasize the acquired meaning of stimuli across situations as determinants of behavior (Mischel, 1969, 1973).

Cheung (1982a) critically reviews the attribution of somatization to Chinese and cautions that generalizations about somatization among Chinese based solely on the behavior of patients may miss the idiographic variations of help-seeking behavior in different situations. In addition to idiographic variations, subcultural and regional differences within the Chinese culture should be noted. The majority of the psychiatric cases attending public mental health services have lower educational levels and come from lower income families (Lieh-Mak, Tam, Yu, and Pun, 1981). Social class differences may be confounded with cultural differences when generalizations are made based on such cases. Kleinman (1977) does qualify his observation on the Chinese tendency to somatize by admitting that white middle-class Americans were used as the reference group. Singer (1975) argues that somatization is not exclusive to Chinese patients but is also commonly found in other non-Western cultures and among the lower social classes and the less educated within Western countries. Differences in behavioral patterns have also been found among Chinese residing in different geographical locales. A large-scale study of 40 cultures by Hofstede (1980) found that people of Chinese origin living in different parts of the world, such as Hong Kong, Singapore, and Taiwan, possessed different patterns of values despite basic similarities in "mental programs." Cultural patterns found among Chinese in one area may not be directly generalized to those living in another geographical region. Therefore, in study forms and manifestations of psychopathology among Chinese, subject variables such as sex, age, education, socioeconomic status, and geographical locale should be included.

Furthermore, conclusions about the dynamics of psychopathology among Chinese are based mainly on cultural impressions and clinical observations. Aspects of the Chinese culture are then cited to explain these phenomena. Such post hoc explanations lack vigor and precision and do not provide a discriminative prediction of the dynamics of behavior. Oversensitivity to generalized "cultural" traits may, at times, impede accurate perception of behavioral determinants (Li-Repac, 1981). A study on the relationship between locus of control and psychological distress among Chinese-Americans (Kuo, Gray, and Lin, 1979) points to the importance of personality variables in affecting symptomatology among Chinese. Variables such as situationism and the locus of control may provide clues to the cognitive schema and the belief system that influence the manifestation of mental illness. Instead of arguing whether Chinese tend to somatize or not (Kleinman, 1977; Singer, 1977), it is necessary to discuss and clarify the conceptual and terminological difference between the psychoanalytic concept of somatization and the tendency of somatic presentation. Furthermore, more specific questions should be asked about the pattern of somatic presentation, such as, Among Chinese, who tends to present somatic complaints? When, to whom, and why do they present somatic complaints? How do they perceive their problems? It will be useful to conduct process study or longitudinal study of cases to trace and to understand dynamically how the patients' pattern of problem-presentation continues or shifts in the process of natural cause or therapy. We should also ask these questions of psychological forms of manifestation. Examination of these questions in depth will help us to understand better the dynamics of psychopathology as well as the dynamics of the Chinese culture.

REFERENCES

Better Mental Health Promoters
    1980   *Street poll on the concept of mental health.* Unpublished report, Better Mental Health Promoters, Hong Kong.
Bowers, K. S.
    1973   Situationism in psychology: An analysis and a critique. *Psychological Review,* 80(5), 307–336.
Briers, N.
    1981   The emperor's new clothes. *Hong Kong Journal of Mental Health,* 10(2), 5–7.

Carney, C. G., and Barak, A.
1976   A survey of students needs and student services. *Journal of College Student Personnel, 17*, 280–284.
Carney, C. G., Savitz, C. J., and Weiskott, G. N.
1979   Students' evaluations of a university counseling center and their intentions to use its programs. *Journal of Counseling Psychology, 26*(3), 242–249.
Chang, J. S.
1980   *Zhong-yi zhi-liao jing-shen-bin* [Chinese medical treatment of psychiatric illness]. Hupei, China: Hupei People's Publishers.
Chen, C. N.
1981   Mental health and education. In T. P. Khoo (Ed.), *Aspects of mental health care: Hong Kong 1981.* Hong Kong: Mental Health Association of Hong Kong.
Cheung, F. M.
1979   MMPI profiles and analyses of normals in Hong Kong. In J. N. Butcher, H. Hama, and Y. Matsuyama (Eds.), *Proceedings of the 6th International Conference on Personality Assessment.* Kyoto, Japan: Doshisha University.
1981a   *Development of the Chinese MMPI in Hong Kong: Comparisons between the Chinese and the English versions.* Paper presented at the 7th International Conference on Personality Assessment, Honolulu, Hawaii.
1981b   Opening Pandora's box on counselling: Comments on Norman Brier's article "The emperor's new clothes." *Hong Kong Journal of Mental Health, 10*(2), 10–12.
1981c   Public Education & Promotion of Mental Health. In T. P. Khoo (ed.) *Aspects of mental health care: Hong Kong 1981.* Hong Kong: Mental Health Association of Hong Kong.
1982a   Somatization among Chinese: A critique. *Bulletin of the Hong Kong Psychological Society*, No. 8, January, 27–35.
1982b   Psychological symptoms among Chinese in urban Hong Kong. *Social Science and Medicine, 16,* 1339–1344.
Cheung, F. M., and Lau, B.
1982   Situational variations in help-seeking behavior among Chinese patients. *Comprehensive Psychiatry, 23,* 252–262.
Cheung, F. M., Lau, B., and Waldmann E.
1980–1981   Somatization among Chinese depressive in general practice. *International Journal of Psychiatry in Medicine, 10*(4), 361–374.
Cheung, F. (Chairperson)
1980   *Counselling and counselors in Hong Kong: A survey.* Hong Kong: Educators' Social Action Council, Counselling Survey Task Force.
Eyesenck, S. B., and Chan, J.
1982   A comparative study of personality in adults and children: Hong Kong vs. England. *Personality and Individual differences, 3,* 153–160.
Friedlander, J.
1978   Student ratings of co-curricular services and their intent to use them. *Journal of College Student Personnel, 19,* 195–201.
Gelso, C. J., and McKenzie, J. D.
1973   Effect of information on students' perceptions of counselling and their willingness to seek help. *Journal of Counselling Psychology, 20,* 406–411.
Hofstede, G
1980   *Culture's consequences: International differences in work-related values.* Beverly Hills, CA: Sage Publications.

Hsieh, T., Shybut, J., and Lotsof, E.
    1969   Internal versus external control and ethnic group membership: A cross-cultural
            comparison. *Journal of Consulting and Clinical Psychology, 33*(1), 122–124.
Hsu, F. L. K.
    1971   Psychosocial homeostasis and jen: Conceptual tools for advancing psychologi-
            cal anthropology. *American Anthropologist, 73,* 23–44.
Khoo, T. P.
    1980   Long hair beggars. *Hong Kong Journal of Mental Health, 9*(2), 1–4.
Kleinman, A. M.
    1977   Depression, somatization and the "new cross-cultural psychiatry." *Social Science
            and Medicine, 11,* 3–10.
Kuo, W. H., Gray, R., and Lin, N.
    1979   Locus of control and symptoms of psychological distress among Chinese-Amer-
            icans. *The International Journal of Social Psychiatry, 25*(3), 176–187.
Kwong, B., and Wong, S. W.
    1981   Physical presentations of psychological problems among Hong Kong Chinese:
            Cultural implications. *Journal of Hong Kong Psychiatric Association, 1,* 33–39.
Kwong, E.
    1981   A response to "The Emperor's New Clothes" by Norman Briers. *Hong Kong
            Journal of Mental Health, 10*(2), 8–9.
Lam, P. T. C.
    1981   Some case histories and their implications for planning of mental health ser-
            vices. In T. P. Khoo (Ed.), *Aspects of mental health care: Hong Kong 1981.* Hong
            Kong: Mental Health Association of Hong Kong.
Lau, B. W. L., Cheung, F. M., and Waldmann, E.
    1981   Morbidity of depression illness in general practice. *Asian Medical Journal, 24*(7),
            518–527.
Lee, R. P. L.
    1974   *The stratification between modern and traditional profession: A study of health services
            in Hong Kong.* Occasional paper of the Social Research Centre, The Chinese
            University of Hong Kong.
    1975   Interaction between Chinese and Western medicine in Hong Kong: Moderniza-
            tion and professional inequality. In A Kleinman, P. Kunstadter, E. R. Alexan-
            der, and J. L. Gale (Eds.), *Medicine in Chinese cultures: Comparative studies of
            health care in Chinese and other societies.* Washington, DC: U.S. Department of
            Health, Education, and Welfare.
    1976   *Sex and social class differences in mental illness: The case of Hong Kong.* Occasional
            paper of the Social Research Centre, The Chinese University of Hong Kong.
    1980a   Perceptions and uses of Chinese medicine among the Chinese in Hong Kong.
            Culture, Medicine and Psychiatry, 4, 345–375.
    1980b   Sex roles, social status, and psychiatric symptoms in urban Hong Kong. In A.
            Kleinman and T. Y. Lin (Eds.), *Normal and abnormal behavior in Chinese culture.*
            Dordrecht, Holland: Reidel.
Li-Repac, D.
    1981   Cultural influences on clinical perception: A comparison between Caucasian
            and Chinese-American therapists. *Journal of Cross-Cultural Psychology, 11*(3),
            327–342.
Lieh-Mak, F., Luk, S. L., and Leung, L.
    1979   Gilles de la Tourette's Syndrome: Report of five cases in the Chinese. *British
            Journal of Psychiatry, 134,* 630–634.

Leih-Mak, F., Tam, Y. K., Yu, K. K., and Pun, P. C.
    1981   Psychiatric unit in a general hospital. In T. P. Khoo (Ed.), *Aspects of mental health care: Hong Kong 1981*. Hong Kong: Mental Health Association of Hong Kong.

Lo, W. H.
    1967   A follow-up study of obsessional neurotics in Hong Kong Chinese. *British Journal of Psychiatry, 113*, 823–832.
    1978   Abdominal pain as a psychosomatic manifestation. *Hong Kong Journal of Mental Health, 7*(2), 33–39.
    1981a   *Culture and depression: With special reference to treatment*. Paper presented at the Symposium on Transcultural Psychiatry, Macau, September 6–11.
    1981b   Government mental health service. In T. P. Khoo (Ed.), *Aspects of mental health care: Hong Kong 1981*. Hong Kong: Mental Health Association of Hong Kong.

Lo, W. H., and Lo, T.
    1977   A ten-year follow-up study of Chinese schizophrenics in Hong Kong. *British Journal of Psychiatry, 131*, 63–66.

Ma, K. S.
    1974   The adverse effects of social stigma on the mentally disordered. *Hong Kong Journal of Mental Health, 3*(2), 8–11.

Mischel, W.
    1969   Continuity and change in personality. *American Psychologist, 24*, 1012–1028.
    1973   Toward a cognitive social learning reconceptualization of personality. *Psychological Review, 80*(4), 252–283.

Ng, V. S.
    1980   Cultural patterns of problem-solving: A comparative study of Hong Kong and American Caucasian students. Unpublished project report. Honolulu: East-West Cultural Learning Institute, East-West Center.

Samaritan Befrienders of Hong Kong
    1981   *Annual Report*. Hong Kong: Author.

Singer, K.
    1975   Depressive disorders from a transcultural perspective. *Social Science and Medicine, 9*, 289–301.
    1976   Culture and mental health. In W. H. Lo, W. Chen, K. S. Ma, A. Wong, and K. K. Yeung (Eds.), *Perspectives in mental health: Hong Kong 1976*. Hong Kong: Mental Health Association of Hong Kong.
    1977   Somatization and new cross-cultural psychiatry: Reply. *Social Science and Medicine, 11*(1), 11–12.

Singer, K., Chang, P. T., and Hsu, G. L. K.
    1972   Physique, personality and mental illness in the southern Chinese. *British Journal of Psychiatry, 121*, 315–319.

Singer, K., Lieh-Mak, F., and Ng, M. L.
    1976   Physique, personality and mental illness in southern Chinese women. *British Journal of Psychiatry, 129*, 243–247.

Singer, K., Ney, P. G., and Lieh-Mak, F.
    1978   A cultural perspective on child psychiatric disorders. *Comprehensive Psychiatry, 19*(6), 533–540.

Topley, M.
    1967   Chinese occasional rites in Hong Kong. In M. Topley (Ed.), *Some traditional Chinese ideas and conceptions in Hong Kong social life today*. Hong Kong: The Hong Kong Branch of the Royal Asiatic Society.

Tseng, W. S.
    1975   The nature of somatic complaints among psychiatric patients: The Chinese case. *Comprehensive Psychiatry, 16,* 237–245.

Tseng, W. S., and Hsu, J.
    1970   Chinese culture, personality formation and mental illness. *The International Journal of Social Psychiatry, 16*(1) 5–14.

White, G.
    1980   *Cultural explanations of illness and adjustment: A comparative study of American and Hong Kong Chinese students.* Paper presented at the Symposium on the Ethnology of Health Care Discussions, 7th Annual Meeting of the American Anthropological Association. Washington, DC, December 4–7.
    1981   *The role of cultural explanations in "somatization and psychologization": American and Hong Kong Chinese.* Unpublished paper.

Wong, C. L.
    1976   An appraisal of psychosomatic symptoms, with special reference to psychiatric private practice in Hong Kong. *Hong Kong Journal of Mental Health, 5*(2), 5–7.

Wong, S. W.
    1979   Hypochondriacal complaints among Hong Kong children: A mental health hazard? *Annals Academy of Medicine Singapore, 8*(3), 244–251.

Wong, S. W. and Kwong, B.
    1981   *Chinese language and hypochondriacal complaints.* Paper presented at the Annual Conference of the Royal Australian and New Zealand College of Psychiatrists. Hong Kong, 12–16 October.

Wu, D.
    1980   *Emotion and mental health in traditional Chinese medicine.* Paper presented at the Conference on Cultural Conceptions of Mental Health and Therapy, East-West Center, Honolulu, June 4–6.

Yap, P. M.
    1965a   Koro—A culture-bound depersonalization syndrome. *British Journal of Psychiatry, 111,* 43.
    1965b   Phenomenology of affective disorder in Chinese and other cultures (Ciba Foundation Symposium). In A. V. S. de Reuck and R. Porter (Eds.), *Transcultural psychiatry.* London: Churchill.
    1967a   Classification of the culture-bound reactive syndromes. *Australian and New Zealand Journal of Psychiatry, 1,* 172-179.
    1967b   Ideas of mental health and disorder in Hong Kong and their practical influence. In M. Topley (Ed.), *Some traditional Chinese ideas and conceptions in Hong Kong social life today.* Hong Kong: The Hong Kong Branch of the Royal Asiatic Society.
    1971   Guilt and shame, depression and culture: A psychiatric cliché re-examined. *Community Contemporary Psychiatry, 1*(2), 35.

CHAPTER 20

An Epidemiological Study of Child Mental Health Problems in Nanjing District

Yu Lian

INTRODUCTION

Childhood is a period of physical and intellectual growth. It is also a period of psychosocial development. During this period, a variety of factors may influence normal growth (Tao, 1980). For the purpose of discovering the most common mental helath problems among children and exploring the possible reasons for such problems so that appropriate preventive work could be developed, the Section of Child Psychiatry of the Nanjing Neuro-psychiatric Institute carried out a mental health epidemiological study of 1246 kindergarten and school-children in Nanjing District from April to May 1981. (In China at the time of this investigation, children under 3 years were cared for at nurseries, attended kindergarten between 3 and 6, and at 7 entered primary school. Therefore, "kindergarten" in this chapter

CHINESE CULTURE
AND MENTAL HEALTH

corresponds to preschool and kindergarten in the American educational system).

DESCRIPTION OF THE METHOD

In order to study children from an urban area, we chose at random two primary schools and two kindergartens in Nanjing City. To study children in a rural area, we selected one primary school and one kindergarten in Jiang Ning County and one primary school and one kindergarten in Chun Hua rural commune.

We used the Child and Mental Health Survey Questionnaire, a research instrument designed by the Division of Child and Adolescence Health, Beijing Medical College, and our Institute. The contents of the questionnaire include (1) personal growth history, (2) past illness, (3) family history, (4) family milieu, (5) behavior at home, and (5) behavior at school. The questionnaire includes 24 questions regarding the child's behavior, to be evaluated and rated by parents for behavior at home and by the teacher for behavior at school. For each question, there are four possible replies: "none," "occasional," "yes (present)," and "(very) often." In this chapter, the focus is confined primarily to child mental health problems at home and at school.

Because the questionnaire covered a variety of areas involving many items and because the work required uniform criteria and universal agreement in order to make the combined data accurate and reliable, we carried out training sessions for the participating workers to familiarize them with the items and the criteria so as to minimize errors. We then held conferences with all the parents and teachers involved to help them understand fully the purpose and meaning of the project and assure their full cooperation. We also explained each item included in the questionnaire. Thus, the teachers and parents could take the responsibility of making accurate assessments of the children's mental health behavior.

RESULTS OF THE INVESTIGATION

We investigated 368 children from two primary schools and 175 from two kindergartens in Nanjing City. We also investigated 450 children from two primary schools and 253 from two kindergartens from rural areas in Nanjing District. The total number of children investigated was 1246, of which 636 were boys and 610 girls. Their ages range from 4 to 16 years, with the distribution between age and gender shown in Table 20.1.

Analysis of the 24 items relating to the 1246 children's behavior at home

Table 20.1 Demographic Data of Children Studied

Area and school	Number of students	Gender		Age		
		Male	Female	4–6	7–12	13–16
Nanjing City						
Nanjing Teacher's College						
Kindergarten	86	40	46	64	22	—
Wu Tai Shan						
Kindergarten	89	43	46	66	23	—
Nanjing Teacher's College						
Primary School	209	110	99	—	206	3
Lhasa Road						
Primary School	159	67	92	—	151	8
Jiang Ning County						
Ton Shan Zhen						
Kindergarten	119	71	48	38	81	—
Chun Hua Commune						
Kindergarten	134	74	60	77	57	—
Ton Shan Zhen						
Primary School	259	134	125	—	223	36
Chun Hua Commune						
Primary School	191	95	96	—	153	38
	1246	634	612	245	916	85

and school showed high rates for some items: for instance, finicky eating behavior (34.1%), overdependence on parents and adults (21%), emotional instability (16.8%), sluggishness in daily life (14%), and nail sucking and biting (11.6%). But for some other items, such as frequently staying away from school (1.3%), failure in school (2%), rudeness in speaking (2.5%), drinking alcoholic beverages (0.3%), and pilfering (0.3%), the rates are comparatively low (see Table 20.2).

Area Differences. Comparing the results of the investigation between urban and rural areas, it was found that although the rates for some items were high in both city and the country, others were higher in the city. Examples are: finicky eating behavior (city 45.1% vs. country 25.6%; $p <$ .01), overdependence on parents and adults (28% vs. 15.5%; $p <$ .01), sluggishness in daily life (16.4% vs. 12.2%; .01 $< p <$ .05), fondness for making mischief (6.4% vs. 2.7%; $p <$ .01), biting and sucking other objects (13% vs. 4.5%; $p <$ .01). Some other items were lower in the city than in

Table 20.2   Mental Health Problems of Children in Urban and Rural Areas

Problem	Nanjing City		Jiang Ning County		Total		p
	n	%	n	%	n	%	
Poor concentration and attention	52	9.5	59	8.4	111	8.9	>.05
Hyperactivity	52	9.5	60	8.5	112	9.0	>.05
Mischief making	35	6.4	19	2.7	54	4.3	<.01
Poor academic performance	30	5.5	70	10.0	100	8.0	<.01
Failure of grade	8	1.5	17	2.4	25	2.0	>.05
Emotional instability	102	18.8	107	15.2	209	16.8	>.05
Sluggishness	89	16.4	86	12.2	175	14.0	<.05
Overdependence	152	28.0	109	15.5	261	21.0	<.01
Finicky eating behavior	245	45.1	180	25.6	425	34.1	<.01
Frequent headaches	19	3.5	31	4.4	50	4.0	>.05
Finger sucking and nail biting	98	18.0	47	6.7	145	11.6	<.01
Biting or sucking other objects	70	13.0	32	4.5	102	8.2	<.01
Stammering	31	5.7	41	5.8	72	5.8	>.05
Slurred speech	52	9.5	67	9.5	119	9.6	>.05
Night bed-wetting	26	4.8	38	5.4	64	5.1	>.05
Breath-holding spells	7	1.3	21	3.0	28	2.2	>.01; <.05
Frowning and winking	21	3.9	17	2.4	38	3.0	>.05
Twitching of face and shoulders	6	1.1	5	0.7	11	0.9	>.05
Lying	11	2.0	21	3.0	32	2.6	>.05
Truancy	0	0	16	2.3	16	1.3	<.01
Physical fighting	6	1.1	35	5.0	41	3.3	<.01
Rudeness in speaking	7	1.3	24	3.4	31	2.5	>.01; <.05
Drinking alcohol	2	0.4	2	0.3	4	0.3	>.05
Pilfering	1	0.2	3	0.4	4	0.3	>.05
	543		703		1246		

the county, including frequently staying away from school (0.0% vs. 2.3%; $p < .01$), low grades (5.5% vs. 10%; $p = .05$), fondness for fighting (1.1% vs. 5.0%; $p < 0.01$), breath-holding spells, rudeness in speaking, and so forth.

Gender Differences.   Analysis of the results by gender discloses some differences (see Table 20.3). Boys showed a higher incidence than girls for difficulty in concentrating (boys 11.4% vs. girls 6.4%; $p < .01$), hyperactivity (13.2% vs. 4.6%; $p < .01$), sluggishness in daily life (17.5% vs. 10.5%;

Table 20.3   Relationship between Children's Mental Health Problems and Gender

Problem	Male		Female		Total		
	n	%	n	%	n	%	p
Poor concentration and attention	72	11.4	39	6.4	111	8.9	<.01
Hyperactivity	84	13.2	28	4.6	112	9.0	<.01
Mischief making	39	6.2	15	2.5	54	4.3	<.01
Poor academic performance	51	8.0	49	8.0	100	8.0	>.05
Failure of grade	14	2.2	11	1.8	25	2.0	>.05
Emotional instability	125	19.7	84	13.7	209	16.8	<.01
Sluggishness	111	17.5	64	10.5	175	14.0	<.01
Overdependence	157	24.8	104	17.0	261	21.0	<.01
Finicky eating behavior	205	32.3	220	36.0	425	34.1	>.05
Frequent headaches	24	3.8	26	4.2	50	4.0	>.05
Finger sucking and nail biting	76	12.0	69	11.3	145	11.6	>.05
Biting or sucking other objects	64	10.1	38	6.2	102	8.2	>.01; <.05
Stammering	44	6.9	28	4.6	72	5.8	>.05
Slurred speech	77	12.1	42	6.9	119	9.6	<.01
Night bed-wetting	42	6.6	22	3.6	64	5.1	>.01; <.05
Breath-holding spells	22	3.5	6	1.0	28	2.2	<.01
Frowning and winking	28	4.4	10	1.6	38	3.0	<.01
Twitching of face and shoulders	5	0.8	6	1.0	11	0.9	>.05
Lying	24	3.8	8	1.3	32	2.6	<.01
Truancy	9	1.4	7	1.1	16	1.3	>.05
Physical fighting	37	5.8	4	0.7	41	3.3	<.01
Rudeness in speaking	25	3.9	6	1.0	31	2.5	<.01
Drinking alcohol	4	0.6	0	0	4	0.3	>.01; <.05
Pilfering	2	0.3	2	0.3	4	0.3	>.05
	634		612		1246		

$p < .01$), overdependence on parents and adults (24.8% vs. 17%; $p < .01$), slurring of speech (12.1% vs. 6.9%; $p < .01$), bedwetting (6.6% vs. 3.6%; $.01 < p < .05$), and so on.

Developmental Differences.   Comparison of the results for kindergarten and elementary school students in terms of age group differences was carried out (see Table 20.4). Among the kindergarten children, only the rate of breath-holding spells is higher (kindergarten 3.5% vs. elementary 1.6%; $.01 < p < .05$); other behaviors show lower incidence than in the elementary school group, for example, difficulty in concentrating (4.7% vs.

Table 20.4   Mental Health Problems of Children in Kindergarten and Primary School

Problem	Kinder-garten n	%	Primary school n	%	Total n	%	p
Poor concentration and attention	20	4.7	91	11.1	111	8.9	<.01
Hyperactivity	27	6.3	85	10.4	112	9.0	>.01; <.05
Mischief making	15	3.5	39	4.7	54	4.3	<.05
Poor academic performance	15	3.5	85	10.4	100	8.0	<.01
Failure of grade	0	0	25	3.1	25	2.0	<.01
Emotional instability	46	10.7	163	19.9	209	16.8	<.01
Sluggishness	24	5.6	151	18.5	175	14.0	<.01
Overdependence	42	9.8	219	26.8	261	21.0	<.01
Finicky eating behavior	138	32.2	287	35.1	425	34.1	>.05
Frequent headaches	7	1.6	43	5.3	50	4.0	<.01
Finger sucking and nail biting	49	11.4	96	11.7	145	11.6	>.05
Biting or sucking other objects	18	4.2	84	10.3	102	8.2	<.01
Stammering	21	4.9	51	6.2	72	5.8	>.05
Slurred speech	44	10.3	75	9.2	119	9.6	>.05
Night bed-wetting	12	2.8	52	6.4	64	5.1	<.01
Breath-holding spells	15	3.5	13	1.6	28	2.2	>.01; <.05
Frowning and winking	7	1.6	31	3.8	38	3.0	>.01; <.05
Twitching of face and shoulders	4	0.9	7	0.9	11	0.9	>.05
Lying	14	3.3	18	2.2	32	2.6	>.05
Truancy	10	2.3	6	0.7	16	1.3	>.01; <.05
Physical fighting	14	3.3	27	3.3	41	3.3	>.05
Rudeness in speaking	4	0.9	27	3.3	31	2.5	<.01
Drinking alcohol	2	0.5	2	0.2	4	0.3	>.05
Pilfering	1	0.2	3	0.4	4	0.3	>.05
	428		318		1246		

11.1%; $p < .01$), hyperactivity (6.3% vs. 10.4%; $.05 < p < .01$), sluggishness in daily life (5.6% vs. 18.5%; $p < .01$), overdependence on parents and adults (9.8% vs. 26.8%, $p < .01$), bed-wetting (2.8% vs. 6.4%, $p < .01$), and so on. Nocturnal bed-wetting is a mental hygiene problem worthy of notice in older children; but for kindergarten children under 5, occasional occurrence may be considered normal.

DISCUSSION

Two factors are taken into consideration concerning the possible causes of the mental health problems found in the investigation.

Psychophysiological Factors

Age.   Psychological development shows its characteristics at every stage of development (Zhu, 1980). Kindergarten children are still very young; and when compared with elementary school students, have not fully developed certain behavioral traits (Whalen, 1980). For example, problems in concentration are not a major issue for kindergarten students since it is relatively unimportant in their daily performance. Some behaviors are normal development phenomena that are recognized as problems at certain ages; night bed-wetting is one such example. This observation explains why the rates for younger children in such items are higher than those for older children (Zhang, 1979).

Gender and Character.   Differences in gender are related to differences in rates associated with particular survey items (Lu, 1980). According to Hsu (1966), Chinese girls, in general, from a very young age, have gentle dispositions and are quiet, timid, and physically weak; they dare not stir up trouble. Therefore, the rates of lying and fighting are lower for girls than for boys. Because, for the most part, Chinese boys are bold and active, most of them show hyperactivity. Additionally, boys' development is not as rapid as girls'. The incidence of difficulty in concentration and of night bed-wetting is comparatively higher for boys than for girls. These observations are broadly generalized, and, of course, all cases should not be viewed in the same light.

Physical Condition.   During the growing process from fetus to adulthood, various factors, such as heredity, infection, trauma, intoxication, and malnutrition, may cause mental hygiene problems. All of these factors should be taken into consideration (Makita, 1978).

Psychological State.   Children usually pay great attention to their status in the family and to the attitudes of their parents and teachers toward them. If they are spoiled at home, they tend to have feelings of superiority and to show sluggishness in daily life and overdependence on others (Kasamatsu, 1971). If parents and teachers are too strict with the children, some of them may become nervous and depressed either at school or at home. These feelings may be manifested in habits of biting fingernails and other objects and stammering.

Psychosocial–Enviornmental Factors

In the data for the 1246 children investigated, the following items are relatively high: partiality for particular foods, overdependence on adults, emotional instability, sluggishness in daily life, finger sucking, and nail biting. In contrast, failure in school, rudeness in speaking, drinking alcoholic beverages, and pilfering are relatively low.

There has been speculation that because Chinese parents tend to be concerned about the physical condition of their children, they pay special attention to eating and nutrition and show their affection by offering food. This may, in a way, increase the importance of the child's eating pattern and be related to concern for the child's diet. Eating problems, as well as overdependence on adults and emotional instability, are reported in families with an only child who is overindulged by the parents (Tao and Chiu, Chapter 11, this volume). In China, education is highly regarded, and elementary schools and kindergartens are expected to provide academic, social, and recreational programs for children to participation in and to enjoy. Therefore, elementary schools and kindergartens are generally well attended, and there is little problem with children refusing to go to school or failing in academic work. This phenomenon is probably reinforced by the parents' strong desire for their children to receive a good education. Because of excellent public morality and highly structured social organization, drinking and pilfering among children is most uncommon.

Many people still consider men to be superior to women, so boys are often treated more favorably and pampered. Because of this tendency of favoritism and indulgence toward boys, boys have more bad habits, such as sluggishness in daily life, overdependence on others, and emotional instability, than do girls.

Certain parents, as well as teachers, neglect moral education and do not expose children to the spiritual side of life. This neglect may be the cause of the children's rudeness in speaking, fondness for lying, and predisposition toward drinking alcoholic beverages and pilfering.

Life-styles and their associated behaviors vary between the urban and rural areas. For instance, children in the city have a very full life. They see films very often, watch TV, listen to the radio, and have more opportunity to take part in social activities. Therefore, they have more experience and knowledge. They also devote more time to study, show less truancy, and usually earn better grades, but they are less able to take care of themselves. This may be due to the fact that the parents tend to do things for the children rather than to allow the children to be selfsufficient (Wu, 1981). Overdependence on parents, sluggishness in living, and other bad habits are common behaviors.

In contrast to this, rural children have less time to study because they usually have responsibility for physical labor at home; they also participate in fewer social activities. In these children, the rates of fondness for making mischief, partiality to particular kinds of food, sluggishness in living, and overdependence on others are lower. However, because many parents in the rural areas pay less attention to the morale and spiritual aspects of education, the rates of fondness for fighting, rudeness in speaking, and so on are higher than for children in the city.

COMMENT

In order to promote normal growth and physical and mental health of children, we emphasize the importance of positive psychosocial development and of using preventive measures. Information on mental health should be popularized, and students majoring in medicine and education should have special mental health courses. Scientific knowledge concerning the mental health of children should be broadly disseminated, and the whole society should be aroused to give attention to the mental health of children and to understand the effects of psychological and social factors on health and disease.

Research on child mental health has already started in mainland China. We have shown some results in this chapter, and we will continue our study of psychosocial factors in order to have a basis for advocating preventive measures to protect children's physical and mental health. Because our social system encourages such endeavors, research on this subject will advance to a new and higher level in the near future.

REFERENCES

Hsu, C. C.
   1966   A study on "problem children" reported by teachers. *Japanese Journal of Child Psychiatry*, 7, 91–108.
Kasamatsu, A.
   1971   Kaku ryoiki no seishin eisei [Various fields of mental health]. In A. Kasamatsu, *Rinsho seishin igaku* [Clinical psychiatry II]. Chugai Medical Publisher.
Lu, L. G.
   1980   *Yi-xue-xing-li-xue jian-je* [A summary introduction of medical psychology]. Unpublished demographic material of the Nanjing Neuropsychiatry Institution.
Makita, K.
   1978   *Yoboteki jidoseinshinigaku* [Preventive child psychiatry]. In K. Makita, *Jidoseishinigaku* [Child psychiatry] (rev. ed.). Iwazaki Academic Publisher.
Tao, K. T.
   1980   *Er-tong xin-li-wei-sheng* [Child mental health]. Unpublished demographic material of the Nanjing Neuropsychiatry Institution.

Whalen, C. K.
    1980   In C. K. Whalen and B. Henker (Eds.), *Hyperactive children.* New York: Aca-
              demic Press.
Wu, F. G.
    1981   *Tan-tan er-tong xin-li de fa-zhang* [Talking about child mental development].
              Science Press.
Zhang, Y. S.
    1979   *Xue-sheng pin-de-bu-liang de i-xie xin-li-fen-xi* [Some psychological analysis of
              students' misconduct]. Psychological Broadcasting Lectures, Tian Su Education
              College.
Zhu, Z. X.
    1980   *Er-tong xin-li fa-zhang de ji-ben gui-lü* [The basic regulation of child mental
              development]. In Z. X. Zhu, *Er-tong xin-li-xue* [Child psychology], Beijing,
              China: Beijing Peoples' Medical Press.

CHAPTER 21

An Investigation of Minimal Brain Disorders among Primary School Students in the Beijing Area

Yang Xiaoling

INTRODUCTION

The Nature of Minimal Brain Dysfunction

Minimal brain dysfunction, also called hyperactive syndrome or attention deficient disorder, is widely considered one of the important problems in the field of child mental health. Although many studies have been carried out relating to this problem, the nature of this dysfunction is not yet well defined nor formalized. It was in 1932 that Kramer, who used the term *child hyperactive syndrome,* initially reported the disorder. In 1947, Strauss, Gesell, and others, thinking that it was the result of minor brain

315

injury, used the designation *minimal brain damage*. In 1962, the International Pediatric Neurology Association in Oxford, England, rejected the theory of brain damage and renamed it *minimal brain dysfunction*. In the ninth edition of *International Classification of Disease* (1978), the condition is referred to as *hyperactivity syndrome;* while in the third edition of *Diagnostic and Statistical Manuals for Mental Disorders* (1980), the term *attention deficit disorder* is employed. In both classification systems, the condition is subdivided into two subtypes, one with and the other without hyperactivity.

Regardless of the variations in diagnostic terminology, all designations refer to a more or less similar clinical syndrome that includes four major symptoms—poor concentration, short attention span, hyperactivity, impulsivity of emotion—which create difficulty in relating well with others. Although this dysfunction is seen commonly among school-age children, the onset of symptoms can be traced to an earlier stage of life. More boys than girls show the dysfunction. Children having this kind of dysfunction are frequently regarded as problem children. Such children do not pay attention to their teacher, but instead look around or play with clothes or other objects. They daydream or talk to surrounding classmates and are restless, moving or shaking the tables and chairs. They are inattentive in class and disturb the class atmosphere by bothering classmates or not responding when the teacher gives them individual attention. Although intellectual endowment is not necessarily low, poor academic performance is not necessary due to inattentiveness, and there is, additionally, interactional difficulty with classmates or family members. Such children cry easily, become impatient, and are temperamental. As a result, a child with this syndrome may be labeled a "naughty child," a "problem child," or "a special child." An individual with a mild case may not be permitted to attend group activities, while the severe case may be dismissed from school.

Some investigators have reported that this disorder is more common among children in families of low socioeconomic levels that live in crowded home environments, and thus, they relate the condition to family background and child-rearing practices. Others have suggested that some of the children have hereditary tendencies or histories of prenatal sickness, premature delivery, low body weight at birth, difficult delivery, or central nervous system infection or injury during infancy. Some researchers view the dysfunction as a developmental problem, suggesting that such children tend to have delayed development and that the dysfunction improves after puberty. Recent studies in psychopharmacotherapy suggest that the dysfunction may relate to a metabolic disorder of the central nervous system.

Recent Concern about Minimal Brain Dysfunction in China

Minimal brain dysfunction among children has received much attention in China since 1979. According to Tao (personal communication, 1982), after the Child Mental Health Clinic was established in 1954 at the Nanjing Neuropsychiatric Institution, there were usually only 30–40 children who were diagnosed each year as suffering from minimal brain dysfunction. However, since 1979, there have been more than 100 children diagnosed annually. The same increase was noted in Beijing, Shanghai, and other major cities. There are several reasons for such a sharp increase of minimal brain dysfunction cases in the child mental health clinics.

During the Ten Year Turmoil (the period of the Cultural Revolution), the educational system was disrupted. Not only higher education, but also elementary schools were affected. Now as the educational system recovers, the teaching curriculum has become more organized, and both academic education and student discipline are emphasized more. Higher education is more accessible, and there is an increased concern for higher entrance rates as a direct result of better preparation for high school and the university. There is a higher expectation for excellence in academic performance from teachers and parents. Therefore, students who have difficulty in concentration in their studies or who show unsatisfactory academic performance, such as children with minimal brain dysfunction, receive more attention. This increasing interest in academic achievement was coincident with the fact that the subject of minimal brain dysfunction was publicized in a popular medical magazine and later in newspaper reports. That children with such problems could be favorably treated by medication encouraged many teachers and parents to send children for psychiatric evaluation.

It is necessary to understand the mainland Chinese educational system and expected classroom behavior and their possible relationship to the behavior and learning problems of students. In China, based on the traditional cultural heritage, most parents are usually very much concerned with the education of their children. It is a common saying that *"Wang zi cheng Long"* (parents expect their son will become a dragon)—the dragon is a symbol of success. Parents expect their children to have not only good academic performance but also good social behavior—to accept discipline, to learn appropriate etiquette, and to respect their elders. In the city, children are usually sent to kindergarten between 4 and 6 years of age. They are brought to kindergarten by their parents early in the morning and are picked up in the late afternoon; they spend 10–12 hours daily at the kindergarten, having three meals and 2–3 hours' nap time there. Small children are taught to behave properly, to follow discipline, to respect teachers, and to have concern for the group.

After the age of 6, children enter elementary school. In general, students have four classes in the morning and two or three classes in the afternoon. Each class lasts 45 minutes, with 10 minutes recess inbetween. In contrast to the kindergarten, a stricter discipline is imposed in elementary school. During the class, students are expected to sit quietly on their seats, and they are not allowed to leave their seats without permission from the teacher. The students are required to raise their hands if they want to speak—either to raise a question or to answer a question. Needless to say, no one is permitted to do anything that conflicts with class activities. There is usually much homework assigned, with the expectation that it will be finished on time. Students who cannot finish the homework or do not follow the discipline of the class, receive public criticism. If they are repeatedly criticized and still do not correct their behavior, the parents are called to the school for an interview in order to obtain their cooperation in correcting the behavior. In other words, students who cannot sit still and concentrate on what the teacher is saying are considered not behaving correctly and receive special attention. Concern is also shown about a student who tends to be active in the classroom and who is less tolerated by teachers than the quiet and reserved student. Consequently, such students are labeled problem students and are referred for clinical assessment.

All the previously described factors—the historical background, the educational system, and social–cultural trends—contributed to the recent concern for minimal brain dysfunction in children in China, at least as reflected by the sharp increase in the number of cases diagnosed as such in children's mental health clinics.

In order to obtain an accurate picture of the frequency of the disorder, studies of the prevalence of minimal brain dysfunction among school children have been carried out by psychologists and psychiatrists in various large cities in China, including Shanghai, Beijing, and Guangzhou (Guangzhou City, Dongshan District Public Health Bureau, 1981). However, the results indicate that the prevalence rate of this disorder varies greatly—between 1 and 13% in different areas—suggesting that such studies may be affected by differences in diagnostic criteria and the method of survey.

INVESTIGATIONS IN ELEMENTARY SCHOOLS OF DIFFERENT AREAS

Based on this background, the present study was carried out in Beijing and had two objectives: first, to develop and to test a reliable screening method for identifying the disorder; and second, to conduct school surveys, using the screening method, in urban, suburban, and rural areas. The aim of the study was to investigate possible social, family life, and other environmental factors that may contribute to the frequency of the disorder.

Three schools were selected for this investigation: one in an urban area with 315 students, one in a suburban area with 424 students, and two in a mountainous rural area with a total of 658 students. Thus, a total of 1379 students were surveyed. Schools from different geographic and economic backgrounds were selected for purposes of comparison.

Backgrounds of the Areas Surveyed

The school in the urban area is located in the cultural district of the western section of Beijing City, where many universities, colleges, and scientific research institutions are located. About one-third of the students in this school are from scientists' and technicians' families. The rest are from workers' and cadres' (office workers') families. About one-third of the pupils' fathers are college educated, while the rest have at least a high-school education. Thus, in general, most of the parents strongly emphasize their children's education.

The school in the suburban area is located in the industrial district of the eastern suburb of Beijing City, and about 45% of the pupils come from workers' families, about 33% from technicians' or scientists' families, 12% from cadres' families, and about 10% from farmers' families. The economic backgrounds of families in the suburban area is very similar to those in the urban area.

The schools surveyed in the rural areas are located in mountainous areas where transportation is not very convenient and there is no industry nearby. The economic backgrounds of families in this area are generally lower than in the other areas studied. Parents do not emphasize their children's education, and children tend to enter elementary school between the ages of 7 and 9, 1 or 2 years later than children in the city areas.

The Design of the Questionnaire

With reference to Rutter's (1967) Children's Behavior Questionnaire and Conner's (1973) simplified rating scale for minimal brain dysfunction, a Children's Learning and Behavior Questionnaire to be scored by teachers for the purpose of screening of minimal brain dysfunction was designed by our institute. The Questionnaire contains four items: poor concentration, short attention span, hyperactivity, and emotional instability. Within each item, various degrees of severity are described in clear and concrete terms so that the questionnaire can be more objectively scored. Each item is to be rated in 5 degrees, with scores from 0 to 4, so that the highest possible score is 16. Based on our past experience and preliminary studies, knowing that Chinese students are less likely to be considered and described as having emotional instability and impulsive behavior, such areas are downplayed in our questionnaire and tailored to our particular situation.

The efficiency of the questionnaire design was pretested with 424 students at a school in the suburban area. A total of 83 students with different questionnaire scores were randomly selected, and clinical examinations of them were carried out to test the validity of the questionnaire design. The clinical examination included attention to present history, developmental history, family history, a physical and neurological examination, and an intelligence assessment (Draw-a-Person Test and review of academic records). As a result, 45 cases were clinically diagnosed as having minimal brain dysfunction. Thus, it was found that the sensitivity, specificity, and efficiency of the questionnaire as a whole were most satisfactory when a score of 7 was used as the cutoff point.

The test–retest reliability of the questionnaire was also tested. A total of 92 pupils in three different classes were reevaluated with the questionnaire by the class master teacher 1 month after the initial scoring. (In each class, there is a master teacher who not only gives a lecture to the class but who is also responsible for the performance and behavior of the entire class. Thus, the class master teacher is considered to be the best person to rate the questionnaire for the whole class of students.) The scores correlated moderately high ($r = .55, .81$, and $.69$ for the three classes, respectively).

Results of the Survey

Even though we found from the pretest that a score of above 7 is significantly correlated with clinical cases of minimal brain dysfunction, we decided, on the side of caution, to use a score of above 9 as the index for positive cases. By using such criteria, the results of the questionnaire survey are as follows:

1. *Geographical areas.* The positive minimal brain dysfunction cases found in the three different areas are distributed as follows: 13 cases per 315 subjects in the urban area (4.1%), 31 per 424 subjects in the suburban area (7.3%), and 48 per 656 subjects in the mountainous rural areas (7.3%). Statistically, there is no significant difference.

2. *Gender.* The occurrence rate of children with minimal brain dysfunction is significantly higher among males (11.1%) than among females (1.5%). This is true in all three areas.

3. *Symptoms.* Each student was rated with regard to four symptoms: poor concentration, short attention span, hyperactivity, and emotional instability. Each item is scored on a 5-degree scale: none (0), occasional (1), frequent (2), always/remarkable (3), always/very remarkable (4). If the rating is above 3, it is considered an indication of the obvious presence of the specific symptom. Marked indications of poor concentration and short attention span were found among pupils in the different areas (about 3.5–7.8% and 3.2–6.6%, respectively), but this was not the case for hyperactivity and emotional instability (1.2–3.8% and 0.3-3.4%, respectively). In other words, the problems of poor concentration and inattention are more frequently scored, while hyperactivity and emotional instability are scored much less frequently. This tendency was observed in all three geographic areas.

4. *Father's occupation.* The father's occupation is categorized as (a) professional worker (technician, scientist, university faculty), (b) cadre, (staff member in the administration), (c) peasant, and (d) worker. The rate of minimal brain dysfunction differs in relation to the father's occupation: it is 3.9% for professional workers, 6.1% for cadres, 7.4% for peasants, and 8.1% for workers.

5. *Father's educational level.* In order to review the intellectual and educational background of the family, the father's educational level is studied. It was revealed that the rate of minimal brain dysfunction is 3.6% for pupils whose fathers have college educations, 8.3% for high school educations, and 10.9% for primary-school educations or no formal education. Results indicate that the prevalence of minimal brain dysfunction differs with respect to the father's educational level, that is, the prevalence rate decreases if the father has a higher educational background.

SUMMARY

Minimal brain dysfunction is an ill-defined mental health problem of children. The diagnosis of the disorder relies on subjective assessment. In order to carry out prevalence studies, it is necessary to have reliable survey instruments. The Children's Learning and Behavior Questionnaire was designed by our institute for the screening survey in China. Our study indicates that our questionnaire design can be used as a valid screening instrument with satisfactory specificity, sensitivity, and overall efficiency.

Utilizing the present questionnaire design, a survey was conducted in primary schools in the Beijing area. Results indicate that the prevalence of the disorder varies within a range of 4.1%–7.3% among elementary school students studied in different geographical areas—urban, suburban, and rural. The prevalence rate of the disorder in China is comparable to that reported in Western societies (e.g., 4% of the school population, Stewart et al. 1966; or 10%, Huessy, 1967).

The disorder is found more frequently in boys than in girls and more commonly among children from families of lower socioeconomic and educational backgrounds. This pattern fits the general impression obtained from other investigations carried out around the world, suggesting that the environmental condition of the children may play a role in the development of minimal brain dysfunction.

For Chinese students, it was found that, in contrast to symptoms of hyperactivity and emotional instability, the problems of poor concentration and inattention are more frequently scored in the questionnaire because they have a more direct impact upon the teachers. This reflects the relationship of classroom behavior to culture; that is, students are expected to sit quietly and concentrate on the teacher, and the teacher notices those who do not conform. In general, Chinese students are less likely to be observed and described as having emotional instability or impulsive behavior.

It has been pointed out that there was—associated with the recent recovery of the basic educational system in China—a revival of serious concern for school children's academic performance on the parts of parents and teachers. Such a tendency, coupled with the increased awareness of minimal brain dysfunction as a treatable child mental disorder, has brought about a sudden increase in community attention to the disorder. This has resulted in a sharp increase in the number of cases referred to, and diagnosed in, the child mental health clinics. This suggests that sociocultural conditioning may contribute indirectly to the recognition of and concern for such mental health problems among children.

REFERENCES

Conners, C.
    1973   Rating scales for use in drug studies with children. Pharmacotherapy of children [Special issue]. *Psychopharmacology Bulletin, 24*–84.
Guangzhou City, Dongshan District Public Health Bureau
    1981   Guang-zhou-shi Dong-shang-qu shi-i-suo xiau-xue ji you-er-yuan duo-dong-zheng diao-cha [An investigation of hyperactive syndrome in eleven primary schools and kindergartens]. *Chinese Journal of Neurology and Psychiatry, 14*(1), 32.
Huessy, H. R.
    1969   Study of the prevalence and therapy of the choreatiform syndrome or hyperkinesis in Vermont. *Acta Paedopsychiatrica, 34*, 130–135.
Rutter, M. A.
    1967   Children's behavior questionnaire for completion by teachers: Preliminary findings. *Journal of Child Psychology and Psychiatry, 8*, 1–11.

Stewart, M. A. et al.
1966   The hyperactive child syndrome. *American Journal of Orthopsychiatry, 36*, 861–867.
Yian, W. W.
1981   Guan-yu nao-gong-neng qin-wei-she-diao de diao-cha bau-gao [A report on investigation of minimal brain dysfunction]. *Information on Psychological Sciences, 4*, 28.
Yie, G. Jun et al.
1982   Er-tong duo-dong-zong-he-zheng de diao-cha bau-gao [An investigation about minimal brain dysfunction in a primary school]. *Chinese Journal of Preventive Medicine, 16*(1), 389.

CHAPTER 22

Some Psychological Problems Manifested by Neurotic Patients: Shanghai Examples

Yan Heqin

INTRODUCTION

Neurosis is one of the commonly diagnosed psychiatric disorders in clinical practice. It includes neurasthenia, anxiety disorder, hysteria, phobia, obsessive disorder, hypochondriasis, neurotic depression, and various organ neuroses, such as cardiac and gastrointestinal neurosis; Among these, neurasthenia is seen in China most frequently. These diseases are generally included in the psychogenic category. Psychological factors are not only an important precipitating factor, but are also closely related to the manifestation of symptoms and the prognosis.

Since Cullen proposed the diagnostic term in 1764, the history of research on neurosis may be divided into three stages:

1. In the nineteenth century, during the development period of cytopathology, the disease was differentiated simply on the basis of the mor-

325

phological changes in cells. All the functional disorders of the nervous system that were not accompanied by obvious changes in cytomorphology were diagnosed as neurosis.

2. As medical research gradually turned toward human psychological phenomena, as exemplified by Freud's psychoanalytic theory, problems were interpreted primarily in terms of conflicts between the conscious and the unconscious and of the psychological defense mechanism. As the theory concerned only the intrapsychic activities of the individual and did not focus on social and environmental factors, many explanations were subjective and limited. Pavlov, in his animal experiments, studied induced factors and mechanisms through functional changes in high-level nervous activities. He used various intensities of stimuli to induce experimental neuroses, providing valuable experimental information. These studies demonstrated that the research had investigated the psychological and physiological functions of the central nervous system. In the meantime, many others also did meaningful research in these fields.

3. Since the early 1950s, work on the relationship between social–psychological factors and disease have absorbed medical workers. They turned their attention from the internal psychological conflicts of the patients to the influences of social environment. As we know, psychological activities are bound up with social and cultural factors. Therefore, in different cultures and under various social conditions, there are different characteristics observable in mental disorders (K. M. Lin, Kleinman, and T. Lin, 1980; Tseng and Hsu, 1970; Tseng and McDermott, 1981).

In traditional Chinese medicine, there was no disease entity that can be equated with neurosis or neurasthenia, and the diagnostic concept was so different to that of modern medicine that it is impossible to make any contrasting comparison. In general, all psychiatric disorders were included in internal medicine.

It was not until the 1930s that neurasthenia as a diagnostic term was introduced in the medical literature in China (Song, 1936). At that time, it was considered to be a common social sickness. In addition to being related to an inherited neurotic trait, it was considered to be a kind of psychiatric disorder due to stress from the environment. At that time, the hysteria, obsessive disorders, phobia, anxiety disorders, and hypochondriasis were all included in the concept of neurasthenia. Because it was associated with the development of psychiatry in China, such diagnostic terminology became popular and was not only adopted by medical personnel in various specialties, but was also used by ordinary people in their daily lives and appeared in medical advertisements. Whenever a person suffered from insomnia, dizziness, headache, mental fatigue, poor concentration, poor memory and related complaints, he or she was labeled neurasthenic.

In the 1950s, with the influence of Soviet medicine, Pavlov's theory of the central nervous system became popular in China. General practitioners adopted Pavlov's concept of stimulation and inhibition, as well as the view that overstimulation, leading to the weakness of internal inhibitions, is the cause of neurasthenia. Practitioners made an attempt to interpret their patients' clinical manifestations accordingly.

Since neurasthenia is one of the most common psychiatric disorders in China, it is one of the main subjects for research. Numerous groups have carried out extensive surveys and studies in this field, all of them concluding that psychological factors are the major contributors to such disorders (Geng, 1960; Psychiatric Department, Sichuan Medical College, 1960, 1965; Xu, 1964; Yan, 1977; Zhong, 1964). However, the focus of the research programs was on the psychology of individuals only. (For further explanation of neurasthenia in mainland China, see Chapter 25, p. 374, this volume.)

More recently, many investigators have begun to pay attention to the cultural aspects of psychiatric disorders and to study the relationship between Chinese culture and the neuroses. For example, *koro,* which is called *suo-yang* (the shrinking of the penis) in Chinese is a mental disorder found in southeast Asia—Malaya, Indonesia, Burma, and parts of sourthern China. The patient manifests panic and tension because he is afraid that his penis is retracting into his abdomen. Some clinicians considered it to be related to Chinese culture (Rin, 1965), since in the fundamental theory of Chinese traditional medicine, the penis was taken as the symbol of masculinity; thus, the patient is in fear of losing his sexual ability and reacting as if he were castrated. Other disorders such as *shen kui* (kidney deficiency syndrome) and *hsieh ping* (*xie bing,* devil's sickness) are considered to be culture-related syndromes. According to traditional Chinese medicine, *shen* (kidney) controls the function of the cerebrum. Thus, a deficiency of *shen yang* (positive element of the kidney) causes dizziness, tinnitus, insomnia, fatigue, and spermatorrhea, which are the common symptoms of neurasthenia (Wen and Wang, 1980). The *hsieh ping* (devil's sickness) is manifested as episodes of clouding of consciousness, tremor, and disorientation and is accompanied by auditory hallucination, "possession by the devil," and so forth. During the attack of possession by the devil, the patient is possessed by a ghost (usually a deceased relative or ancestor), who attempts to communicate with family members through the patient. The cause of the attack usually relates to family discord. Patients with this disorder are generally adult females with impoverished backgrounds, from rural and traditional areas. They have little or no education and are prone to deeply religious fanaticism (T. Y. Lin, 1953).

Some authors note that Chinese patients have fewer complaints of emotional conflict and tend to express their emotional disturbance through somatic symptoms. This tendency was reported by nearly 70% of the psychiatric outpatients presenting somatic complaints to the psychiatrist at their first visit in Taiwan in 1975. It has been pointed out that the psychiatrist needs to be therapeutically oriented toward the deeper meaning of the patient's somatic complaints (Tseng, 1975). Other investigators have reported that the prevalence rate of neurosis has increased rapidly owing to expanding urbanization and to the potentially adverse effects of uprooting. For example, following a period of 15 years (1946–1948 to 1961–1963) in the same region, using epidemiological survey methods, researchers did not find marked changes in major psychosis, but the prevalence rate of neurosis increased from 1.2‰ to 7.8‰; among immigrants to that region, the prevalence rate went up to 16.1%. (T. Y. Lin, Rin, Yeh, Hsu, and Chu, 1969). Noting these reports, it is valuable for us to study the relationship between psychosocial factors and neurosis in order to understand the nature of the disease and explore appropriate measures in prevention and treatment. The neurotic patient's consciousness is clear; he or she has full insight into the disease, asks for treatment eagerly, and complain of symptoms and psychosocial problems freely. Because only the patients themselves can express the internal psychological conflicts clearly, the investigation of the psychological problems of neurotic patients is an important subject for research (Tseng, 1973).

COMMON PSYCHOLOGICAL PROBLEMS

This chapter discusses the kinds of relationship between psychological problems and social culture found in neuroses. According to cases observed in Shanghai, the common psychological problems of neurosis can be categorized as described in the next six sections. (The patients' names have been changed.)

DEPRESSION DUE TO DISSATISFACTION WITH THE ENVIRONMENT

This includes inability to study, displeasure with work, and unhappy love life.

Mr. Liu is a 27-year-old factory worker. The youngest child in the family, he was raised indulgently by his parents, who hoped that he would have a successful future. Therefore, even as a small child, he was determined to study at the university and to become a doctor. But he attended school during the Cultural Revolution. After graduation from junior middle school (equivalent to U.S.

seventh through ninth grades), he found that he could not fulfill his wish, as all the universities were closed, and was assigned to work in a factory, where he became unhappy and depressed. After the Gang of Four was crushed, the university entrance examination system was reestablished. He thought then that he might have a chance to enter the university and studied diligently in his spare time for this purpose. But he failed because of his poor academic preparation, so he suffered greatly from further dejection. He knew he should not react in that way, but he could not control himself. The situation was aggravated when his mother died of cancer and, in the meantime, he developed unhappy relationships with his colleagues at work. He began to suffer from sleep disturbances and developed some unusual ideas without being able to rid himself of them. For example, he would have ideas such as jumping into the river when he walked over the bridge, and tasting the stool or licking up the dirty water with his tongue when he went to the toilet. Furthermore, he even developed the desire to kill persons who were antagonistic to him. The patient recognized the abnormalities of his mind but could not control himself. He suffered dizziness, distraction, and impairment of memory. He could not review his lessons, felt sad, and asked to see a psychiatrist. He was diagnosed as having obsessional neurosis.

DISCORD IN INTERPERSONAL RELATIONSHIPS

This includes family disharmony and discord with colleagues. Because subjects live or work with these people all the time they have continual emotional problems.

Mr. Zhang, 29 years old, was a bus driver for nearly 10 years. He worked hard and well and was often on the nightshift. Of a calm temperament, he was often able to control himself during unpleasant occurrences and did not discuss his problems with anyone. He did not have any emotional disturbance until a conflict developed between his wife and his mother over financial matters and his wife had several hysterical attacks. Although he was sympathetic toward his wife's situation, he dared not to do anything against his mother for fear of being criticized by others for unfilial behavior. The patient tried to patch up the quarrel between his wife and mother but failed and felt very depressed. He felt responsibility to his work and believed that household affairs should not influence him in his work situation. Thus, he made efforts to control himself but found he could not concentrate on his driving. He was exhausted but had difficulty falling asleep in the evening. Over a period of time, he began to suffer from headaches, dizziness, fatigue, and forgetfullness. He could not free himself from his family trouble and was easily irritated. He was treated at the hospital, where his condition was diagnosed as neurasthenia. There was no marked improvement after either medical or acupuncture treatments. Then from explanations of the nature of the disease by his psychiatrist, the patient realized that his illness was related to the frustration caused by his family problems. Thus, his anxiety began to disappear, and his response to medical treatment was better. With the therapist's encouragement, he finally found a place for his mother to live apart from him and his wife, and, at the same time, he urged his wife to visit his mother frequently with gifts to please her. Based on this arrangement, the wife and mother regained harmony in their relationship, and the patient and his wife were soon reconciled.

FEAR AND ANXIETY ABOUT HEALTH AND FUTURE

Miss Wei, age 28 and unemployed, did not leave the house for 8 years because of her fear of sudden death due to heart failure. Several members of her family forced her to go to the hospital for treatment. At the outpatient clinic, she appeared tense, closed her eyes tightly, held her head, and expressed her fear of impending death through trembling lips. She was unsteady on her feet and tended to fall down.

According to her past history, she was very overprotected during her childhood by her mother. Whenever she fell down, her mother would send her to the hospital immediately for fear of serious injury. As a result, the patient had been timid since childhood. After entering primary school, she overheard her schoolmates talking about heart disease, which could result in sudden death. She then developed the idea that heart disease was to be feared.

When she was 14 years old, she had rheumatic heart disease. In spite of the fact that the condition of her heart was healthy for many years, the patient's parents and relatives continually advised her to rest and related stories to her of people with heart disease who died at an early age. This constant reminding made her think of heart disease all the time. She was fearful and hopeless and considered heart disease to be an imprisonment; she worried about her own sudden death. She was sent to the hospital several times by her family—whenever she felt anxiety and a fear of death. Each time, medical examination revealed that there was no obvious cardic dysfunction. At the age of 20, on the way to the hospital one day, she suddenly felt tenseness, palpitations, dyspnea, and difficulty in moving, and she thought that she would die immediately. After the symptoms had gone, she promptly returned home. After that, she refused to leave the house for fear of sudden death from heart disease. At home she was able to take care of herself, to do the daily household chores, such as cooking, dishwashing, and knitting. Except for the phobia of going out, there was no other mental abnormality. She was annoyed by her phobic condition and eventually wrote a letter to the psychological association for help. Though interpretational psychotherapy and behavior modification therapy, she was able to resume normal activity. The diagnosis was agoraphobia.

Mr. Huang, age 54, was an engineer in a pharmaceutical factory who had no past history of mental disorder. When he was a child, his father had a tendency to discipline him severely, while his mother, who was very close to him, overprotected him and indulged him with tenderness. His personality was characterized as being timid, obedient, always following orders, and never doing anything contrary to his parents' expectations of perfection. At one time during the Cultural Revolution, he made the mistake of carelessly splashing ink on a newspaper portrait of Chairman Mao, which frightened him and he was afraid of being punished. Afterwards, he became more obsessional and checked every piece of paper in the wastepaper basket and lavatory. He checked his own pockets continually. This behavior troubled him because of its great influence over his daily life. The only thing he could do was to sew up the pockets on his clothes, as well as on those of his family. Gradually, his obsession progressed to the point that whenever he saw a piece of paper, he would close his eyes and become very anxious. His problem was diagnosed as obsessive neurosis, and he was hospitalized for about 6 months but showed no improvement. After the smashing of the Gang of Four, there was a significant change in the social environment. This and in addition to the combined therapy of modern medication, traditional medicine, psychotherapy, and behavior therapy, resulted in the patient completely regaining his mental health.

PARTICULAR ALARM OVER ACCIDENTS

Types of accidents include natural disasters, psychic trauma, and severe stress.

> In a girls' nursing school, there were numerous students between the ages of 17 and 19. One day in the dormitory, one of the girls, because of her own carelessness, fell from the upper berth of a double-deck bed during the night and sustained a severe head trauma with a serious wound. She died after rescue measures proved ineffectual. All the students were frightened by this accident. One girl suddenly developed difficulty in breathing and made the sounds, "ah-san" and "ah-shi." This phenomenon quickly spread through the whole dormitory; ultimately, more than half of the girls in the class were suffering from the same symptoms. During class, if anyone coughed or sneezed, the whole class would respond with the same sounds, and the teacher did not know what to do. A special epidemic disease was suspected. After consultation, a psychiatrist diagnosed the disease as epidemic hysteria. The patients were separated and psychotherapy was applied. The epidemic was soon controled.

ACHIEVEMENT PROBLEMS

These occur when subjects set high demands for work and study, but their abilities fall short of their goals.

> Mr. Han, age 30, was a third-year student in the department of pedagogy of a university. When he passed the entrance examination and went to the university, he established a very ambitious plan for himself and planned to study harder than he ever had. He did not leave for summer vacation but, instead, stayed at school and forced himself to pursue his studies. He did nothing but read all day. He was thinking of questions in his leisure time and even during the night. His mind was always under stress, and his life was disordered. When school reopened, he found a contradiction between his living style and university schedule. He became very tired and grew nervous because he suffered from insomnia. He found it difficult to concentrate, his attention span and his memory faded. He eventually suffered severe headaches, which he described as a rope around his head. At the same time, he suffered from tinnitus and could not wear his glasses. He felt a bit better only when he held his head in his hands. He could not read or

rest and had no interest in any outside social activity. He was doubtful that this disease could be cured. In low spirits, he had a strong desire to seek medical relief. Finally, doctors diagnosed the illness as neurasthenia.

OTHER REASONS

These include the death or departure of a family member, the loss of an important function of a body part, and the feeling of being wronged because of being "framed" or receiving unjust criticism. These give the patient a feeling of loss.

COMMENTS

We have commonly encountered the psychological problems discussed in the preceding section. What impact do these problems have on the patient's mind and how do they cause the disease? All sorts of psychological stress cause corresponding emotional reactions. Weak stress may lead to anger, anxiety, and fear, while serious stress may cause rage, depression, and panic. Chinese traditional medicine relies upon the theory of *qi qing* (seven sentiments)—*xi* (happiness), *nu* (anger), *yu* (depression), *si* (anxiety), *bei* (sadness), *kong* (fear), and *jing* (panic)—in similar circumstances.

It is not true that all psychological stress causes disease in everyone. Stress is unavoidable in the social environment. Under the same psychological stress, one person may suffer from mental illness while another may respond to the stress as a stimulus to overcome difficulties. For example, during the 10-year period (1966–1976) of civil turmoil in China, many innocent people were subjected to persecution. The majority withstood it, yet someone like the Mr. Huang, who only splashed ink on the Chairman's portrait in the newspaper, was obsessed with fear. While heart disease sufferers are not rare, Miss Wei suffered from a cardiac phobia because of her fear. Therefore, it is not appropriate to seek relationships between the mental disorder and the nature and intensity of the psychological problem alone. The individual's attitude and coping ability when faced with psychological stress must also be considered.

Additionally, emotional reactions caused by a single type of psychological problem can result in different types of neurosis. For instance, Miss Wei's reaction of fear is manifested as phobia, while Mr. Huang's is manifested as obsession, and in other patients, as neurasthenia or anxiety. All these reactions relate to the character of the individual patient. While I am not going into further detail in this chapter, it should be noted that an individual's character, attitude toward psychological stress and tolerance level have to do with environment, education, and childhood experiences. Therefore, there is a close relationship between individual character and psychosocial environment.

Based on the cases of illnesses we have encountered, psychological factors affecting mental disorders can be divided into two types: one is mainly associated with natural factors—natural disasters, such as floods, earthquakes, loss of family members, and sudden loss of sight; it is not, or is little, affected by differences in social and cultural surroundings. The other type occurs in a particular social environment and/or cultural circumstance. Obsession in Mr. Huang, who repeatedly examined a piece of paper, is related to the given condition of the Cultural Revolution in our country. When the Gang of Four was smashed and the social environment changed, his mental threat was eliminated, and he recovered.

Since the late 1950s, cultural psychiatry has given significant attention to the influence of the cultural background on mental disorders in different geographical areas. Our experiences show that even in the same area, when the environment has changed, the causes and symptoms of mental disease affecting patients changed also. For example, prior to the late 1940s, many patients believed that spermatorrhea was an important causal factor for neurasthenia. This attitude had to do with the state of medical knowledge as well as with the influence of unscientific propaganda. At that time, sperm was recognized as man's vitality. It was said that "one drop of seminal fluid is equal to 90 drops of blood." Therefore, the discharge of semen in nocturnal ejaculation or in masturbation was treated as a serious matter. Accordingly, the patient who discharged semen in these ways became nervous and worried and took large quantities of medicine to prevent this loss. Because since 1949, scientific medical knowledge has been gradually popularized, people no longer fear this natural discharge. There are, therefore, few cases of this kind of neurathenia.

During the 1950s, neurasthenia was one of the most common mental health disorders in China. It was previously treated by individual therapy, but due to the extreme shortage of mental health workers, such limited treatment did not meet the needs of society. The Nanjing Neuropsychiatric Institution began group therapy for neurasthenic patients in 1956. Subsequently, so-called comprehensive group therapy was further developed by the collaboratory work of the Institute of Psychology of Academia Sinica and the Insitute of Psychiatry of Beijing Medical School in 1958 (Chen, 1955; Li, 1958). The treatment is referred to as comprehensive group therapy because it treats patients collectively, as a group, and makes use of various kinds of therapeutic maneuvers that include drug therapy, psychotherapy, accupuncture, physical therapy, and traditional physical-training exercise. The candidate patients are screened for the indication, and the treatment is carried out while the patients work half-time and participate in the treatment program half-time. The treatment, as a course, lasts for 14–24 days.

Psychotherapy is carried out in both group and individual interviews. The purpose of group therapy is to provide instruction about the nature of the disorders and the correct way to treat the disorders. Its aim is to establish an accurate understanding of the problem and develop self-confidence in the patient to overcome the problem. Sometimes a patient who has recovered is invited to share with the group his or her experience of recovery. Besides group therapy, individual counseling is provided, and attempts are made to understand the background of the individual, to answer questions, and to encourage active engagement in improvement.

As physical therapy, traditional Chinese exercises such as *tai ji quan* (*tai chi chuan*, shadow boxing) and meditation are practiced. The regularity and variation of daily activities is emphasized as a way of improvement, and patients are encouraged to participate in both intellectual and physical activities as part of their lives.

According to research results from the Psychiatric Department, Beijing Medical College (1966), among 1837 cases treated in this manner at their clinic during $7\frac{1}{2}$ years, 60.0% obtained complete recovery and another 31.1% showed improvement. The effectiveness of this therapy was thus confirmed, and since that time, such treatments have been applied broadly in China for neurasthenic patients.

At the present time, the office workers who have relatively higher prevalence of neurasthenia balance their activities with both work and rest, and the incidence of this disorder among them has dropped markedly. Among students, however, because they bear heavy stresses due to their studies, the incidence of neurasthenia is increasing. Mr. Han is an extreme case of this tendency.

We have seen few cases of psychosexual disorders in our clinic. Due to traditional custom and the cultural influences in China, the Chinese people have a controlled attitude toward sexual desire and are not liable to disregard this cultural control. Therefore, it is very rare to hear about psychosexual problems. In Shanghai, it is also very rare to see typical hysterical attacks or possessions by devils, whereas in culturally backward areas, such cases may still occur. The foregoing discussion indicates that the psychosocial environment really has great influence on the incidence of neurosis.

Sociocultural psychological factors not only relate to the occurrence and prognosis of neurosis but also have an impact on the patient's illness behavior and help-seeking pattern. One of the characteristics of Chinese patients' illness behavior is that very few patients present their psychological or emotional problems as the primary complaint. Most of them will visit a general hospital to request a check-up for a somatic disorder. For a long time, the Chinese have been occupied with the traditional idea about the function of medical practice, namely, "To examine the disorder and give the prescription." Everyone considers it the doctor's function to make the diagnosis and prescribe the drug for treatment. Even neurotic patients expect to obtain "good" medicine to cure their sickness. Therefore, psychotherapy alone would not satisfy them even though some of them deny psychological problems as their major concern. It takes time and patient procedure to obtain the patient's trust and understanding before he or she is willing to reveal psychological problems. In addition, because of the traditional family system, the patient usually prefers to reveal any emotional problems only to parents, spouse, or other family members. Therefore, it is essential to obtain the assistance of the patient's family members in order to facilitate the treatment. In mainland China, there is a well-organized system in the work place and in the neighborhood, and all the people are related as close comrades. It is very important to utilize such existing assets in the treatment of neurotic patients.

In summary, it is difficult to identify the exact cause of the psychological problems involved in neurosis because patients may deny their existence; but if we analyze these problems from the psychosocial point of view, we can find interacting relationships. Psychological problems are conditioned by the social and cultural environment. Differences in world outlook and value concept have an impact on the coping mechanisms related to psychological problems. We cannot neglect, therefore, the relationship between neurosis and the following factors: psychosocial influences, the nature of the psychological problem, and the individual constitution. We must do more work in investigating the incidence of neuroses in different situations and different time periods in order to learn more about the previously mentioned factors. Only when we have more knowledge of these relationships can we take more effective measures in the prevention and treatment of neurosis.

REFERENCES

Chen, Z.
1955   Nanjing jing-shen-bin fan-zhi-yuan dui shen-jing-shuai-ruo huan-zhe kai-zhan la ziti-jing-shen zhi-lia huo-de chu-bu cheng-xiao [The preliminary results of group therapy for neurasthenic patients carried out by Nanjing Psychiatric Hospital]. *Chinese Journal of Neurology and Psychiatry*, *1*(2) 104—106.

Geng, Z.
1960   Yi-bai-li shen-jing-shuai-ruo lin-chuang fen-xi [Clinical analysis of 100 cases of neurasthenia]. *Chinese Journal of Neurology and Psychiatry*, *6*(2), 112—115.

Li, Z.
1958   Shen-jing-shuai-ruo de kuai-shu-zhi-liao [Short course comprehensive group therapy of neurasthenia]. *Chinese Journal of Neurology and Psychiatry 4*(5), 351—356.

Lin, K. M., Kleinman, A., and Lin, T.

1980   Overview of mental disorders in Chinese culture: Review of epidemiological and clinical studies. In A. Kleinman and T. Y. Lin (Eds.), *Normal and abnormal behavior in Chinese culture.* Dordrecht; Reidel.

Lin, T. Y.

1953   A study of mental disorders in Chinese and other cultures. *Psychiatry 16,* 313–336.

Lin, T. Y., Rin, H., Yeh, E. K., Hsu, C. C., Chu, H. M.

1969   Mental disorders in Taiwan: Fifteen years later. In W. Caudil and T. Y. Lin (Eds.), *Mental health research in Asia and the Pacific.* Honolulu: East-West Center Press.

Psychiatric Department, Beijing Medical College

1966   Qi-nian-ban lai shen-jin-shuai-ruo zong-he-zhe-liau gong-zuo de jing-yan zong-jie [A study of comprehensive therapy of neurasthenia for seven years]. *Chinese Journal of Neurology and Psychiatry, 10*(2), 115–118.

Psychiatric Department, Sichuan Medical College

1960   Shen-jing shuai-ruo de bin-yin fen-xi [A study of etiological factors of neurasthenia]. *Chinese Journal of Neurology and Psychiatry, 6*(2), 102–106.

1965   Dui shen-jing-shuai-ruo bin-yin he zhi-liao de kan-fa [On etiology and treatment of neurasthenia]. *Chinese Journal of Neurology and Psychiatry, 9*(3), 258–260.

Rin, H.

1965   A study of the aetiology of koro in respect to the Chinese concept of illness. *International Journal of Social Psychiatry 11*(1), 7–13.

Song, M.

1936   Neurasthenia. *Tong Ji Medicine, 6*(1), 87–89.

Tseng, W. S.

1973   Psychopathologic study of obsessive-compulsive neurosis in Taiwan. *Comprehensive Psychiatry, 14,* 139–150.

1975   The nature of somatic complaints among psychiatric patients: The Chinese case. *Comprehensive Psychiatry, 16,* 237–245.

Tseng, W. S., and Hsu, J.

1970   Chinese culture, personality formation and mental illness. *International Journal of Social Psychiatry, 16,* 5–14.

Tseng, W. S., and McDermott, J. F., Jr.

1981   Minor psychiatric disorders. In W. S. Tseng (Ed.), *Culture, mind and therapy.* New York: Brunner/Mazel.

Wen, J. K., and Wang, C. L.

1980   Shen-k'uei syndrome: A culture-specific sexual neurosis in Taiwan. In A. Kleinman and T. Y. Lin (Eds.), *Normal and abnormal behavior in Chinese culture.* Dordrecht: Reidel.

Xu, S.

1964   Guan-yu shen-jing-shuai-ruo he hysteria de mou-xie bin-li xin-li te-den [Some psychopathological characteristics of neurasthenia and hysteria]. *Chinese Journal of Neurology and Psychiatry, 8*(1), 85–90.

Yan, D.

1977   Effects of psychological conflicts. *Foreign Medicine, 2,* 49–53.

Zhong, Y.

1964   Shen-jing-shuai-ruo bin-ren dui xin-yin de fou-ren [Denying of psychological factors among neurasthenic patients]. *Chinese Journal of Neurology and Psychiatry, 8*(3), 282–286.

PART V

MANAGEMENT AND PREVENTION OF MENTAL ILLNESS

In this part, attention moves to the management and prevention of mental illness. Two reports from Shanghai and Beijing are presented, which consider how the social, political, and cultural system is utilized to develop mental health programs in China.

Xia (Chapter 23) first describes the sociodemographic background of Shanghai: the rapid increase of population, coupled with the extreme shortage of exisiting mental facilities, and the need to fulfill the government's policy of providing service primarily for the common people. He then reports on how a comprehensive community mental health system is developing in Shanghai on municipal, district, and neighborhood levels. He discusses how the already developed and well-organized neighborhood organization, the readily available paramedical personnel, and the cultural emphasis on family and neighborhood relationships are maximally utilized. Details are supplied about how the work rehabilitation station was developed on the neighborhood level. An example of a mental health team attached to a factory illustrates the effect of such a community-rooted mental health program.

Shen (Chapter 24) tells of the home care program in the Beijing area,

339

which cares for decompensated psychiatric patients in home settings in rural areas, rather than in hospitals. This is based on the rationale that severely decompensated patients need not only medical treatment, but also emotional support from family and the opportunity to participate in familiar household activity and occupational work for social rehabilitation. This meets the cultural emphasis on family, solves the problems of shortage of mental hospital facilities in rural areas, and makes good use of an already existing, well-distributed, public health system in rural areas. After describing the program setting, training of staff, and evaluation of the program, Shen points out that the results of such home care programs are very good: The frequency of relapse is decreased, social rehabilitation is promoted, and the treatment approach is, of course, more acceptable to the patient and family.

CHAPTER 23

The Mental Health Delivery System in Shanghai

Xia Zhenyi

INTRODUCTION

Shanghai has a difficult task utilizing the support of government, the assets of the family and social system, and the cultural environment to develop an adequate mental health delivery system in a big city with a total population of more than 11 million. This effort is challenged by the fact that virtually no mental health service system existed in the past, and there is an urgent need to develop and expand the present mental health care system in a relatively short period of time to serve the majority of the people.

Shanghai is the largest city in China. Administratively, it contains 12 districts in the city areas and 10 counties in the suburban areas. The total population is 11,620,000. Before 1949, there were only 12 psychiatrists and 454 psychiatric beds for the population of more than 5 million at that time. Needless to say, such facilities were too far away to adequately serve such a large population. In fact, most of the psychiatric patients never had

341

the opportunity to be cared for in the psychiatric facilities available at that time.

Since 1949, with the support of the government, mental health facilities and human resources have been developed and expanded rapidly throughout the country (Xia and Zhang, 1981). In Shanghai, the number of psychiatric beds increased to 1562 in 1958, to 2920 in 1965, and to 5319 beds in 1981. Presently, in Shanghai, there is a total of 441 psychiatrists and 837 psychiatric nurses. There are 25 psychiatric institutions, among them, one municipal psychiatric hospital with its branch hospital, 20 district (or county) psychiatric stations, and three sanitaria. These provide a total of 5319 beds for mental patients, with an average of 46 beds per population of 100,000.

Beginning in the 1960s, there has been a unique development of a comprehensive, three-level scheme of a mental health care system that provides for the delivery of community service at the neighborhood level. It is based on the support of different levels of governmental administrative systems, the utilization of the neighborhood committee staff, paramedical personnel, volunteer retirees, and the cooperation of the family to provide such neighborhood-rooted mental health service.

Problems of Developing the Service

Merely increasing the number of psychiatric beds and improving the quality of psychiatric service have not met the actual needs of the mental health service in Shanghai. Its development is challenged by serious problems, most significantly by the increasing prevalence of psychiatric patients through the years.

In order to obtain a figure of the frequency of mental illness in the community, we at the Shanghai Psychiatric Institute carried out a psychiatric census survey in 1958. The foci of the survey were major psychoses, moderate to severe mental retardation, and severe neurotic disorders with impairment in life and occupational work. The prevalence of the these mental disorders was found to be 3‰, while that of schizophrenia was 0.98‰ (Chi et al., 1964). Twenty years later, in 1978, we carried out a similar census survey. This time, we found that the prevalence of total mental disorders was 7.3‰, and that of schizophrenia was 4.‰ (Xia et al., 1980). Clearly, the prevalence of all mental disorders increased 1.4 times, while schizophrenia increased 3.3 times, within two decades.

This increase in the prevalence rate is not at all due to the increase in incidence rate. (Prevalence rate refers to the number of cases at a certain time; while incidence rate, the number of new cases found at certain period of time.) For example, the incidence rate of schizophrenia was steady (between 0.15 and 0.2‰) in the 1960s and 1970s, without any remarkable change. The increase of prevalence of schizophrenia is related to two facts: the extension of life-span and the accumulation of relapsed cases. Before 1949, people's life-span in Shanghai was less than 40 years. Associated with the improvement of the quality of life and the development of health care, the expected life-span at the end of the 1970s was more than 70 years. This increase of life-span also applies to schizophrenic patients. We studied the survival rate of schizophrenic patients in two different time periods. The first group of patients, who were first admitted to the hospital during the period between 1935 and 1957, were followed up 10 years after their discharge. It was found that 26 among 79 cases were deceased, with a mortality rate of 32.9% and a ten-year survival rate of 67.1% (Hsia, She, Zhang, Lin, Hu, and Chen, 1958). For the second group of patients, who were first admitted to the hospital in 1958–1959, a 10-year follow-up study disclosed that 272 among 1472 cases were deceased, a mortality rate of only 18.5% (Xu, 1979), indicating that even among schizophrenic patients, there is a longer life expectancy nowadays.

Superimposed on this phenomenon is the fact that the relapse rate of schizophrenia remains high. Even in the last quarter of a century, there has been a remarkable improvement in the treatment of psychiatric patients. Nevertheless, the rate of complete cure has not increased significantly. It is particularly notable that the relapse rate of schizophrenia remains the same (Zhang and Xia, 1980). With the life-span of schizophrenic patients being prolonged, while the relapse rate remains the same, the consequence is obvious: The number of schizophrenic patients needing psychiatric service will snowball.

How are we to deal with the ever-increasing number of psychiatric patients and to solve a situation wherein the supply never meets the need? There are only two alternatives. One is to continuously increase the number of psychiatric facilities to accommodate the ever-larger number of psychiatric patients. Another is to utilize the nonpsychiatry resources available in the society in order to develop a community mental health delivery system. This was the challenge awaiting our response in Shanghai.

Sociocultural Background of the Development of a Mental Health Delivery System

After having discovered that there was a great need to develop and expand the psychiatry service, our next task was to make appropriate decisions leading to the development of a style of mental health service that would fit the needs of the particular society. Every society or nation has its own unique sociocultural background, and when a mental health care system is to be developed in the community, it should not be viewed as merely a medical program. Consideration should be given to the sociocultural nature of the community. The experience and developments of other societies can be considered but cannot be duplicated. We must design and develop a system which has a foundation on our own political, philosophical, social, and cultural conditions, a system that will be fully supported by government, have roots in the neighborhood community, and maximally utilize lay volunteers for the delivery of service.

In order to obtain the full support of the various administrative levels of government, it is essential that our design of a mental health delivery system follow the government's political policy. The four main principles of health work in China country are (1) primary concern for laborers, farmers, and soldiers; (2) emphasis on prevention; (3) the combined use of Chinese traditional medicine and Western medicine; and (4) combined mental health work and mass socialist movements. The mental health delivery system we have in mind meets at least three of these four fundamental principles. Our proposed system is aimed at the early discovery, diagnosis, and treatment of psychiatric patients and the promotion of better rehabilitation for patients in the community. In other words, it is directed primarily toward secondary and tertiary prevention. Our system will extend the areas of service to the neighborhood level so that ordinary people—most of them laborers, farmers, and soldiers—will benefit from such community-oriented care. To convince people in the community to jointly share in the concern for mentally ill persons is certainly a part of combining health work with mass socialist movements. We presented our idea of design, explained the rationale associating political ideology with practical need, and we obtained the government's enthusiastic support.

The sociocultural environment of China is an asset for developing a family- and community-based mental health delivery system. For many centuries, China has maintained a strong family system. Even though there has been some recent change in family structure, generally speaking, the family is still a very important organizational unit in the society. In Shanghai, the majority of the people still maintain three-generation family relationships. Based on the influence of tradition, the concept of family is still very deep. If anyone in the family has mental illness, then the rest of the family members—be it parents, siblings, spouse, or children—feel responsibility to care for the sick family member. Therefore, the family members always welcome and accept care from mental health workers and join in the care of their sick relative.

There exist not only good family relationships, but also close neighborhood relationships in China. Traditionally, many people have lived together as neighbors for many generations. Additionally, due to environ-mental factors, most of the households live in such close proximity to neighbors that everyone knows what is happening in the neighborhood and is always willing to extend help in time of need. Even if there is a quarrel or conflict in a household, the neighbors are always willing to step in and mediate between the quarreling persons in order to solve the prob-lem. The official neighborhood organization established after the 1950s—the residential committee, or street committee—further promotes these close neighborhood relationships. The committee was formed to function as the fundamental administrative unit in the community. It was also developed to function as a self-help organization. To provide assistance in taking care of old, weak, sick and handicapped persons is one example of the committee's function. The existence of good neighborhood relation-ships and tight neighborhood organization are additional assets for devel-oping community-rooted mental health program.

The virtue of mutual concern and help is a reflection of traditional Chi-nese philosophical thought. As early as 2000 years ago, Confucius and his follower, Mencius, had already introduced the concept of *ren* (mutual benevolence) as the core of interpersonal relationships. Later, people sum-marized Confucian thought and described the moral standards for inter-personal relations into *wu-chang* (five principles), namely: *ren* (mutual benevolence), *yi* (moral obligation), *li* (etiquette), *zhi* (wisdom), and *xin* (trust). Among these five principles, *ren* (mutual benevolence) is primary. From the calligraphic point of view, the Chinese word *ren* is composed of two parts: *two* and *person*, which refer to interpersonal relationships. Con-fucius and Mencius advocated a moral principle: *"Ji suo bu yu, hu shi yu ren"* (Don't force on others what you hate to be done by others). Philoso-phers later developed this idea into the concept *"Zhu ren wei le"* (It is a pleasure to help others). In traditional folklore, the individual is taught to *"Jiu ren ji nan"* (help others when they are in danger), *"Fu lau ji you"* (help the old; assist the young), and *"She ji jiu ren"* (sacrifice oneself to others). Such philosophical ideas are familiar to ordinary people and deeply influ-ence their thoughts and behavior. Many people in actual life would not care about gain and would not mind hardship if they can provide service and help for others. It is because of the traditional thought and attitudes that are a part of Chinese society that we can encourage hundreds of thousands of people, retired laborers and neighborhood residents, who are willing to participate in the voluntary work for the mental health services. The community-based mental health delivery system designed and devel-oped in Shanghai is based on the assets that are integral to our political, philosophical, social, and cultural background.

A THREE-LEVEL SCHEME OF THE MENTAL
HEALTH CARE SYSTEM

As we know, mental health service cannot be delivered only by medical personnel, but must incorporate support from various other groups and agencies. Thus, it must have a structured and coordinated organizational system in order to carry out its function. With the support of the government and the administrative system of the city of Shanghai, we have developed a system of mental health care in a three-level scheme, namely, municipal, district (or county), and street (or commune) (see Figure 23.1).

At the municipal level, the representatives from the Municipal Bureau of Health, the Civil Welfare Agency, and the Police form a coordinating committee that has the responsibility to:

1. establish the policies and rules of mental health service system at the municipal level,
2. coordinate methods and projects developed by various divisions or agencies,

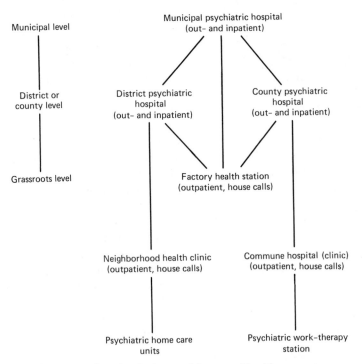

Figure 23.1 Three-level scheme of the mental health care system.

3. organize and mobilize medical personnel and existing social groups to implement mental health work, and
4. provide supervision and guidance for a corresponding mental health system at the district level to carry out the service.

With the assistance of this advisory committee, the Shanghai Psychiatric Institute has been named the executive institution, which plays the leading role in the development of the overall municipal mental health project. Shanghai Psychiatric Institute is a unique municipal mental hospital composed of a branch hospital and provides inpatient as well as outpatient services.

At the district and street level, there have also been established similar coordinating committees, which have their own defined functions as well as responsibilities to relate upward and downward to the corresponding coordinating committees. At the district level, the district psychiatric hospital or county psychiatric hospital that has the facilities to provide both inpatient and outpatient care is assigned as the executive agency. At the street level, the neighborhood health clinic or commune health clinic that provides outpatient and house-call service is responsible for supervising the psychiatric work therapy station and the psychiatric home care unit, providing service at the grass roots level.

Following the establishment of this three-level mental health system scheme, many projects have been carried out among which are mental health education, training of the basic mental health staff, development of street-level mental health clinics, establishment of psychiatric work-therapy stations, and home care units as well as factory mental health services, all of which serve to bring about remarkable benefit for the people in need of service. According to 1980 statistics, 32.6% of the psychiatric patients have visited municipal psychiatric hospitals, 23.5% have visited district psychiatric hospitals, and 43.9% have utilized the neighborhood-level facilities at street (or commune) mental health clinics, indicating that such a three-level mental health service has been extensively used by the people.

Publicizing Mental Health Knowledge

Successful community mental health service depends greatly on the support and cooperation of the general public. Promoting and publicizing the concept of and information about mental health are important tasks. Since the late 1970s, we have utilized various available communication channels, including television, radio, newspapers, and magazines, to expand mental health information among the people. We have shown short programs on television about the life and activities of psychiatric patients in the settings of hospitals and neighborhood clinics and in the process of psychiatric treatment, thus familiarizing people with mental illness, psychiatric patients, and mental hospitals. Through such communication media, we have tried to increase people's knowledge about emotional disorders and to build an understanding of mental health programs, as well as to educate the general public about how to care for emotionally disturbed patients.

Many psychiatric workers have also written numerous articles to introduce various subjects, such as mental health of the single child and of youth. We edit a popular scientific monograph on the topic of psychiatric illness, of which more than 80,000 copies have been distributed within 3 years and which has been favorably commented on by the public as one of the most helpful popular scientific monographs.

Mental health workers have also visited many neighborhoods and factories, have periodically given talks to people about mental health, and have noted a beneficial effect on people's understanding of mental health problems. Originally, many people did not understand psychiatric illness and looked down on mental patients. But there has been a radical change. Now, many people show their concern about psychiatric patients and are willing to join the work of the mental health service.

Training Basic Mental Health Workers

An effective mental health program needs not only the understanding and support of the people in the community, but also requires a group of basic staff members who carry out the projects. Obviously, a professional psychiatrist is one of the important components of such a staff. However, the presence of a psychiatrist alone is not enough. We need the considerable involvement of nonpsychiatric medical staff as well as paramedical personnel. In the past, we have provided psychiatric training for 630 basic medical staff from neighborhood health clinics, commune hospitals (or clinics), and factory health clinics, as well as a large number of paramedical personnel, in order to form a large group of basic mental health workers.

Psychiatric training for medical personnel working at the grass roots level in neighborhoods, communes, and factories has been provided. The training course lasts 6 weeks, 2 weeks of which is devoted to theoretical lectures and 4 weeks to clinical practice. The object of such training is to provide the trainee with basic and practical knowledge about psychiatric symptomatology, diagnosis, psychopharmacology, and psychiatric care so that the medical personnel can provide practical clinical psychiatric service at the neighborhood and factory level and also provide assistance to the psychiatric work-therapy stations or psychiatric home care units that are providing service in various corners of the community.

Although most of the medical staff know very little about psychiatry prior to the training period, they are able to increase their psychiatric knowledge sufficiently for practical usage after the short-term training. Several follow-up studies of medical staff who completed the training course reveal that most of the trained medical staff can accurately identify most of the psychiatric symptoms (more than 70% of the positive symptoms identified by professional psychiatrist); nearly 90% of them are able to function satisfactorily and more than 40% are very satisfactory as judged by professional psychiatrists. The most crucial point is that 99% of the patients and their families served by such trained medical staff are satisfied by the clinical service offered to them. Our experience illustrates that if the medical personnel are properly trained, they can easily become a vital asset in providing neighborhood-level psychiatric care.

Psychiatric Work-Therapy Stations

Among the tasks of community psychiatry are the reduction of psychiatric hospitalization, helping patients to adjust to social life, and promoting patients' rehabilitation. We have developed and established psychiatric work-therapy stations at the neighborhood level as one of the important ways to promote patients' sociooccupational rehabilitation.

The psychiatric work-therapy stations we refer to here are, in certain ways, similar to day hospitals, half-way houses, or patients' factory programs, as they are referred to in other countries. Our psychiatric work-therapy stations are characterized by the following four points. First, stations are organized under the auspices of the community administrations, that is, the neighborhood committees, communes or factories. Second, the staff of the stations is composed of paramedical personnel from the community who volunteer their work. Third, the stations are formed for the combined purposes of psychiatric therapy and social control. Fourth, occupational work, supplemented with drug therapy and recreational therapy, is the primary mode of therapy.

The psychiatric work-therapy stations accommodate mental patients who have partially recovered but are not yet capable of returning to take up their previous jobs and patients who have had no previous job experience. Most of the staff members at the stations are retired laborers, though there are also community personnel from the neighborhood committee or communes and paramedical personnel. At this point, it is appropriate to describe the retirement system in China. At present, the retirement age is rather young: 60 years for men and 50–55 years for women. After retirement, people receive 70–80% of their previous working salary to support themselves. As most of their children have already grown up and no longer require their support, these retired persons are relatively free of responsibility. Most of them are still very healthy. As life expectancy has increased, the number of retired persons is steadily increasing, and they are a good source of volunteer workers. As a matter of fact, many of them are interested in providing service to society in order to enrich their own lives. Thus, we have utilized retired workers as volunteer staff for our work-therapy stations.

In the establishment of the stations, the local government provides housing space, while the expenditures are borne by the neighborhood committee in addition to small loans that welfare agencies may allocate. The number of patients in each station varies from 10 to 90; most of the stations accommodate about 20 cases. Each person works 6 hours a day, 6 days a week. Most of the work is light handwork, such as sewing, making match boxes, and other kinds of handicraft, and processing work. Depending on the number of work hours and the quality of the work, patients can receive a small wage. Therefore, these stations are welcomed by the patients and their families.

In each station, there are one or two paramedics or health workers who have received a short course in psychiatric training. They keep simple case histories of patients, supervise patients for the administration of drugs, observe and made records of patients' psychiatric conditions, and maintain contact with the regional psychiatric doctors for professional advice. In the meanwhile, they conduct basic, supportive, individual and group counseling. They also try to help patients whenever there is some life stress or family conflict that disturbs the patients. This arrangement, to some degree, provides the service of crisis intervention.

At present, there is a total of 103 psychiatric work-therapy stations in Shanghai, providing care for about 2600 patients, of whom the majority are schizophrenic. Some stations began to accommodate moderately mentally retarded persons, providing work therapy as well as educational therapy.

By participating in the work-therapy stations, the patients are able to take medication regularly with systematic follow up, making the drug therapy more effective. Additionally, patients can participate in social activities, undertake work, obtain some income, decrease their insecurity, and broaden their daily experience. Thus, the experience is beneficial to their rehabilitation by preventing them from deteriorating. Most of the retired workers who serve as staff in the stations are sincerely concerned about the patients they are caring for and usually treat them as if they are their own family members. Because of this, patients develop affection for staff members and become actively involved in activities, relating to the staff as well as to fellow patients as members of an extended family. It certainly promotes patients' ability for social adjustment and prevents them from deterioration and relapse.

The Shanghai Psychiatric Institute has carried out an assessment of such a program (Qu, n.d.). One hundred cases were randomly selected for follow-up evaluation—54 males and 46 females, with an age range of 18–58 (average, 34), an average duration of illness of 12.3 years, and an average duration of participating in the program of 2.3 years. Comparing the before and after periods of participating in the stations, it was found that 86% of the patients showed some degree of improvement in symptomatology, particularly regarding withdrawn tendencies and disturbing behavior; 97% of them showed improvement in social adjustments; and the frequency of relapse and rehospitalization has been decreased remarkably—70 rehospitalizations required among 44 cases before attending the program, and 18 rehospitalizations among 15 cases after program involvement. These figures illustrate that such a work-therapy program is a useful project for rehabilitation within the socioculture setting of China.

Psychiatric Home Care Unit

The psychiatric home care unit is another important community psychiatric project developed in Shanghai. From the general survey, we have learned that in Shanghai there are about 20–50 mental patients living within each neighborhood area. Among them, some have fully recovered and returned to work and are being followed up by the factory health clinic; some have not yet fully recovered, and they participate in the previously described psychiatric work-therapy stations, with some staying at home for convalescence. It is usually a difficult task in the field of community psychiatry to take care of those who have not fully recovered. This is particularly so in Shanghai, since most of the adult family members of patients are working and are not at home during the day to take care of the patients. Therefore, it becomes the task of the psychiatric home care unit to take care of them.

The psychiatric home care units are composed of patients' neighbors, retired workers, and family members, who assist in the care of mental patients. It usually takes two or three persons as a team to take care of one patient. The retired workers in the team are usually familiar with and have good relations with the patient and, therefore, are devoted to their volunteer work. Their responsibilities are to observe the patient's condition, to supervise patients in taking medications, to contact regional medical staff whenever necessary, to have concern for the patient's well being and interests, to provide guidance and education, and to help the patient and his or her family in solving any psychological problems that may arise.

The home care teams within a particular residential area form a home care unit or network under the neighborhood committee of that particular area. The members of all the teams in the neighborhood area meet once monthly to share their experiences. Occasionally, psychiatric staff members participate in such meetings in order to provide psychiatric education and consultation about any particular problems team members may encounter. The member of the home care team acts as bridge and mediator among patient, family, hospital, and society. As a matter of fact, they function as nonprofessional psychiatric social workers.

At present, more than 40% of the neighborhood committees have established these psychiatric home care units with home care teams. At the end of 1980, in Shanghai, there was a total of 462 neighborhood committees supervising home care units, which were staffed by 18,561 volunteers taking care of 7719 psychiatric cases. After the establishment of the psychiatric home care system, there were improvements in follow-up care, a development of close contact between discharged patients and medical personnel, and the prevention of disturbing behavior by patients, all of which were beneficial.

Closely related to this program is the home treatment project. Instead of hospitalizing the actively sick patient, psychiatric or medical staff from the district or county mental hospitals make home visits and provide necessary treatment for the patient at home including medication and counseling. In 1980, there was a total of 816 patients who were treated in their homes. This kind of home treatment program not only makes it convenient to treat patients, but it also indirectly solves the problem of the shortage of psychiatric beds in Shanghai.

Care of Mental Patients in Large Factories

In Shanghai, there are many industrial factories. If the factories are relatively large in size (more than 2000 workers) a mental health service is established in the factory's health clinic as part of the health care system and is closely integrated into the administrative system of the factory.

The coordinating committee for the care of mental patients in the factory is composed of representatives of the administration, the worker's union, the personnel department, and the health station. The factory health station is assigned as an executive unit to carry out the functions of the mental health service. In each factory station, there are usually one or two medical doctors or health workers who have received short-term psychiatric training from the psychiatrists in municipal or district mental hospitals, and these people are able to provide basic psychiatric service. When there are many psychiatric patients in the factory, the staff works full-time to provide psychiatric services; otherwise, the staff is available on a part-time basis.

With regard to psychiatric service, the factory health stations function similarly to other community-level health clinics to carry out registration of psychiatric patients, to provide outpatient clinical services, and to treat patients either at the clinic or at the patients' homes. Sometimes, work-therapy stations associated with the factory are established so that those patients who have not recovered completely and are not able to return to work can receive work therapy at the stations. According to statistics for 1980, there was a total of 329 factories in Shanghai providing psychiatric service to a total of 4524 patients, of whom 293 were treated by the home-treatment program. In addition, 3528 home visits have been carried out— a significant achievement.

Such an achievement can be illustrated from the example of a large cigarette factory in Shanghai that has 4837 workers. Since 1973, the factory has provided psychiatric service. The leaders of this factory pay great attention to this effort. They selected a health worker, a former staff member of a worker's union who is devoted to the welfare of the workers, as a key person for such a project. He received psychiatric training and provided enthusiastic service, particularly in the early detection of cases for treatment. According to the assessment, there were 53 persons who became psychiatric cases prior to 1973, and it took about 3 years for them to visit psychiatric facilities for treatment after the onset of mental illness. After the establishment of the mental health service in this factory, there were 47 persons between 1973 and 1978 who had psychiatric breakdowns. However, it took an average of only $4\frac{1}{2}$ months for them to visit the clinic for treatment. This improvement in early treatment, without a doubt, has brought about better treatment results and has also decreased the rates of relapse and readmission.

SUMMARY AND FUTURE PERSPECTIVES

So far, we have described this project as a grass roots community mental health delivery system developed in Shanghai. It has been developed with consideration of the mainland Chinese health situation (an extreme shortage of mental health facilities) and in consonance with a political ideology that strives to serve the general public, particularly laborers, farmers, and soldiers. We have maximally utilized paramedical personnel and volunteer retired workers in order to expand the scope of service horizontally, but we have also strengthened the supporting vertical network of well-coordinated, three-level mental health program among the municipal, the district (county), and the neighborhood (commune). Importantly, we have made use of our traditional sociocultural system—with its close family ties and interpersonal relationships in the neighborhood, backed up by a formal street (neighborhood) committee organization—to develop a home- and neighborhood-oriented and work-emphasizing mental health program in Shanghai. With the support of the government on one hand and with the collaboration of the community on the other, we are proud to have been able to develop such an operating mental health delivery system within a relatively short period of time. We have attained many obvious successes. The programs have eliminated the communities' past prejudice about the mentally ill and have facilitated reintegration of patients into the community, reduced relapses, and promoted the patients social rehabilitation.

The results obtained so far are most encouraging, though there is plenty of room for future improvement. For example, our work has been focused primarily on the practical aspects of service delivery. We need theoretical consideration in order to make full use of the knowledge and theories from the disciplines of psychology, sociology, and anthropology and must integrate this information with psychiatric knowledge in order to promote a more comprehensive and scientifically based understanding of the nature and objectives of community mental health. There is a need for more systematic assessment and research to evaluate the programs for future improvement.

We also realize that the mental health delivery system has not developed evenly in Shanghai, and this is true for the country as a whole. For various reasons, the mental health program has not yet been developed in some areas. In 1980, we held the Second National Conference on Preventive Mental Health in Shanghai. At the conference, we made presentations on the mental health programs developed in Beijing and Shanghai. We took the conference delegates from various parts of the country to some of the successful mental health projects in Shanghai, encouraging them to use these projects as models for them to learn from in order to develop their own mental health programs with appropriate modifications based on their own local social conditions.

The patients we have served through our present mental health program have, thus far, been primarily psychotic patients—most of them schizophrenic. We are aware of the many other groups of psychiatric patients calling for our attention. For example, from our previous census survey in Shanghai (Liu et al., 1980; Qu et al., 1980), we learned that there are a number of mentally retarded persons in the community who are presently being cared for at home but who are in need of professional care. In some communities of Shanghai, we have already begun the establishment of several work-therapy stations for the mentally retarded. We also realize that, as in most societies, there is a relatively large number of patients with minor psychiatric disorders such as neuroses who also live in our society. Paralleling the prolongation of life-span, there is a gradual increase of geriatric psychiatric disorders among the elderly. Providing a comprehensive service for these groups of patients is our future concern and task.

Finally, a major issue is providing continuous psychiatric education for the program staff. The basic medical and paramedical staff, whom we trained in the past, have worked in the field of mental health for some time. Combined with the increase in their working experience, they also need more education. The periodic provision of continuing education programs to increase and update their knowledge and skills is another task needing our future attention.

A comprehensive and successful community mental health system depends on various elements. We need the continuous effort of the working staff, enthusiastic support from the government, cooperation from the community, and participation and support from the people. Above all, success depends on the people's views, attitudes, and understanding of mental health. In this regard, it is critical to give careful consideration to all aspects of the sociocultural background of the society in developing an appropriate and successful mental health delivery system.

REFERENCES

Chi, M., et al.
   1964   Shanghai di-qu jing-shen-fen-le-zheng huan-zhe 1,196 li de yi-chuan-shen-wu-xue diau-cha yan-jiu [A genetic survey of 1,196 cases of schizophrenia in Shanghai]. *Chinese Journal of Neurology and Psychiatry, 8,* 80–81.
Hsia, C. Y., She, H., Zhang, F., Ling, Y., Hu, Y., and Chen, S.
   1958   2000 li jing-shen-fen-le-zheng de lin-chuang-fen-xi ji sui-fang-yan-jiu [A clinical and follow-up study of 2,000 cases of schizophrenia]. *Chinese Journal of Neurology and Psychiatry, 4,* 89–94.
Qu, G. Y.,
   n.d.   Results of rehabilitation in psychiatric work therapy station: An analysis of 100 schizophrenics. Internal report of the Shanghai Psychiatric Institute.
Xia, Z. Y.,
   1980   Mental health work in Shanghai. *Chinese Medical Journal, 93,* 127–129.
Xia, Z. Y., and Zhang, M. Y.
   1981   History and present status of modern psychiatry in China. *Chinese Medical Journal, 94,* 277–282.
Xu, T. Y.,
   1979   [Clinical and follow-up investigation of 2,000 schizophrenics.] *Journal of Nervous and Mental Diseases, 5,* 244–247.

Zhang, M. Y., and Xia, Z. Y.
    1980   Jing-shen-fen-le-zheng de fu-fa-wen-ti [The relapses of schizophrenia.] *Journal of Nervous and Mental Disease, 6,* 257–259.

Liu, J. et al.
    1980   Shanghai-shi Xuhui-qu jing-shen-bing liu-xing-bing-xue diau-cha [An epidemiological investigation of mental disorders in Xuhui District of Sharghai]. *Chinese Journal of Neurology and Psychiatry 13,* 1–6.

Qu, G. et al.
    1980   Jing-shen-fa-yu-bu-quan liu-xing-bing-xue diau-cha [An epidemiologic study of mental retardation]. *Chinese Journal of Neurology and Psychiatry, 13,* 19–21.

CHAPTER 24

The Mental Health Home Care Program: Beijing's Rural Haidian District

Shen Yucun

INTRODUCTION

The mental health home care program is a community mental health program in which the patient is cared for at home through treatment and rehabilitation. The program makes good use of the assets of the family's and the community's living environment in order to improve the patient's mental condition and to decrease the chance of relapse. It is one kind of mental health program with emphasis on prevention and differs from the usual program of hospitalization or outpatient treatment. By analyzing the social and cultural background of mainland China, we introduce this program with the hope of finding a more practical way of helping the mental patients in rural areas where mental health services are not yet adequate.

In order to develop this pilot program for study, three major considerations were made:

357

CHINESE CULTURE
AND MENTAL HEALTH

1. In the course of treatment, patients who suffer from mental illnesses are in special need of sympathy, understanding, and concern from those around them. In other words, they need support not only from medical workers, but also from family members, friends, and the community. If they are deprived of the opportunity to take part in the activities of the collective group and forced to live in isolation, the benefit of drug treatment can hardly be evaluated. They may also have relapses. In order to keep them from reverting to illness, community mental health care is absolutely necessary.

2. According to cultural tradition, Chinese family members have a closer relationship than do members of Western families. Chinese usually consider it their duty to help one another economically as well as in other respects. They tend to think it is also their responsibility to take care of those members who are ill. As a rule, the family would not consider sending sick relatives to mental hospitals. So, in mainland China, most of the mental patients are kept at home and looked after by other members of the family. That is why home care of mental patients is more acceptable to us Chinese.

3. In China, there are already quite a number of primary health care centers in the villages. There is a hospital for each commune, and there are "barefoot" doctors (paramedical staff who provide neighborhood-based health care) in ecah production brigade. This makes it much easier to develop mental health care in villages and provide sick-beds in the homes of the villagers.

In June 1974, the Institute of Mental Health of Beijing Medical College began to set up a health care network for mental diseases in 11 communes in the Haidian District which has a population of nearly 190,000. A series of procedures were followed, including the training of barefoot doctors and doctors from commune hospitals, and the identification of severely ill mental patients in the district. While giving the patients various kinds of treatment, the doctors and barefoot doctors paid visits to their families from time to time. If the patients' conditions improved, they were encouraged to join in more social activities. They either did housework or took part in collective labor. In this way, they got improved steadily, and the results were quite satisfactory. More than 200 schizophrenic patients received drug treatment in combination with this kind of home care. Since 1976, good remission and marked improvement have been achieved in 60% of the schizophrenic patients. Such improvement could never have been achieved by hospital treatment alone. Thus, this pilot project supports the idea that the home care program for schizophrenic patients works well for the rural areas of China.

GENERAL INFORMATION ABOUT THE HAIDIAN DISTRICT PROJECT AREA

The Haidian District lies in the northwestern suburbs of Beijing, covers nearly 433 Km², and had a population of 185,148 in 1981. There has not been significant population movement—less than 1.0% per year moving in or out in the last 4 years. The birth rate is 17‰, and the death rate is 7.7‰ with the natural growth of the population averaging 9.2‰ a year. According to the census study in 1979, 27.4% of the population were ages 1–14, 62.7% ages 15–59, and 9.9% over 60. The male to female ratio is 1 : 1.2. The structure of families has been changing in recent years. There are few extended families. When children grow up and get married, they form their own families, but they usually still live in the same courtyards so that they can still help one another. Each family consists of an average of four members. And on an average, each person occupies 12 square meters of housing.

The income of most of the peasants in this district has grown to nearly compare in amount with that of city dwellers. The communes that run factories or other enterprises and those whose chief income is from growing vegetables and fruit are naturally richer than the communes in distant or mountainous areas that plant nothing but grain. The average income for each member of the richer communes is double that of the poorer ones. In four communes close to the city, the commune members enjoy free medical care, their children can be sent to the kindergartens free of charge, and even funeral expenses are paid by the collectives. All children enjoy a 10-year schooling at public expense. In the outer suburbs, the communes are not so rich, so the peasants can enjoy only partly free medical service and other kinds of public welfare. The density of population in this district varies from 278.4 to 550.2 persons per square kilometer. Junior high schools have been generally accessible since 1949 and senior high schools since 1975. Only a few illiterates can be found, and they are in the age group above 60.

PROCEDURES USED IN SETTING UP THE COMMUNITY MENTAL HEALTH CARE NETWORK

A team of four or five psychiatrists from the Mental Health Institute of Beijing Medical College was organized to set up a mental health care network in each commune by focusing on the following:

1. *Psychiatric training of medical personnel:* Attention was given to the training of one or two doctors from commune hospitals for period of 4–6

months and one or two barefoot doctors from each productive brigade for 1 week. A total of 240 barefoot doctors and 14 doctors from commune hospitals were trained. The average ratio between the number of barefoot doctors trained and the population of village was 1 : 750, while the ratio between the number of medical workers of commune hospitals and the commune population was 1 : 13,000.

2. *Field survey:* A list of suspected mental patients in each production brigade was provided, chiefly by the barefoot doctors in charge. Key information was collected from the head of brigades, the police, and the psychiatric department of the district polyclinic. A psychiatric interview of each suspected case was carried out by an experienced psychiatrist. The average time spent in examining each patient was about 1 hour, which included a case history taken from the patient's relatives. Among the diseases investigated were different kinds of psychoses, mental retardation, and epilepsy.

3. *Drug treatment:* Systematic drug treatment was provided for those indicated. Psychiatrists from our department together with the barefoot doctors in charge and medical workers from the commune hospitals periodically called on the patients under treatment.

The investigation and organization of mental health care service throughout the district were completed by February 1977. A total of 1333 severely ill mental patients was identified, and 787 home beds were created by the end of February 1977 (Department of Psychiatry, Beijing Medi-

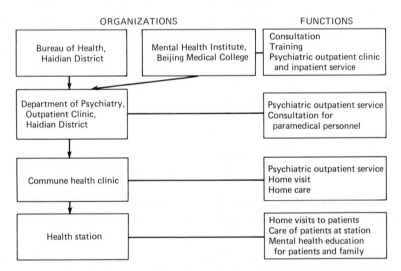

Figure 24.1 Community mental health care network in the Haidian District, Beijing.

cal College, 1980). The establishment of mental health care services in the district and the function of the different levels of services are as shown in Figure 24.1.

FINDINGS OF THE PSYCHIATRIC SURVEY
IN THE HAIDIAN DISTRICT

A systematic field survey of psychiatric disorders in the project site of the Haidian District revealed a total of 1333 cases. The prevalence rate of various disorders are shown in the Table 24.1. The prevalence rate of schizophrenia is 1.8%, reactive psychosis 0.3%, manic–depressive psychosis 0.1%, other psychoses, which include involutional, arteriosclerotic, senile, presenile, psychosis due to intoxication or infectious disease, 0.3%, epilepsy and mental disorders that are epileptic in origin 2.1%, and oligophrenia 2.6%. No alcoholism or drug addiction was found (Shen et al., 1981). This distribution pattern is similar to that reported from various parts of China, such as the survey from Taiwan (Lin, 1953), the survey of Dayangben in the Xiangtan District of Central China by Hunan Medical College in the fifties (Li and Shen, 1982); the surveys in eastern China by the Shanghai Psychiatric Institute and by the Nanjing Neuropsychiatric Institute, and western China survey by the Sichuan Medical College in the 1970s (Shen, 1981).

Since schizophrenia is the most common major psychosis found—300 cases among 156,200 people in the 10 communes we investigated—the clinical data for this disorder are described in more detail.

Prevalence Rate.   The overall prevalence rate is 1.9‰; for males, it is 1.2‰ (87 out of 74,500) and for females, 2.6‰ (213 out of 81,700), with

Table 24.1   Diagnostic Findings of the Psychiatric Survey in 11 Communes in the Haidian District of Beijing, 1977

Diagnosis	Number of patients	Percentage	Prevalence rate(‰)
Schizophrenia	341	25.6	1.8
Reactive psychosis	49	3.7	0.3
Manic–depressive psychosis	14	1.0	0.1
Other psychoses	52	3.9	0.3
Oligophrenia	481	36.1	2.6
Epilepsy and epilepsy-related mental disorders	396	29.7	2.1
	1333	100.0	7.2

the ratio 0.46 : 1. Prevalence for both sexes rises in the 25–29 age group, peaking in the 40–49 age group. Male prevalence is comparatively higher than female under ages 30–34, and female prevalence increases after age 35, then rises sharply for ages 40–49. The male–female ratios become 2.5 : 1 and 3.2 : 1, respectively.

The prevalence rate in each of the 10 communes ranges from 1.0‰ to 3.2‰. The highest prevalence of schizophrenic patients is found in Yuyuantan commune, which borders the city and has the highest population density. Difference in prevalence does not seem to have any relationship to the average income or with the geographic position of the communes in the district.

Clinical Features. The general clinical features of schizophrenia in this district indicate the high degree of chronicity and the long duration of the disease course. Onset of the disease is chronic and subacute in 71.1% of cases and acute in 28.9%. The disease course above 5 years constitutes 68.5%, and that above 10 years, 39.3%; 19% (61 out of 300) obviously deteriorate. Among them 46.8% have a chronic course (symptoms persist), 16.8% a progressive course, 26.9% a remittent course, and 9.4% have only one episode.

Mental Status during the Field Survey. During the field survey, 77.7% (233 out of 300) were found to have obvious psychiatric symptoms, 7% (21 out of 300) were in partial remission, 15.3% (46 out of 300) were in good remission. Clinical types include paranoid (54.3%), chronic (19.7%), hebephrenic (11%), simple (2%), pseudoneurotic (0.7%), catatonic (0.3%), and others (12%). As a rule, these chronic patients are looked after by a family member and live in a separate room. They are kept isolated from social life for a long time and do not participate in collective labor. The survey also shows that among the patients, 62.3% have received treatment, 7.5% have been treated for only a short time, and 30.1% have never received any previous treatment. The reasons vary: Some of them are skeptical about the treatment, saying that mental illness can never be cured. Others believe that mental illness is due to the fault or immorality of their ancestors. Still others are reluctant to be treated in any way simply for economic reasons.

DEVELOPMENT OF THE HOME CARE PROGRAM

As a first step, mental health education for family members of the identified patient was carried out by the community-based medical personnel— doctors and barefoot doctors. It was aimed at correcting preexisting bias and negative attitudes toward mental illness. Knowledge about how to provide care during drug therapy was introduced, and the usefulness for patients to participate in family and community life was explained so that active cooperation and participation from family members could be assured.

Whenever there was improvement in the mental condition, the patient was encouraged to participate in whatever work he or she could carry out, such as raising chicken or ducks, planting vegetables, sewing clothes, cooking, and so on.

A course of 2–3 months of active drug therapy is usually carried out followed by a drug maintenance therapy. For chronic schizophrenia, drug therapy was maintained at least 1 year, or even 2 years, in order to obtain apparent improvement or remission. Either long-acting or short-acting antipsychotic drugs were given to most of the patients. The patients were urged to participate in family activities or collective production work for improvement of socialization and work competency.

The medical personnel regularly and periodically do home visiting, even after patients have reached remission. Whenever there was fluctuation in the mental condition of a patient or an occurrence of family conflict, necessary drug therapy and/or counseling was provided. Annually, psychiatric consultation from the Department of Psychiatry of Beijing Medical College was given for the future therapeutic plan.

RESULTS OF THE HOME CARE PROGRAM

The schizophrenic patients treated in the home care program were followed up annually to assess the results of the service. After 7 years, the results proved to be promising. As illustrated in Table 24.2, at the end of

Table 24.2   Clinical Evaluation of Schizophrenia Patients in the Haidian District Treated through the Home Care Program, 1974–1980

Year	Number of patients	Remission		Marked improvement		Improvement		No improvement	
		n	%	n	%	n	%	n	%
At time of survey									
1974–1976	211	0	0.0	137	64.9	54	25.6	20	9.5
After the program									
1977	232	102	44.0	69	29.7	44	19.0	17	7.3
1978	234	115	49.1	51	21.8	59	25.2	9	3.8
1979	206	74	35.9	66	32.0	52	25.2	14	6.8

Table 24.3   Working Capacity of Schizophrenic Patients in the Haidian District, before and after Participating in the Home Care Program ($N = 206$)

	Before onset		At time of survey (1974–1976)		After the program (1979)	
	n	%	n	%	n	%
Full-day farm work	157	76.2	6	2.9	97	47.1
Half-day farm work	3	1.5	11	5.3	32	15.5
Full-time housework	22	10.7	4	1.9	37	17.0
Part-time housework	7	3.4	16	7.8	30	14.6
At school	11	5.3	0	0.0	0	0.0
Unable to work	6	2.9	169	82.0	12	5.8
	206	100.0	206	100.0	206	100.0

1979, clinical assessment was carried out on the condition of the 206 patients who received home care service. Among them, 74 cases (35.7%) were found to be in good remission, and 66 cases (32%) were markedly improved with some residual symptoms (Shen, 1981).

When the working capacities of the patients in the family or in the community are reviewed, the effect of the service becomes more apparent (see Table 24.3). Before the program was instituted, only 6 out of 206 cases (2.9%) were doing normal farm work on a full-time basis; after the beginning of the program in 1979, the number of cases increased to 97 (47.1%). For a full day of housework, from 4 cases (1.9%) to 35 cases (17%). The number who did not participate in either housework or farm work dropped from 169 cases (82.0%) to 12 cases (5.8%). The result of such improvement was rechecked in 1981, and it was found that it remained the same, maintaining results difficult to achieve by hospitalization.

Reevaluation of the Program Results

A systematic follow-up evaluation was carried out in 1981 to assure that the previous clinical impression of improvement was correct. Standardized questionnaires designed by the World Health Organization for the evaluation of the patients' condition were utilized. One of the largest communes, Sijiging (Forever Green) Commune was chosen for this evaluation.

From January to February 1982, a team of two senior psychiatrists and one psychiatric resident was sent to Sijiging Commune for an intensive investigation. A total of 106 schizophrenic patients had been diagnosed in that district by the end of 1981. Among them, 99 cases were identified to be schizophrenic at the time of investigation for reevaluation. (The other 7 cases did not fit the diagnostic criteria.) Besides the ordinary form of clinical interview the Present State Examination Schedule and the Diagnostic Assessment Schedule designed by the World Health Organization were used in this reevaluation.

The result of the treatment in the seventh year was still quite satisfactory—36 cases (36.4%) were in good remission, 41 cases (41.4%) were in marked improvement, 13 cases (13.1%) were improved with some residual symptoms, 9 cases (9.1%) were either still symptomatic or deteriorated.

The recovery of the patients in their social and family functioning in this commune in 1981 was about the same as in 1979 for the whole district. The patients who took part in normal farm work or household work in the year 1981 make up 44.2% and 11.6%, respectively. Only 10 of the patients could not work, 5 due to chronic deterioration, 1 to a new episode, and other 4 to exacerbation of psychotic symptoms.

This systematic reevaluation shows that the previous clinical investigation obtained almost the same evaluation accuracy as could be obtained by standardized evaluation techniques, indicating the previous report of the whole district (11 communes) is rather reliable. At the same time, it also illustrates that the result of the service was the same in seventh year follow-up as in the fifty year follow-up, meaning that the effect of service is quite long standing.

DISCUSSION

Our study revealed that the mental health home care program that views the community as a whole, with the family as base and a foundation of a community care network, can provide excellent results. For the treatment of chronic schizophrenic patients based on the psychopharmacological control of symptoms, it is essential to have a healthy family and social milieu and an opportunity for collective work experience in order to decrease the chance of relapse as well as to recover ordinary socialization, working capacity, and emotional life. A 5-year follow-up visit to 206 chronic schizophrenics and a 7-year follow-up investigation has provided the data to support this belief. The results indicate that instead of deteriorating further, about one-third of the cases remain in remission, two-fifths of the cases can maintain ordinary family and social life even with some symptoms, and about half of the cases could participate in collective productive farm work or housework after receiving the home care service.

The World Health Organization studied the prognoses of schizophrenic patients in the WHO International Pilot Study of Schizophrenia from nine

study centers around the world and found out that the prognosis of schizophrenia is related to the sociocultural background of the patients. The
patients in developing countries have a more favorable course and outcome than those in developed, urbanized, industrialized countries (Sartorius, Jablensky, and Shapiro, 1977). Based on these findings, it has been
speculated that the family background, the nature of interaction between
family members, as well as the occupational, economic, and cultural environment, may relate to the outcome of the illness of schizophrenic patients.

From our study, we may say that what we have done over these years in
the rural areas is based on our understanding of the principles of mental
health, the social environment of the patient, the importance of normal
social activities and family support to the patient's psyche, and the patient's
own state of mind. This probably explains why we have obtained some
fairly good results in our research program. Another very important factor
is the socialist system in China. For without the support of the Health
Bureau of the Haidian District and the close cooperation of the patients'
families as well as the whole community, we would not have been able to
achieve what we did. The work of developing mental health home care on
the primary health level not only benefits the patients and lightens the
burden on the state; it also promotes socialist ethics throughout the country.

REFERENCES

Department of Psychiatry, Beijing Medical College
    1980   Beijing-shi Haidian-qu jing-shen-ji-bing de diau-cha bau-gau [Investigation of
            mental disorders in Haidian District, Beijing]. *Journal of Chinese Neurolology and
            Psychiatry*, *13*(1), 10—12.
Li, C. P., and Shen, Y.
    1982   Wo-guo mou-xie shen-shi di-qu jing-shen-bing liu-xing-xue jin-nian diau-cha
            zhi-liau de gai-shu [Recent psychiatric epidemiologic surveys in China]. A
            review. *Journal of Chinese Neurology and Psychiatry*, *15*(2), 120—125.
Lin, T. Y.
    1953   A study of the incidence of mental disorder in Chinese and other cultures.
            Psychiatry, *16*, 313—336.
Sartorius, N., Jablensky, A., and Shapiro, R.
    1977   Two-year follow-up of the patients included in The WHO International Pilot
            Study of Schizophrenia. *Psychological Medicine*, *7*, 529—541.
Shen, Y.
    1981   [The psychiatric services in the urban and rural areas of the People's Republic
            of China.] *Clinical Psychiatry*, *275*, 1165—1169.
Shen, Y. et al.
    1981   Investigation of mental disorders in Beijing Suburban District. *Chinese Medical
            Journal*, *94*(3), 153—156.

PART VI

SUMMARY AND SUGGESTIONS FOR THE FUTURE

Based on accumulated clinical studies and epidemiological observations on Chinese psychiatric patients in various communities in the last several decades, Lin (Chapter 25) summarizes the characteristic features of Chinese patients' manifestation of psychopathology, that is, the relative favorable prognosis for schizophrenia, the low prevalence of depressive disorders with their predominantly somatic symptoms, the relatively common manifestation of neurasthenic disorders, the still low occurrence of juvenile delinquency and alcoholism, and the existence of some culture-related specific syndromes such as impotence panic (*koro*) and "frigophobia." He further analyzes Chinese patients' help-seeking behavior, familys' coping patterns, and the delivery system of mental health services in the context of Chinese society and culture. He urges that more knowledge and theory be developed in the future, based either on clinical study or on research input from various Chinese communities for understanding the system of psychiatry related to Chinese culture.

Finally, concerning future research in culture and mental health, Tseng and Wu (Chapter 26) suggest the need for a more interdisciplinary approach by the cross-comparative method to investigate the complex phe-

367

nomena of culture, behavior, and mental health. More specifically, they emphasize the importance of the dual micro- and macroscopic approach, with more focus on the subject of psychologically and culturally related mental health issues rather than mere concern about mental disorders. The mental health of the child, the family, and the elderly are some of the issues that need to be focused on and investigated in the rapidly changing society of our time; and the value system, which may contribute to mental well-being, needs to be explored not only for the Chinese people but also for the people of the world.

CHAPTER 25

Mental Disorders and Psychiatry in Chinese Culture: Characteristic Features and Major Issues

Tsung-Yi Lin

INTRODUCTION

Since its inception at the turn of the twentieth century, modern psychiatry in China, as well as in other Chinese societies, has made a conscious effort to make Western psychiatry its basic frame of reference and has attempted to apply Western concepts and methodological tools to develop its system of knowledge and psychiatric services (T. Lin, 1953, 1982a; Xia, 1981). The pursuit of the Western psychiatric mode, and the pervasiveness of its effects are evident in almost all spheres of psychiatric activities: in daily clinical work with patients, in the management of psychiatric hospitals, and in the methods and content of teaching and research, including the logic and theories used for sorting out the acquired information and experiences.

A growing body of accumulated scientific observations, especially since

369

the early 1950s, has begun to point out certain differences Chinese patients manifest in psychopathology and in the course of mental disorders as well as in the ways the family and society treat and cope with the mentally ill. This has led to such important questions as the relative vulnerability and tolerance of the Chinese to specific stresses and the extent to which Chinese culture with its traditional health beliefs and health practices influences the perception and management of mental illness and mental health–related behavior.

In this chapter, I address a set of four questions in order to investigate the role Chinese culture plays in shaping psychiatry and mental health services:

1. Are there psychiatric phenomena that are characteristic of the Chinese?
2. Are there psychiatric treatment modalities that are unique to the Chinese or commonly practiced by the Chinese but not by others?
3. Have the Chinese, with their social and cultural traditions, developed unique coping skills that have expressed themselves in a pattern of help seeking and delivery of mental health services?
4. Do the Chinese have a system of psychiatric knowledge or theory closely related to Chinese culture, especially regarding factors affecting the causation, manifestation, and evolution of mental illness and its intervention?

It is my view that the term *Chinese psychiatry* can have specific scientific meaning of practical value only when one or more or, preferably, all of these questions are answered in the affirmative.

CHARACTERISTIC FEATURES OF MENTAL DISORDERS AMONG THE CHINESE

It should be pointed out first that there are basic similarities in the psychopathology of mental disorders between the Chinese and the people of Western and other cultures. Two major similarities have been observed and reported by various investigators in the past, which are substantiated by the World Health Organization's (1973) International Pilot Studies of Schizophrenia and other international collaborative studies (Rin, Schooler, and Caudill, 1973). First, the entire range of psychopathology observed in Western or other cultures in terms of symptoms or syndromes have also been observed in the Chinese. Second, all types of mental disorders, including their subtypes, as discussed in Western literature and textbooks, have been identified among the Chinese when standard Western diagnostic criteria are applied. The confirmation of these similarities is of fundamental importance because it assures basic common ground for the development of Chinese psychiatry by first learning from the West as has been done over the past 80 years. It also enables Chinese clinicians and scientists to compare notes with their counterparts from the West for validating their respective observations.

The overall prevalence rates of mental disorders, as well as the rates for psychoses among the Chinese, have been reported to be roughly equivalent to, or slightly lower than, the reported rates from other cultures (K. M. Lin, Kleinman, and T. Lin, 1981). Such observations cannot yet, however, be regarded as conclusive or meaningful. Epidemiological studies that have been carried out in Chinese and other cultures up to the present vary significantly in scope, methods of case finding, diagnostic criteria, sociodemographic measurements, and data analysis and thus have yielded no data for meaningful comparisons, especially as far as overall rates of mental disorders are concerned.

Major Psychoses

Observations of certain specific types of mental disorders are amenable to comparison with other studies by virtue of the utilization of better-defined diagnostic criteria.

SCHIZOPHRENIA

The prevalence rates of schizophrenia in various studies range from 1.1 to 4.0 per 1000, which stand in the lower range of reported rates from other cultures (K. M. Lin, et al., 1981; T. Lin, 1953; T. Lin, Rin, Yeh, C. C. Hsu, and Chu, 1969; Shen et al., 1981). It should be noted, however, that this research requires further confirmation through systematic epidemiological studies using standardized research methodology and well-defined criteria.

Two significant features among Chinese schizophrenics seem to stand out from the reported findings. First, a high percentage of schizophrenic patients in Taiwan are diagnosed as paranoid, in both clinical and systematic comparative studies (Rin et al., 1973; Yeh, Fan, and Tien, 1979). Second, the data obtained from Taiwan and Hong Kong seem to indicate a considerably more favorable prognosis for Chinese schizophrenics. The Chinese schizophrenic patients in the International Pilot Study of Schizophrenia (IPSS), conducted by World Health Organization (1973), showed better prognoses than those of Western countries after 2 years and after 5 years. In Hong Kong, two-thirds of the schizophrenics were found to have either lasting remission or to evidence only mild deterioration at the 10-year follow-up (Lo and Lo, 1977). The hospital statistics obtained during my visits to the Chinese mainland in 1981 and 1982 also suggest a benign prognosis of schizophrenics there.

Additionally, in order to investigate the possible role biogenetic factors play in the favorable outcome of schizophrenia, the contribution of psychosocial factors peculiar to Chinese culture should be explored. It is conceivable that the strong supportive network imbedded in the traditional Chinese family system and in the community may play a key role. It is also possible that preindustrial Chinese social structure, with its well-defined roles and functions for each individual, may place a lower demand upon the sick individual and thus make it easier for that person to regain his or her place with its prescribed roles and functions. This last hypothesis might conceivably apply to the other three developing centers of IPSS—Cali, Columbia; Ibadan, Nigeria; and Agia, India—all of which have certain preindustrial social characteristics similar to those of the Chinese in Taiwan. The testing of this hypothesis would be a worthwhile area of inquiry. It is interesting that the labeling hypothesis of mental disorders (Waxler, 1974, 1979) appears not to apply to the Chinese case, where mental illness is stigmatized and chronicity is expected. Field research needs to be done in mainland China as well in order to determine the current beliefs and explanations that influence the particular course of illness.

AFFECTIVE PSYCHOSES

Prevalence rates of affective psychoses in Taiwan and Hong Kong point to a lower range that is generally assumed in other cultures (T. Lin, 1953, T. Lin, Rin, Yeh, Hsu and Chu, 1969; Liu, 1980b; Yap, 1965b). Manic patients are in the majority in most studies. Whether this finding is due to the underreporting of depressive patients or to overreporting of manic patients, which might be traced to differing cultural tolerance of the Chinese, deserves further study.

SENILE PSYCHOSES

In sharp contrast to the West, care for the aged suffering from senile psychoses has not constituted a major problem for the family, society, or psychiatric institutions in Chinese societies. The prevalence rates of senile psychoses in the community observed in Taiwan (T. Lin, 1953) and rates of hospitalized psychotics over the age of 60 in Hong Kong (Yap, 1965b) are relatively low.

These findings should not be taken to indicate that the Chinese do not develop senile dementia or suffer from senile psychoses. The age-specific rates of senile dementia and psychoses in the Taiwan study are found to be comparable to those reported from Bavaria and Thuringia. It is conceivable that the low hospital admission rates of senile psychiatric patients reflect the protective attitude of the Chinese toward the elderly, sick or well. In the commune of Haidian, near Beijing, the 200-bed Old People's Home had an average of only 50 residents, at any one time (Shen et al., 1981). It is postulated that the Chinese community has a higher tolerance for the elderly, encouraging them to function actively and making them feel loved, wanted, respected, and useful, which gives them a sense of self-respect and belonging. How much such traditional attitudes help retard the aging process or influence the onset and course of senile psychoses would be a subject of future medicosocial inquiry.

Minor Mental Disorders and Culture-Bound Syndromes

In this group of disorders, three findings stand out prominently in most studies regardless of whether they are based on hospital statistics or community surveys; the very low prevalence rates of depressive illness, especially neurotic depression, the large number of patients diagnosed as having neurasthenia, and the relative paucity of obsessive–compulsive neuroses among the Chinese.

DEPRESSIVE ILLNESS

It is fair to state that depressive illness among the Chinese has so far received little attention, largely due to their perceived low prevalence rates. The author's observation on the statistics of hospitalized patients and outpatient clinics in mainland China further confirms the generally held view that depressive illnesses are rarely diagnosed. For example, less than 3% of the outpatient clinic patients and about 1% of the inpatients are diagnosed as depressives in most institutions. Several reasons have been put forward to account for these reports:

1. The manifestations of depression—mainly dysphoric mood change, self-depreciation, and guilt feelings—do not fit the traditional concept of madness in Chinese society, which emphasizes outward antisocial or bizarre behavior as pathognomonic features. Therefore, the people with dysphoric conditions neither seek psychiatric help nor are they reported in the epidemiological surveys.

2. The Chinese reluctance to express or discuss one's feelings, especially to anyone outside of one's family, may also play a part in inhibiting the manifestation of a depressive condition (F. L. K. Hsu, 1981).

3. Somatization, a prevalent form of symptom manifestation in Chinese psychiatric patients, especially those with minor mental disorders, is regarded as playing an important role in influencing the diagnosis of depression (Kleinman, 1977; K. M. Lin et al., 1981; Rin, Chu, and Lin, 1966; Tseng, 1975). The application of Western diagnostic criteria for depression, which consist mainly of psychological dysphoric symptoms, would leave out a large number of Chinese depressives whose prevalent symptoms are predominantly somatic and vegetative (T. Lin, 1983). The report on research findings in Changsha, Hunan, where 87 out of 100 consecutive patients of neurasthenia seen as outpatients are rediagnosed as having depressive disorders, provides further support to the important role of somatization in depressive psychopathology among the Chinese (Kleinman, 1982).

An indirect, but potentially important, supportive evidence of somatization can be found from linguistic studies. It has been pointed out that the Chinese words expressing dysphoria or depression are surprisingly limited when compared to the richness of somatic expressions that denote certain emotions (Cheung, Lau, and Waldman, 1980–1981, K. M. Lin, 1981).

4. One cannot overlook the real possibility that, indeed, the Chinese people suffer less depression. It is hypothesized that pathogenic conditions for depression, such as divorce, alcholism, and drug abuse, are less prevalent, wheras mutual help through an extended family or neighborhood alliance is more readily available for those under stress in Chinese society. This hypothesis deserves a systematic inquiry.

NEURASTHENIA

The writer's visits to mainland China confirmed the many reports of visitors and Chinese psychiatrists that neurasthenia stands out as the most frequent diagnosis given to psychiatric outpatients (Bermann, 1968, Chao, 1965, Kleinman, 1982). There was even a nation-wide campaign against neurasthenia in the late 1950s and 1960s (Yan, Chapter 22, this volume).

The term *neurasthenia* seems to be defined variously and is often used as a synonym of neurosis or even of minor mental disorders including neurotic depression, anxiety states, hypochondria, and hysteria. The vague and idiosyncratic usage of the term makes it difficult to analyze objectively many of the psychiatric findings reported on this condition, whether they be concerned with its epidemiology, causation, treatment, or clinical and social significance. Most Chinese psychiatrists seem to be of the view that there exists a group of patients suffering from a similar morbid condition of neurasthenia, probably of similar biological or neurological causation as orginally reported by Beard (1880) and Ballet (1908).

The whole issue of neurasthenia calls for an intensive systematic and comprehensive, clinical, epidemiological, and laboratory investigation. This research should use standard operational diagnostic criteria for redefining several subgroups that are given the label of neurasthenia.

OBSESSIVE–COMPULSIVE NEUROSIS

The rarity of obsessive–compulsive neurosis among the Chinese has been reported in the past by a visiting observer (La Barre, 1946), through epidemiological survey (T. Lin, 1953), and by clinical impression (Rin, 1959). I made similar observations during two visits to mainland China in 1981 and 1982. However, the epidemiological study in Shanghai by Liu et al. (1980) revealed that the prevalence of obsessive–compulsive neurosis is 0.03% in the community population studied. Hospital statistics from Taipei indicate that approximately 5% of the neurotic outpatients at the university psychiatric clinic are diagnosed as obsessive–compulsive (Department of psychiatry, National Taiwan University Hospital, 1980), a figure compatible with that reported from the West. Whether these findings represent a change in the frequency of the disorder among Chinese deserves further study. Tseng (1973b) regards the strong ties of the affected individual to a domineering and perfectionist mother to be the major psychodynamic of pathology in 10 cases of obsessive–compulsive neurosis in the young males he studied, which is a different formulation from that of the Western analytic one. For obtaining more objective infomation on the prevalence of obsessive–compulsive neuroses and understanding its psychocultural factors, it would be worthwhile to conduct large-scale careful epidemiological research combined with in-depth clinical studies.

CULTURE-BOUND SYNDROMES

A number of syndromes such as *koro,* "frigophobia," and *shen-k'uei* occur almost exclusively among the Chinese. *Koro* is characterized by panic due to a perceived shrinking of the penis into the abdomen among young men of lower social classes with minimal education in South China, Hong Kong, and Taiwan (Rin, 1965, Yap, 1965a). An epidemic was reported in Singapore (Ngui, 1969, Koro Study Team, 1969). Frigophobia patients suffer from an excessive fear and intolerance of cold, in terms of temperature and food of a cold (*yin*) nature (Chang, Rin, and Chen, 1975). *Shen-k'uei* is characterized by weakness, fatigue, insomnia, anxiety, and hypochondria. It is believed to be caused by excessive masturbation, nocturnal emission, or intercourse and is often called sexual neurasthenia.

All these syndromes have an important characteristic in common; somatization of anxiety or fear. It should be noted that traditional Chinese medical beliefs rooted in the Yin–Yang theory play an essential role in the manifestation, perception, and interpretation, of the these conditions. To what degree culture-specific treatment modalities have been applied to deal with these syndromes is not known, as no such reports are yet available.

Another reported culture-bound syndrom, *hsieh-ping* (evil sickness), is a form of possession and trance state often associated with guilt or fear over laxity in ancestor worship (Kleinman, 1979; T. Lin, 1953; Yap, 1960). It may be regarded as a form of religiously sanctioned behavior or a coping mechanism. Similar pathological possessions occur in other cultures (Rao, 1978) but are not related to ancestor worship as in the Chinese case.

It is interesting and somewhat surprising that all of the preceding reports about culture-bound syndromes were reported from Chinese communities outside of mainland China. I would be most curious to learn if any of the these syndromes exist in contemporary China. If so, information on its extent or social epidemiology, as well as the handling or treatment of such syndromes by professionals and the society, would be most valuable in understanding its sociocultural significance. Although I have not encountered any report of such cases during my visits, it would be premature to rule them out. Most probably, cases of culture-bound syndromes are handled by traditional medical healers or folk healers outside of the established health care system.

Children's Mental Health

The commonly held view that Chinese children suffer little from poor mental health seems to encounter increasing challenge from recent reports. For example, 14 Chinese children (13 boys and 1 girl) with autism, who manifest close similarity to non-Chinese autism, have been reported from Hong Kong (Ney et al., 1979). Cases of autism are also observed in mainland China and Taiwan. Learning difficulties are now found to be as prevalent among school children of Taiwan as among their American and Japanese counterparts. This observation is based on a collaborative, comparative, multicultural study using standardized research methodology (Hsu, 1982).

The sudden surge of interest in minimal brain dysfunction among Chinese children in mainland China since 1978 is worth noting. The reported prevalence rates are extremely high, even up to 10% of school-age children in extreme cases (Shinfuku and Kalicinski, 1982). It is almost epidemic by virtue of its sudden and widespread high morbidity, which deserves a systematic study through epidemiological and clinical research. It would be of great importance to find out whether such a sudden increase is caused by category fallacy or is due to true increase. The category fallacy refers to the possibility that the introduction of this concept following the resumption of international exchange of scientific communication in 1978 triggered a special interest among certain psychiatrists, and thus, the diagnostic criteria of minimal brain dysfunction has been indiscriminately applied. Should the factor of category fallacy be ruled out, then the situation of such a high prevalence rate would be most alarming to all concerned with the mental health of children in mainland China.

The increase of juvenile delinquency or conduct disorder among Chinese children has become an issue of increasing concern in Taiwan, Hong Kong, and North America since the 1960s, although the overall prevalence rate is still favorable compared to those of children in Western cultures (Ho, 1981; C. C. Hsu, 1966; C. C. Hsu and Lin, 1969). Such factors as influences of Western cultures on the behavior of children and youth, the social disorganization and family breakdown caused by urbanization and population pressure, adoption of the Western, individual-oriented value system and life style have, among others, been regarded as contributory to this increase (T. Lin, 1958, Rin, 1981).

Information on conduct disorder and juvenile delinquency from mainland China would be of enormous interest because of the profound social changes that have taken place since 1949 and, especially, subsequent to the Cultural Revolution in 1965. The contrast between the usual reports of well-behaved Chinese children with no evidence of juvenile delinquency and those of the Red Guards, who actively took part in the destructive and rebellious rampage against traditional cultural heritage and authority during the Cultural Revolution is most striking. It is hoped that more facts and information will become available to fill the present hiatus regarding our knowledge of Chinese youth. We will then be in a position to understand them better in terms of their views on education, occupation, sex and marriage, family, identity, political ideology, and relationship with the outside world.

An interesting, provocative hypothesis is made by Breiner (1980). He postulates that conformity, so typical of Chinese children, may be indicative of their psychopathology rather than of their good conduct or virtue as commonly assumed. He argues that the very early separation of babies from their working mothers might have deprived the children of the constant physical, human, and loving contacts that are essential for healthy brain development. This hypothesis, however, has a serious snag, as the good behavior of children is not new in Chinese history but was the rule in periods when children had sufficient and constant contact with their mothers. These periods of history occurred well before the revolution of 1949. At any rate, combined biomedical and biosocial research projects on child development in Chinese culture deserve special efforts in order to answer such questions.

Other Problems Related to Mental Health

ALCOHOLISM

Alcoholism has never been a social or medical problem in Chinese society at any time in its long history, a fact that can be regarded as most a remarkable cultural distinction (Cerny, 1965; Chu, 1972; T. Lin, 1953, Loewinger, 1973; Singer, 1972, Wang 1968). The rarity of alcoholism among the Chinese assumes more significance in view of the popular use of alcohol for medicinal, culinary, social, and religious purposes, which is ingrained in their everyday living.

The Chinese have a high sensitivity to ethylalcohol, due to a genetic peculiarity, and this may, in part, account for their resistance to consuming large amounts of alcohol regularly and thus, developing alcoholism (Wolff, 1972). The social control mechanism of traditional Chinese society seems to play a more significant role in preventing alcohol abuse (Harrel, 1981; T. Lin and D. T. C. Lin, 1982). It is conceivable, therefore, that social change in terms of Westernization of the life-style, accompanied by social disorganization and family breakdown as seem in certain segments of Chinese society in Hong Kong, Taiwan, and certain North American locations, contributes to an increase in alcohol consumption, leading to alcoholism. Concerns to this effect have been expressed in Hong Kong (Lee, 1982; Singer, 1972, 1974) and Taiwan (Yeh, Chapter 18, this volume), but no noticeable increase has been observed in a community survey carried out in Vancouver (T. Lin and D. T. C. Lin, 1982) or in mainland China (Shen, 1981).

HOMOSEXUALITY

In contrast to the frequent reference to homosexuality in Chinese literature, it has not been an issue of concern to psychiatry in Taiwan or mainland China. In the author's 18 years in Taiwan, only three cases came for psychiatric consultation: two males suffering from reactive depression due to pressure by the family for marriage and one male in a paranoid state. Wen (1973, 1978) made two successive surveys among about 200 college students in Taipei and found that 4% and 14%, respectively, of male and about 1% of female students had had some homosexual experiences.

It would seem plausible to speculate that homosexuality is as prevalent in Chinese culture as in other cultures, but the lack of stigmatization might make society tolerant or indifferent to its practice. Homosexuality comes to the attention of psychiatrists and mental health agencies only when the homosexuals experience psychiatric problems caused by serious psychological or social and familial pressures that attempt to force them to conform to traditional social acts such as marriage or producing children for the continuation of the family line.

TREATMENT MODALITIES OF MENTAL DISORDERS

The armamentarium of Western psychiatric treatments, with the notable exception of psychotherapy, has found wide application in China and, to a considerable extent, general acceptance among the Chinese people. It is, however, premature to conclude that Western psychiatric treatment modalities are effective with Chinese patients, as evaluative studies using comparable standardized criteria and research techniques seem scarce. Even the widespread use of psychotropic medication, electroconvulsive therapy, and insulin shock treatments have yet to be objectively assessed for their effectiveness on Chinese patients through careful clinical research that takes into consideration various biological, psychological, and sociolcultural factors.

Cross-cultural psychopharmacology is an issue of importance for consideration. For example, in my clinical experience, Chinese manic patients seem to require smaller doses of lithium carbonate per body weight and a lower blood level. The Japanese obtained similar findings through large-scale collaborative, evaluative research (Takahashi et al., 1975). Similarly, observations made on antipsychotic medication in mainland China and Malaysia also deserve careful scientific inquiry. The antipsychotic drugs like phenothiazine derivates can be effective on Chinese patients with only about half the dose required by their Western counterparts.

Psychotherapy

That Western insight-oriented psychotherapy is not acceptable to the Chinese and that its effectiveness is in doubt has become almost a conviction (Brown, Stein, Huang, and Harris, 1973; Kleinman and Mechanic, 1981, Tsai, Tseng, and Sue 1981). The fact that professional psychotherapy is not legitimized or available for the general population in Taiwan, mainland China, or Hong Kong corroborates this general notion (Kleinman, 1979). It seems however, that such a common notion merits critical scrutiny, as psychotherapy is, and should be, a central focus of psychiatry in any culture, for it distinguishes psychiatry from all other medical specialties, either as a system of science or as a healing art.

I find it premature to accept the notion that insight-oriented psychotherapy is not applicable to Chinese patients for the following reasons:

1. Insight-oriented psychotherapy has not been properly and sufficiently tried on Chinese patients by, for example, well-trained Chinese psychoanalytic psychotherapists, to a degree that would warrant a conclusive assessment of its effectiveness. The number of well-trained Chinese psychotherapists is extremely small, and in-depth reports are not available from the few well-qualified psychotherapists regarding their personal experiences or well-considered views. Whether there is a single psychoanalyst capable of treating Chinese patients in mainland China or in other Chinese societies in Asia is undetermined. Therefore, some of the comments regarding psychotherapeutic results on Chinese patients by psychiatrists not fully trained in insight-oriented psychotherapy can only be regarded as anecdotal and, therefore, of little consequence. The same criticism also applies to views expressed by Western psychiatrists by virtue of their linguistic limitations and their lack of familiarity with Chinese culture, including traditional modes of verbal or nonverbal communication, medical beliefs, and doctor–patient relationships.

2. Most of the available reports lack clear descriptions of the type and method of specific psychotherapy applied. The development of psychotherapy, both in its theory and techniques since the 1910s, has been such that psychotherapy includes literally hundreds of different psychological interventions. It is, therefore, almost meaningless to state that Western psychotherapy works or does not work. It requires a clear description of the patient and his or her problems and background, as well as the actual method, psychotherapeutic orientation, frequency and duration of treatment, targets or goals of treatment, and assessment of the results of the intervention, in order to understand the effectiveness of the psychotherapy rendered.

Given the preceding reservations, the fact remains that there exists a considerable resistence to insight-oriented psychotherapy on the part of both Chinese people as patients or family members and the Chinese medical system, including the psychiatrists' therapeutic orientation. This resistance merits clarification. Four hypotheses have been advanced to explain this deep-seated resistance:

1. Chinese philosophy emphasizes harmonious interpersonal relationships, interdependence, and mutual moral obligation or loyalty for achieving a state of psychosocial homeostasis or peaceful coexistence with family or other fellow beings (F. L. K. Hsu, 1971). It seems to have conditioned the Chinese to look for the cause of their stresses or

adjustmental difficulties in their relationships with people rather than in themselves.

2. For the Chinese, emotion and sex are private matters that are jealously guarded from anyone outside the immediate family circle. The Chinese are taught to avoid, at all costs, talking to outsiders about their private lives, feelings, and emotional lives with family members (F. L. K. Hsu, 1981).

3. The medical belief system in Chinese culture, because of its emphasis on organic causation of mental illness and tendency to somatization, seems to act as a deterrant against the use of psychotherapy as a means of conflict resolution, (K. M. Lin, 1981).

4. The reliance on verbal communication as the sole or major tool for psychotherapy may be difficult for Chinese people to accept, for they, by tradition or training, rely a great deal on nonverbal communication or symbolic figurative expression in conveying their emotions.

Testing the preceding hypotheses would make it possible to identify certain elements in psychotherapy that can be used effectively in treating Chinese patients. For instance, it is conceivable that family or social therapy is a preferred approach in restoring the patient's interpersonal equilibrium with members of his or her immediate circle of significant people. An effective use of nonverbal communication, including body language, should be encouraged for inclusion in the armamentarium of treatment techniques in Chinese culture. It is conceivable that a psychotherapist might take a more direct approach in manipulating the doctor–patient relationship, at least in its early stages, to make the patient accept the psychotherapeutic treatment modality. Through such experimental studies, one can test the hypotheses, which would further refine psychotherapeutic techniques for Chinese patients.

Traditional Medicine

The world's psychiatric community has awaited, with keen expectation, news from mainland China regarding scientific developments or breakthroughs in psychiatric treatment with the use of traditional medicine and acupuncture. This expectation has not as yet been fulfilled, however, as confirmed by an overview by Liu (1981). The two treatment modalities are widely used in mainland China. Acupuncture is used for treatment of schizophrenia, especially for patients experiencing auditory hallucinations. Several needles were inserted around both of the patient's ears for 20 minutes each day, 6 days a week. Most psychiatrists involved in this treatment program claimed that the auditory hallucinations had been treated successfully within 3–6 weeks. The other treatment involves the use of a combination of certain herbs claimed to be effective for patients exhibiting agitation and excitement. It is essential to conduct well-designed control studies to objectively assess the effectiveness of the acupuncture therapy and herbal therapy in clearly defined psychiatric conditions.

There is another practical research issue that also deserves careful attention: the treatment of neurasthenia. Some patients diagnosed as having neurasthenia are sometimes rediagnosed as depressive when they show marked improvement in response to tricyclic medication (Kleinman, 1982). It would be most useful to find out, through clinical trials, which types of neurasthenia respond to antidepressant tricyclics. Such research would also help distinguish the diagnosis of neurasthenia and other minor disorders from depression and, at the same time, contribute to the treatment.

The intensive treatment method called comprehensive group therapy, which was employed widely for neurasthenia in the late 1950s and early 1960s in China deserves special attention. It combines group and individual psychotherapy and other forms of medical, dietary, and physiotherapeutic treatments for a group of neurasthenic patients for 3–5 weeks. The results are reported to be extremely favorable (Chao, 1965; Chen, 1955), with remarkable improvement evident immediately after the treatment in about 85%, and after 3 months follow-up in 76.8% (Yan, Chapter 18 this volume). Two questions may be raised. Which aspects of the total comprehensive program are critical to its success? If the program was as successful as has been reported, why is it no longer in use? One should not overlook the significant role of politics of "Mao's thoughts" in the whole issue of neurasthenia and its intensive therapeutic treatment. The group sessions had the function, parallel to the self-criticism sessions in the political arena, of correcting deviant behavior that conflicted with the norms prescribed by the party line. Since neurasthenia is still a major psychiatric problem in China, clarification of these questions may have clinical usefulness.

COPING, HELP-SEEKING, AND DELIVERY OF
MENTAL HEALTH SERVICES FOR THE
MENTALLY ILL IN CHINESE CULTURE

One finding common to Chinese communities all over the world is that the family plays a key role in coping and help-seeking when a member of the family becomes mentally ill. However, some changes are being observed in Hong Kong and other rapidly Westernizing Chinese communities, in which the family appears to play an increasingly diminishing role in taking care of the sick (Brown, Stein, Huang, and Harris, 1973; Lee, Chapter 14, this volume).

From research in Vancouver, it was found that the Chinese family has a specific coping pattern in dealing with a serious psychiatric illness in the family (T. Lin and M. C. Lin, 1978, 1981; T. Lin, Tardiff, Donetz, and Goresky, 1978). The Chinese pattern is characterized by five distinctive phases which, as a rule, follow a typical sequential order. Phase 1 starts with a protracted phase of exclusively intrafamilial coping, sometimes lasting 10–20 years. The family attempts to influence the abnormal behavior of the sick member with every possible remedial means and resource within the family to their limit of tolerance. This is followed by Phase 2 in which trusted outsiders, such as friends and elders of the community, are asked to help the family in coping with the problems of correcting the abnormal behavior of the sick member. Phase 3 is characterized by inviting outside helping agencies, such as herbalists, physicians, or religious healers, to help the family in attempting to treat the psychotic individual who is still kept inside the family. Phase 4 starts when the sick member is labeled a mentally ill person by a physician or a trusted outside agency, a diagnosis to which the family consents. This labeling also implies that the family has come to the limit of its resources in dealing with the psychotic member within the family. The specialist's help is sought first on an outpatient basis and then through admission to a medical institution. When the hope for the recovery of the sick individual fades and the psychological and financial burden of caring for a mentally ill family member becomes unbearable, the final Phase 5 of rejection and scapegoating sets in. Either the family members give up hope and are reconciled to their "fate" of having a mental patient in their midst for the rest of his or her life, or an arrangement is made to keep the individual in a distant mental hospital, an option that precludes thinking about the family member. Certain events of life or persons or, sometimes, bad spirits or bad *feng-sui* (geomancy) are blamed for the family's fate in being burdened with an unfortunate, ill-starred, mentally ill member.

With regard to minor mental disorders, the pattern of help-seeking differs greatly from that relating to major psychoses. It seems, instead, to resemble the pattern of dealing with physical disorders (Lee, 1980). It commonly starts with self-medication, and is followed by consulting Western-style doctors, then Chinese-style practitioners, and finally, by going to a Western-style hospital. The sequential order of this help-seeking course may vary in some cases depending on the availability of services and the educational or social and economic condition of the family. Seldom do such patients end up in psychiatric facilities with inpatient services. As a rule, traditional Chinese medical practitioners play a more prominent role in neurotic cases involving sexual dysfunction such as *shen-k'uei*.

The preceding findings concerning patterns of help-seeking in Vancouver and Hong Kong seem to apply generally to most Chinese communities outside of mainland China, although no comparable studies are available. It would be of special interest to examine the role the family plays in the sequence of help-seeking and the handling of psychiatric problems at home or in the community in mainland China, where the role and function of the family in caring for the sick has apparently changed greatly since 1949.

The system of delivery of mental health services being developed in mainland China since 1949 has attracted the attention of the psychiatric world by virtue of its uniqueness and promise (Bermann, 1968; Cerny, 1965; Chin and Chin, 1969; Leung, et al., 1977; T. Lin, 1983; Sidel, 1973; D. Y. F. Ho, 1974; Visher and Visher, 1979; Worth, 1965). Such a system has the following major characteristics:

1. It attempts to make mental health services accessible to both urban and rural populations at the grassroots level by (1) emphasizing primary health care through linking mental health care with general health services especially at the commune and brigade levels, (2) providing continuity of care to all patients in every phase of their treatment and rehabilitation, and (3) making full use of available human resources, including barefoot doctors and volunteers, to supplement the limited supply of mental health workers.

2. It encourages self-reliance, that is, involvement of community leaders and administrators in the planning and operation of mental health rehabilitation projects and also in making family members and neighbors of the patient share responsibility in the treatment and care of the mentally sick. In fact all the Occupational Therapy Stations in Shanghai are self-supporting and run by volunteers who are mostly retired workers (Xia, 1980).

3. It attempts to amalgamate traditional Chinese medicine with Western-oriented psychiatric treatments. This approach has the merit of making mental health care more accessible and acceptable to the general populace, in addition to providing opportunities and paving the way for closer cooperation between the two distinct medical systems through clinical services and research. It may also help to reduce costs.

4. Therapeutic optimism seems to be the prevailing mood that underlies the development of the delivery system. This is evident in the actual therapeutic milieu of the mental health services and in the mental health workers' attitudes toward the patients. The revolutionary spirit generated by the government's commitment to carry out the new social order and to improve the living standard of the masses with a positive outlook undoubtedly plays an important role in creating the obvious therapeutic optimism (D. Y. F. Ho, 1974; Sidel, 1973). The unambiguous dramatic improvement in the delivery system of mental health services with therapeutic optimism

since 1949 contrasts sharply to the neglect of the past and the therapeutic pessimism prevailing in the pre-revolutionary era.

Another feature of therapeutic optimism in China lies in the fact that it extends beyond the psychiatric institutions. In a sense, it may be said that a therapeutic society seems to be in the making beyond the four walls of psychiatric institutions to which the concept of the therapeutic community applies (Jones, 1963).

One word of caution may be necessary in this connection. The previously described development of the system of delivery of mental health services takes place unevenly and with considerable variation in different localities (Liu, 1980a). What has been observed or reported should be regarded as models or prototypes for future development. The task ahead is arduous and tedious. Continued commitment of the government and political stability are the keys to the maintenance and development of this highly politicized system of delivery of multiservices in mainland China.

THEORIES AND HYPOTHESES ABOUT MENTAL DISORDERS

Traditional Chinese medicine has maintained its theoretical frame of reference and medical beliefs into the modern age and is still exerting an important, pervasive influence on the symptom formation of mental illness and mental health–related behavior of patients and their families (Chan and Chang, 1976; Kleinman, Kunstadter, Alexander, and Gale, 1975, 1978; Topley, 1976).

The theoretical basis of mental disorders can be summarized (Lieh-Mak, 1982; K. M. Lin, 1981; Ogren, 1982; Tseng, 1973a). In Chinese medical thought, psychosomatic integration characterizes the relationship between psychological and physiological functions. According to this theory, each of the five major emotions has a corresponding internal organ: Happiness is in the heart, anger is in the liver, worry is in the lung, fear is in the kidney, and desire is in the spleen. The imbalance of emotions disturbs the functional balance of these organs, and vice versa. Excess, incongruence, and lack of harmony of emotions are regarded as pathogenic; and high value is placed upon moderation and inhibition of emotions or affective expression. Once, however, physiological balance has been disturbed subsequent to psychological imbalance, methods of treatment are sought through physiological or medical intervention rather than through avenues of psychological treatment. The training of body–mind unity in activities like *tai ji quan* (*tai-chi chuan*, shadow boxing) is more valued as a preventive means than as therapy to restore the emotional imbalance.

Chinese traditional medicine seems, therefore, to have exerted an inhibiting effect on the development of psychiatry as an independent system of psychological medicine as it is in the West. Indeed, psychiatry has been given a marginal place in the total medical system throughout Chinese history. Modern psychiatry in China has largely ignored traditional Chinese medicine until very recently, even after the renewed interest in traditional Chinese medicine evident since 1949, when it acquired a status equal to that of Western medicine. Some of the pharmacotherapeutic and physiological treatment methods such as herbal therapy and acupuncture are incorporated in the treatment of mental disorders but without established standardized methods or proven effects.

Nevertheless, one should not underestimate the significant influence of traditional medical beliefs peculiar to Chinese culture on the manifestation and treatment of mental disorders. For instance, the prominent role somatization plays in the psychopathology of mental disorders and in illness behavior, as discussed previously, has its origin in the traditional medical thought that is deeply imbedded in the everyday life of the Chinese. It clearly influences the preferred modes of treatment. It also offers an effective defense against shame and guilt associated with the stigma attached to mental illness because the psychological burden of the sick individual or the family is greatly relieved by somatization, which represents an acceptable explanatory model to all concerned. Although somatization is not exclusively confined to the Chinese people or culture alone, its intensity and pervasiveness are such that Chinese somatization has a unique quality (Kleinman, 1982; Marsella, 1978).

A hypothesis of externalization may be advanced to explain Chinese somatization, in tandem with the finding that paranoid symptomatology is prevalent among psychotic patients (Lin, 1983). Both somatization and paranoid symtomatology represent a similar defense of turning away from intrapsychic mechanism—the former through bodily manifestation, and the latter projecting to person(s) or happenings in the outside world.

This hypothesis offers a plausible explanation for Chinese somatization in light of its cultural emphasis on a situation-oriented approach to life. It is postulated that the Chinese view a human as a relational being, living and interacting in a massively complicated role system (King and Bond, Chapter 3, this volume). Chinese cultural emphasis singles out harmonious personal relationships as the fundamental element in achieving psychosocial homeostasis (F. L. K. Hsu, 1971, 1981). To the Chinese mind, harmony, interdependence, and loyalty are keys to survival, peace, and happiness. The unique quality of Chinese somatization can thus be regarded as having two major cultural roots, namely, traditional medicinal beliefs and a situation-related approach to life.

It is conceivable that the Chinese concept of a human as a relational being oriented to the myriad situations of the surrounding world has far-reaching mental health implications. For example, the resistance of the Chinese to insight-oriented psychotherapy and the dominance of intra-familial coping in response to mental illness may be explained in this basic cultural emphasis, where resolution of conflicts is attempted, consciously or unconsciously, by extrapsychic rather than intrapsychic mechanisms. In addition, the rarity of alcoholism and of conduct disorder in children can also be explained by this hypothesis.

These hypotheses need vigorous testing to examine their validity. It should be emphasized, however, that they must be reconceptualized into a set of subhypotheses with clearly defined criteria in order to become testable. For example, the statement that humans are relational beings is by itself too abstract to be tested scientifically, as it includes such components as a person's self-concept, his or her view of the surroundings and the world, the pattern of interaction between him or her and the people in the immediate family circle, and so on. The concept of psychosocial homeostasis and its meaning to individuals would be a worthwhile philosophical concept for scientific inquiry.

Finally, one should always keep in mind that Chinese culture varies in different communities and is constantly changing in spite of the common notion concerning its stability, durability, and continuity for over 20 centuries. The fact remains that it is changing with time and place through contacts with outside influences as well as through its own evolution and revolution. This factor of variation and change should be taken into consideration when one looks at certain observed facts or attempts to grasp the conceptual frame of reference of any observation.

CONCLUDING REMARKS

A summary of the foregoing review may be made corresponding to the four questions raised at the outset of this chapter.

1. A number of significant features of psychiatric disorders have been observed that are characteristic to the Chinese; for example, the relatively favorable prognosis of schizophrenia, the low prevalence rates of depressive illness with its predominant symptomatology of somatization, and the relative paucity of obsessive–compulsive neuroses and of such mental health–related behavior as juvenile delinquency and alcoholism. In addition, there exist several culture-bound syndromes peculiar to Chinese culture, namely, *koro*, frigophobia, *shen-k'uei*, and *hsieh-ping*.

2. No definitive studies have demonstrated the effectiveness of any treatment modalities specific to Chinese culture. The efficacy of Western psychiatric treatments, especially psychotherapy, on the Chinese patients has yet to be objectively assessed.

3. The typical pattern of coping with severe mental illness observed in Chinese society reflects the key role the family plays in handling mentally ill individuals at home and in help-seeking; and this pattern, in the main, is influenced by traditional concepts of insanity and the pervasive social stigma. The delivery system of mental health services in mainland China represents not only a distinct departure from the past, but also an innovative attempt to provide primary mental health care to the masses. Presumably, the socialist social, economic, and administrative structure and the politicized community orientation form the basis for this new approach and its therapeutic optimism.

4. No unified psychiatric theory has been developed or advocated by Chinese psychiatrists on the causation, symptom manifestation, or course and outcome of mental illnesses; nor is there a culture-specific system of classification of mental disorders. A number of hypotheses that have been advanced to explain certain characteristic features of mental disorders as described in the text will have to be vigorously tested.

It is evident from the preceding that the generic question, Is there a Chinese psychiatry? cannot be responded to affirmatively at this stage of psychiatric development. There is hope, however, that some of the gaps in psychiatric knowledge and theory, both in clinical endeavor and research input, will be bridged to arrive at a more cohesive scientific system in a not too distant future, particularly if the current lively psychiatric activities in Chinese communities, especially in mainland China, Taiwan, Hong Kong, Singapore, and North America can be continued.

REFERENCES

Ballet, G.
    1908   *Neurasthenia*. London: Henry Kimpton.
Beard, G.
    1880   *A practical treatise on nervous exhaustion (neurasthenia)*. New York: William Wood and Co.
Bermann, G.
    1968   Mental health in China, In A. Kiev (Ed.), *Psychiatry in the Communist world*. New York: Science Home.
Breiner, S.
    1980   Early child development in China. *Child Psychiatry and Human Development*, *11*(2), 87–95.

Brown, T. R., Stein, K. M., Haung, K., and Harris, D. E.
   1973   Mental illness and the role of mental health facilities in Chinatown. In S. Sue,
            and N. Wagner (Eds.), *Asian-Americans: Psychological perspectives*. Palo Alto, CA:
            Science and Behavior Books.
Cerny, J.
   1965   Chinese psychiatry. *International Journal of Psychiatry 1*, 229–239.
Chan, C. W., and Chang, J. K.
   1976   The role of Chinese medicine in New York City's Chinatown. *American Journal
            of Chinese Medicine 4*, 31–46, 129–146.
Chang, Y. H., Rin, H., and Chen, C. C.
   1975   Frigophobia: A report of five cases. *Bulletin Chinese Society of Neurology and
            Psychiatry, 1*, 9–13.
Chao, Y.
   1965   Neurology, neurosurgery and psychiatry in new China. *Chinese Medical Journal,
            84*, 714–742.
Chen, Z.
   1955   Nanjing jingshenbin fanzhiyuan dui shenjingshuairuo huanzhe kaizhan la jīti
            jingshen zhiliao huode chubu chengxiao [The preliminary results of group
            therapy for neurasthenia patients carried out by Nanjing Psychiatric Hospital].
            Chinese Journal of Neurology and Psychiatry, 1, 104–106.
Cheung, F., Lau, B., and Waldman, E.
   1980–   Somatization among Chinese depressives in general practive. *International Jour-
   1981   nal of Psychiatry in Medicine, 10*, 361–374.
Chin, R., and Chin, A. L. S.
   1969   *Psychological Research in Communist China: 1949–1966*. Cambridge: The M.I.T.
            Press.
Chu, G.
   1972   Drinking patterns and attitudes of rooming-house Chinese in San Francisco.
            Quarterly Journal of Studies on Alcohol, 33(1, 2).
Department of Psychiatry, National Taiwan University Hospital
   1980   *Statistics of the Department of Psychiatry, National Taiwan University Hospital,
            1969–1979*. Taipei: National Taiwan University Hospital.
Harrell, S.
   1981   Normal and deviant drinking in rural Taiwan. In A. Kleinman and T. Lin
            (Eds.), *Normal and abnormal behavior in Chinese culture*. Dordrecht, Holland:
            Reidel.
Ho, D. Y. F.
   1974   Prevention and treatment of mental illness in the people's Republic of China.
            American Journal of Orthopsychiatry, 44, 620–635.
   1981   Childhood psychopathology: A dialogue with special reference to Chinese and
            American cultures. In A. Kleinman and T. Lin (Eds.), *Normal and abnormal
            behavior in Chinese cultures*. Dordrecht, Holland: Reidel.
Hsu, C. C.
   1966   A study of "problem children" reported by teachers. *Japanese Journal of Child
            Psychiatry, 7*, 91–108.
   1982   *A study of reading disabilities among Chinese fifth graders*. Paper presented at the
            World Psychiatric Association Regional Symposium, Kyoto, Japan.
Hsu, C. C., and Lin, T.
   1969   A mental health program at the elementary school level in Taiwan: A six-year
            review of the East-Gate project. In W. Caudill and T. Lin (Eds.), *Mental health
            research in Asia and the Pacific*. Honolulu: East–West Center Press.

Hsu, F. L. K.
  1971   *Under the ancestors' shadow: Kinship, personality and social mobility in China.*
            Stanford: Stanford University Press.
  1981   *Americans and Chinese: Passages to differences.* Honolulu: The University Press of
            Hawaii.
Jones, M.
  1963   *The therapeutic community.* New York: Basic Books.
Kleinman, A.
  1977   Depression, somatization and the "new cross-cultural psychiatry." *Social Science
            and Medicine, 11,* 3–10.
  1979   *Patients and healers in the context of culture: An exploration of the borderland between
            anthropology, medicine and psychiatry.* Berkeley: University of California Press.
  1982   Neurasthenia and depression: A study of somatization and culture in China.
            Culture, Medicine and Psychiatry, 6, 117–190.
Kleinman, A., and Mechanic, D.
  1981   Mental illness and psychological aspects of medical problems in China. In A.
            Kleinman and T. Lin (Eds.), *Normal and abnormal behavior in Chinese culture.*
            Dordrecht, Holland: Reidel.
Kleinman, A., Kunstadter, P., Alexander, E., and Gale, J.
  1975   *Medicine in Chinese Cultures.* Washington, DC: U.S. Government Printing Office
            for Fogarty International Center, National Institutes of Health.
  1978   *Culture and healing in Asian Societies: Anthropological, psychiatric and public health
            studies.* MA: Schenkman.
Koro Study Team
  1969   The koro epidemic in Singapore. *Singapore Medical Journal, 10,* 234–242.
LaBarre, W.
  1946   Some observations on character structure in the Orient: The Chinese. Part I and
            II. *Psychiatry 9,* 215–237, 375–395.
Lee, R.
  1980   Perceptions and uses of Chinese medicine among the Chinese in Hong Kong.
            Culture, Medicine and Psychiatry, 4, 345–375.
Leung, S. et al.
  1977   *A simple Chinese recipe for responsibility: Serve the people.* Paper presented at
            the 130th annual meeting of the American Psychiatric Association, May 2–
            6.
Lieh-Mak, F.
  1982   The Yin-Yang concept in the treatment of mental illness. In Ogawa, T. (Ed.),
            History of psychiatry. Tokyo: Saikon.
Lin, K. M.
  1981   Traditional Chinese medical beliefs and their relevance for mental illness and
            psychiatry. In A. Kleinman and T. Lin (Eds.), *Normal and abnormal behavior in
            Chinese culture.* Dordrecht, Holland: Reidel.
Lin, K. M., Kleinman, A., and Lin, T.
  1981   Overview of mental disorders in Chinese cultures: Review of epidemiological
            and clinical studies. In A. Kleinman and T. Lin (Eds.), *Normal and abnormal
            behavior in Chinese culture.* Dordrecht, Holland: Reidel.
Lin, T.
  1953   A study of mental disorders in Chinese and other cultures. *Psychiatry, 16,* 313–
            336.
  1958   *Taipau* and *liu-mang:* Two types of delinquent youths in Chinese society. *British
            Journal of Delinquency, 8,* 244–256.

1982   *Mental health in the Third World.* Margaret Mead Memorial Lecture, World
        Congress on Mental Health, Manila, Philippines, July 27–August 1.
1983   Psychiatry and Chinese culture. *The Western Journal of Medicine, 139*, 862–867.
Lin, T., and Lin, D. T. C.
1982   Alcoholism among the Chinese: Further observations of a low-risk population.
        Culture, Medicine and Psychiatry, 6, 109–116.
Lin, T., and Lin, M. C.
1978   Service delivery issues in Asian North-American communities. *American Jour-
        nal of Psychiatry, 135*(4), 454–456.
1981   Love, denial and rejection. In A. Kleinman and T. Lin (Eds.), *Normal and
        abnormal behavior in Chinese culture.* Dordrecht, Holland: Reidel.
Lin, T., Rin, H., Yeh, E. K., Hsu, C. C., and Chu, H. M.
1969   Mental disorders in Taiwan, fifteen years later. In W. Caudill and Y. Lin (Eds.),
        Mental health research in Asia and the Pacific. Honolulu: East–West Center Press.
Lin, T., Tardiff, K., Donetz, G., and Goresky, W.
1978   Ethnicity and patterns of help-seeking. *Culture, Medicine and Psychiatry, 2*(1), 3–
        14.
Liu J. et al.
1980   Shanghai-shi Xuhui-gu jing-shen-bing liu-xing-bing-xue diau-cha [An epi-
        demlological investigation of mental disorders in Xuhui District of Shanghai].
        Chinese Journal of Neurology and Psychiatry 13, 1–6.
Liu, X.
1980a   Mental health work in Sichuan. *British Journal of Psychiatry, 137*, 371–376.
1980b   Sichuan jingshenbing fabingqingkuang diaucha [Survey of mental disorders in
        Sichuan]. *Chinese Journal of Neurology and Psychiatry 13*(1), 7–9.
1981   Psychiatry in traditional Chinese medicine. *British Journal of Psychiatry, 138*,
        429–433.
Lo, W. H., and Lo, T.
1977   A ten-year follow-up study of Chinese schizophrenics in Hong Kong. *British
        Journal of Psychiatry, 131*, 63–66.
Loewinger, P.
1973   How the People's Republic of China solved the drug abuse problem. *American
        Journal of Chinese Medicine, 1*(2), 275–282.
Marsella, A.
1978   *Towards a conceptual framework for understanding cross-cultural variations in de-
        pressive affect and disorder.* Paper presented at the Psychocultural Aspects of
        Ethnicity Seminar, School of International Studies, University of Washington,
        April 18.
Ney, P. et al.
1979   Chinese autistic children. *Social Psychiatry, 14*, 147–150.
Ngui, R. W.
1969   The koro social epidemic in Singapore. *Australian and New Zealand Journal of
        Psychiatry, 3*, 263–266.
Ogren, H.
1982   Concepts of psychiatric interest in Chinese traditional medicine. In T. Ogawa
        (Ed.), *History of psychiatry,* Tokyo: Saikon.
Rao, V.
1978   Some aspects of psychiatry in India. *Transcultural Psychiatry News. 15*, 17–38.
Rin, H.
1959   Psychotherapy with six cases of obsessive-compulsive neuroses. *Journal of For-
        mosan Medical Association, 59*, 189–220.

1965   A study of the etiology of Koro in respect to the Chinese concept of illness. *International Journal of Psychiatry, 11,* 7–13.

1981   The effect of family pathology in Taipei's juvenile delinquents. In A. Kleinman and T. Lin (Eds.), *Normal and abnormal behavior in Chinese culture.* Dordrecht, Holland: Reidel.

Rin, H., Chu, H. M., and Lin, T. Y.

1966   Psychophysiological reactions of a rural and suburban population in Taiwan. *Acta Psychiatrica Scandinavica, 42,* 410–473.

Rin, H., Schooler, C., and Caudill, W. A.

1973   Symptomatology and hospitalization: Culture, social structure and psychopathology in Taiwan and Japan. *Journal of Nervous and Mental Diseases, 157,* 296–312.

Shen, Y. et al.

1981   Investigation of mental disorders in Beijing suburban district. *Chinese Medical Journal, 94*(3), 153–156.

Shinfuku, N., and Kalicinski, K.

1982   *Report on attendance at the National Seminar on Child Mental Health, Nanjing, China, Nov–Dec, 1981.* WHO (WP) MNH/M4/80/2(WP)MNH/M3/81/1. Geneva: World Health Organization.

Sidel, R.

1973   Mental diseases and their treatment. In J. R. Quinn (Ed.), *Medicine and public health in the People's Republic of China* (DHEW No. (NIH) 72–67). Washington, DC: U.S. Government Printing Office.

Singer, K.

1972   Drinking patterns and alcoholism in the Chinese. *British Journal of Addiction, 67,* 3–14.

1974   The choice of intoxicant among the Chinese. *British Journal of Addiction, 69,* 257–268.

Takahashi, R., Sakuma, A., Itoh, K., Itoh, H., Kurihara, M., Saito, M., and Watanabe, M.

1975   Comparison of efficacy of lithium carbonate and chlorpromazine in mania. *Archives of General Psychiatry, 32*(10), 1310–1318.

Topley, M.

1976   Chinese traditional etiology and methods of cure in Hong Kong. In C. Leslie (Ed.), *Asian medical systems.* Berkeley: University of California Press.

Tsai, M., Teng, L. N., and Sue, S.

1981   Mental health status of Chinese in the United States. In A. Kleinman and T. Lin (Eds.), *Normal and abnormal behavior in Chinese culture.* Dordrecht, Holland: Reidel.

Tseng, W. S.

1973a   The development of psychiatric concepts in traditional Chinese medicine. *Archives of General Psychiatry, 29,* 569–575.

1973b   Psychopathological study of obsessive–compulsive neurosis in Taiwan. *Comprehensive Psychiatry, 14,* 139–150.

1975   The nature of somatic complaints among psychiatric patients: The Chinese case. *Comprehensive Psychiatry, 16,* 237–245.

Visher, J. S., and Visher, E. B.

1979   Mental illness in China. *American Journal of Psychiatry, 136,* 28–32.

Wang, R. P.

1968   A study of alcoholism in Chinatown. *International Journal of Social Psychiatry, 14,* 260–267.

Waxler, N. E.
 1974 Culture and mental illness: A social labelling perspective. *The Journal of Nervous and Mental Disease, 159*(6), 379–395.
 1979 Is outcome for schizophrenia better in non-industrial societies? The case of Sri Lanka. *The Journal of Nervous and Mental Disease, 167*(3), 144–158.
Wen, J. K.
 1973 *Social attitudes towards homosexuality.* Unpublished manuscript, College of Medicine, National Taiwan University, Taipei, Taiwan.
 1978 Sexual attitudes of college students. *Ching-Hsing* [Green Apricot], *46*, 160–107.
Wolff, P.
 1972 Ethnic difference in alcoholic sensitivity. *Science, 175*, 449–450.
World Health Organization
 1973 *International pilot study of schizophrenia.* Geneva, Switzerland.
Worth, R.
 1965 New China's accomplishments in the control of diseases. In M. Wegman, T. Lin, and E. Purcell (Eds.), *Public health in the People's Republic of China.* New York: The Josiah Macy, Jr., Foundation.
Xia, Z. et al.
 1980 Mental health work in Shanghai. *Chinese Medical Journal, 93*(2), 127–129.
 1981 History and present status of modern psychiatry in China. *Chinese Medical Journal, 95*(5), 277-279.
Yap, P. M.
 1960 The possesion syndrome: A comparison of Hong Kong and French findings. *Journal of Mental Science, 106*, 114–137.
 1965a Koro: A culture-bound depersonalization syndrome. *British Journal of Psychiatry, 3*, 43–50.
 1965b Phenomenology of affective disorders in Chinese and other cultures. In A. V. S. DeReuck and R. Porter (Eds.), Transcultural psychiatry. Boston: Little and Brown.
Yeh, E. K., Fan, B. Y., and Tien, S. J.
 1979 A statistical study of the discharged patients from the Taipei City Psychiatric Center during 1969–1978. In *10 years' report, Taipei City Psychiatric Center.* Taipei: Taipei City Psychiatric Center.

CHAPTER 26

Directions for Future Study

Wen-Shing Tseng
David Y. H. Wu

INTRODUCTION

There are two basic ways to explore the subject of culture and mental health: by focusing on a selected issue to cross-compare culture and mental health among a number of different cultural samples (Brown and Torrey, 1973; Caudil and Lin, 1969; DeReuck and Porter, 1965; Lebra, 1976; H. B. M. Murphy, 1982; Opler, 1959; Westermeyer, 1976) or by focusing on a single culture to explore comprehensively various matters of mental health in relation to that particular culture (T. S. Lebra and W. P. Lebra, 1974; Kleinman and Lin, 1981). In this book, we choose the second approach— to study culture and mental health within the context of Chinese culture. It is definitely a historical event that, for the first time, Chinese scholars from various parts of the world—mainland China, Southeast Asia, and Western countries—gathered to address the common concern: how Chinese culture affects the emotional problems, mental illness, and mental health care of the Chinese people. Although the scholars come from many locations and their backgrounds include various disciplines, nearly all have the same

395

Chinese ethnic background in common. This allows us to address the issue of Chinese culture and mental health from the "insider's" point of view.

Because this is the first work of its kind, we chose to review aspects of Chinese culture and mental health broadly and generally in order to obtain a comprehensive picture. We have addressed prevailing characteristics of Chinese culture and society, examined the Chinese personality, discussed family and child, and reviewed the adjustment of Chinese in different settings. This led to analysis of mental health problems and their management.

IMPORTANT APPROACHES TO STUDYING CULTURE AND MENTAL HEALTH

Culture and mental health concerns the effect of culture on the mind, behavior, and mental health. Its objectives are to explore how cultural factors influence the nature of stress in society, the forms psychopathological of manifestation, and the patterns of coping mechanisms and styles of care delivery. The ultimate concerns are how to modify life styles and adjust the culture for better mental health (Favazza and Oman, 1978; Leighton and J. M. Murphy, 1965; Tseng and McDermott, 1981; Wittkower and Prince, 1974). In a scientific exploration concerning the cultural aspect of mental health, several basic approaches need to be borne in mind, and these approaches are discussed next.

The Need for an Interdisciplinary Approach

Human life and behavior are very complex phenomena. In order to pursue knowledge in culture and mental health, it is necessary to make full use of knowledge in various disciplines and to combine the work of social and behavioral scientists and mental health workers (Foulks, 1977).

Lack of such interdisciplinary work may result in many scientific pitfalls. Many mental health workers, such as psychiatrists and clinical psychologists, approach the subject of culture and mental health with a loose concept of culture and an insufficient understanding of society, which results in incorrect interpretations or overgeneralizations of the sociocultural aspects of mental health. In contrast, many social and behavioral scientists, such as sociologists and anthropologists, study the matter of culture and mental health without adequate knowledge of psychiatry or mental health, which results in loose or inaccurate use of clinical concepts or neglecting clinical and applied implications.

There are many studies by social scientists that neglect implications in mental health or interpret impact on mental health prematurely. And, conversely, many clinical studies do not trace the cultural impact precisely or specifically. Many psychiatric epidemiological studies have been carried out that successfully reveal the prevalence of various mental disorders within the Chinese communities. However, without input from social scientists in the data collection stage of research design, there was a shortage of systematic information to illuminate the sociocultural variables that might contribute to the frequency of certain mental disorders. Collaboration between psychiatrists and social scientists definitely minimizes the shortage of such monorail-style investigation of sociocultural mental health. If—or, more positively, when—each researcher makes full use of the knowledge of other disciplines, we shall all benefit. Human life, culture, and mental health are very complex phenomena. Researchers from many disciplines working with one another will advance the understanding of these complexities.

The Benefits of Cross-Comparison

In the study of culture and mental health, there is a need for—and there will certainly be benefits to be gained from—cross-comparison (Brislin, Lonner, and Thorndike, 1973; Draguns, 1977; Draguns, 1982; Marsella, 1979; H. B. M. Murphy, 1969). Culture is an abstract term, describing a particular set of living patterns observed and transmitted through generations. Culture is impossible to express concretely, and difficult to operationalize. Thus, to determine and validate the influence of cultural factors, we need to compare findings cross-culturally and, preferably, cross-multi-culturally to highlight certain elements of culture. For instance, it is desirable to cross-compare the findings among Chinese ethnic samples in various geographic settings that have different sociogeographic and political backgrounds but share a common culture root. For example, cross-comparison of elementary school systems in different social settings, such as Shanghai, Hong Kong, Singapore, and Taipei, will help us to determine the common cultural element that molds the basic educational pattern and the socioeconomic and political influences that shape the variations of the school system in those settings. During various periods, for various reasons, many Chinese migrated from mainland China and settled in many parts of the world. Comparative studies of various groups of overseas Chinese residing in various parts of the world will bring out interesting information to answer questions such as, What is the common pattern of adjustment observed among overseas Chinese in various social settings? What is the influence of cultural attitudes that contribute to their success or failure in adjusting to a new environment? and, What are the common mental health problems observed among these subgroups that may have common roots in Chinese culture?

It is also desirable to compare cross-ethnically so that ethnic or culture specificity can be tested. For example, finding the somatization tendency among people in Korea, Japan, and non-Asian countries—if this tendency is indeed common to various ethnic–cultural groups—can challenge us to discover in what specific ways it is—or is not—unique to Chinese culture. A cross-comparison of the language and identity problems of ethnic groups in various multilanguage societies, such as Hawaii, New York, Kula Lumpur, and Singapore, will assist us in analyzing more meaningfully the relationships between culture and language and identity. As another example, cross-comparison of the modern high-rise housing environment and its possible effects on the mental health of children and families who live in this setting, carried out in cities such as Shanghai, Hong Kong, Singapore, and Taipei, certainly will allow us to examine how Chinese children and families adjust to the housing environment of different societies. Of particular concern are the variables of physical environment, children, family behavior, and mental health. But if we cross-compare these matters further in other communities and cultural groups, such as New York, Berlin, and Stockholm, then the additional variables of ethnicity or culture may emerge for analysis. Such cross-comparison can prevent us from making premature speculations on cultural causality and can validate interpretation based on our findings.

The Need to Update Knowledge

Science is founded on the endless search for knowledge, and there is constant need for new knowledge and new approaches. The field of culture and mental health is no exception to this. This field has made remarkable progress in the past several decades: Formerly, students of culture and mental health were concerned with minority groups or primitive peoples; they have now shifted their focus. The attempt now is to study the majority group and one's own culture and mental health as well (J. J. Schwab and M. E. Schwab 1977). This new attitude is reflected in this book: We study our own Chinese culture and mental health. Another significant change is that cultural psychiatrists no longer limit their interest to examining so-called culture-bound specific psychiatric syndromes. Instead, they are interested in seeing how cultural factors influence the manifestation of psychopathology in its every aspect. Questions they ask include, What is the universal pattern of manifesting anxiety, depression, anger, or frustration? What is the cultural variation of expressing such emotional problems? What is the common, universally observed symptom of depression? and, What is the ethnic variation in handling depressive reaction?

Finally, the mental health worker who was once preoccupied with studying folk or primitive healing now also considers how the cultural factor has impact on the delivery of modern mental health service. Many investigators are interested in studying help-seeking behavior patterns among people in the community and are concerned with how cultural factors affect the economic aspects of mental health delivery. There are also many explorations focusing on how various forms of therapy, such as group therapy, family therapy, and occupational rehabilitation, may be more adequately and effectively utilized by different sociocultural subgroups. This shift of concern has made culture and mental health a discipline that is focused, not just on research, but also on the practical application of research. Thus, it becomes necessary for all of us to keep abreast of progress and to remain in contact with scholars around the world so that our knowledge will be kept up-to-date.

FUTURE DIRECTIONS

We next outline in detail four main paths that future culture and mental health studies can profitably follow: (1) a shift to dynamic investigation rather than mere descriptive study, (2) the combination of micro- and macrolevel studies, (3) a change of emphasis from major psychiatric disorders to minor ones, and (4) the extension of concern from clinical patients to the community as a whole. We consider each in turn.

The Shift to Dynamic Investigation

The descriptive study of mental health refers to systematic observation and objective description of psychopathology and mental health conditions; dynamic study means investigating the dynamic correlation or causality of stress and emotional disorders and finding meaningful interpretation of the phenomena.

Obviously, systematic observations and objective descriptions of phenomena are essential in any scientific exploration. However, this should be the *means* to an end—not the end in itself. Attempts should be made to explore the dynamic correlation of the phenomena and to seek meaningful interpretation of the phenomena. This is particularly true in the study of culture and mental health. There is a danger of becoming preoccupied with the scholarly comparison of symptom manifestation and frequency of occurrence, and a study must not stop here. These comparisons must be the background for an attempt to disclose the possible reasons for phenomena. An example is the study of the phenomenon of suicide behavior. Exploring the frequency and method of suicide is a beginning; the study becomes more useful when it goes on to explore the social–cultural–individual dynamic causes for self-destructive behavior. The study of conduct behavior among children in different settings leads to the interesting and potentially helpful inquiry: What are the possible sociocultural factors that contribute to the observed differences in behavior disorders?

Another example is the investigation of the cultural pattern of somatic presentation among Chinese psychiatric patients. After we have learned the descriptive phenomena—how frequently Chinese patients tend to present somatic symptoms (rather than emotional and psychological symptoms) or how educational background, age, of patients in various diagnostic categories of psychiatric disorders do or do not correlate with such phenomena, then we should move to explore further the nature of such patterns. Are they related to the individual's cultural concept of problems, orientation of problem presentation, or underlying psychological problems? Are they serving as a coping mechanism by focusing and presenting somatic symptoms instead of psychological problems? A careful longitudinal follow-up investigation of cases, tracing the fate of such somatic presentation pattern by means of psychotherapy is one method for such dynamic exploration.

The Dual Approach of Micro- and Macrolevel Studies

We also suggest a need for a combination of micro- and macrolevel studies. This is a combination that calls for the joint and cooperative efforts of several different disciplines. The clinician generally has the skill and experience to examine a single case in depth, that is, to provide a microlevel study. The social scientist, used to dealing with the mass—with the group—is especially skilled in macrolevel studies. We suggest that these two approaches should be combined. With this dual approach, what is learned from individual cases can be generalized to group situations. At the same time, group findings can provide meaningful interpretations based on the insights gained from the case analysis.

The best example of this is the investigation of the sociocultural influence on the psychological problems of neuroses. Careful clinical analysis of characteristic psychological problems presented by individual neurotic cases will lead us to gain an insight about the possible reflection of common psychological problems existing in the society concerned. However, such microscopic analysis will only lead us to formalize such speculation, pointing to the need for further macroscopic examination. Studying large group samples in the society and testing speculated correlations will enable us to verify that certain psychological problems are commonly observed in the society and that these problems are reflected in the characteristic complaints and symptoms of neurotic patients in that society.

As another example, the speculation that homosexuality is rare among Chinese people cannot be fully tested without the combination of micro- and macrolevel investigations. Through case study, the manifestation of an underlying homosexual tendency among the Chinese patients can be explored intensively. Then, based on resulting information, a culturally relevant homosexuality-study questionnaire can be designed for a large group survey that would reveal the prevalence of this psychosexual phenomena within the Chinese population in the community.

Change of Focus from Major to Minor Psychiatric Disorders

As our third point, we suggest a changed emphasis in research from major psychiatric disorders (psychoses) to minor psychiatric disorders such as neuroses, psychosomatic disorders, and adjustmental reaction.

In the past, cultural psychiatrists conducted their investigations with great emphasis on major psychiatric disorders, such as schizophrenia and affective psychoses. A change in emphasis now seems due. Recent developments indicate that major psychiatric disorders—schizophrenia is a prime example—are influenced predominantly by biological factors. Minor psychiatric disorders, such as neuroses, substance abuse, and alcohol-related problems, are attributed more to psychological factors. Therefore, from the perspective of culture and mental health, it makes very good sense to emphasize the study of the minor disorders. These are more or less reactive in nature and related to situations; thus, the cultural dimensions involved can be more meaningfully analyzed. Studying cross-cultural aspects of the symptomatology of schizophrenia or the frequency of major depression may yield relatively little new and useful knowledge in culture and mental health, whereas studying the cross-cultural aspects of suicide attempts, neurotic depression, or ethnic-identity crisis may be very enlightening.

Practical Application

Although students of culture and mental health started this field as a research science, it is now time to expand our concern to applied aspects of mental health. For example, in addition to investigating the characteristic pattern of Chinese family interaction and the related area of family dysfunction or psychology, it is necessary to explore the cultural aspect of family therapy for Chinese clients. Does the Chinese saying, "*Jia chou bu ke wai yang*"(family disgrace should not be revealed to the outsider), actually affect the process of family counseling? Does the cultural emphasis of parental authority over the children and the value of harmony (rather than confrontation) within the family influence the therapeutic strategies of family therapy? These are some of the questions that need to be investigated and answered for culturally relevant family therapy.

The study of traditional Chinese folk therapy, such as shamanism, divination in temple or fortune telling is interesting. We could gain a great deal of insight about how culturally sanctioned coping mechanisms are utilized in such folk counseling and about how universally important therapeutic elements such as the provision of hope, the provision of interpretation, and the opportunity for ventilation are found in the traditional healing arts. But is there room for modern counseling to make use of such therapeutic variables to maximize the treatment effects? This is another example of a challenging question waiting for clinical application.

Extension of Concern from Clinical Patients to the Community

Our fourth point is based on the often quoted statement, "clinicians see sick people, not healthy ones"; that is, they focus on pathology and neglect observing normality. In individual practice, this is usually unavoidable and necessary. Where culture and mental health research studies are concerned, it is a serious imbalance. Studies tend to be based on the pathological group; hospital data are used heavily. Thus, a narrow view of mental health results and data are apt to be biased and may not be applicable to the general population. Especially when cultural factors are being investigated, the focus must move away from the clinician's office and the hospital ward. Adequate samples of people who represent the ordinary life in the community must be studied. Society- and community-related issues need to be focused on.

Questions must be asked, based on existing Chinese culture: How should the process of modernization, industrialization, or urbanization be adjusted? What possible cultural attributes can be utilized for maintaining mental health equilibrium in a process of sociocultural change? What are the possible cultural elements that serve as obstacles or resistence to this necessary progress? How can the obstacles be dealt with or modified? What is the desirable Chinese personality for better mental health in contemporary society? and, How can optimistic personality traits be developed? These questions need to be addressed jointly by mental health workers, social and behavioral scientists, government administrators, and many other people who are concerned with the matter of cultural planning for the health of the individual and the society.

CHINESE CULTURE AND MENTAL HEALTH: REVIEW

In this section, we review the specific matter of Chinese culture and mental health to see what we have learned about it. Certain characteristics of Chinese culture and mental health need comment.

One of these is the Chinese attitude toward mental health and mental illness. It is obvious that most of the Chinese, either in mainland China or overseas, still attach a marked stigma to mental illness. As a result, the Chinese, in general, are reluctant to go to a mental health facility. To overcome this reluctance, the present-day concept of mental health care must be actively promoted. It must be understood that mental health care does not mean only the treatment of severely disturbed persons, but also has a positive and hopeful meaning: to attain, maintain, and retain the health of mind of all people. The Chinese have a long history of civilization, and, in spite of many disasters in the past, they have maintained a large population over many centuries. Based on our general impression that relatively few mental health problems have existed, some characteristic of Chinese culture and the basic personality of Chinese must maintain remarkable mental equilibrium. It is worthwhile to learn more about what kinds of attributes have contributed to this mental health.

From the mental health point of view, the Chinese need to recognize that culture is not static, but undergoes change, and they should be prepared to accept and adjust to the changing culture. For example, although traditionally, great emphasis has been placed on the extended family, this may no longer be practical in view of the fact that the majority of dwellings house only the nuclear family. The traditional view of many children as a blessing and family treasure must now make way for family planning concerns and restricted family size. Instead of the expected time of "golden old age," the elderly must now learn to live independently of the younger generation. The child, the family, and aging are some of the key areas on which, from the mental health point of view, we should concentrate.

As we all know, the matter of identity plays a significant role in our personalities, minds, and behavior. Identity includes self-identity, family identity, social identity, ethnic or cultural identity, and so forth, all of which help us to define self and provide us with a sense of self. Due to the long history of their civilization, Chinese in general have maintained their ethnic identity and are proud of being Chinese. This contributes to the stability of their self-image and mental health. However, during the past century, the Chinese self-image has been challenged and severely weakened through the deterioration of dynastic rule, foreign invasion, and delay in modernization. With recent improved standards of living and upgrading of sociopolitical status in mainland China and in Chinese populations overseas, the situation has shown remarkable progress since the early 1970s, and most Chinese have begun to regain ethnic confidence and cultural identity, which are so important for mental health.

Socioanthropological studies support current views on ethnicity: that the identity is not fixed and unchangeable and that ethnic boundaries can be fluid and loosely defined. From our observations, there are strong indications that Chinese living in various places demonstrate not only variation in their subculture, but are characterized by multiple ethnicity, depending on the sociocultural and political situation. What are regarded as Chinese characteristics or attributes may be quite different from place to place and generation to generation and are subject to both individual and group manipulations. It is very important for us to realize this so that we can be comfortable in accepting the diversity we see among ourselves in terms of sociopolitical and subcultural background while at the same time sharing a common ethnic and cultural heritage and identity.

In the past, directly or indirectly, China had a significant impact on the development of world civilization. We believe that in some way Chinese mental health may also have influenced world mental health. China is characterized by a large, ethnically homogeneous population, which is a unique laboratory for the observation and validation of many scientific theories regarding mental health. It will, for example, be very interesting to compare epidemiological data regarding mental illnesses, such as schizophrenia and minimal brain syndrome, and information about child temperament between ethnic Chinese and other groups for the sake of validation or challenge. The special issue of mental health problems among Chinese people, with regard to the individual, the family, or a particular group, remains a fascinating subject for cross-cultural comparison. Of great interest to the outside world is the adjustment of the Chinese population to the present rapid culture change in China, and the impact it will have on the children, the family, and the aged.

Mainland China has demonstrated the utilization of a sociocultural–political system to provide a community-oriented mental health delivery system that is effective with certain kinds of mental health patients and is helpful in solving or minimizing certain mental health problems. This provides a very valuable example for other areas of the world, one that they can take into consideration when developing their own mental health programs.

Finally, the ethnic Chinese continue to emphasize marriage, family, and child rearing, to value the humanistic side of life, and to stress harmony, mutual benefit, and personal growth as their basic philosophy. The Chinese value system may contribute to the mental well-being of the Chinese and provide a unique example of life-style and mental health for the whole world to watch.

It is our responsibility as social scientists and mental health workers to work with people in the society for the improvement of mental health for people everywhere.

REFERENCES

Brislin, R. W., Lonner, W. J., and Thorndike, R. M.
   1973   *Cross-cultural research methods.* New York: Wiley.
Brown, B. S., and Torrey, E. F. (Eds.)
   1973   *International collaboration in mental health.* Rockville, MD: National Institute of Mental Health, DHEW Publication.
Caudil, W., and Lin, E. F.
   1969   *Mental health research in Asia and the Pacific.* Honolulu: East-West Center Press.
DeReuck, A. V. S., and Porter, R. (Eds.)
   1965   *Transcultural psychiatry.* Boston: Little, Brown & Company.
Draguns, J. G.
   1977   Advances in methodology of cross-cultural psychiatric assessment. *Transcultural Psychiatric Research Review, 14,* 125–143.
   1982   Methodology in cross-cultural psychopathology. In I. Al-Issa (Ed.), *Culture and psychopathology.* Baltimore, MD: University Park Press.
Favazza, A. R., and Oman, M.
   1978   Overview: Foundation of cultural psychiatry. *American Journal of Psychiatry, 135,* 293–303.
Foulks, E. F.
   1977   Anthropology and psychiatry: A new blending of an old relationship. In E. F. Foulk, R. M. Wintrob, J. Westermeyer, and A. R. Favazza (Eds.), *Current perspectives in cultural psychiatry.* New York: Spectrum Publications.
Kleinman, A., and Lin, T. Y. (Eds.)
   1981   *Normal and abnormal behavior in Chinese culture.* Dordrecht, Holland: Reidel.
Lebra, T. S., and Lebra, W. P. (Eds.)
   1974   *Japanese culture and behavior: Selected readings.* Honolulu: University Press of Hawaii.
Lebra, W. P. (Ed.)
   1976   *Culture-bound syndromes, ethno-psychiatry, and alternate therapies.* Honolulu: University Press of Hawaii.
Leighton, A. H., and Murphy, J. M.
   1965   Cross-cultural psychiatry. In J. M. Murphy and A. H. Leighton (Eds.), *Approaches to cross-cultural psychiatry.* Ithaca, NY: Cornell University Press.
Marsella, A. J.
   1979   Cross-cultural studies of mental disorders. In A. J. Marsella, R. G. Tharp, and T. J. Ciborowski (Eds.), *Perspectives on cross-cultural psychology.* New York: Academic Press.
Murphy, H. B. M.
   1969   Handling the culture dimension in psychiatric research. *Social Psychiatry, 4,* 11–15.

1982   *Comparative psychiatry: The international and intercultural distribution of mental illness.* Berlin: Springer-Verlag.

Opler, M. K. (Ed.)
1959   *Culture and mental health.* New York: Macmillan.

Schwab, J. J., and Schwab, M. E.
1977   The future of cultural psychiatry. In E. F. Foulk, R. M. Wintrob, J. Westermeyer, and A. R. Favazza (Eds.), *Current perspectives in cultural psychiatry.* New York: Spectrum.

Tseng, W. S., and McDermott, J. F., Jr.
1981   *Culture, mind and therapy: An introduction to cultural psychiatry.* New York: Brunner/Mazel.

Westermeyer, J. (Ed.)
1976   *Anthropology and mental health: Setting a new course.* The Hague: Mouton.

Wittkower, E. D., and Prince, R.
1974   A review of transcultural psychiatry. In S. Arieti (Ed.), *American handbook of psychiatry* (2nd ed.). New York: Basic Books.

INDEX

A

Aborigines, of Taiwan, 61, 63
Achievement, 7, 11, 18, 41, 100, 119, 126, 200, 207, 209, 218, 221, 225, 332
Acupuncture, 73, 79
Adaptation, 215–226, *see also* Adjustment
Adjustment, 216, 179
  of migrants, 57, 64, 65, 199, 210
Aggression, 34, 129–131, 198
Alcohol, 76, 89
  drinking in ancient China, 76
Alcoholism, 278, 378
Ancestor worship, 18, 100, 127, 206, 208
Anti-Rightist Movement, 20
Assimilation, 216, 224
Attachment, *see also* Bond
  mother–child, 84, 116, 118, 120, 122
Authority, 87, 131
  Chinese family, 33, 34, 83, 97, 98
  leadership 60

B

Back door, 9, 41
Bao (reciprocity), 42
Behavior disorders, and temperament, 140
Bond, 116, 121, 131, 204
Breast feeding, 117
Buddhist, 63, 207
Business (commerce), 11, 114, 194, 218, 220, 205

C

Caucasians, 217, 218, 221, 224
Child mental health, 157, 166, 305, 376

Child rearing
  Chinese, 8, 34, 35, 36, 37, 84, 86, 96–97, 113–132
  in Hong Kong, 197–198
  in Mainland China, 8, 86–88
  in Papua New Guinea, 84, 113–132
  in Taiwan, 8
Chinatown, 219, 223
Chinese
  behavior, 29–222
  character, 2, 29, 47–55
  cultural characteristics, 3–12, 82, 85, 114, 215, 216, 222
  cultural values, 3–12
  dialects, 181–192
  language, 105, 181–192
  in Singapore, 229
  tradition, 63, 85–86
  youth, 86
Chinese medicine, 67–79
Chinese novels, in relation to mental disorders, 75–79
Chinese young, 10, 24–25, 54, 86, 92, 210
Christian, 127
  church, 58, 61, 62, 63
  missionary, 217
Civil Service examination (in China), 77
Commune, 19, 20, 24, 37
Community mental health, care network, 359
Competition
  in Hong Kong, 202–208
  in school, 202
  in society, 60, 202, 204, 205, 208

Conformity, 33, 34, 198
Confucian
  concept of humanity (man), 1, 30–32
  individualism, 36, 40, 42
  paradigm, 1, 7, 30–42 (*passim*)
  social theory, 31, 32, 40
  thought, 53–54
  values, 187, 223
Confucianism, 1, 7, 10, 29–42, 63, 85
  defined, 30
Confucius, 29–42
Consciousness, 59, 64
Coping, 104–5, 219
  coping mechanism, 197, 198, 208, 209,
    216
Criticism, 20
  self, 20
Cultural identity, 61, 181, 182, *see also*
    Ethnic identity
Cultural Revolution, 5, 14, 19, 20, 21, 22,
    23, 25, 26, 79
  Chinese response to, 5, 23
Culture
  characteristics of Chinese, 3–12, 114,
    201, 207, 209, 216, 222
  Chinese cultural tradition, 114, 120, 215,
    222
  concept of, 3, 16
  new Chinese, 1, 3–12
  norm, 106
Culture-bound syndromes, 375
Culture change, 4, 17, 18, 116, 216
  in China, 5, 15–27, 86
  in Taiwan, 264
Curing (healing) ritual, 61, 62, 65

D

Depressive illness, 373
Dian (insane or epileptic), 68, 69–70, 72,
    73
Discrimination, 221, 223, 225
Divination, 72–73
Divorce, 207
  in China, 87–88

E

Education, 54, 201, 207, 210, 216
  Chinese, in Singapore, 182, 185–
    186

  as social control, 87
  value of, 11, 218, 221, 225
Elderly (aged people), 88–93, 128, 194,
    198
Emotion, 100, 105, 116, 194, 195, 199,
    202, 203, 205, 208
  of Chinese, 2, 7–8, 10–11, 100, 105,
    195–208
  and Chinese mental illness, 70, 72, 73,
    75, 79
  control, 34
  emotional expression of Chinese child,
    34, 100
  emotional illness, 195
Epidemiological study (or psychiatric sur-
    vey), 305, 361
Epilepsy, 70, 77
Ethnic group, 183, 215–218, 223
Ethnic identity, 179, 181–192, 215, 221–
    226
Ethnic minority, 65, 223, 225, *see also*
    Aborigines

F

Face, 7, 37, 39, 100
  Chinese concept of, 7, 37, 100
Family (*Jia*), 39
  Chinese, 7–8, 32–41, 82, 88, 90, 92, 93,
    95–110, 194, 198, 204, 223, 225
  and effect on mental health 85, 96–98
  extended, 18
  health, 96–98
  hierarchical structure, 38–39
  oriented, 30, 222, 225
  planning, 153
  problem, 95–110
  and psychotherapy, 7, 94–112
  responsibility, 7, 95–110
Father–son relation, 30, 33, 60, 99, 108,
    216–225
Fear, 116, 121–125
Feng (wind, insane), 68
Feng shui (geomancy), 206–207
Filial piety (*Xiao*), 26, 33, 34, 38, 88, 90,
    91, 99
  defined 88
Filipinos, 217, 218
Five cardinal relations (*wu lun*), 32, 33, 38,
    41

Five moral standards and four "beauties," 25, 26, 54, 93
Food preference, 159
Formality
   in ritual, 60, 64
Four Modernizations, 25, 27, 54, 93
Freud, 78, 116
Friendship, 38–39, 41, 87, 89, 92, 99, 198, 203, 204, 207
Fu-ji (spirit writing), 64

G

Gang of Four, 20, 24, 25
Generation gap, 102–103
God (spirits, ghosts, supernatural beings), 18, 60, 61, 62
Government
   participation in, 216, 218, 220
   role of, 202, 203, 210
Great Leap Forward, 19
Group
   control, 60
   identity, 61, 181
   pressure, 19
Group-oriented, 1, 30, 36, 58–59, 114
   Chinese and Japanese difference, 36
Guan-xi-xue (relationology), 41

H

Han nationality (ethnic group), 50
Harmony, 10, 27, 30, 34, 37, 90
   family, 34, 38, 90
   he (harmony), 34
   social, 30, 35
Hawaiian, 218, 222, 224, 225
   Hawaiian Chinese, 126
Help-seeking, 382
Hippies, 61, 76
Home care, 351, 357
   program, 362
Homosexuality, 378
Hundred Day Reform, 20
Hundred Flowers Movement, 21
Husband–wife relationship, 103–106, 108–109
Hyperactive syndrome, 173, 176, *see also* Minimal brain disorders
Hysteria, 71

I

Identity, *see also* Cultural identity
   crisis, 61
   self, 32
   of traditional Chinese society, 33
Ideology, 18, 19, 25, 54, 99
   ideological campaign, 20, 21
   socialist, 19, 54
   of traditional Chinese society, 33
Immigration (immigrants), 182, 193, 197, 209, 210, 216, 217, 223, 225, 251, *see also* Migration, Migrants
Individualism, 30–31, 35, 36, 40, 42, 58–59, 60, 82, 97, 99, 113, 198, *see also* Confucian, individualism
Industrialization, 5, 82, 132
   in Hong Kong, 41, 206
   in Taiwan, 64
Instrumentalism, 204, 205
Intellectuals, 21, 22
Interpersonal relationship, 41, 60, 63, 90, 92, 93, 103, 128, 204, 205, 207, 329

J

Japanese, 217, 218, 223, 224
Jews, 224
Juvenile delinquency, 194, 227

K

Kinship
   group, 19
   network, 19, 26, 34, 40, 128, 203, 204, 205
   organization, 127
   relations, 7, 8, 40, 89, 90, 115
   system, 96, 101
Kuang (insane), 68, 69–70, 72, 73

L

Land reform, 18
Language, *see also* Chinese, dialects
   identity, 181–192
   Mandarin, 181–192
   multilingualism in Singapore, 184–192
   policy in Singapore, 184–187
Li (propriety), 30, 33, 34, 54, 60
Loneliness, 88–93

Love, 54, 77, 87, 92, 105
  qing chi (love sickness), 77
  universal, 54
Lun, 30–41 (passim)

M

Manic depression, 78
Marriage, 87–91, 207, 218, 224, 225
  intergroup, 188
Materialistic, 24
  Chinese youth, 27
Mental cultivation (*dao*), 18
Mental health, 116, 132, 199, 205, 206
  of children, 87, 88
  delivery system in Shanghai, 341
  of students, 274
Mental illness (disorder), 113, 194
  in ancient China, 67–79
  in China, 87, 88
  Chinese concept, 2, 11, 67–79
  Chinese pattern of disorder, 4, 75–79
  original meaning in Chinese, 68–69
  therapy, in ancient China, 73–75, 77
Migrants
  China to Hawaii, 216–225
  China to Hong Kong, 93, 197, 209
  China to Taiwan, 61
  rural–urban, 61
Migration, 5, 9, 61, 64, 99
Millennial cult or movement, 62–63
Minimal brain disorders, 315
MMPI (Minnesota Multiphasic Personality
  Inventory), 48–53, 48, 289
  in China, 49–53
Modernization, 82, 93, 98, 108, *see also*
  Four Modernizations
Moral (morality), 10–11, 54, 78–79, 86,
  201
  autonomy, 32
  Confucian, 10, 40
  standards, 60, 64, 65, *see also* Five moral
    standards
  traditional Chinese, 63, 64, 78–79
Moslem, 63
Moxibustion, 79

N

Narcotics, 194
Nationalism, 24

Nativistic movement, 63
Neurasthenia, 374
Neurotic disorder (or neuroses), 87, 325,
  401
  among outpatient population in Taiwan,
    273
  among Singapore Chinese, 240
Noise, 122–123

O

One-child-per-couple policy, 93, 153
Only child
  advantages and disadvantages, 157
  negative behavior patterns, 160
Overseas Chinese, 7, 11, 132, 191, 223–
  224

P

Parent–child relation, 7, 34, 88–93, 100–
  108, 114, 115, 116, 132
Personal network, 9, *see also* Friendship,
  Kinship
Personality, 30, 113, 114, 116, 129
  adjustment, 3
  Chinese, 1, 29–42, 47–55 (passim), 57
Physiological symptoms, 195
Population density (high density living),
  179, 196, 197, 198, 199, 206, 209
Population growth, 193, 218
Pragmatism, 9, 27, 60, 201, 204, 222
Privacy, 198
Propriety, 99, *see also* Li
Psychological problems, 324
Psychopathology, 215–218
  psychoneurotic symptoms, 195
Psychophysiological disorders, community
  survey, 272
Psychosexual problems, 245
Psychotherapy, 379

Q

Qing chi (love sickness), 77

R

Rabies, 68–69
  Chinese therapy of, 69